ATBMS AND WESTERN SECURITY

ATBMS AND WESTERN SECURITY
Missile Defenses for Europe

Edited By
DONALD L. HAFNER
and
JOHN ROPER

A Study Done under the Auspices of the
American Academy of Arts and Sciences and
the Royal Institute of International Affairs,
London

BALLINGER PUBLISHING COMPANY
Cambridge, Massachusetts
A Subsidiary of Harper & Row, Publishers, Inc.

Copyright © 1988 by Ballinger Publishing Company. All rights reserved. No part of this publication may be reproduced, stored in a retrieval system, or transmitted in any form or by any means, electronic, mechanical, photocopy, recording or otherwise, without the prior written consent of the publisher.

International Standard Book Number: 0-88730-232-7

Library of Congress Catalog Card Number: 88-8615

Printed in the United States of America

Library of Congress Cataloging-in-Publication Data

ATBMs and Western security : missile defenses for Europe / edited by Donald L. Hafner and John Roper.
   p. cm.
   "A study done under the auspices of the American Academy of Arts and Sciences and the Royal Institute of International Affairs, London."
   Includes index.
   ISBN 0-88730-232-7
   1. Europe—National security.   2. Anti-tactical ballistic missiles—Europe.   3. Europe—Air defenses, Military. I. Hafner. Donald. II. Roper, John, 1936– . III. American Academy of Arts and Sciences. IV. Royal Institute of International Affairs.
UA646.A84 1988
355'.03304—dc19   88-8615
                                                                                CIP

CONTENTS

List of Figures		vii
List of Tables		ix
Acknowledgments		xi
Introduction —Donald L. Hafner and John Roper		xiii
1	The Nature of the Debate —James Eberle and Alain Baer	1
2	ATBM Technologies and NATO —Benoit Morel and Theodore A. Postol	21
3	The Soviet Threat: New and Enduring Dimensions —Dennis M. Gormley	57
4	A Technical Assessment of the Soviet TBM Threat to NATO —Benoit Morel and Theodore A. Postol	93
5	Alternatives to ATBMs —David Rubenson and James Bonomo	133
6	TBMs, ATBMs, and NATO Doctrine —Peter Volten	155

7	TBMs and ATBMs: Arms Control Considerations —*Ivo H. Daalder and Jeffrey Boutwell*	179
8	The Politics of ATBMs: The United States and the Alliance —*Catherine McArdle Kelleher*	209
9	ATBMs and Alliance Politics in Europe —*Phil Williams*	237
10	Perspective and Commentary: ATBMs and the Middle East —*Shahram Chubin*	261
11	Perspective and Commentary: China, Japan, and ATBMs —*Gerald Segal*	273
12	Perspective and Commentary: ATBMs: An Opportunity for the Alliance —*François DeRose*	285
13	Perspective and Commentary: Of Allies and ATBMs —*Josef Joffe*	299
	Index	311
	About the Editors	321
	About the Contributors	323

LIST OF FIGURES

1–1 Approximate Target Coverage by NATO and Warsaw Pact TBMs in the Central Region

2–1 Comparison of Warsaw Pact TBM Trajectories and Potential NATO Surveillance Radar Coverage (for Various Radar Beam Elevation Angles)

4–1 Comparison of Total Bombing Capabilities of Soviet/Warsaw Pact TBMs and Ground-Attack Aircraft at Various Ranges

4–2 Probability That a TBM Destroys a Radar

4–3 Probability of TBM Submunitions Hitting a Bunker

4–4 Probability of Achieving Various Levels of Damage against a Target Composed of Twelve Sub-units

4–5 Probability of TBM Submunitions Hitting a Sub-bunker

4–6 Main Runway, Taxiways, Aircraft Shelters, and Main Base Operations Buildings of Major NATO Airbase at Bitburg, West Germany

4–7 Probability That a TBM Will Impact at a Range in Excess of Distance R from a Runway Centerline

LIST OF FIGURES

4–8 Submunition-Armed TBM Attack on Runway and Taxiway of Major NATO Airbase at Bitburg, West Germany

4–9 Expected Number of Submunitions Hitting a 50 Meter Wide Runway for Various Submunition Dispersal Radii

4–10 Probability of a TBM Hitting a Square Bunker (for Various TBM Accuracies)

4–11 Approximate Arrangement of Trucks, Vans, and Armored Vehicles in Deployed Main Divisional Command Post (DMAIN)

5–1 Additional Runway and Taxiways That Could Be Constructed to Complicate Soviet TBM Attack on Major NATO Airbase at Bitburg, West Germany

7–1 Approximate Target Coverage by NATO and Warsaw Pact TBMs with a 300 Km Range Limitation

LIST OF TABLES

2–1 Radar Detection Ranges for Various Missiles

3–1 Current Soviet and Warsaw Pact TBM Launcher Deployments by Soviet Theater of Military Operations (TVD)

4–1 Surface-to-Surface Missile Characteristics

4–2 Take-off and Landing Runs for NATO Aircraft

4–3 Baseline Soviet TBM Characteristics

4–4 Missile and Reentry Vehicle Characteristics

ACKNOWLEDGMENTS

We wish to express our gratitude to those who have made this book possible: to the Johnson Foundation, the Sloan Foundation, the Carnegie Corporation, and the Ford Foundation for their financial support; to the participants in our conferences at Wingspread, Chatham House, and the American Academy whose advice and directions helped guide us from error; and to the members of our transatlantic steering group who gave both good advice and encouragement in generous measure. We are grateful as well to Carolyn Casagrande and her associates at Ballinger Publishing for their patience and good humor as we labored to forge book from manuscript.

Although our study of the ATBM issue was carried out under the auspices of the American Academy of Arts and Sciences and the Royal Institute of International Affairs, we wish to emphasize that the opinions expressed and the conclusions reached by the ATBM study group members should not be mistaken to be the formal position of either the Royal Institute or the American Academy.

Donald L. Hafner
John Roper

INTRODUCTION
Donald Hafner and John Roper

DOES EUROPE NEED MISSILE DEFENSES?

The chapters in this book, addressing this question in detail, are the product of a European and American study group assembled in late 1986 under the auspices of the American Academy of Arts and Sciences and the Royal Institute of International Affairs. At the time the study group began its work, turmoil was already spreading within the Alliance not only over the answer to this question but even about how the question should be framed: what kind of missile defenses, and against what manner of threat? The turmoil was compounded by a sense of urgency and frustration. For political and military reasons, it appeared that NATO must answer the question soon, and yet the issue seemed intractably complex, presuming answers to so many other questions that the Allies have found difficult to resolve.

The cause of this turbulence within the Alliance was in part new Soviet threats, in part new doubts about NATO's accustomed solutions. Europe has long been exposed to Soviet nuclear missiles. Nevertheless, the Soviet Union's modernization of its intermediate- and shorter-range ballistic missile forces in the late 1970s and early 1980s inevitably provoked concern that the Soviets might use the new technologies in missile guidance and munitions to penetrate and destroy NATO's military shield. By the 1990s, some argued, Soviet forces might be able to trigger a collapse of NATO's forces in Europe without ever crossing the nuclear threshold, through adroit use of nonnuclear ballistic missiles equipped with precision guidance and modern chemical or high-explosive warheads. In addition, early in the 1980s the Soviets began developing one new air defense system and flight-testing another that were judged to have an anti-missile defense capability against NATO's theater weapons. The new threats to NATO were thus multifaceted — nuclear and nonnuclear, posing problems for both offensive and defensive forces.

At the same time, the NATO Alliance was already developing new weapons and concepts with which to reinforce its strategy of flexible response. In the nuclear field, the Allies had agreed to modernize NATO's theater forces by the deployment of Pershing IIs and ground-launched cruise missiles. The United States had started to develop conventionally armed, precision-guided cruise and ballistic missiles. SACEUR was developing its concept of Follow-On Forces Attack (FOFA), which envisioned the use of such weapons for deep strikes into Warsaw Pact territory. But all of these implied an "offensive defense" policy for NATO, an idea that was becoming constrained by political developments in Europe, of which the growth of the peace movement was foremost. The development of ATBMs as a "defensive defense" thus appeared as an attractive option. Yet if NATO intended to have an ATBM defense in time to meet the developing Soviet threat, it had to act soon.

Compounding the sense of urgency was the challenge posed by President Reagan's Strategic Defense Initiative. If the United States were to become immune to Soviet missile attack, what of Europe? Clearly, a place had to be found for the European allies within the SDI. Recognizing that European support would be indispensable in gaining congressional approval and funding for the SDI, the Reagan administration sought a response to European defense concerns and a channel for European endorsement and participation in the SDI. From a variety of motives, including an anxiety neither to be denied a voice in so profound a shift in U.S. policy nor to risk industrial backwardness by being denied access to SDI technologies, Europeans also sought a mode of participation that would be in harmony with distinctive European political and military requirements.

Therefore the sense of political and military urgency was almost palpable in late 1985 when German Defense Minister Manfred Wörner publicly endorsed a plausible solution: "The only politically and strategically acceptable alternative for NATO is a direct defense against Soviet missiles" — ATBM. General Bernard Rogers, Supreme Allied Commander-Europe, added his voice in urging that NATO quickly agree to deploy ATBMs. Indeed, there was much to argue for ATBMs as a solution. If the advocates were correct, ATBMs would bolster the Alliance's political cohesion and military effectiveness by enhancing the policy of forward defense, helping NATO postpone the moment at which it must resort to theater nuclear weapons in the event of Soviet conventional attack, and providing a basis for European-American collaboration on advanced technologies.

Few things in life are unmixed blessings, however, and ATBMs are no exception. The study contained in this volume derived in part from a concern that, in its sense of urgency, the Alliance not rush to judgment on ATBMs until the arguable benefits were carefully assessed against potential hazards. ATBMs would confront the Alliance with delicate questions about where such defenses would be deployed and for what purposes, who would bear their cost, and most important, what impact they would have on the overall military balance. At issue is not NATO's advantage if it alone deployed ATBMs, but how the balance would weigh — in both conventional and nuclear contexts — when the Soviets also deployed ATBMs. For example, if conventionally armed theater ballistic missiles are vital to NATO's military strategy because they could offset Warsaw Pact quantitative superiority in manpower, armor, aircraft, and air defenses, then deployments of ATBMs by both sides may not be to NATO's net advantage. Moreover, a Soviet deployment of a dense network of ATBM might blunt the effectiveness of nuclear options that are a necessary part of NATO's flexible response policy.

ATBMs also have implications at the strategic nuclear level. Defenses against theater ballistic missiles, after all, occupy an anomalous position in the arms control arrangements that have helped preserve nuclear deterrence and NATO's security. The ABM Treaty regulates defenses against strategic missiles, but it does not define *strategic*. A distinction between strategic and nonstrategic missiles can be extracted from the SALT accords on offensive weapons and the 1987 treaty on intermediate- and long-range theater missiles, although the distinction is more legal than technical: ballistic missiles are nonstrategic if they are land-based and have a range of less than 5,500 km or submarine-based and have a range of less than 1,400 km. If it is permissible for the Soviets to give their ATBMs a capacity to intercept the longest-range nonstrategic missiles, they could in principle also defend against strategic missiles fired from comparable ranges. Such defenses could challenge all the strategic nuclear forces of the European Allies—and thus the nuclear voice of Europe within the Alliance— because all current European nuclear missiles (and a substantial portion of U.S. SLBMs) have ranges under 5,000 km.

As ostensibly nonstrategic defenses, Soviet ATBMs could well depart from ABM Treaty limitations in other significant ways, with mobile deployments, rapid-reload and "MIRVed" interceptors, or new technologies based on "other physical principles." At the least, ATBMs of this sort could provide a substantial R&D base in defense technologies that were deliberately restrained in 1972; at worst, they could establish a deployment base for strategic breakout from the ABM Treaty. Verifying that the treaty's limits on strategic defenses were still being honored—a vital matter even for SDI advocates who hope eventually to replace the treaty—could become exceedingly complicated, perhaps pointless.

This brief summary in no way exhausts the list of complications posed by ATBMs. Yet it is quite long enough to confirm that the ramifications extend to every corner of NATO's military and political structure.

While the members of the study group were wrestling with these issues, events were in flux on both sides of the Atlantic. In the United States, the future direction of the SDI became increasingly ambiguous. President Reagan's unflagging determination to see the program through was matched by congressional refusal to fund the initiative at requested levels and insistence that the program comply with the ABM Treaty, narrowly construed. To the extent that a European ATBM was conceived as a strategic, political, and technological bridge to the SDI, its status became ambiguous as well. Far more important, however, was the sudden resolution of remaining differences between the superpowers on an arms control agreement covering intermediate-range nuclear forces. When Reagan and Gorbachev met in Washington in December 1987 and signed the treaty banning all theater ballistic missiles with ranges between 500 and 5,500 km, they seemingly swept away much of the argument for ATBM defenses as well.

Yet the new U.S.-Soviet treaty governing theater ballistic missiles leaves a number of important issues still to be resolved. With the Pershings and ground-launched cruise missiles removed, their assigned tasks must now be met by the Alliance's remaining nuclear and conventional forces. But the bulk of NATO's forces, from the German border to the English Channel, and the control network that binds them together, will still lie within reach of Soviet short-range theater missiles that are not banned by treaty. The appropriate way to protect these forces remains an issue. In addition, NATO's own missiles continue to play a significant role in theater deterrence, and the Alliance therefore cannot be indifferent to Soviet deployments of ATBMs.

Nor have the political and strategic complications posed by the SDI disappeared for the European allies. Despite its modest technological achievements, the SDI has generated increased political support for continued research on defense technologies and a widespread view that some forms of defense—for instance, site defense of crucial military targets—should be reconsidered. Continuing research in the United States means a continuing technological and industrial challenge to Europe. And each advance in technology for site defense will undoubtedly provoke questions about whether it might be adapted as an ATBM for Alliance purposes.

The impact on the ATBM issue of several other events that have occurred since our study began can only be surmised. In December 1987 Germany's Manfred Wörner was selected as the new Secretary-General of NATO, thus bringing Europe's most prominent advocate of ATBMs to the head of the Alliance. General John Galvin, who replaced Bernard Rogers as SACEUR in 1987, has insisted that NATO implement its 1983 Montebello decision by acquiring a modern theater ballistic missile with a range just under the new treaty limitation of 500 km, thus again begging questions about the interaction between the Alliance's offensive forces and Soviet defense programs. Also of potential importance is an emerging Alliance controversy over whether the remaining short-range missiles in Europe, those with ranges under 500 km, should be constrained or even abolished through an arms control agreement with the Soviet Union. German interests in limiting these weapons, because the threat they pose is aimed principally at Germany, may not be easily reconciled with the opinions of other Allies who worry that further constraints will undermine NATO's nuclear options and nuclear resolve. Although the ATBM systems that could be deployed within the next decade do not promise an effective technical response to Soviet short-range nuclear missiles, some observers may come to view an Alliance ATBM program as a useful political response to German sensitivities.

So, does Europe need missile defenses? The question is still urgent.

In assembling our study group to address these matters, we brought together experts with long experience in military and alliance affairs, and our purposes were wider than just subjecting the ATBM issue to thorough examination. Unavoidably, any Alliance discussion of ATBMs would heighten awareness that each ally faces grave dangers and accepts risks on behalf of all, yet no two allies confront precisely the same risks. We judged it important, therefore, that voices from many corners of the Alliance be heard on the ATBM issue and that Europeans and Americans together search out common grounds for discourse and decisions on whether NATO would be better off in a world of missile defenses. Accordingly, we invited both U.S. and European experts to be study participants and arranged for a vigorous and candid exchange of views in a set of workshops held in the United States and Britain. And recognizing the American proclivity for discussing such issues primarily in technical terms, and a European inclination to view them as quintessentially political, we sought out participants who could move with ease between both realms. Finally, when our group members were drafting the papers that follow in this book, we encouraged them not to understate the complexities of the ATBM issues, but at the same time to present those complexities in terms accessible to the wider publics who will share the benefits and bear the burdens of Alliance decisions on ATBMs. We hope the reader will agree that the study group performed its tasks well and that this was indeed a fruitful transatlantic collaboration.

1 THE NATURE OF THE DEBATE
James Eberle and Alain Baer

This book is about a new Alliance debate, one that thus far has been conducted chiefly among military experts and has been primarily concerned with the future security of Western Europe. But it also has strong roots in the United States and has important implications for the whole NATO Alliance. The debate is concerned primarily with issues of defense against conventional weapons but has nuclear overtones as well. Its outcome will affect the future balance of offense and defense within the overall strategy of the Alliance. It also has wide-reaching ramifications for arms control; its outcome may affect the strength and direction of future technological development in Europe. It is therefore an important debate.

The crux of the debate is whether antimissile defenses should be deployed in Western Europe. The debate has arisen for two fundamental reasons. The first is that the Soviets have been deploying a new generation of tactical and theater missiles, both ballistic and cruise. Ballistic missiles with ranges between tens and several thousand kilometers have been deployed with Soviet forces opposite NATO since the late 1950s. But until now these missiles had been judged so inaccurate that, if armed with conventional warheads, they posed only a marginal threat. And the use of nuclear warheads on these missiles by the Soviets would have risked nuclear retaliation by NATO. In the early 1980s, however, the Soviets began improving the newest generation of Soviet shorter-range ballistic missiles to give them greatly improved accuracies. Concern is now voiced that in the future these Soviet missiles will be able effectively to attack key NATO installations, with little warning and without crossing the nuclear threshold.

The second reason this debate has arisen stems not from Soviet but from U.S. programs. President Reagan's announcement of the Strategic Defense Initiative (SDI) in 1983 was a radical and unanticipated departure from existing policies, certain to provoke debate about its meaning for the cohesion of the Alliance and security of Western Europe. In the past, NATO had been able to plan its security doctrine on the assumption that the Soviet Union would be vulnerable to—and thus deterred by—the threat of nuclear escalation. And NATO's cohesion rested in part on an assumption of shared risk, that all members of the Alliance were equally exposed to the Soviet nuclear threat. A surge in high-technology missile defense programs in the United States and the Soviet Union called into question both assumptions. The implications of missile defense for Europe were injected into the SDI debate from the outset by a panel of technical advisers who urged the president to harness the SDI first to Europe's defense needs.

It is a sign of both the complexity and contentiousness of this debate that dispute exists over what to call the objects of discussion. The label most frequently used is anti–tactical ballistic missile (ATBM) systems. But many would argue the label is misleading on several grounds. For one, the *T* in *ATBM* should stand for *theater* as well as *tactical* because the Soviet missiles of concern include both those that might be used in the immediate battlefield area as well as those that might be launched from areas remote from the battlefield, against targets also remote from the battlefield. Prior to the 1987 INF treaty, ATBM defenses were envisioned against the Soviet theater missile, the SS-20 (range: 5,000 km), as well as the theater/tactical SS-21, SS-23, and SS-22 (ranges: 120 km, 500 km, and 900 km).[1] Under the new treaty, TBMs with ranges up to 500 km are still permitted. In addition, one might equally drop the *B* from *ATBM* because in many formulations, these defenses would be called on to intercept all manner of missiles, whether ballistic, semiballistic, or cruise, whether ground-launched, air-launched, or sea-launched. For our purposes here, we will stay with the label we have inherited—ATBMs.

There are those who would argue that the ATBM debate is an "artificial" one, where the arguments heard in public do not correspond with the real motives of those using them. Not all are convinced that the Soviet conventional missile threat is either imminent or serious. Those who are so convinced are more likely to be found in the United States than in Europe. Others are persuaded that the clamor for ATBMs is primarily intended to enlarge popular and commercial support for the SDI in the United States. Some suspect that support for ATBMs is merely an expedient to overcome European objections to SDI and to the new U.S. doctrine of strategic defense. There are also those who believe European interest in ATBMs stems less from the Soviet missile threat than from the commercial and industrial challenge posed by U.S. high-technology advances under the SDI program. And there are military leaders who see the ATBM debate as a distraction from more important issues, such as the effect that shorter range "smart weapons" may have on the future battlefield. But whatever the origin of the debate, it is clear that *if* the Soviets were able to carry out an effective attack with conventional weapons at a very early stage of a war in Europe that would cripple NATO's airfields, its command, control, and communication centers, and its nuclear weapon storage sites, *and if* there were no effective defense against such an attack, then the whole basis of NATO's military strategy would be placed in serious jeopardy (see Figure 1–1). In this sense, the debate is genuine and important.

NATO DOCTRINE

The NATO Alliance's strategy of "flexible response" was adopted in 1967, after a long debate during which France withdrew from the integrated military structure. This strategy demands that NATO have the capability for direct defense at each level of attack and the capacity to escalate if necessary, in order to convince the attacker that his aggression cannot succeed. This escalation may require the use of nuclear weapons—including, in the ultimate, U.S. strategic forces. NATO is also committed to "forward defense." This means that in response to Soviet aggression, the forces of the Alliance cannot trade territory for time, an exchange that would allow more opportunity for reinforcements from the United States to arrive at the fighting front in Europe. NATO forces must resist "forward" and, as far as is possible, contain a Warsaw Pact attack without yielding Allied territory. This requires strong conventional forces, placed as near as possible to the Alliance's borders, and able to absorb the brunt of the initial attack.

Figure 1–1. Approximate Target Coverage by NATO and Warsaw Pact TBMs in the Central Region.

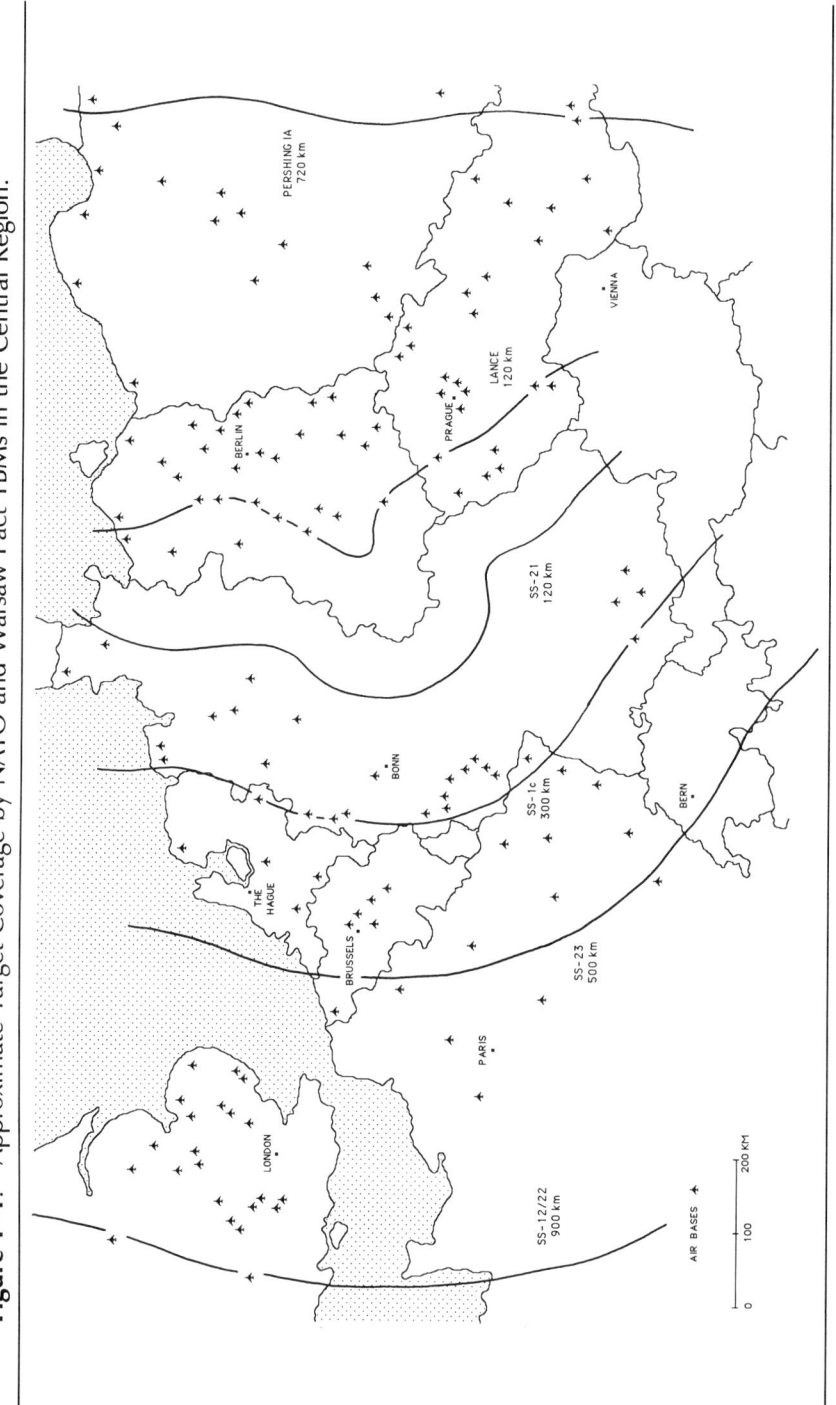

Although anything that undermined the strategy of flexible response would inevitably have serious military consequences and implications for NATO's military force structure, its impact in the political field and on deterrence itself would likely be even greater. This is because one of the peculiarities of the Atlantic Alliance is that it combines nations whose concepts of deterrence are not identical. The United States, for instance, has on the one hand announced progressive refinements in its nuclear doctrine to allow selective and limited nuclear use as a means of increasing the coupling between the security of North America and that of Europe. On the other hand, the argument has also been voiced in prominent places in the United States that the credibility of extended nuclear guarantees in an era of superpower strategic parity is uncertain. Officially, the United States has called for larger conventional forces and, more recently, has urged the strengthening of forces able to carry war deep into Warsaw Pact territory to attack follow-on forces, thus placing on the Soviets the onus of whether or not to use nuclear weapons first in order to prevail. In contrast, many European members of NATO have resisted larger conventional forces for a variety of reasons, including the economic burden they would pose, and the fear that the nuclear threshold might be raised so high that a conventional war in Europe might once again become "thinkable." European members of the Alliance, with the exception of France, have also had to cope with a greater divergence of domestic political opinion about NATO's policies and the wisdom of confrontational military strategies than has the United States.

France, as a nuclear power, has tended to dismiss the possibility of a prolonged conventional conflict in Europe, as well as that of a limited theater nuclear exchange. Arguing that "disuasion du faible au fort" ("deterrence by the weak, of the strong") has different characteristics and consequences from deterrence between the superpowers, France asserts that nuclear weapons used against its territory, whether described as "tactical" or "strategic," will bring about a nuclear response against the urban or industrial centers of the aggressor. Britain, on the other hand, in effect has two policies, one involving NATO use and the other national use. In contrast to France, Britain in 1962 pledged its nuclear forces in support of Alliance strategy, so that the targeting of its nuclear weapons would be planned as part of Supreme Allied Commander, Europe's (SACEUR's) overall nuclear response. Yet Britain reserves its right, should supreme national interests be at stake, to initiate an independent national nuclear response against targets of its own choosing.

However, even when differences of view have been quite sharp, the need for political solidarity in the Alliance has been sufficiently strong to allow doctrinal difficulties among members of the integrated military structure to be overcome by mutual compromises. Thus, although the result has never been entirely satisfactory from the standpoint of any one member, it has been sufficient to encourage each member to believe that its own view about how "flexible response" would be implemented in the event of actual war has been respected. And while the disagreements among Allies might encourage the Soviets to believe that NATO will dissolve in disarray under attack, the ambiguity about the precise nature of the NATO response creates uncertainties that complicate Soviet planning and so strengthen deterrence. Thus a strength of "flexible response" is that it neither promises nor demands anything in precise detail. NATO has in some measure sacrificed clarity and coherence in military doctrine in order to sustain political solidarity. Flexible response represents a compromise among allies who have diverse security threats, disparate domestic economic and political circumstances, and different ideas about how best to ensure their own and the collective security; and for most NATO countries, the doctrine provides an acceptable bridge between nuclear and conventional force strategies. It recognizes that both nuclear and conventional forces play a part in deterrence as well as war fighting; and that their capabilities are necessarily complementary and supportive. Flexible response has been sufficiently resilient to accommodate more than two decades of technological and doctrinal change, and the perceived ebbs and flows of the state of East/West relations. If NATO's flexibility in response were to be undermined, the actual and doctrinal consequences for the Alliance would be deep and almost certainly damaging.

THE CHANGING NATURE OF THE SOVIET THREAT

We noted above that one of the provocations for this debate has been the changing character of Soviet missile forces. The significance of those changes is also an element of the debate. The older Soviet missiles were relatively inaccurate, but their inaccuracy was offset by the large destructive radius of their nuclear warheads. Had these missiles been fitted with nonnuclear warheads, the combination of low accuracy and reduced destructive power would have rendered them insignificant as a threat to NATO. Recently, however, improved midcourse guidance accuracy, the development of terminal guidance, and improvements in nonnuclear warhead performance (for instance, the development of individually guided submunitions) makes the use of ballistic missiles with conventional warheads a contingency that has to be seriously examined from the military point of view. It is also likely to attract increasing public concern in a number of European countries due to a growing interest in nonnuclear defense. Furthermore, developments in chemical weapons technology present the prospect that ballistic missiles might be fitted with chemical warheads.

The effectiveness of NATO's defensive capabilities depends in good measure on the survival and continued functioning of key facilities, some for the duration of a conflict and others for at least the opening hours or days. Such facilities include command-and-control centers, main airbases, air defense batteries, ports and airfields for the arrival of reinforcements, nuclear warhead storage sites, and NATO's own theater nuclear forces. They are all potential targets for enhanced Soviet TBMs, and were they to be effectively and swiftly disabled, NATO could find itself immediately confronted with little choice but to surrender or to escalate the war to a nuclear level. If the issue were this uncomplicated, and this narrow, there would be little debate about what Allied governments ought to do.

However, as the subsequent chapters in this volume explain in greater detail, there is a continuing debate that is being conducted in a wider context, one that includes questions about

- How the Soviet TBM threat is to be understood, within the framework of Soviet strategic and operational doctrine;
- How NATO ought to respond, within the framework of NATO's strategic and operational doctrine, taking into account other demands on resources;
- The arms control implications of ATBMs, both the impact of agreements limiting theater and tactical ballistic missiles, and the impact of ATBMs on ABM Treaty limits covering strategic ballistic missile defenses;
- ATBMs as an avenue for Europe or the United States to exploit emerging defense technologies, with broader implications for industrial and technological competitiveness;

- How the Alliance should deal with potential divisiveness in the ATBM issue, where allies have differing views about the urgency of the TBM threat and differing levels of willingness and capacity to cooperate in a solution;
- How Alliance solutions on these matters will affect security relationships in regions beyond Europe.

The mere existence of new Soviet missile technologies does not in itself constitute a direct threat to the Alliance. To be a direct threat, new Soviet systems must be deployed in such numbers, and matched with a credible military concept for their operational use, that NATO would be unable to counter their effect. Too often, Western observers succumb to the temptation of assuming that any potentially threatening technology within Soviet grasp will be deployed at a rate and in a way that is most threatening to Alliance interests, as defined by *Western* observers. More sensibly, we should assume that Soviet deployments and practices will be defined by historical and organizational imperatives, as the *Soviets* understand them. It matters a great deal in assessing the Alliance's proper response whether enhanced technology missiles will be fully deployed with Soviet forces within five years or fifteen; whether they will be deployed only with conventional warheads or with chemical warheads as well; whether in numbers that merely replace existing missile forces or significantly enlarge them; and whether they are operational adjuncts to other weapon systems or replacements for them. When the Soviets deploy any weapon system, they need to make such choices, choices that are by no means clear cut, because the Soviets also face constraints both on the availability of technological resources and on the ability of their existing organizations to absorb new programs.

Sound predictions about how soon and in what manner a new Soviet technology may threaten the West must, therefore, start with the wider context of Soviet military policy and tactical doctrine. Yet many crucial parts of that context are concealed from Western observers and are therefore the subject of controversy. For instance, when the threat posed by new Soviet missiles is discussed, a scenario is often invoked in which NATO command posts, nuclear warhead storage bunkers, and airfields have to be "destroyed" with conventional weapons. It may then be suggested that the Soviets would allocate this task to missiles alone. This would mean that the Soviets must acquire missile inventories of a certain size, and by extrapolating from current deployment rates, the Alliance could predict how soon this threat might emerge. Indeed, if the required inventories seemed too large for Soviet resources, NATO might conclude that the threat is not one to which it need pay serious attention. But if Soviet tactical doctrine does not envisage "destroying" these NATO sites by missile attack but only disabling them temporarily until other weapons can be brought to bear, a very different picture of overall Soviet capabilities may emerge. This picture might suggest a more modest Soviet missile force inventory and a threat that would emerge sooner rather than later.

It must be remembered as well that the NATO Alliance has its own purposes and internal dynamic, and it does not follow, even if a Soviet TBM threat were plausible, that NATO's response should be merely reflexive. When confronting a new threat, the wiser course for NATO is to return to its own doctrinal and operational foundations and devise a response that fits its fundamental objectives. A return to the cornerstone of its own policy also provides a sense of perspective on the whole structure of alliance security. The threat posed by the Warsaw Pact in Central Europe is a good deal more diversified than just theater ballistic missiles. It includes manned aircraft, short- and medium-range air-to-ground missiles, and long-range cruise missiles launched from the ground, sea, or air. The Soviets regularly update all of these systems to improve their performance. A defense policy for the Alliance that focused excessively on the TBM threat would merely invite the Soviets to concentrate their offensive efforts on other weapons that could circumvent ballistic missile defenses. For the same reason, a debate on ATBMs that focused only on the ballistic missile threat would risk downgrading other threats from the air. In recognition of this, the discussion of ATBMs in Europe has increasingly been conducted within the broader framework of "extended air defense." This label itself serves as a reminder that the Alliance faces a spectrum of threats from the air, which has now been extended to include improved Soviet theater ballistic missiles. Air defense has also become "extended" in the sense that the longer ranges of new Soviet missiles and aircraft expand the threat to a wider geographical area in Europe. The ATBM issue, therefore, must be set in the broader context of a set of assumptions about how the Soviets might use the panoply of weapons available to them and how NATO might tailor a response that best serves its needs while thwarting Soviet plans.

The consequence of setting the ATBM issue in this broader context can be illustrated by a basic problem that the Alliance must confront.

Should it cope with the TBM threat by building a defense devoted to this purpose, or should it upgrade the capabilities of the existing air-defense system to encompass the ATBM mission? Some proponents of ATBMs have indeed argued for treating the ballistic missile threat in isolation and building a specialized ATBM system on the grounds that only such a system would provide effective defense. Built specifically as a missile defense against theater-range missiles, it could also provide a foundation for extended defense against longer-range missiles. It might thus provide a bridge between European theater defense and U.S. strategic defense. Yet unless NATO could also defend against the evolving Soviet aircraft and cruise missile threats, a specialized ATBM network would be of limited value in Europe.

NATO is committed to an upgrade of the present air defense network, involving the deployment in some countries of the Patriot and improved Hawk interceptor missiles. Both of these surface-to-air missile (SAM) systems have reportedly been tested in an ATBM role, though only in one-on-one encounters at test ranges (a complex ATBM network would have more formidable tasks in wartime). A number of existing U.S. and European anti-aircraft missile systems could be upgraded to provide some ATBM protection. Yet for technical reasons, such upgrades are likely to entail some loss of efficiency as an anti-aircraft system, a loss that would also reduce their effectiveness against cruise missiles and air-launched weapons. Hence, when viewed in the broader context, the ATBM issue can be recognized as a debate over the relative importance of different NATO missions and vulnerabilities.

In the face of attack by Warsaw Pact aircraft, the Alliance's freedom of military action can be defended by passive as well as active measures of protection. Passive techniques include electronic jamming, deception, dispersal of forces, mobility, redundancy, hardening of sites, and rapid damage repair facilities. Offensive counterair operations also provide a valuable means of reducing the enemy's attack potential. The variety of measures is significant because many or most of them might also be effective against missile attacks. Advocates of ATBM tend to characterize such passive countermeasures as at worst inadequate and at best mere adjuncts to active ATBM defense. On the other hand, those who are skeptical of ATBMs have endorsed passive techniques as being sufficiently effective and point to their very low cost in comparison with an ATBM system. Thus far, however, the public debate on ATBM has not benefited from a careful and systematic analysis of precisely which countermeasures might best serve the

Alliance's needs, how difficult and costly they would be to implement, or how effective they would be.

ATBM: "EXTENDED AIR DEFENSE" OR "THE SON OF SDI"

Not the least difficulty the Alliance will face in addressing the ATBM issue is deciding how it should be framed: Are ATBMs to be the next step in the natural evolution of current air defenses, or are they the first step in a revolutionary transformation of Alliance doctrine — are ATBMs "the son of SAM" or "the son of SDI"? As subtle as the distinction may seem, it is not inconsequential. As an extension of air defenses, ATBMs would focus on nonnuclear threats. Although it may be a matter of indifference to the defense weapons themselves whether the missiles that they intercept carry conventional or nuclear warheads, it cannot be a point of indifference to the defense designer. The performance standards demanded of nuclear defense will be far higher, dictating different technologies and tactics. Viewed as "son of SAM," in contrast, ATBMs might perform quite adequately with readily available technologies, without requiring or providing a channel to more exotic SDI technologies. As such, ATBMs might be compatible with, and perform far better in the context of stringent arms control restraints on strategic defenses and offensive missiles. Not least, conceived as an extension of air defenses, ATBMs might legitimately be viewed as a responsibility and burden to be shared by all of the allies.

An alternative view of ATBMs as "the son of SDI" would examine how the ideas of the U.S. Strategic Defense Initiative might be adapted and extended to provide antimissile defense of Europe as well as that of North America. Such an approach raises difficult technical and political questions. Unlike the ATBM debate, SDI primarily addresses the issue of defense against nuclear missiles, a much more demanding requirement than defense against conventionally armed missiles. In the nuclear case, even a very small number of missiles getting through to their targets would be potentially disastrous. The shorter time of flight of Soviet missiles aimed at targets in Europe, compared with targets in the United States, not only provides less opportunity for warning but makes it much more difficult to have a "layered" defense — that is, one in which there are opportunities to intercept the attacking missile in its boost phase, in its midcourse flight, and in its terminal descent.

In some measure, the view that development of ATBM systems *ought* to be linked to the SDI stems from a sense that, for alliance cohesion, there *must be* a "son of SDI" if there is an SDI. It is argued that the vast conceptual, scientific, and industrial endeavor being made in the United States on SDI neither can nor should disregard the problem of defending Europe against Soviet missile attack. Unavoidably, the question arises about who should bear the burden of providing the European "layer" of defense. There is the view that, in the present state of transatlantic relationships, the security of European countries and their future influence on Alliance policies requires that Europeans initiate their own solutions to this problem, independent of the SDI program. Cooperation with the United States, on the basis of a partnership between the U.S. SDI program and a European ATBM program, would be widely seen as beneficial to the Alliance as a whole. Raised as "the son of SDI," a European ATBM program would evidently presume the demise of the ABM Treaty and any other arms control arrangements with which the treaty is linked.

STRATEGIC CONSIDERATIONS

In strategic political terms, the development of effective missile defenses by the two superpowers, providing near-perfect protection for their territories, would make them sanctuaries from nuclear retaliation. It is argued by some that this would produce a more stable strategic balance between the two superpowers. But others believe that it would make Europe, including the satellites of the USSR, the neutrals, and the Alliance countries, feel much less secure. Insofar as the U.S. SDI system might also provide some protection for its European allies against Soviet strategic missiles, this sense of insecurity might be lessened. But it would not disappear because Western Europe would continue to be directly vulnerable to all other Soviet forces. Under these conditions, the security of the European nations would have been decoupled from that of the United States, a goal that the Soviet Union has long sought.

The Reagan administration appears to have been mindful of this predicament for its allies from the beginning. In his speech of 23 March 1983, President Reagan acknowledged the importance of the links between the United States and its allies, not only in the context of the existing strategy of deterrence based on nuclear retaliation but also in a future alternative strategy based on defense:

> As we pursue our goal of defensive technologies, we recognize that our allies rely on our strategic offensive power to deter attack against them. Their vital interests and ours are inextricably linked. Their safety and ours are one. And no change in technology can or will alter that reality. We must and shall continue to honor our commitments.

And a White House pamphlet issued under President Reagan's signature in January 1985 affirmed that "U.S. policy has always been one of deterring aggression and will remain so even if a decision is made in the future to deploy defensive systems. The purpose of the SDI is to strengthen deterrence."

Statements by senior members of the Reagan administration have also stressed the need for linkage between strategic missile defense in the U.S. and theater missile defense in Europe. The Hoffman Panel, in its report advising the president on the security implications of strategic defenses, proposed that defense deployment proceed in stages, starting most immediately with ATBM defenses for Europe, based on available (and thus nonexotic) technologies, for a ground-based terminal defense against both conventional and nuclear missiles. Subsequently, despite "official" enthusiasm of those who support the "grand design" of SDI, and the key role it assigns to space-based exotic weapons, there has been growing pressure for the more step-by-step approach to strategic defense by those who consider that a less ambitious system should be developed with technologies that exist now, rather than waiting for the exploitation of what might be available in the more distant future. These views were reflected in U.S. action during 1986 in awarding contracts to Europeans for the study of a "European architecture" for defense against both strategic and theater nuclear missiles. This suggests not only the Reagan administration's wish to get as wide a European research backing as possible for the technologies of the SDI program but also an understanding that a vigorous program to develop European theater missile defenses is important to the political survival of SDI within the United States. It also suggests that there could be considerable convergence between the "extended air defense" and the "son of SDI" approaches to TBM defense in Europe.

TECHNOLOGICAL AND INDUSTRIAL ISSUES

As European governments were considering the strategic, diplomatic, and political implications of SDI, serious concern arose among them over the foreseeable consequences in the scientific, technological, and industrial spheres if Europe failed to keep pace with a vast U.S. research program in emerging technologies. The fears that Europe might cease to be master of its own future were underscored by the peremptory action of the Reagan administration in announcing to the Europeans that they had a deadline of sixty days to answer proposals for cooperation with the United States on SDI. The subsequent rescinding of this deadline and the attempts of the administration to allay European concerns by explaining the good intentions behind this have not been sufficient to remove the fear that spin-offs from SDI technology, particularly in the computer field, would enlarge an already growing high-technology gap between the United States and Europe. Western Europeans also feared a "brain drain" of scientists to the other side of the Atlantic, attracted by the scientific challenges of SDI and the research resources and facilities that would be generated by it. They feared that unless radical measures were taken in Europe, European countries would not, in the future, have the technological know-how to design and build advanced weapon systems; and as a result, Europe would become effectively dependent on the United States for its security for all time.

The depth of the European quandary, and the complexities of the politics surrounding the ATBM issue, are suggested by the European response. France stepped forward in April 1985 with the EUREKA initiative, a proposal for European research cooperation, broadly defined to exploit the opportunities of the newly emerging technologies so that the competitiveness of key sectors of European industry, including those concerned with advanced weapon development, could be protected in an increasingly global market. But this was not enough for several European governments that, while not wishing to be seen giving wholehearted political support to the ideas of SDI, were nonetheless anxious to share the technical benefits that might accrue from it. It did not thus prove possible to reach agreement on a common European response to the U.S. administration's invitation to participate in the SDI research program.

Although defense industry companies in Britain, France, Germany, Italy, and the Netherlands are now participating in the SDI program, there continue to be reservations expressed about the attitude and commitment of U.S. industry to the genuine sharing of the mutual benefits of research. Not only is it feared that the U.S. Congress or government might impose its own rules to limit technology transfer and adopt measures to regulate the wider exploitation of SDI research on the grounds of security but also that the difference in size between the research facilities of most European companies and those of the major U.S. laboratories, would result in skimming off the most attractive and advanced results of European research for the prime benefit of the United States. Most of the research areas in which SDI is concerned are those where the gap separating Europe from the United States is the widest and in which the European position is most vulnerable.

Thus, it is argued that the mobilization of European industry and European technological research facilities behind a cooperative European ATBM research program would be attractive from the standpoint of maintaining European autonomy in advanced weapons development. Technical links would be maintained with the SDI program, thereby providing a continuing political linkage on the strategic issues and possibly reducing the cost burden of antimissile defense in Europe. Whatever the merit of these arguments, there is no denying that they are part of the wider context within which the ATBM issue must be understood and addressed.

SOVIET RESPONSES AND ARMS CONTROL

In considering the strategic consequences of NATO's ATBM decisions, we need also to examine the effect of possible reactions by the Soviets. A plausible reaction would be for the Soviets to expand their offensive forces, so as to overcome NATO's ATBM defenses by saturation. There would therefore be a very strong case for ensuring, as is planned with SDI, that the deployment of the defensive systems would be "cost effective at the margin" — that is, ensuring it would be significantly more expensive for the Soviets to deploy more offensive systems than it would be for NATO to deploy the defensive systems necessary to counter them. Whether this argues for active defenses such as ATBM or passive, whether for revolutionary "son of SDI" technologies or evolutionary "extended air defense," is part of the debate.

Soviet offensive counters to NATO defenses are only half the issue. Widespread deployment of new Soviet defenses against NATO's offensive missiles could pose an additional direct challenge to NATO by undermining its ability to deter Soviet aggression through the threat of escalation. Thus an important element in the ATBM debate is an assessment of whether developments in Soviet ATBM capabilities, as well as Soviet TBM capabilities, present a threat to NATO's existing strategy. At present, Soviet ATBM capability appears to be modest. The SA-10 system, which is now being deployed at some hundred sites inside the Soviet Union, has some antimissile capability—but it seems unlikely that it would place any effective limit on NATO's capacity for limited nuclear response and selective nuclear employment options. The SA-10 could certainly do little to blunt a massive nuclear blow by the Alliance. The SA-X-12 missile, which is still under development, is alleged to have an ATBM capability and may have the potential to intercept some types of strategic ballistic missiles. This could provide a significant advantage for the Soviets by blurring the distinction between theater and strategic missile defense in the context of the ABM Treaty. In these circumstances, NATO's own choices regarding the balance between active and passive defensive measures against Soviet TBMs cannot help but be influenced by the prospects of the Soviet ATBM defenses.

The ATBM issue cannot be fully debated without considering the implications of and for arms control. There is, first, the connection to possible strategic arms limitation agreements and to possible deployment of strategic missile defense systems. If the United States were to go ahead with SDI deployments, then it would effectively have to renounce the fundamental provisions of the 1972 ABM Treaty. In this case, the ATBM issue is no longer principally one of defense against Soviet conventional missiles, in a context where options for nuclear escalation against Soviet territory still exist as an action of last resort. The issue then becomes one involving the need for theater defense against nuclear missiles, in a context where the options for nuclear escalation against Soviet territory may be increasingly limited. This, of course, has particular importance for the lesser nuclear powers within the Alliance.

The second major consideration is the extent to which the development and deployment of a European ATBM defense would be consistent with the provisions of the ABM Treaty. To many in Europe, the ABM Treaty is both strategically and politically important because it is the one piece of arms control that has been successfully negotiated and that seems to provide an effective brake in one area of the arms race. It has thus become a political symbol in Europe. Even though the ABM Treaty binds only the two superpower signatories, the Alliance members cannot be indifferent to the potential impact of European defense programs on the treaty regime. This raises a question on which there has not been much discussion: Are there limits within which ATBM defense programs—NATO's and the Warsaw Pact's—ought to be confined, as much to preserve the Alliance's escalation strategy as to preserve the ABM Treaty?

A third important arms control consideration is the effect that limitations on the deployment of tactical and theater missiles may have on the case for ATBM. It is a quirk of East/West relations that although the most immediate threat to NATO's strategy comes from the shortest-range TBMs, the 1987 INF arms control treaty focuses instead on longer-range TBMs. One might suppose that a new agreement banning three of the four categories of Soviet TBMs (the SS-20, SS-22, and SS-23) would diminish the need and enthusiams for ATBMs. But this would underestimate the variety of arguments being pressed forward on behalf of ATBMs. From the military standpoint, the progress being made toward reductions in theater nuclear weapons in Europe places an increased importance on the balance of conventional forces; on the possible use of longer-range ballistic missiles with conventional warheads; and on the continuing Warsaw Pact advantage in numbers of shorter-range TBMs. Moreover, the enthusiasm for ATBMs in some circles results as much from political and technological concerns as from military ones. So the new INF agreement has changed the content of the debate on ATBMs rather than brought it to an end.

RESOURCES

Unavoidably, NATO must consider the resource implications of its ATBM decisions. Nobody can yet tell with any certainty how much a European antimissile defense system or extended air defense system would cost. Nor can we be sure that such a system would be cost-effective when the countermeasures that are likely to be developed against it are taken into account. But it seems certain that the costs involved are likely to be very substantial and that money to meet them has not been earmarked in the budget projections of most European countries. That "we cannot afford it" is clearly not, in itself, a complete argument against an ATBM project. What the Alliance can afford is a matter of priorities. But the priority given to ATBM has to be considered against all the other priority tasks that the Atlantic Alliance will have to meet by the 1990s. Demands for command and control, air defense, weapons intended for ground, naval and air forces are queuing up for the attention of governments at a time of increasing resistance to calls for larger defense budgets. Even more important is the manpower challenge. At a time of declining birth rates—particularly but not only in West Germany—the requirement for manpower for the armed forces is likely to be an almost overriding consideration during the 1990s. Thus Alliance governments will undoubtedly face increasingly difficult decisions in setting their defense priorities.

THE CONTINUING DEBATE

The ATBM debate has a fascinating combination of political, economic, strategic, scientific, technological, military, and industrial considerations woven into it; and the relative balance of these elements will have a significant effect on the outcome of the debate. At the same time, the debate carries all the seeds of a new transatlantic misunderstanding. These complex issues need to be widely understood in public and official circles throughout the Alliance if this is to be avoided. But the debate also provides an opportunity for the European members of the Alliance, either within their own program or as part of the development of the U.S. SDI program, to make an important contribution to the building of a stronger European pillar to the NATO Alliance.

The chapters that follow in this volume could not conceivably exhaust all the issues raised in the ATBM debate, but they do explore important matters that must be part of decisions both in Europe and in the United States on the issues of ATBM defense, the outcome of which could result in the expression of a renewed commitment to the common goal of Atlantic security.

NOTES

1. The confusion over proper terms extends to the labels given to the ballistic missiles as well. The Soviets have placed the SS-20 under the command of the *Strategic* Rocket Forces, and they distinguish the "operation-tactical" SS-23 and SS-22 from the "tactical" SS-21. In the West, the SS-20 was originally referred to as part of Soviet theater nuclear forces (TNF), then subsequently as part of Soviet intermediate-range nuclear forces (INF). When arms control proposals linking limitations on the SS-20 with constraints on the SS-23 and SS-22 arose, the latter two missiles were in some circles labeled as SRINF or "short-range intermediate-range nuclear forces." In other circles, both the press and officials have referred to the SS-20 and NATO's Pershing II as "medium-range" missiles and all TBMs with ranges between 500 and 1,000 km (the SS-23 and SS-22) as "shorter-range" missiles. The 1987 INF treaty designates missiles with ranges between 1,000 and 5,500 km as "intermediate-range," and those with ranges between 500 and 1,000 km as "shorter-range" missiles.

   There is added possibility of confusion from the use of NATO designators for Soviet missiles—that is, Scud, Frog, Scaleboard, SS-21, SS-22, SS-23, and so forth. In particular, up until a few years ago, the U.S. Department of Defense repeatedly stated its expectation that the missile designated as the SS-12 Scaleboard would be replaced by the SS-22. When the newest version of the SS-12 finally appeared, some observers judged it so little changed from the SS-12 that they designated it as the SS-12 Mod (modification); others refer to it as the SS-12/22. For the purposes of the new INF treaty, the United States adopted the designation SS-12, although the Soviets label the missile as the OTR-22.

   The authors of the chapters that follow in this volume have been persuaded to adopt common terminology, where possible. The term *TBM* will refer to ballistic missiles with ranges up to the 5,000 km SS-20; the term *shorter-range TBMs* will refer to ballistic missiles with ranges under 1,000 km; and the term *shortest-range TBMs* will refer to ballistic missiles with ranges under 500 km. In many instances, however, the authors must resort to the labels used by officials and other analysts.

2 ATBM TECHNOLOGIES AND NATO
*Benoit Morel and
Theodore A. Postol*

One of the many modernization options currently being debated within NATO is the upgrading of air defenses to protect critical NATO assets from attack by a new generation of Soviet tactical ballistic missiles (TBMs). Because these shorter-range missiles might possibly combine great precision of delivery with a short flight time to targets, some observers have argued that they could provide the Warsaw Pact with effective nonnuclear weapons for use in a conventional surprise attack on NATO. In order to offset the destabilizing influence of these missiles, it is argued, anti-TBM (ATBM) defenses are required for NATO.

Any analysis of an ATBM response would have to answer several basic questions before cost-effectiveness comparisons with other possible defense responses could be made. These questions would include:

- If a near-term, active defense is desirable, is it possible to upgrade an existing air defense system to provide either limited or extensive intercept capabilities against Soviet TBMs?
- How well will ATBM systems function if they are subjected to countermeasures that are commonly used in warfare today?
- What are the prospects for new defense technologies, available in the mid- or long-term, that might be used in future versions or upgrades of ATBM defenses?

- Are there new classes of countermeasures that might also be successful against applications of new ATBM-related technologies that are currently being discussed and developed?

Because there are also arms control issues raised by missile defenses, we should add a fifth question: Are there significant technical distinctions among anti-aircraft, ATBM, and strategic ABM defense systems? This chapter presents a short descriptive summary of a detailed technical analysis of these and other related questions.[1]

TASKS THAT ACTIVE DEFENSES MUST PERFORM

Whether defenses consist of medieval walls to protect against footsoldiers, or modern systems that use interceptors and radars to protect against ballistic missiles, they must be designed so that a resourceful and intelligent adversary cannot circumvent them. There are five distinct and interdependent tasks that an active missile defense must perform. Because these interdependent tasks must be performed rapidly even if the defense system itself is under attack, any enemy action that delays or prevents even one critical defense task can begin a chain of events that causes degraded performance — or even the collapse — of the entire defense.

Detection

Potentially threatening objects must be detected at great enough range to allow time for the defense to perform all the distinct tasks required of it. The range at which TBMs must be detected depends on the amount of time the defense system needs to assure its own protection and that of the site it is to defend. Even if a defense could react instantly to approaching TBMs, interceptors still need time to fly out and intercept attacking warheads. The speed of approaching objects and the speed at which defense interceptors can fly to intercept points therefore are important determinants of the range at which sensors must be able to detect approaching objects. If the properties of objects make them difficult to detect (for instance, if the attacker has designed his missiles to be "stealthy"), and their high speed of approach requires a large detection range to allow time for the defense to react, the demands on the detection sensor and its susceptibility to enemy countermeasures will generally be increased.

An enemy seeking to thwart detection can also accomplish this if he can introduce spurious signals into a defense system's sensors (jamming). When the false signals are of a strength comparable to the signals from real objects, they effectively blind the sensor by making it impossible for the defense system to distinguish between real objects and spurious ones, or even to determine whether any real objects are present. If an attacker combines countermeasures of this sort with stealth technology, it creates synergisms that can have a devastating impact on a defense system's ability to perform the task of detection. Where the sensor must scan at a high rate to detect distant, high-speed, stealthy objects, even weak signals introduced by enemy countermeasures may be indistinguishable from those observed from real objects.

Discrimination

An attacker might try to defeat or degrade the performance of a defense by presenting it with a large number of credible decoys. The defense must be able to discriminate between threatening and non-threatening objects, or it will expend interceptors against decoys rather than against genuine attackers. Such discrimination is possible only if the signals from decoys and real objects are dissimilar in ways that the sensor can measure. For example, if decoys wobble but TBMs do not, the signal from a decoy may fluctuate at a different rate. If drag effects in the atmosphere cause a decoy to slow down more rapidly than a TBM, the differences in velocity change may be discernible. If the reflected radar signal from the longer body of a TBM is stretched in time relative to the signal from a small decoy, a radar might be able to discriminate between TBMs and decoys by observing such variations in reflected pulses.

Again, the defense must expect countermeasures. If an attacker could generate spurious signals of random intensity that overlapped the signals from TBMs and decoys, the added signals might disrupt or even eliminate a sensor's ability to observe differences between the two types of objects. Against a radar sensor system, this countermeasure could be implemented with low-power jammers carried on both decoys and TBMs. Variations of this technique could also be used against heat-sensing, long-wave infrared sensors (LWIR). Decoys and

TBMs might be made indistinguishable to LWIR sensors by encasing them in reflecting balloons or surrounding them with clouds of aerosols that brightly reflect radiation welling up from the earth—or reradiate heat from the sun. Other masking techniques might be to create false infrared signals with reflectors, gas clouds, or flares.

Tracking

The objective of tracking is to provide data on the location, speed, and path of threatening objects so that the defense can estimate their future positions and dispatch defense interceptors for engagements. The precision with which tracking must be done is related to the lethal range of the interceptor's warhead and to the interceptor's ability to home in on the target. If the defense interceptors are armed with nuclear warheads, which can destroy a target at considerable range, the demands on the accuracy of tracking sensors external to the missiles are greatly reduced. Interceptors that are armed with conventional fragmentation warheads, or those that are designed to destroy their targets by direct impact, on the other hand, must be guided much closer to their intended targets—indeed, the probability of kill may be very low unless the interceptor has an on-board capability to locate and home on the target.

Hostile TBMs may be surrounded by clouds of decoys or small jamming devices, making it difficult or impossible for interceptors to discern their intended targets. If nuclear-armed interceptors are substituted for conventional ones, the large lethal radius of a nuclear detonation could be used to destroy both TBMs and nearby objects in the "escort" cloud. The need for extremely precise tracking dictated by the use of nonnuclear or hit-to-kill interceptors therefore makes defenses susceptible to countermeasures that utilize decoys and/or jammers to disrupt precision homing.

Guidance of Interceptors

To intercept approaching targets, a defense must know the location of both the attacking objects and its own interceptors. If interceptors have no on-board guidance units, the defense must track them and communicate very detailed guidance commands that direct them to intercept points. A problem with this kind of defense is that the enemy may be able to jam or disrupt communication links to the interceptors. Such countermeasures have been successful against relatively unsophisticated, command-guided anti-aircraft systems like the Soviet SA-2 system, but modern antijam communication techniques can greatly reduce the effectiveness of such countermeasures if the defense is carefully designed and properly operated.

Modern command-guided anti-aircraft systems generally use "hybrid" interceptors that are controlled in part by on-board systems and in part by communication links from ground-based elements of the defense. For example, the Patriot system, one of the major air defense weapons in NATO, utilizes an interceptor that is in constant communication with its ground control station, even though it has its own internal navigation and target sensing capabilities. When launched, the Patriot interceptor is initially guided toward the target by commands from a ground-based control unit. As the interceptor nears its target, the target is illuminated by the system's ground-based radar with very complex coded radar pulses, and the missile homes on the radar signal reflected from the target. During this process of homing, radar data obtained from sensors on the interceptor is transmitted to the ground for analysis by fast, powerful computers. Homing commands are then generated and quickly transmitted back to the missile. If the target is an airplane that is attempting to disrupt the homing process by jamming the ground-based radar, it must either mimic the radar's coded signal or overwhelm the interceptor's on-board sensors with a powerful jamming signal. If it tries the latter, the interceptor can be instructed by the ground-based unit to home on the jamming signal. Because the interceptor itself does not illuminate the target, it is very difficult for the aircraft to sense its approach, which makes it hard for the aircraft operator to know when to maneuver and activate jammers. These circumstances combine to make it very difficult for unaided aircraft to counter the homing process in a track-via-missile system like Patriot.

In contrast to aircraft, TBMs reflect much smaller amounts of radar energy, they must be engaged at greater range, and they operate where minimal atmospheric drag effects make it possible to surround them with escort clouds of accompanying jammers or decoys for extended periods during flight. Because radars must illuminate TBMs at great distances and the fraction of incident radar energy reflected from TBMs is small, missile homing must take place using much weaker signals. As a result, escort jammers do not need to be especially powerful to overwhelm homing sensors on interceptors. Because a jammer can escort a TBM for extended intervals without being attached to it, if the defense adopts a strategy of homing on jammers (in the same way it might home on jammers carried by aircraft), intercept of the actual TBM will be improbable. Thus, TBMs present different engagement conditions from those of aircraft, and antihoming measures that are likely to fail when used by aircraft may succeed when used by TBMs.

Destruction of Targets

Once the interceptor has been guided sufficiently close, it can accomplish destruction of its target with a nuclear warhead, or with fragments from a conventional high-explosive warhead, or by direct impact. The range of lethal effects from a nuclear detonation are quite large, relative to those of a conventional warhead of practical size. For example, a nuclear warhead weighing a few tens of kilograms might have an explosive yield of 1 to 10 KT and would probably destroy an approaching TBM if detonated within 100 to 200 meters of it. In contrast, a well-designed 100 kg fragmentation warhead might fail to do enough damage to an approaching TBM even if detonated within 10 to 20 meters of it. Hit-to-kill interceptors, of course, must actually collide with the TBM target.

The effectiveness of a nonnuclear interceptor against aircraft does not ensure lethality against TBMs. The cross-sectional area of an aircraft that contains components critical to its function (engines, fuel tanks, electronics and control units, pilot, aerodynamic surfaces, and so forth) is much larger than that of a TBM, so a fragmentation warhead detonated nearby is much more likely to strike an important component of the aircraft. Even light damage from an interceptor could well result in a mission abort and loss of the aircraft. The susceptibility of TBMs to damage from a fragmentation warhead is more problematic. As the TBM approaches its target, there is no longer any propellant in the rocket motor to detonate if a fragment passes through the motor casing. The TBM's warhead might be constructed with insensitive high-explosives, which might not detonate even if hit by a fragment. The TBM is falling toward its target at high speed, under the influence of gravity, and may not deviate from its ballistic path even if struck.[2]

On the other hand, conventionally armed TBMs can achieve high accuracy only if they can make small maneuvers in the lower atmosphere to adjust for the accuracy-degrading effects of wind and guidance errors. This is usually asccomplished with small aerodynamic surfaces that change the TBM's angle of attack as it falls (the U.S. Lance and Pershing II missiles enhance their accuracy in this manner). If an attempt to intercept a TBM results in damage to any of its critical maneuvering and guidance elements, the accuracy would be drastically degraded, greatly increasing the likelihood that its intended target will not be hit. Hence, in order to damage a well-designed and hardened TBM enough to stop it from destroying its target, it is likely that a conventional fragmentation warhead must score a near-direct hit.

FUNCTIONAL DESCRIPTION OF PATRIOT-LIKE DEFENSE OPERATIONS

We can get a better impression of the functional interaction of the five defense tasks, as well as the distinctions among anti-aircraft (SAM), ATBM, and ABM defense systems, if we look in greater detail at the illustrative case of Patriot, the long-range air defense system deployed with NATO forces in Europe that some propose upgrading for an ATBM role.

Each Patriot air defense fire unit (or battery) is composed of a radar, interceptor launchers, an engagement control station, power generators, and communications facilities. Each battery can in principle operate as an autonomous defense unit, receiving no external information about incoming threatening objects and depending entirely on its own radar for detecting attackers. But as deployed, each Patriot fire unit is to operate in conjunction with five other batteries, sharing radar data and defense tasks. For intercepts to be possible, the defense radars must detect approaching TBMs far enough away to allow time for interceptors to accelerate and fly to intercept points. The shortest range at which such detections must take place is the required detection range. There is also a minimum range at which intercepts must occur, because the defense unit or defended site will be damaged if an attacking missile detonates too nearby. This range is called the *keepout* range, and its size will vary, depending on how far the sites to be defended are from the defense unit and on how lethal the secondary effects of an intercept might be. If the attacker has "salvage fuzed" a nuclear-armed TBM warhead so that it detonates when intercepted, for instance, it may damage a "soft" target (such as exposed forces or the defense unit itself) from considerable distance away.[3] Nearby intercepts of TBMs armed with chemicals may also fail to protect targets, if winds carry the chemicals to targets anyway. These instances therefore require intercepts at greater distances. In actual engagements, the defense will prefer to intercept TBMs long before they reach the keepout zone, so the keepout range should be thought of as a minimum performance requirement, not the most desirable.

In cases where the size of the keepout range must be increased, there are very few easy choices available to the defense designer. Additional time must be created for interceptors to fly to intercept points at greater range, or additional speed must be given to interceptors to reach greater range more quickly (or both). If extra time to reach intercept points is sought by increasing the detection range, a radar with considerably greater power and antenna size would be required. If extra interceptor speed is sought through an increase in the interceptor's rate of acceleration and top speed, then a choice must be faced between the interceptor's size and its range—a choice with vital implications if the system has a dual role as an anti-aircraft and anti-TBM defense.

To illustrate this last point, suppose the Patriot interceptor were modified for higher-speed flight by simply increasing the burn rate of propellant in its motor, without changing its size.[4] As a first example, assume the missile were to accelerate at a uniform rate of about 20 Gs for about 5 seconds until it achieves a speed of 1 km/sec (Mach 3). On achieving this "cruise speed," the booster's thrust drops to a much lower value, so the motor's thrust merely cancels the decelerating effects of aerodynamic drag and gravity. The interceptor would then continue along its path at constant speed, climbing out of the dense lower atmosphere until it reached a maximum altitude of about 9 km, its motor having burned for about 50 seconds until all propellant is consumed. Under these conditions, the interceptor's maximum range would be about 45 km. In contrast, if the burn rate of propellants were modified so the missile could accelerate to a cruise speed of 1.25 km/sec, it would have a range of less than 20 km; if accelerated to a cruise speed of 1.5 km/sec, the range would drop to less than 8 km. The sharp range reductions occur because a much larger amount of fuel is needed to accelerate to a higher speed, and once the higher speed is achieved, the interceptor must continue to produce larger thrust to offset the added aerodynamic drag on the vehicle.

These calculations suggest why proposals for upgrading Patriot to an ATBM role include considerable modifications to the interceptor. Interceptors with cruise speeds in excess of 1 km/sec will have to be much larger than the current Patriot missile, or they will have considerably shorter engagement ranges—so short that their anti-aircraft role would be severely compromised. For example, a new interceptor designed to reach the 45 km range at a cruise speed of 1.5 km/sec under the assumptions above would weigh about twice as much as the current Patriot interceptor. This doubling in weight occurs in part because more propellant is needed, in part because the higher fuel load and acceleration entail the added weight of a larger airframe and more powerful flight control systems.

If the defense unit is to have a dual anti-aircraft and anti-TBM role, it will therefore require either a mix of small, special-purpose interceptors, some for use against aircraft and others for use against TBMs, or completely new and much larger interceptors that can fly to long range against aircraft. This in turn probably means new missile launchers, transport and support equipment for these launchers, modifications of computer control equipment to manage new and/or modified mixes of interceptors, and upgrades to electronic interfaces that support communications and control to the missiles and launchers.[5] Although the character and feasibility of such modifications is still uncertain, we can get some sense of how extensive the upgrade must be by illustrating our subsequent discussion with the baseline Patriot system—that is, one with no major size or propulsion modifications to its interceptor.

If we assume a set of performance characteristics for the interceptor, other important capabilities of an effective ATBM defense can then be sketched out. For instance, if the Patriot interceptor accelerates at a rate of 10 Gs, it will take slightly more than 10 seconds to achieve its maximum speed of 1 km/sec. Maximum speed would be achieved at about 5 km from the launch point where, we will assume, it intercepts an attacking TBM warhead that is arriving at 1 km/sec. Because a large defended site such as a major NATO airfield might well span 3 to 4 km on a side, a 5 km keepout zone might be a sensible performance requirement.[6]

In the 10 seconds it takes the interceptor to reach the 5 km keepout point, the TBM has also been closing in at 1 km/sec, from a point

15 km away down to the 5 km intercept point. So, assuming instantaneous launch of the interceptor on detection of an approaching TBM, 15 km is the minimum range at which the 1 km/sec TBM must be detected if the defense is to protect a 5 km keepout zone. In a real defense system, when a threatening object is detected, time must be consumed verifying the reported detection, tracking the object, predicting its impact point, determining an intercept point, and initiating an interceptor launch sequence. If the defense system takes 5 seconds to perform these functions and a 5 km keepout is still to be enforced, the minimum detection range must be increased from 15 to 20 km.

Not all missiles would approach the intercept point at a speed of 1 km/sec, however. The 120 km range Soviet SS-21, for instance, arrives at a speed of about 1 km/sec. But the 500 km range SS-23 arrives at about 2 km/sec, the 900 km range SS-12/22 arrives at about 3 km/sec, and the 5,000 km range SS-20 arrives at about 6 km/sec. For comparison, the 1,800 km range Pershing II would arrive at about 4 km/sec and a 10,000 km range ICBM at a speed of about 7 km/sec. So if the Patriot defense unit cannot execute an interceptor launch for 5 seconds after the initial detection of an approaching TBM, the engagement time requirements against the faster arriving SS-23 will dictate a detection range of about 35 km. And the very fast arriving SS-12/22 and SS-20 missiles will demand detection ranges of about 50 km and 95 km, respectively.

The performance demands placed on the radar are a function not only of the required detection range but also the area of the sky that must be scanned for attacking TBMs—the search solid angle. The required size of the radar search solid angle is determined by the variety of azimuths and elevations from which attacking missiles might arrive. A quick examination of a map of Europe suggests that if defense units in West Germany have to search for TBMs fired from anywhere along the central front, from northern Germany to the northern border of Yugoslavia, about 90 or more degrees of azimuth must be searched.

To determine the size of the vertical angle that must be searched, we need to know which ballistic trajectories might be followed by Soviet TBMs. By combining the sparse and sometimes contradictory public information on these missiles with well-established data on the properties of rocket propulsion systems, we can estimate the variety of trajectories that could be achieved. These include "minimum energy" trajectories, which result when a fully loaded missile achieves its maximum range by burning all its fuel, as well as shorter range trajectories that result when fully loaded missiles are programmed to burn out at loft angles that are larger (lofted trajectories) or smaller (depressed trajectories) than the maximum range loft angle.

Our analysis suggests that kinematically accessible ranges and loft angles for fully and partially loaded SS-12/22s and SS-23s would allow those missiles to arrive at a defense unit at angles larger than 75 degrees with respect to local horizontal, as well as at elevation angles smaller than 15 degrees. But on the most extreme trajectories, the Soviets would pay penalties in reduced payload or missile range, or both. So as a practical matter, the Patriot radar set would have adequate search capability against Soviet TBMs in Europe if it were able to search for missiles arriving at any loft angle between 15 and 75 degrees above the local horizon. Assuming the missiles might arrive from any direction within 90 degrees of azimuth, this translates into a search solid angle requirement of about 3,600 square degrees.

We noted earlier that, according to operational plans, each Patriot fire unit will be deployed with five other batteries, in a mutually supporting battalion. Hence, it might at first appear that a significant gain in system capability could be achieved by having each radar carry out only part of the entire search function. However, precisely how a battalion would divide up the search labors is unclear. For instance, because each radar that is used for anti-aircraft search can only search about 120 degrees of azimuth, three radars might be needed to search 360 degrees of azimuth, or else defended sites will be vulnerable to attack from the flanks or rear. Because enemy direction finding can be used to locate and attack radars that are emitting signals, it would be unwise to have all radars operating at the same time. It is likely that three of the six radars would be in motion or not operating most of the time, so that they can quickly replace any radar that is being suppressed or has been destroyed in raids against the air defense. If in spite of these operational constraints it proves feasible to use two or even three radars dedicated exclusively to the TBM search task, then two radars might have to search only 1,800 to 2,000 square degrees each, and three would need search only 1,200 to 1,400 square degrees each (we assume each radar's search fan will have some overlap with those of adjacent radars). Still another concern are demands placed on Patriot radars by the dual requirements of anti-air and anti-TBM missions. Reportedly Patriot fire units performing dual tasks will require different computer software and will suffer some loss of effectiveness against aircraft.[7] Such degradations in performance are both significant and expected, as a radar can use its available radiated power for only a finite number of tasks. We will assume, however, that radars dedicated to ATBM search and track functions are totally committed to this role. In reality, such an assumption would mean that those units would cease to function in their air defense role.

As we will discuss shortly, having several radars operate in conjunction with each other would have almost no impact on the effectiveness of most antiradar electronic countermeasures that may defeat Patriot in its anti-TBM role. Nevertheless, we will look first at the case where the ATBM search task is shared by two radars, each searching about 2,000 square degrees. Then to show how this defense might degrade with the suppression or loss of radars, we will also look at the cases where a single radar must search a full 3,600 square degrees.

The ability of a defense radar to search a given solid angle at a particular range depends on its radiated power, the size of its antenna, the speed of approaching objects that must be detected, and the amount of radar energy that is reflected back to the defense unit by the objects. The first two quantities—the radar power and antenna size—define what is called the "power-aperture product" of the radar. Because the power-aperture product is a property of the radar, its magnitude is determined by design choices and technologies available to those who build the radar. However, the second two quantities that have a critical impact on a radar's search capability—the amount of energy reflected by TBMs and their speed of approach—are properties of the attacking weapons and thus are determined by design choices and technologies available to the attacker.

The algebraic expression that defines the relationship among these factors is as follows:

$$\Omega \sim \frac{P_a A \, \sigma}{R_d^3 V}$$

where:

Ω is the size of the search solid angle,
P_a is the average power of the radar,
A is the area of the radar antenna,
σ is the radar cross-section of the target to be detected,
R_d is the minimum range at which the target must be detected,
V is the target's speed of approach relative to the radar.

We have relegated a detailed explanation of this equation to an endnote, and focus here on several key implications.[8] First, the solid angle that can be searched is a function of the cube of the detection range required. Hence, for a given radar, even modest changes in the required range greatly alter the area of the sky that can be searched for attacking TBMs within a given period of time. If a defense system is forced to increase the required detection range by 30 percent, from 15 km to 20 km for instance, the solid angle it could search in the given time period will drop roughly by half. The reason is that when a radar must search for approaching objects at a greater range, where its illuminating power is greatly reduced, the radar must scan more slowly so that the radar-target will be illuminated for a longer time as the radar beam scans across it. The weaker signal from the more distant target can then be collected over a longer period of time, making it possible for the radar to detect the presence of a target despite the weak reflected signal.

The hazard of the slower scan rate, of course, is that while the radar is carefully searching one segment of the sky, it may miss the approach of an attacker coming from another segment, perhaps aimed at the defense unit itself. Consequently, if a particular radar *must* search a given solid angle often enough to protect its keepout zone against particular TBMs, the above equation defines the greatest range at which the radar will be able to detect the attacking missiles.

We return now to the example of the Patriot radar. The general characteristics of the Patriot radar can be obtained by combining data from the open literature with general principles of electronic and signal processing technologies.[9] We need a value for the radar cross-section (radar reflectivity) of Soviet missiles to complete the equation. The radar cross-section (RCS) of an object is determined by the object's intrinsic features and its orientation with respect to the radar. Radar signals are reflected from many physical features of an object of complex shape. When such an object made up of many materials with high reflectivity has numerous flat or curved surfaces, sharp edges, sharp changes in body geometry, protruding features, or openings through its surface, it will generally be a good reflector of radar waves at many orientations with respect to a radar. Aircraft generally have these features and therefore have relatively large radar cross-sections. Even when observed front-on, a small fighter, for example, is likely to have an RCS of several square meters.

The aerodynamic circumstances of a ballistic missile, on the other hand, encourage the use of materials and shapes that incidentally result in lower RCS values over a wide range of orientations. When a bullet-shaped TBM with a seamless metal body exterior is viewed within about 60 degrees of a nose-on orientation, its RCS will be determined by weak scattering of radar waves from its nosetip, aft end, and complex weak currents that travel along the length of its body. Significant scattering from its nosetip will not be present if the nose is very sharp. Because even the fastest traveling TBM does not create a shock wave much hotter than 3,000 degrees K at its nosetip, a sharp nosetip that will essentially remove this contribution to the RCS can be used. The aft end contribution to the RCS may also be insignificant, because radar absorbing material can be attached to sharp edges at the aft end (and along edges on the missile's body), or the TBM may be designed with an aft end that has rounded edges, or both. Thus, when observed within 60 degrees of nose-on orientation, the main contribution to the RCS of a TBM designed to have a small RCS will be from weak travelling currents induced by radar waves along the cylindrical length of its metallic body. In these circumstances, the RCS observed by Patriot radars would be an astonishingly small value, of about 0.001 square meters.

For conventionally armed TBMs, however, the demands of maneuver and terminal guidance can add physical features to a missile that can substantially alter the overall RCS. For example, wings or aerodynamic control surfaces used for TBM maneuvers have sharp edges that scatter radar signals. If a tail wing has a front or rear edge of 0.25 meters length, when it is viewed at normal incidence by a radar, it alone can have an RCS of 0.02 square meters. When the wing-edge is viewed at only a few degrees off normal, however, its RCS could be considerably smaller than 0.001 square meter. Still other potential contributions to the RCS can result from a guidance system that uses an active radar because radar waves from the defense unit can pass through TBM radomes or windows and be reflected by internal components. This contribution to the RCS can also be greatly reduced by judicious use of radar-absorbing materials, shaping of components and edges, and with shutters to shield components from illumination until they are to be used. In fact, active radar systems might not even be used by high-accuracy TBMs because satellite-borne beacons like the U.S. Global Positioning Satellite System (or the Soviet GLONASS system) could be used by guidance systems to help maintain high accuracy. The bodies and components of modern missiles may also be constructed of woven glass, polymer, or carbon fiber materials, tailored to be poor reflectors and good absorbers of radar waves. If current TBMs have not been designed with RCS reduction as a priority, numerous contributions to radar scattering can result in a TBM RCS as large as 0.01 to 0.1 square meters. However, because today's technology makes it a modest effort to build low-RCS TBMs, the only sensible way to evaluate a defense is to explore its capabilities in the face of at least modest enemy countermeasures. We will therefore assume a span of RCS values from 0.1 to 0.001 square meters, and we will assume that an RCS value of 0.001 square meters is the likely RCS value for a reactive Soviet adversary in the 1990s.[10]

Table 2-1 summarizes required and achievable radar detection ranges against various missiles, under the assumptions we have made. To provide some sense of the challenge confronting Soviet ATBMs, if they have performance characteristics comparable to the Patriot, the table includes figures for Pershing II. It also includes the U.S. Trident SLBM, just to give some sense of how a defense system comparable to Patriot might fare in a strategic defense role. Current French and British nuclear SLBMs have ranges comparable to the SS-20. The table presumes that *no countermeasures* are employed by the attacker. To give an impression of how an upgraded interceptor and improved defense reaction-time could change the size of the minimum detection range, we have included figures for a hypothetical high-performance missile *significantly* more capable than the current Patriot. Because some of the countermeasures to be discussed below would still be effective against such an upgraded system, the reduced detection ranges shown in the table should not be construed as assuring the effectiveness of a future ATBM defense system.

The figures in Table 2-1 must be viewed with caution. They are approximations, so not too much should be made of small differences. And while we have confidence in our underlying assumptions, the figures can of course be no better than our assumptions. That being said, several points are worth highlighting, keeping in mind that these points only apply to situations where there are no Soviet countermeasures:

- Achievable detection ranges for a radar such as Patriot appear adequate to protect a 5 km keepout zone against TBMs such as the SS-21 under all the cases we examine, even if the radar must function autonomously against a "stealthy" TBM;
- Achievable detection ranges might be adequate to intercept TBMs such as the SS-23, even with the current interceptor, provided the defense system's reaction time is less than 5 seconds and Soviet missiles do not currently have the lowest value of RCS;

Table 2-1. Radar Detection Ranges for Various Missiles

Missile	Missile Range[a]	Achievable Detection Range[b]						Required Detection Range[c]	
		2,000 sq Degree Search			3,600 sq Degree Search				
		RCS 0.1 sqm	RCS 0.01 sqm	RCS 0.001 sqm	RCS 0.1 sqm	RCS 0.01 sqm	RCS 0.001 sqm	Current Interceptor	Upgraded Interceptor
SS-21	120 km	185 km	86 km	40 km	152 km	71 km	33 km	20 km	11 km
SS-23	500 km	147 km	68 km	32 km	121 km	56 km	26 km	35 km	16 km
SS-12/22	900 km	128 km	60 km	28 km	105 km	49 km	23 km	50 km	21 km
Pershing II	1,800 km	117 km	54 km	25 km	96 km	44 km	21 km	65 km	27 km
SS-20	5,000 km	102 km	47 km	22 km	84 km	39 km	18 km	95 km	33 km
Trident	7,400 km	97 km	45 km	21 km	79 km	37 km	17 km	105 km	38 km

a. Required detection ranges are related to the target's speed of approach, not its range. This table assumes minimum energy trajectories and missile warhead speed at the 5 km intercept point equal to speed at reentry. These assumptions are easily justified, as aerodynamic drag effects do not significantly alter the trajectory of approaching TBMs until they reach altitudes well below that of the assumed intercept point.

b. For indicated radar cross sections (RCS), assuming the characteristics for the Patriot radar indicated in end-of-chapter note 8.

c. Current interceptor assumes a five-second reaction time and interceptor characteristics stated in end-of-chapter note 4. Upgraded interceptor assumes general system improvement for a two-second reaction time and an interceptor with 100 G acceleration capability and 2 km/sec cruise speed.

- Achievable detection ranges are likely to be *inadequate* to enforce a 5 km keepout zone against a TBM such as the SS-12/22, unless the TBM has a large radar cross-section or an upgraded interceptor is added;
- Achievable detection ranges would be severely inadequate against a missile such as the SS-20 (or longer-range SLBMs and ICBMs), unless the warhead has a large radar cross-section; even an upgraded interceptor cannot help.

Similarly, a Soviet defense system with interceptor and radar capabilities comparable to Patriot would likely be unable to protect a 5 km keepout zone against Pershing II, Trident, or French or British SLBMs, unless they have large radar cross-sections. But such a defense might have adequate radar capabilities for intercepting the current Lance, Pershing I, and Pluton missiles deployed with NATO forces, and perhaps even a longer-range replacement resembling the Soviet 500 km SS-23 — in the absence of NATO countermeasures.

For those concerned with technical distinctions among SAM, ATBM, and ABM defenses, a number of very important points are worth noting. First, with respect to the radar capacity of a stand-alone defense unit, there is a substantial gap in required performance between a system to cope with 500 km range TBMs and strategic missiles such as Trident. Second, it cannot be simply assumed that if an "ATBM" system is competent enough to deal with the SS-20, it will either be able, or not able to deal with other long-range missiles. For example, because a 7,400 km range SLBM like Trident can arrive from many azimuths and loft angles, an ATBM defense would have to search an enormous solid angle, between 10,000 and 15,000 square degrees, for this faster-arriving missile. On the other hand, U.S. ICBMs can be launched from only six silo fields of known location. Achievable ballistic trajectories from very long range are severely constrained, so for each silo field, a radar need scan only an interval of loft angles of less than 25 degrees and a span of azimuths of about one degree. An ATBM radar would therefore need to search only from 120 to 150 square degrees for arriving ICBM warheads. A third point of significance is that modest RCS reduction measures can drastically limit the capability of an ATBM system to engage these long-range missiles. A fourth point, to be discussed shortly, is that fairly modest decoy and electronic countermeasures can be expected to degrade severely the antimissile performance of all SAM and ATBM systems, except systems that are so robust that their performance is indistinguishable from those with full ABM potential. A fifth point is that long-range surveillance sensors can greatly enhance the ABM capabilities of SAM and ATBM systems, provided, or course, that countermeasures are not used to offset the contributions of such surveillance sensors.

A final point is worth making for those interested in the formulation of policy. The diversity of the above considerations indicates that evaluations of SAM, ATBM, and ABM potentials is a complex subject with many technical subtleties. Sound policies on these matters can be derived only from an equally sound understanding of the technical issues discussed here and later in this chapter.

Because radar capacity appears to be such a prominent constraint on a defense system such as Patriot, we need to examine the ease with which this constraint might be overcome. As the radar search equation suggests, there are ways to address the shortcomings of a defense radar. One would be to increase the power-aperture product of the radar (P_aA in the equation). Another would be to reduce the solid angle that the radar must search, either by providing the defense unit with cues from another surveillance sensor about where specifically to look for attacking TBMs or by deploying more radars so that each can narrow its search angle. None of these approaches is without its complications. We have been assuming a mean emitted power of about 10,000 watts and an antenna aperture of 4.5 m^2 for the Patriot, yielding a power-aperture product of 45,000. Extending the detection range against a SS-12/22 with low RCS (0.001 m^2), for instance, from the 28 km achievable to the 50 km required for Patriot to scan a 2,000 square degree search solid angle and protect a 5 km keepout zone with a 5 second reaction time would mean multiplying the P_aA product by a factor of more than six, to 285,000. Extending the range from 22 km to 95 km, so that Patriot could engage an SS-20 under the same conditions, would require a power-aperture product on the order of 3 million watt-meters-squared, indistinguishable from radars limited by the ABM Treaty.

An alternative approach to enhancing defense capacity would be to share the search task among more radars. In the case of Patriot, if five of the battalion's radars could simultaneously scan from the horizon to 75 degrees elevation for aircraft and TBMs, each would have to cover only a portion of the total 5,000 square degrees to be searched (assuming coverage of 90 degrees of azimuth is adequate for the anti-air function). This could push TBM detection ranges out by perhaps 20 percent. Rather than divert radars from the anti-air task, NATO could add several more batteries to each battalion to aid the TBM mission, although it is not at all obvious that extra fire units could be pasted on to a battalion without other, major changes in communication and battle management equipment. We will return shortly to a third option, cueing the defense unit's radar from another surveillance sensor.

COUNTERMEASURES AND COUNTER-COUNTERMEASURES

In the prior discussion, we examined required and achievable detection ranges in the *absence* of countermeasures. In an actual military engagement, an important objective of the attacker will be to suppress the opposing defenses by disrupting or blocking the execution of one or several critical defense tasks. We can think of several schemes that an attacker might use to overwhelm the defense—and counter-countermeasures available to the defense. None of these is simple; all remind us that the great complexity of offense-defense engagements should caution us against excessive confidence in the performance of defenses. The diversity of suppression methods that are technically and tactically possible is great, and our omission of some methods from discussion here should not be construed as a suggestion that they are less attractive, efficient, or cost-effective than those mentioned.

As we noted earlier, the countermeasure called *jamming* works by directing so many spurious signals at a defense radar that the system is no longer able to distinguish between real signals and false ones. The radar in response can counter the jamming by concentrating its search at a shorter range, where the reflected signals from real targets will be much stronger, making them distinguishable from the weaker masking signals of a jammer. But if this reduced search range becomes too small to allow time for the defense to make intercepts, the defense will fail catastrophically.

Precisely which jamming technique an attacker might employ would depend on the sophistication of technology and the effort an attacker is willing and able to devote to the task. The general tactic would be to place multiple small jammers within tens of kilometers of the defense unit radar and activate them long enough to mask attacking TBMs. The jamming devices might be carried to an appropriate altitude and dispensed by cruise missiles, remotely piloted drones, aircraft, or by a TBM; they could be held aloft by parachutes or balloons or aerodynamically designed to accompany an attacking TBM on its trajectory. The simplest of such jammers would need to radiate no more than tens of watts of power. They would be turned on immediately before the TBM reached the maximum search range of defense radars. Since a radar can readily determine the direction of a jammer by radio direction finding, the tactics used in jamming attacks on defenses can influence the outcomes of engagements. For example, the most effective tactical use of jammers requires that TBMs and jammers be launched from different directions—so victim radars would have to perform the impossible task of searching all directions for TBMs in the presence of jamming. It is also possible that battlefield conditions could force an enemy to launch TBMs and jammers from the same locations. This situation would result in an attack where TBMs and jammers arrive from the same azimuth. If the defense correctly "guessed" that this was the case, the radar could then concentrate all its search power in that sector, slowly and deliberately scanning the range of elevations from which TBMs might arrive. This concentrated search would result in the collection of much larger reflected signals from approaching objects, requiring that the jammer be tens or hundreds of times more powerful for it to still overwhelm the radar. In this way, a radar can "burn through" a jamming attack, if the attack is not implemented properly.

On the other hand, if TBMs are placed on trajectories that are close to those of jammers, radars might have to observe them while looking directly at approaching jammers. This would place the radar in an impossible circumstance—similar to that of a baseball player trying to observe the approach of a ball arriving from the direction of the sun.

In this situation, radars would not be able to measure the range of TBMs. Still another possibility is that TBMs and jammers might not be launched on similar trajectories. They would then each arrive at radars from different elevation angles. If the jamming is powerful enough to overwhelm the radars in spite of attempts to "burn through" the jamming signals, then the defense would not be able to measure either the range or the elevation of approaching TBMs. In either case, the defense would then have to launch interceptors in the hope that an interceptor can be guided to an intercept without range data. Even in the unlikely event where luck resulted in the interceptor's arriving at a location close enough to allow last minute maneuvering and homing on signals, it would then be overwhelmingly likely that an escort jammer, rather than the TBM, would be intercepted.

The defense is not without its resources. One way a defense such as Patriot might attempt to defeat this enemy countermeasure is by cross-fixing on the jammer signal with its multiple radars. One radar might be placed 10 km up-range, or better, 10 km up-range and 10 to 20 km cross-range of the other. Because each radar could observe the direction to the jammer to a resolution of about one and a half degrees, this could provide adequate range information to allow for timely launch and guidance of interceptors. Nonetheless, if the jammer were close enough to the TBM, the weak signals from the TBM would be masked by the strong ones from jammers—and the defense would still be able only to track jammers. When interceptors then attempt to home on their targets by homing on signals from jammers, it will be overwhelmingly likely that an escort jammer rather than a TBM will be intercepted.[11] If in addition the escort jammers were configured as decoy TBMs, they might thwart discrimination even where the defense could discern jamming from true reflected signals.

The jamming devices themselves could take a variety of forms. Although none of these is utterly simple, they would utilize technology that has been available in the West for many years. One example of a jammer using currently available technology would be a 100 watt device with a directional antenna of modest size ($\frac{1}{3}$ meter in diameter) designed to focus jamming power into a 10 degree cone aimed in the direction of the defense radars. Another equally effective jammer—that is technologically more sophisticated but nevertheless uses currently available technology—might radiate 25 watts through a $\frac{2}{3}$ meter diameter electronically scanning antenna, able to lock electronically onto the signal from the defense radar and focus energy into a 5 degree cone. Each jammer would need some mechanism for determining its orientation so it could point its focussing antenna in the direction of the defense unit. (If the jammer's antenna had no directionality, it would need a power of 25 kilowatts to achieve comparable effects—an unpromising approach for the attacker.) Because the Patriot radar has the capacity for "nulling" the signals of up to five separate jammers, multiple jammers operating simultaneously would be needed. Properly designed and employed, a half dozen or so devices deployed at a range of perhaps 70 km might sufficiently reduce the radar detection range against a low-RCS version of the SS-21 to assure TBM penetration to the target. Because still longer detection ranges are required against the SS-23 and SS-12/22 TBMs, such jammers, if properly employed, would also defeat defenses against these TBMs as well.

Each jammer need only operate for a very short period of time during an attack, so it would not need large and heavy power supplies. Expendable jammers of the type that can be dropped from aircraft can readily achieve radiated powers of 50 watts/kg or more. Even if we assumed a weight of 10 to 20 kg per jammer, a special SS-23, SS-12/22, or cruise missile modified as a "jammer launch vehicle" could deliver up to fifty jamming devices to a range of about 1,000 km.

Of particular concern is the possibility that numerous, less complex and less powerful jammers might be delivered much nearer to defense radars, thus directing as much or more jamming power against the defense. An example of such a simplified device might be a 20 watt jammer with a 0.05 to 0.06 meter downward pointing directional antenna. If such a device were suspended on a parachute at 5 km altitude, radars within 2 to 3 km of the ground-point directly below it would suffer the same disruption as they would from the more distant jammers described above. A more sophisticated version of this jammer, with a 0.2 meter antenna directing the jamming power into a 15 to 20 degree cone might jam Patriot radars so effectively that they could not even search a solid angle as small as 25 square degrees at a large enough range to engage the SS-23. In this circumstance, even the addition of external surveillance systems that helped narrow the search solid angle would not be sufficient to offset the effects of a well-implemented jamming attack.[12]

When the radar search demands posed by aircraft are compared to those of TBMs, we can see why search-denial by jamming may be more likely to succeed with TBMs and fail with aircraft. For purposes of illustration, we can consider the search task for aircraft as the same as that for TBMs.[13] Aircraft or cruise missiles might approach the defense unit at any altitude from close to the ground to as high as 20 km, and this means the defense must search from the horizon to about 45 degrees elevation. If we assume the air defense must scan only about 90 degrees of azimuth (a highly favorable assumption for the defense), this corresponds to a search solid angle of about 3,600 square degrees — comparable to the TBM task.

However, the speed of approaching aircraft or cruise missiles will generally be between 0.2 to 0.3 km/sec, rather than 1 to 3 km/sec for an attacking TBM. This means the radar can scan more slowly, raising the strength of signals reflected from targets, and still have time for intercepts. A jammer therefore must be five to ten times more powerful, if the speed of the aircraft is one-fifth to one-tenth that of a TBM. Additionally, the radar cross-section of an approaching airplane is likely to be greater, closer to 1 m^2 rather than the 0.1 to 0.001 m^2 of a TBM. To mask a radar cross-section ten to a thousand times larger means a jammer with ten to a thousand times the power. Altogether, the combination of these factors could result in a scale change of well over several thousand in the search equations for approaching aircraft relative to TBMs, suggesting that correspondingly more powerful jammers would be needed to have a similar disruptive effect on radar-search against aircraft.

On the other hand, aircraft and especially cruise missiles can be equipped with stealthy technologies that greatly reduce their radar cross-sections. An aircraft also has modes of defeating defenses that are not available to TBMs, including the ability to devote greater payload to electronic and other countermeasures, to exploit terrain for masking, to apply the cleverness and adaptability of an on-board pilot, to launch stand-off munitions, and if it can outflank the defense unit, to attack from unexpected azimuths. To the extent that appropriate defense responses to these measures include more powerful radars, more capable interceptors, and closer coordination among multiple defense sensors, anti-air (SAM) defenses and ATBMs may demand comparable technical capacities.

Another countermeasure that could be adopted by a TBM attacker would be to modify the missiles so they can deploy decoys. For the decoys to be convincing targets to the defense, they would have to follow TBM-like trajectories when subjected to atmospheric drag and reflect radar signals in a manner indistinguishable from a TBM. Although these are not insubstantial requirements, decoy countermeasures that could overwhelm and exhaust ATBM defenses are certainly easier to devise and implement than they would be against ABM systems based on similar levels of technology.

Long-range strategic missiles reenter the atmosphere at low angles (about 20 degrees above the local horizon) and at high speeds (about 7 km/sec). It is difficult to design a low-weight decoy that can stand such aerodynamic stress and not be quickly stripped away. In contrast, TBMs reenter at higher angles and lower speeds. Low-weight decoys can be designed for such conditions. For instance, a decoy designed to simulate a SS-21 might be a cone-shaped object with a front end made of tungsten, no more than 30 cm in length, and weighing between 6 and 13 kg. The decoy's ratio of aerodynamic drag to weight would be the same as that of the SS-21, which means that aerodynamic and inertial effects will cause it to follow the same trajectory as an unpowered SS-21. Each TBM might carry two to four such decoys.

Decoys could be dispensed from the TBM on the upward arc of its trajectory, immediately after burnout. At this point, atmospheric drag would still be substantial, so that if the drag-to-weight ratios of the decoys were varied, the decoys would begin to slow up at different rates immediately after dispersal. As decoys and TBM arrived over the defense unit, the defense would be challenged to find which, in the dispersed pattern of objects, was the real TBM and which the imposters. Alternatively, if the decoys were released at the TBM's apogee where aerodynamic forces are low, dispersal would not occur until they were subjected to drag effects as they reenter the denser atmosphere at lower altitudes. Even if the defense could discriminate between TBMs and decoys as they got closer, discrimination might occur at too short a range for interceptors to fly out and make intercepts.

Decoys, it might be argued, are not a foolproof countermeasure. If the defense radar can detect and track each one, and they are not all dispersed on trajectories that would be expected to impact near defended targets, the defense could concentrate its attention only on the threatening ones. However, accurate conventionally armed TBMs must be able to maneuver to offset the unpredictable effects of winds as they fall toward their targets. In order to allow time for interceptor fly-out, interceptors must be launched while TBMs are still tens of kilometers away, yet final accuracy-enhancing maneuvers that put the TBM on a "threatening" trajectory need take place only at short distances before the TBM impacts on target. In addition, if the ATBM interceptor is nonnuclear, TBMs and decoys would have to be separated by only tens of meters in order to force the defense to commit a separate interceptor to each credible attacking object.

Yet other issues of defense effectiveness are raised by the decoy design strategy of antisimulation. Instead of trying to make decoys and TBMs all look alike, this strategy would aim at making decoys and TBMs all appear different. One tactic would be to escort TBMs with numerous decoys that have small electronic transponders on them, which would radiate a signal only when they detect the arrival of signals from the defense radar. Because every transponder could be designed to radiate a slightly different signal, each returning pulse observed by a radar would be a different mixture of transponder signal and reflected radar wave. Transponders would also be mounted on TBMs. All approaching objects would then be observed as a confusing diversity of signals, making it impossible for a radar to recognize any differences between signals reflected from TBMs and decoys. A less elegant but perhaps more effective version of this tactic is simply to deny a radar all but the crudest data on approaching objects, by mounting small jammers, each radiating a few watts of power, on all attacking objects.

Finally, it is sometimes asserted that decoys are difficult to implement on TBM trajectories. The shortest-range TBMs (the SS-21) rise only to an altitude of 30 to 40 km; they have short flight times and very high weight-to-drag ratios after their engines have burned out; and most of their trajectory traverses regions of the atmosphere where air drag is high. This makes the design and deployment of decoys more challenging than for TBMs such as the SS-23 or SS-12/22. However, the density of air at SS-21 apogee is only 1 to 2 percent of that at sea level, which makes it possible to dispense decoys without seriously perturbing the trajectories of either the TBM or the decoys. Our calculations clearly show that properly designed decoys, weighing perhaps 10 kg each, could accompany an SS-21 TBM to impact.

THE ROLE OF EXTERNAL SURVEILLANCE IN AN ATBM SYSTEM

As we have seen, the demands on a search radar can be very great if the speed of the approaching target is large and its radar cross-section is small. Even in situations where a search radar is up to its task, offensive countermeasures could result in seriously degraded performance. If defense unit radars are the only means of detection used, the result of radar countermeasures could be the collapse of the defense.

Traditional ABM defense systems deal with this problem by shifting the burden of the search function to a large surveillance (or battle management) radar. When an object is detected, it is tracked by the surveillance radar, its trajectory and impact point are estimated, and this data is then "handed over" to the defense unit that is best located to manage the final intercept. With such data, the defense unit radar can concentrate its search on a very small area of sky, increasing its detection range and its "burn through" capacity against jammers. In addition, because the object's approximate time of arrival is known, an interceptor can be launched before the object has been detected by the defense unit radar. When the the object is finally close enough to be detected, the in-flight interceptor can be redirected to make the final intercept. Using this technique of netted radars and a precommit strategy, a very large area can potentially be defended because a relatively slow interceptor can engage and intercept objects at otherwise prohibitively long ranges from its defense unit.[14]

It is useful to examine several external surveillance systems that might offset the shortcomings of a radar such as Patriot's. The technologies that are — or may be — available for this external surveillance role are potentially quite diverse and powerful. They might include: very large, ground-based search radars; airborne long-wave infrared (LWIR) optical systems that would sense the faint heat radiating from TBMs as they coast through the cold, near-vacuum of the upper atmosphere; and space-based short-wave infrared (SWIR) sensors that would detect the very hot exhaust of TBM rocket motors as they rise out of the dense lower atmosphere.

Among ground-based radars, the most promising candidate would be a large, fixed phased-array radar, similar in concept to the early warning radars at Fylingdales Moor in Great Britain. Fylingdales' distance from the central front in Germany has the advantage of granting it some protection from prompt attack. Unfortunately, due to the curvature of the earth's surface, many TBM trajectories would be below the line-of-sight of a surveillance radar located so far from NATO's Central Region, even if the elevation angle of the radar beam is no more than 5 to 10 degrees (see Figure 2–1). In addition, because the reflected signals from objects at such distances would be fairly weak, low-powered jammers could be used by the attacker to mask TBMs on trajectories over Germany. (The Soviets would confront similar problems if they sought to use an early warning radar to support Warsaw Pact ATBM defenses in Central Europe; the nearest such radar in the Western Soviet Union lies 600 km from the West German border.)

Building a surveillance radar closer to NATO defense units would make defeating it with jammers more difficult, and the radar would have better line-of-sight capability against TBM trajectories. However, phased-array surveillance radars are fixed and very large, and what radars built closer to the front might gain in capability, they could lose in vulnerability. Because without them, the individual defense units would be severely disabled, the Soviets would have great incentive to attack the surveillance radars directly or focus intense jamming efforts on them. Moreover, if the attacker can devise convincing decoys or antisimulation tactics, even large surveillance radars would be unable to provide local defense units with enough information about which were real TBMs and which were decoys to assist local defense units.

Figure 2–1. Comparison of Warsaw Pact TBM Trajectories and Potential NATO Surveillance Radar Coverage (for Various Radar Beam Elevation Angles).

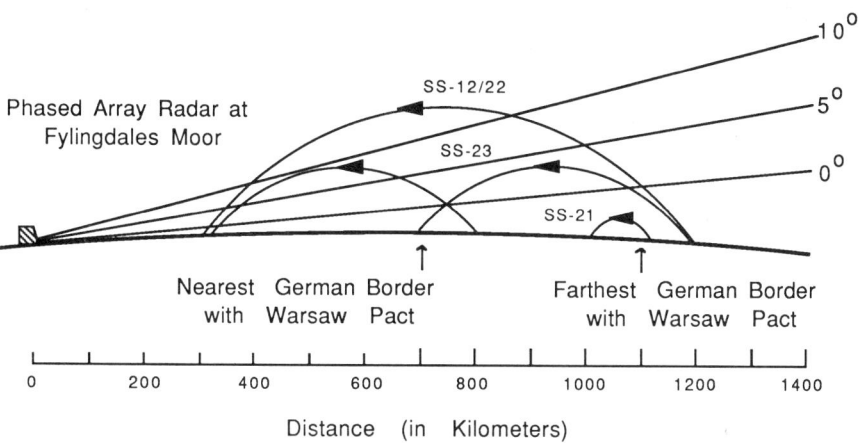

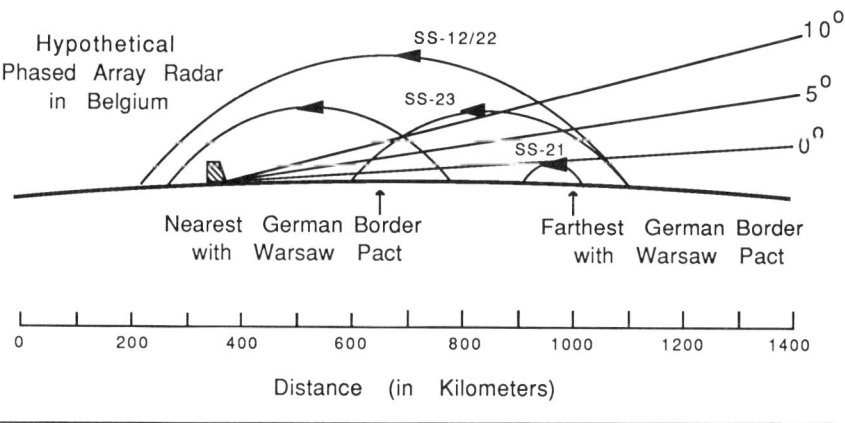

Another candidate for external surveillance would be airborne long-wave infrared (LWIR) sensors. Unlike radars, these sensors would be mobile and thus would be less vulnerable to direct attack. Because each of many (perhaps 100,000) LWIR sensors on a mosaic array would look into its own small section of sky for TBMs, conventional infrared jamming of such a system would not be possible unless tens or hundreds of thousands of jammers could be launched to fill the skies with a blinding infrared signal. On the other hand, LWIR sensors are potentially susceptible to masking, antisimulation, and decoy countermeasures. Accurate predictions of the flight path of a TBM can be calculated from data obtained with a laser range finder, working in combination with passive sensors. Reliable defense coverage would demand several sensors mounted on separate platforms, some of them operating quite close to forward battle areas.

The platforms for LWIR sensors pose their own problems, however. Because the atmosphere is itself a very intense LWIR background, aircraft carrying sensors must fly at high altitudes to reduce the "sky" background so that faintly luminous approaching missiles could be detected. Altitudes in excess of 10 to 15 km would routinely be required, and still higher altitudes might be needed in circumstances where gigantic updraft effects accompanying thunderstorms created high-altitude clouds that masked LWIR signals. Extended operation at these altitudes could best be done with large-wing, subsonic aircraft similar to the U-2 or TR-1. Structural and aerodynamic constraints on such large-wing aircraft make them poorly suited for evasion of air-to-air and surface-to-air missiles, however, and such high-flying aircraft may be readily identifiable during a NATO-Warsaw Pact conflict and subject to attack by long-range stand-off weapons. There are also upper atmospheric phenomena, called noctilucent clouds, that scatter LWIR radiation and may pose substantial problems for reliable LWIR sensor operation. Hence, the reliability and survivability of an airborne LWIR sensor system cannot be taken for granted.

Satellite borne short-wave infrared (SWIR) sensors could also perform the surveillance function, by observing the hot exhaust plume of missiles as they rise out of the atmosphere. Because cloud cover, carbon dioxide, and water vapor in the lower atmosphere absorb SWIR radiation, reliable detection of TBMs would be difficult at altitudes below 10 to 15 km. Our calculations suggest that the SS-21 is likely to burn out at altitudes of about 15 km or less, so this missile probably could not be reliably detected with space-based SWIR sensors. The

SS-23 and SS-22, however, are likely to be above 15 km altitude for perhaps 20 to 30 seconds of booster burn, and should be observable with SWIR. Even though observation times are potentially short, a pair of SWIR satellites with large mosaic sensors could furnish detailed information on a missile's trajectory, provided they were in orbits that permitted stereoscopic viewing of east-to-west launch trajectories. A single SWIR satellite could most likely furnish only information about launch locations and times. Such information would, nevertheless, reduce the search burden on local defense radars, if the total number of attacking TBMs is not too large. Each local radar could use this information to search a limited area of sky along the azimuth of detected launch sites.

Although SWIR sensors might be of use against at least part of the Soviet TBM threat, reliance on them would also raise Soviet incentives to employ new countermeasures. One would be to replace their SS-23s and SS-22s with TBMs designed to minimize SWIR emissions at higher altitudes. Such missiles might have two stages and a somewhat smaller payload than a current-day booster of the same weight. The first stage would burn at about twice the rate of current boosters. After first-stage burnout at a 10 to 15 km altitude, a second low-observable, low-thrust stage would take over and would burn for an additional 20 to 40 seconds. Such a missile would be more difficult to observe with space-based SWIR sensors. (It would also be considerably more complex to design, build, deploy, and operate.) A second countermeasure would be to attack the satellite sensors directly, although the attack timing problems and escalation risks if these satellites were also the ones used to provide early warning of strategic nuclear attack could be high.

CONCLUSION

We opened the discussion in this chapter with a set of questions that needed technical assessment as part of any cost-effectiveness comparisons between ATBMs and alternative methods of protecting NATO from Soviet TBMs. It is to those questions that we now return.

The first question is provoked by an ongoing debate in the United States and NATO: If a near-term ATBM defense is desirable, could an existing or upgraded air defense system—like Patriot, for example—provide either limited or extensive intercept capabilities against Soviet TBMs? Our analysis suggests that Patriot, in its current configuration, does have some self-defense and point-defense potential *but* only against the shortest ranged Soviet TBMs *if* the Soviets do not choose to incorporate stealthy features in their missiles or develop electronic countermeasures. Upgrading the Patriot system with a high-performance interceptor and additional radars would give it a larger performance margin. But we imagine concern would be expressed over three problems. First, shortcomings in the lethality of the interceptor warhead against TBMs may prove more troublesome than the interceptor's acceleration or speed potential. Second, an upgrade incorporating new interceptors and additional radars would be expensive and might not add much to the margin of ATBM capability. Third, while none of the countermeasures to ATBMs appear utterly simple, they are almost certainly far more simple and less costly for the Soviets to implement than for NATO to offset with ATBM improvements.

Unless an upgraded Patriot were equipped with a nuclear warhead (and perhaps even if it were), it would appear to have little or no prospect of providing reliable defense against the longer-range Soviet nuclear or conventionally armed TBMs. In that sense, an upgraded Patriot or comparable ATBM would not be a foundation block for a comprehensive European missile defense.

Countermeasures were at the heart of the second question we posed: How well will ATBM systems function if they are subjected to countermeasures that are commonly used in warfare today? Undeniably, the potential interactions between the offense, the defense, offensive countermeasures, and defensive counter-countermeasures are complex. Analysis is made even more complex when neither the offense (Soviet TBMs with countermeasures) nor the defense (an enhanced Patriot ATBM) have been observed in action. Nevertheless, by the time an upgraded Patriot might be deployed in the 1990s, the Soviets will have had over a decade in which to observe the system from development through deployment, they will have numerous platforms on which to mount and dispense countermeasures, and the countermeasure techniques we have described in this chapter seem likely to be cost-effective for the Soviets, even when discounted for the complexities they would add to an attack.

Our third and fourth questions looked to the future: What are the prospects for new defense technologies that might overcome shortcomings in ATBM systems? What are the prospects for new countermeasures against those new technologies? New ATBM advances that might matter most would be the integration of multiple sensors into the defense network, to improve detection, discrimination, and tracking and thus to complicate the attacker's task of designing countermeasures. There is a good deal of excitement in some circles these days over sensor technologies; it is a technical realm in which the West enjoys advantages over the Soviets, and imaginations have been encouraged by the SDI's needs and ambitions. NATO is accumulating R&D and operational experience on a number of advanced sensor platforms: AWACS, the U.S. Joint Surveillance Target Attack Radar System (Joint STARS), and the Precision Location Strike System (PLSS) are three examples of airborne sensor programs. The progress and expense of those programs may help NATO judge the distance that lies between imagination and realization in advanced sensor technologies.

The final question we posed was of importance to arms control: Are there significant technical distinctions among anti-aircraft, ATBM, and strategic ABM defense systems? The strict technical answer is no; the practical answer is maybe. Properly conceived and supported, even SAM systems have *some* antimissile capability in some circumstances. As we noted above, to the extent that more powerful radars and higher-performance interceptor missiles prove useful against an air threat equipped with stealthy technologies and stand-off weapons, SAM and ATBM systems may evolve in parallel. Nonetheless, the anti-air mission imposes its own demands, and while some of its systems might be adaptable to the ATBM task (guns firing projectiles for close-in defense), others may not (acoustic sensors to augment radars in detecting stealthy aircraft). Because the approach speeds and radar cross-sections of some advanced, air-launched stand-off weapons may well resemble those of the shortest-range TBMs, SAM and ATBM defenses may continue to overlap.

Practical distinctions between ATBMs and ABMs, on the other hand, could be influenced by several factors. If the threat against which ATBMs are designed spans from the SS-21 to the SS-20, then any technical distinctions will probably evaporate; if the threat consists only of the shortest-range TBMs, distinctions may be feasible. So the range capabilities of the Soviet TBM force facing NATO are important. Additionally important is the extent to which ATBM units are linked with external surveillance sensors capable of assuming a significant portion of the detection, discrimination, and tracking burdens.

As our earlier discussion noted, there are inherent tensions, technically and operationally, between systems optimized for the surveillance and detection tasks and those optimized for discrimination, tracking, and interceptor guidance. Being linked with an external surveillance sensor cannot help much if the defense unit is unable to refine the coarse-grained data it receives in the time available and respond with sufficient precision. Put differently, the more capable an ATBM defense unit is in operating autonomously, the more formidable it can become when linked with external sensors. Once again, because the incentive to build more capable ATBMs will stem from the TBMs they face, the efficacy of distinctions between ABM and ATBM systems will inevitably be linked to the perceived character of the TBM threat.

NOTES

1. The full technical analysis will be published as a report of the Center for International Security and Arms Control, Stanford University.
2. It is occasionally argued that because conventionally armed TBMs must have exceptional accuracy to destroy targets, an ATBM defense might succeed if it merely deflected the TBM warhead from its path. However, conventional TBMs must have some maneuvering capability to achieve high accuracy, so even in the unlikely event that an intercept attempt caused a small deflection of a TBM's trajectory, unless severe damage were done to the TBM itself, it would likely still be able to correct its path to a target.

    Reportedly, the 100 kg fragmentation warhead on the Patriot interceptor will be upgraded for anti-TBM missions by increasing the size of its fragments and incorporating a "focused effect" in the fragmentation pattern ("U.S. Develops Antitactical Weapon for Europe Role," *Aviation Week and Space Technology*, 9 April 1984, p. 47). The fact that this change is being made suggests that the lethality of a warhead that uses small fragments has been found to be much lower against TBMs than against aircraft. A modified warhead with a smaller number of larger fragments would generally have a lower likelihood of hitting the TBM with a fragment, but a higher probability of causing severe damage if it achieved a hit.
3. If Soviet TBMs were armed with 100 KT warheads (quite feasible, given their estimated payload capacities), such warheads would generate blast pressures of 2 to 3 psi at a range of 5 km, great enough to damage unsheltered aircraft, for instance.
4. For baseline Patriot interceptor characteristics here, we assume missile weight of 1,000 kg; propellant weight of 500 kg; body structure, warhead, guidance, and radome summing to 500 kg; propellant specific impulse of 250 seconds; propellant density of 0.0018 kg/cm^3; volumetric

loading of 0.95; sustainer thrust of 0.10 boost; axial acceleration (boost) of about 10 G; and cruise speed of Mach 3. The U.S. Department of Defense reports Patriot's range as "80+ km" (*Soviet Military Power 1987* (Washington, D.C.: U.S. Government Printing Office, 1987), p. 74).

5. One published account reports that: "Martin Marietta is working on an upgraded version of the [Patriot] missile for the ATM role. Improvements would include an enhanced radar, an upgraded software package to enable the Patriot to track high speed missiles, and a new motor or possibly an additional boost stage to increase its velocity. . . . Other possible candidates include a hypervelocity missile." *Aviation Week and Space Technology*, 19 January 1987, p. 22.

6. During peak acceleration after launch, an interceptor's center of mass will change rapidly as propellant is burned, affecting its aerodynamic stability. Until this phase of flight is over, it may be difficult for the interceptor to maneuver in order to engage a target. Consequently, for these and other reasons, there will be a limit on how small the minimum intercept range can be made.

7. See "U.S. Develops Antitactical Weapon for Europe Role," *Aviation Week and Space Technology*, 9 April 1984, pp. 46–49.

8. Since the power used to illuminate the target propagates outward in a diverging beam from the radar, the area illuminated by the beam increases as the square of that range. The illumination power per unit area within the beam therefore diminishes inversely as the square of the range. Radio waves reflected by objects in the beam also diverge as they travel back to the radar, resulting again in the power per unit area within the reflected beam diminishing by the inverse square of the range. These two inverse square factors combine to give a reflected signal strength at the radar that varies inversely as the fourth power of the range. Thus, the rate at which a radar will be able to scan for objects must change with the inverse fourth power of the range if it is to collect the same total reflected signal energy as its beam scans across approaching objects.

Next consider the amount of time the radar has to complete a search cycle. Before approaching objects reach the minimum detection range R_d, the reflected signal power seen by the radar changes so rapidly with range that the scanning radar can only detect targets when they are in a relatively well-defined range interval between R_d and $R_d + k$. Since the size of the range interval k grows in direct proportion to the choice of detection range R_d, and the approaching object crosses the range interval at approximately constant speed, the time available for the radar to search is directly proportional to the choice of detection range R_d.

The solid angle that can be searched by the radar can be found by multiplying the scan rate by the time available for a scan cycle. Since the radar scan rate varies with the inverse fourth power of range, and the time available for the radar to complete a scan cycle varies in direct proportion to range, the product of these two factors leads to the conclusion that the search solid angle varies as $1/R^3$ with the choice of detection range.

The source of the other terms in the equation that describes the behavior of the radar search angle should now be evident. The amount of time an approaching object is in the search volume is inversely proportional to its average speed as it crosses the volume. This leads to the factor $1/V$. The radar will be able to scan at a faster rate if its average power is increased, or if its antenna is enlarged so it can collect more of the reflected signal from a radar-target, or if the radar-target reflects a larger fraction of the power in the beam (i.e., if the radar cross section of the target is larger). The search rate of the radar therefore varies in direct proportion to all these factors. This leads to the terms P_a, A, and σ in the above equation.

9. See Eli Brookner, *Radar Technology* (Dedham, Mass.: Artech House, 1977), p. 27; and "Expensive, But Necessary: The Patriot Surface-to-Air Missile System", *Military Technology*, October 1984, p. 33. For our analysis here, we are assuming: a space-fed, phased-array radar; 5,161 ferrite phase shifters; peak power of about 100 KW; average power of about 10 KW; signal frequency of 5 GHz; antenna aperture of 4.5 m^2; prime power for engagement control and radar stations from two 150 KW/400 Hz turbine generators.

10. For further discussion, see T. B. A. Senior, "A Survey of Analytical Techniques for Cross-Section Estimation," *Proceedings of the IEEE*, August 1965, p. 822; J. W. Crispin and A. L. Maffett, "Radar Cross-Section Estimation for Complex Shapes," *Proceedings of the IEEE*, August 1965, p. 833 and 972; Eugene Knott et al. *Radar Cross Section* (Dedham, Mass.: Artech House, 1985), Chpt. 14; R. E. Kell and R. A. Ross, "Radar Cross Section of Targets," in M. Skolnik, ed., *Radar Handbook* (New York: McGraw-Hill, 1970); George Ruck et al., *Radar Cross Section Handbook* (New York: Plenum Press, 1970), vols. 1 and 2.

11. Jammers, like decoys, need not be aerodynamically well-matched to TBMs for them to remain close enough to a TBM to mask it from defense radars. Given the short flight times of TBMs, even a ballistically mismatched jammer will not drift far from the missile. Consequently, the separation angle between the TBM and the jammer observed by a single defense radar may be less than the radar's angular resolution up to the very last moments of flight — too late for the defense to intercept the real TBM.

12. The ability of a radar to resist jamming can be greatly enhanced if the radar can "hop" over many frequencies to avoid jamming. It can also be

enhanced if the radar duty cycle (the ratio of the time the radar is radiating its signal to the time it is off) is small. The Patriot duty cycle is about 0.25, but we assume that the application of signal processing and phase-coded pulse compression results in an "effective" duty cycle of 0.01. We also assume that the radar gains additional antijam capability by frequency hopping over a bandwidth that is 10 percent of its carrier frequency. A side-lobe rejection ratio of 0.001 is assumed for situations where jamming does not occur through the mainlobe. Patriot's five side-lobe cancellers are assumed to be defeated by deployment of more than five jammers. Jammers are assumed to be "dumb" barrage jammers that simply cover all radar frequency bands with noise at all times. Required jamming power would, of course, be greatly reduced if an adversary's electronic countermeasures (ECM) can be properly tailored to defeat the electronic counter-countermeasures (ECCM) of the radar.

13. In practice, the search task for aircraft is not the same as for TBMs. In contrast to TBMs, distant aircraft near the horizon will be observed at low elevation angles regardless of their altitude, while aircraft observed at high elevation angles can only be relatively near the radar. Hence, much less power is needed when a radar searches high elevations for aircraft. Air defense radars take advantage of this fact by concentrating their search power at low elevation angles, thereby varying the range at which different sections of a search solid angle are scanned. Search for TBMs, however, is inherently less efficient because it demands that the radar concentrate the same amount of search energy into each section of the search solid angle at all elevation angles.

14. This method of supporting an air defense system in an antimissile role by linking it with powerful external radars is presumably what the U.S. Department of Defense refers to when it asserts that the Soviet SA-10 and SA-X-12 SAM systems "may have the potential to intercept some types of strategic ballistic missiles" and thus "could, *if properly supported*, add significant point-target defense coverage to a nationwide Soviet ABM deployment" (*Soviet Military Power 1986* (Washington, D.C.: U.S. Government Printing Office, 1986), p. 57, emphasis added). Because, as we argued above, an ordinary anti-aircraft, fragmentation warhead is unlikely to destroy an incoming missile, the Defense Department is almost certainly assuming nuclear warheads for the SA-10 and SA-X-12 interceptors in an antimissile role.

3 THE SOVIET THEATER THREAT
New and Enduring Dimensions
Dennis M. Gormley

Western planners now face still another challenge to NATO's Flexible Response strategy. Growing concern about the modernization and expansion of Soviet shorter-range missiles (SS-21, SS-22, and SS-23) in Eastern Europe has stimulated debate on the merits of antitactical ballistic missile defenses (ATBMs) and European participation in the U.S. Strategic Defense Initiative (SDI). Compounding the controversy are the prospects that a nascent Soviet ATBM program could substantially degrade NATO's few remaining escalatory options after a preemptive Warsaw Pact conventional missile and air attack. Despite the seriousness of the issue, Western planners have yet to comprehend properly the operational benefits that shorter-range missiles and ATBMs furnish the Soviets and consequently what the most effective and affordable means are for NATO to blunt them.[1]

Any balanced appraisal of the Soviet theater warfare threat must rest on correct assumptions about weapon roles and capabilities, as seen from a *Soviet* analytic context. Too many Western analysts, applying Western rather than Soviet perspectives, have exaggerated the Soviet TBM threat by asserting a near-term Soviet capacity to substitute conventional for nuclear warheads on TBMs and to destroy such complex targets as NATO airfields, using conventional TBMs alone.[2]

Warsaw Pact specialists, by contrast, seem less sanguine about directly substituting a conventional weapon for a nuclear one.

Although they see emerging conventional weapons approaching nuclear weapons in levels of effectiveness, they are far more likely to view the effects of conventional weapons in a true combined-arms context. In this view, TBMs would take over primary responsibility for suppressing NATO air defenses and disrupting airbase and nuclear dispersal operations for short intervals only, providing a form of sequential leveraging for subsequent aircraft strikes. Thus, what many Westerners view as the cost ineffective use of expensive missiles to deliver conventional payloads, Soviet planners see as just the opposite: Missiles do not simply replace aircraft for certain missions but multiply the effectiveness of more expensive and reusable manned platforms, each of which can deliver several times the payload of a missile.

An exaggerated view of new Soviet shorter-range missiles can lead to oversimplified assessments of defenses against this emerging threat. Too often in Western analysis, the role of TBMs in the Soviet combined-arms (conventional) air operation is simplified until it resembles something akin to strategic counterforce targeting. Such simplifications may be useful for analyzing SDI architectures, but they have little use in a theater conventional context where missiles are rarely the exclusive damage mechanism.

Only by considering the role of missiles in the proper context can we gauge the full implications of the emerging Soviet threat and derive the best means to cope with it. The essential analytic milieu is the Soviet notion of a strategic operation in a theater of military operations. This chapter, therefore, focuses on several strategy and operational issues central to the European theater context. To set the stage for discussion of contemporary theater issues, the chapter begins with the evolution of Soviet theater strategy and forces, particularly the dilemmas the Soviets have faced in preparing for multiple theater warfare contingencies.

COPING WITH MULTIPLE CONTINGENCIES

The historical antecedents of contemporary Soviet force planning reveal a thirty-five-year history of rather abrupt changes in military thought and force structure. After first appearing to ignore the implications of nuclear weapons for combat operations under Stalin, Soviet military authorities shifted emphasis to nearly an exclusively nuclear orientation in the first half of the 1960s. After the mid-1960s, Soviet military thought shifted again and today reflects a more even-handed approach to assessing the threats inherent in Western strategy and to establishing requirements for military procurement. Indeed, the last two decades of Soviet military thought and development represent a persistent search for, and in large measure the achievement of, increasingly more flexible military power.

Broadly outlined, Soviet planners today see three probable courses of theater conflict, each of which has different implications for the required mix of conventional and nuclear forces, and each of which has had its historical emphasis in Soviet thought.

1. Massive nuclear strikes used at the outset of conflict to the full depth of relevant theaters of military operations (TVDs).
2. An escalating conflict in which an initial (and relatively short) period of conventional operations precedes use of nuclear weapons.
3. A conventional-only conflict in which major strategic operations are successfully carried out within one or more TVDs without recourse to nuclear weapons.

Massive Nuclear-Use

Creation of the Strategic Rocket Forces (SRF) in December 1959 and Khrushchev's announcement of a new military doctrine before the fourth session of the Supreme Soviet in January 1960 became the twin symbols of the massive-use option. Khrushchev's new military doctrine specified that a future war involving the USSR would be an all-out, coalitional conflict with inevitable nuclear escalation. Massive nuclear strikes would occur immediately, or almost immediately, on the outbreak of war. The new nuclear missiles of the SRF would decisively determine the conflict's course and outcome.

The campaign in European TVDs would be fought within the framework of a general war opening with massive nuclear exchanges. The Soviets pictured that the outbreak would be initiated by the West's massive surprise attack, to which the SRF would respond with rapid strategic nuclear strikes, followed by a full-scale theater offensive against NATO Europe. Soviet ground forces were to exploit the nuclear strikes of the theater component of the SRF and Long-Range Aviation (SS-4 and SS-5 missiles and Badger medium-range bombers, later to be replaced by the SS-20 and Backfire bomber). First- and second-generation Soviet shorter-range missiles (Frog-3/7 and Scud-A/B), deployed between 1957 and 1965, were fitting products of the massive-use option. The need to compensate for accuracy errors (CEPs) on the order of a kilometer dictated massive use.

Soviet military doctrine, strategy, and force development have evolved dramatically since the origin of the massive-use option. Although massive nuclear use may be the least preferred of the three contingencies today, it nonetheless still warrants the attention of Soviet planners.[3] Indeed, there is danger in ignoring a Soviet attack option that involves nuclear first use. With projected increases in missile range, launcher numbers, and, most important, missile accuracy, the emerging force of shorter-range ballistic missiles deployed with Soviet ground units in East Germany and Czechoslovakia may be capable by 1990 of destroying many NATO targets in a single strike using 10 KT warheads for large-area targets and subkiloton warheads for small point targets.

The Escalating Contingency

The second contingency that shapes Soviet military requirements — an escalating conflict — grew out of the Soviet military's post-Khrushchev reaction to an overreliance on nuclear weapons. The constituents of this reaction and consequent search for new options were three: the reemergence of the military as the dominant force in the development of military science; the Soviet achievement of strategic nuclear parity with the United States, which hastened the search for new forms and methods of combat; and recognition that NATO had eschewed sole reliance on massive retaliation and sought more flexible forms of response.

By late 1968, several authoritative Soviet military figures had acknowledged the USSR's intent to base planning requirements on a more flexible view of potential conflict contingencies, and to prepare Soviet shorter-range forces for possible "tactical nuclear wars" preceding escalation to theaterwide and general nuclear war.[4] By the end of the decade, the Soviets had charted a clear course foreshadowing (indeed, stimulating) large-scale conventional and limited nuclear warfare options.

Theater forces that were limited in number and quality were tolerable when operational-tactical nuclear systems were intended merely to augment SRF and LRA medium- and intermediate-range nuclear forces. But an escalating contingency meant an expanded role and, therefore, expansion in the front commander's dual-capable theater forces. Without dramatic improvements in conventional preemptive capabilities, Soviet military authorities would never have enough confidence that they could prevent NATO's use of nuclear weapons. While major investments in Soviet strategic forces challenged the credibility of U.S. strategic first use, improvements in theater nuclear forces were required to render NATO's resort to tactical nuclear use self-defeating.

The Soviet force modernization process was already improving military instruments by the mid-1960s. The Scud-B demonstrated an 87 percent increase in range over its predecessor, while the Frog-7 showed a 40 percent range increase. Additionally, in the late 1960s or early 1970s, missile units were enlarged: Frog battalions expanded from three launchers per battalion to four, while Scud brigades went from nine launchers to twelve. But in front-organic offensive power, tactical aviation improved most substantially. From 1965 to 1977, the offensive load capacity of Soviet frontal aviation in Eastern Europe grew by 90 percent.[5] In about a decade the Soviet inventory of operational-tactical nuclear delivery systems (Frog, Scud, dual-capable aircraft, and nuclear artillery) doubled in size and represented roughly a 2.5-to-1 advantage over equivalent NATO systems by the mid-1970s.[6] At the operational-strategic level, older SS-4s and SS-5s, insufficiently survivable or sustainable for any purpose other than massive theaterwide use at the outset of hostilities, were replaced by mobile SS-20s, providing a more secure and enduring theater-strategic nuclear reserve.

Soviet planners have never expressed unequivocal confidence that they could dominate the escalation process and avoid the expansion of a European conflict into general nuclear war. The difficulty of predicting precisely when a conflict would escalate to nuclear operations confronted Soviet decisionmakers with a dilemma: not abandoning a conventional advantage too soon and not exercising a nuclear option too late. By the late 1960s, Soviet planners foresaw the conventional phase of a major European campaign lasting no more than four or five days.[7] During this phase, the Soviets placed highest priority on destroying NATO's theater nuclear weapons by conventional means. But success in this endeavor was highly uncertain, given the difficulty of locating large numbers of mobile nuclear launchers. An even more complex task involved preparing Soviet forces to make a smooth transition from conventional to nuclear operations. The Soviet military saw a decisive advantage accruing to the side that successfully preempted the other's effective use of nuclear weapons. Preemption hinged critically on at least three interdependent conditions: (1) detecting the enemy's preparations to use nuclear weapons; (2) locating enemy nuclear forces; and (3) having an adequate number of one's own nuclear weapons in constant readiness to respond.

Today Soviet planners face deficiencies in each of the necessary conditions for effective preemption in an escalating contingency. NATO's efforts over the last decade to reduce the "noise" associated with the escalation process probably make detecting NATO's preparations for first-use somewhat more problematical than during the early 1970s. Although Warsaw Pact target acquisition systems show substantial improvement, the complexity of the problem is daunting: It requires combining highly perishable targeting information with the proper mix of fully prepared nuclear strike systems, all within a narrow warning time provided by Soviet intelligence. But it is in the third condition (readiness) that Soviet planners fell short in the early 1970s and where, even today, vastly improved dual-capable missiles create planning dilemmas for Soviet decisionmakers.

Certainly the advent of truly dual-capable short-range missiles furnishes Soviet planners greater confidence of conventional success without nuclear escalation. But Soviet command must now confront the nuclear withhold dilemma for both air and missile forces. Even though they believe their chances of winning conventionally are good, Soviet planners know they must convey a clear threat of preemptive theaterwide nuclear use to deter NATO from employing what remains of its nuclear arsenal after conventional operations. Under the conventional contingency, it is far more likely that Soviet planners would allocate all or nearly all available shorter-range missile launchers initially to support of the conventional air operation and subsequently to conventional support of divisions, armies, and fronts. Contemporary Soviet planning for conventional conflict now envisions the possibility of conventional wars lasting up to thirty days.[8] It is doubtful that Soviet planners would have confidence that sufficient numbers of shorter-range missile launchers would remain after prolonged conventional war to fulfill the wholly uncertain needs of nuclear preemption. Under prolonged circumstances, it is far more likely that Soviet planners would rely on more survivable homeland-based nuclear forces for nuclear preemption. Nonetheless, to the extent that military planners can never be certain of predicting anything beyond the first operation, the dual-capability dilemma will create worrisome problems for the Soviet command.

Soviet classified (*Voyennaya msyl'*) and open military sources furnish rich details about conventional and nuclear operations, but they refrain from similar discussions of offensive chemical operations. What does get attention is the need for protective measures. Chemical weapons are lumped together with nuclear and biological ones as "weapons of mass destruction." Despite purposeful ambiguity with respect to offensive chemical intent, Soviet ground and air units are reputedly equipped with a vast stockpile of chemical agents, with estimates ranging up to 700,000 agent tons. What is perplexing, however, is the lack of evidence regarding detailed planning and troop training for the widespread use of chemicals in offensive operations. This may suggest Warsaw Pact plans for more limited chemical use. Precise missile-delivered chemical attacks on just a few rear-area targets in NATO—reinforcement depots, for example—would produce devastating military effects. According to recent congressional testimony, chemical attacks on POMCUS sites alone would create delays in reinforcement of at least several days and require "most of Europe's decontamination units." Moreover, the rapid supply of incoming units to Europe would undergo serious disruption because POMCUS sites depend heavily on local civilians "who may not have enough equipment and be well trained for operations in chemical conditions."[9]

The Conventional-Only Option

The third contingency—conventional-only warfare—culminated an evolutionary process that began in the mid-1960s with the Soviet search for operational flexibility. Soviet military planners initially saw the conventional phase of a major war as brief, lasting a few days at best, during which time preparations for operational-tactical and then strategic nuclear phases would occur. By the mid-1970s, however, they saw the conventional stage expanded to a strategic operation (an ascription previously reserved for nuclear-related operations) lasting up to thirty days. By 1982, Soviet military writers were discussing entire wars between major coalitions conducted without nuclear weapons.[10]

Soviet military authorities make clear the continuing need for nuclear options at the tactical, theater, and strategic levels. Indeed, the Soviet notions of conventional strategic operations and entire wars fought only with conventional weapons were developed in the context of constraints imposed on all combatants by rough nuclear parity. Nonetheless, the efficacy of plausible nuclear options for Soviet planners lies in the coercive power these options hold in peacetime and the intrawar deterrent leverage they provide should war occur. And despite the Soviet unilateral declaration of no first use of nuclear weapons, the need to maintain the capability to conduct operational-tactical and strategic nuclear preemption remains an unremitting requirement for Soviet nuclear forces.[11]

Optimism in early 1980 Soviet military commentaries was no doubt based on both political and military factors. Politically, Soviet foreign policy successes during the 1970s were in no small measure seen as the product of the restraining influence of strategic parity on U.S. global freedom of action. Militarily, emerging conventional technologies — longer-range, highly accurate, dual-capable delivery systems in particular — foreshadowed conventional solutions for nuclear problems. Yet improvements in conventional weaponry were necessary but insufficient. At least two additional conditions seemed in order: development of new operational concepts of war that would capitalize on new and better conventional weapons; and the restructuring of Soviet armed forces to execute these new operational concepts.

The following examples illustrate a few of the many operational and organizational changes instituted in the mid- to late-1970s:

- Soviet planners reorganized the air force and air defense force to provide greater employment flexibility, and they refined the air operation, which, in effect, substitutes for an initial mass nuclear strike against high-value military targets throughout the depth of NATO's defense.
- They revived the World War II "mobile group" concept in the guise of operational maneuver groups (OMG), whose function is to penetrate NATO lines rapidly and create paralysis and eventually complete collapse before NATO can employ nuclear weapons.
- They streamlined logistics command and control and prestocked large quantities of ammunition (sixty to ninety days), fuel (ninety days), and other war supplies in forward areas. NATO can no longer

count on detecting an impending offensive by monitoring the movement of supplies from rear-area dumps to forward positions.[12]
- They made major improvements in the mobility and firepower of Soviet airborne divisions and helicopter-borne air-assault brigades, suggesting a highly coordinated approach to deep-penetration attacks against NATO high-value targets.
- Defense Minister Ustinov in 1982 declared the highest peacetime readiness norm ("combat alert duty") for "troops and naval forces stationed on the forward edge of our motherland and the socialist community." Previously, only the Strategic Rocket Forces and, occasionally, SSBNs and the National Air Defense Troops had been singled out for the performance of combat alert duty. Upgrading the readiness of ground forces presumably included corresponding improvements in organic missile readiness, and thus would serve Soviet planners admirably in their quest to achieve preemptive surprise in the air operation.[13]
- With front commanders now possessing weapons with ranges capable of influence well beyond a front's area of interest, Soviet planners reestablished the concept of the High Command in the TVD, which is designed to control the complex timing and execution of multi-front air, missile, airborne, and ground activity of a conventional strategic offensive in a continental TVD, thus placing Soviet and Warsaw Pact forces in a more streamlined posture to respond to modern war conditions that dictate surprise and preemptive action.

The 1970s brought improvement in Frontal Aviation's range and offensive load capacity, placing aircraft along side army and front missiles as coequal participants in front-based nuclear strikes. The principal contributors to Frontal Aviation's new offensive punch include the SU-24 Fencer, the SU-17 Fitter D/H, and the MIG-27 Flogger D/J, and accompanying improvements in ground-attack avionics, target acquisition, all-weather versatility, and increasingly sophisticated air-to-ground munitions (antiradiation and other standoff munitions) for specialized missions.

Frontal Aviation's dramatic turn from defense to offense signaled more than just an interest in participating in nuclear attack missions; it also corresponded more closely to the fundamental military requirements of the escalating and conventional-only contingencies, in which ground-attack aircraft play a critical role in reducing reliance on medium-

and intermediate-range nuclear missiles and aircraft to destroy NATO's theater nuclear capability. Instead, new high-performance aircraft would strike high-value targets throughout the entire depth of NATO Europe's defenses. To achieve surprise and preemptive shock power, forward deployment and resubordination of aircraft had to be minimized. The Soviet military dissolved Long-Range Aviation (LRA) and Frontal Aviation (which had been formed into Tactical Air Armies (TAA)), and restructured Soviet Air Defense Forces. LRA and some TAA have now become five new Strategic Air Armies. The remainder of the TAA and about half of the strategic interceptor force are now organized as air forces of specific military districts or external Groups of Forces.

The primary shock power for the air operation is furnished by longer-range air assets (including Backfires) of the Strategic Air Armies. One of these armies is reportedly reserved for intercontinental and maritime strike missions (36th Air Army, Headquarters, Moscow), while the other four are structured to support various theater missions. For example, the 24th Air Army, with headquarters in Legnica, Poland, is equipped with five SU-24 Fencer regiments, which would be assigned to the Western TVD in war.[14] Overall, the first mass strike of the air operation in the Western TVD could be configured — without forward movement and consequent loss of surprise — entirely from Soviet air units in the German Democratic Republic, Poland, and Czechoslovakia and the Legnica and Smolensk air armies.[15]

While Soviet frontal and strategic aviation underwent significant growth in the 1960s, the tactical and operational-tactical missile force experienced hardly any development. This ten-year hiatus in short-range missile development is probably explained by the Soviets' inability to produce a sufficiently accurate guidance system to make a new generation of missiles truly dual-capable. But the Soviets initiated new development programs in earnest beginning in 1971 (SS-21) and continuing into the decade (SS-12/22 in 1973 and the SS-23 in 1975). They even reportedly began a Scud product-improvement program, which seems to have culminated in the deployment of a 400 km range Scud-C toward the end of the 1970s.[16] It now appears that the initial version of the three new missiles did not possess the terminal effectiveness (a combination of high accuracy and tailored munitions) needed for full-scale conventional use.[17] But by the end of the decade, follow-on versions apparently demonstrated major improvements in guidance and munition effectiveness. NATO officials now affirm that the Soviets are developing submunition payloads for the SS-22 and SS-23 missiles, while the SS-21 is already deployed with such a conventional payload.[18]

As far as improved accuracy is concerned, the U.S. Undersecretary of Defense for Research and Engineering has disclosed that upgraded models of the SS-21, SS-22, and SS-23 have accuracies (CEPs) on the order of 30 meters.[19] Soviet military specialists claim that such accuracies are obtained by combining upgraded inertial guidance and either an in-flight update or terminal guidance.[20] By comparison, U.S. terminal guidance systems for ballistic missiles such as the Pershing II produce roughly the same accuracies as those reported for upgraded Soviet missiles. All in all, it seems prudent to assume that the earliest of the new generation of missiles (the SS-21) already possesses sufficient accuracy to deliver conventional submunitions effectively and that by the end of this decade the longer-range SS-23 and SS-22 missiles could be deployed with guidance systems roughly comparable to Pershing II.

The 120 kilometer range SS-21 ballistic missile is replacing the 70 kilometer range Frog-7 in Soviet divisions. All of the seventy-six Soviet Frog launchers with Soviet divisions in East Germany have apparently been replaced by the SS-21 system at a reported rate of four per month.[21] To date, over 130 SS-21 launchers have been deployed in the Western TVD, with around 100 forward deployed with Soviet, East German, and Czech ground-force units.[22] Overall, approximately 600 Frog/SS-21 launchers face NATO, more than 200 of which are deployed with non-Soviet Warsaw Pact forces (see Table 3–1).

According to official reports, the army- and front-level SS-23 missile system (500 km range) began to replace the SS-1C/Scud-B missile during 1985 in one missile brigade in the Byelorussian Military District.[23] In view of the fact that the SS-23 first became operational in early 1980, it is curious that only one brigade has received the new missile to date. Perhaps the unavailability of a suitable guidance system promising 30 to 50 meter accuracy has been the constraining factor in the SS-23's deployment rate; alternatively, the adverse consequences of initiating a broad-scale one-for-one deployment (SS-23 for Scud) in the midst of delicate INF negotiations may explain Soviet behavior. Were the SS-23 to begin replacing the Scud-B or perhaps the Scud-C in Soviet units in East Germany at a pace similar to the SS-21's, all Soviet Scud brigades could be fully converted to the new missile system by 1990.

Table 3–1. Current Soviet And Warsaw Pact TBM Launcher Deployments by Soviet Theater of Military Operations (TVD).

TVD	Total for TVD	SS-21/Frog		SS-23/Scud		SS-12/22	
		Soviet	Non-USSR	Soviet	Non-USSR	Soviet	Non-USSR
Western	798	265	120	265	83	65	—
Northwestern	98	36	—	50	—	12	—
Southwestern	349	85	94	110	60	—	—
Southern	190	115	—	75	—	—	—
Far Eastern	363	225	—	100	—	38	—
Central Reserve	125	75	—	35	—	15	—
Totals	1,923	828	214	635	143	130	—

Source: International Institute for Strategic Studies, *The Military Balance 1986–87* (London: IISS, 1986).

Nearly 600 Scud launchers face NATO, with 140 or so deployed in non-Soviet Warsaw Pact units.

The front-level, 900 kilometer range SS-22 missile replaces the SS-12 Scaleboard. It appears that the SS-22 does not represent a wholesale generational change over the SS-12, in that it uses the same launcher and has no reported improvement in range.[24] An estimated fifty Scaleboard launchers, probably configured into three or four brigades, reportedly were deployed into East Germany and Czechoslovakia beginning in late 1983 or early 1984, ostensibly in retaliation for NATO's Pershing II and cruise missile deployments.[25] This is the first time that Soviet missiles of such an extended range have been deployed outside of Soviet borders. From launch locations in East Germany, the SS-22 extends Soviet operational-tactical missile coverage to more than half of the United Kingdom; its movement forward also avoids the loss of surprise that would result from the 700 kilometer trek from the western USSR into Eastern Europe.

Coincident with modernization, army- and front-subordinated missile brigades are expanding from twelve to eighteen launchers per unit; this increase represents the addition of another two-launcher battery to each of the brigade's three battalions.[26] In addition, Soviet shorter-range ballistic missile units opposite the NATO region have as many as four reload missiles per launcher.[27] Given the dramatic improvement in accuracy for the new generation of Soviet shorter-range ballistic missiles, one should expect to see consequent growth in missile stockages in order to support the anticipated increase in the volume of conventional fire support. In fact, the estimated annual production rate for Soviet shorter-range ballistic missiles increased from 300 to 350 in 1983.[28] The increases in shorter-range missile launchers would also add to the volume of fire delivered and could compensate for the possible need to withhold part of the force for a rapid change from conventional to nuclear warfare.

The details of the INF agreement will directly influence the future course of Soviet shorter-range missile development. Now that agreement has been reached to eliminate missiles with ranges between 500 and 1,000 km, the Soviets will still have strong incentives to deploy a new army- and front-level (operational-tactical) missile to replace the aging Scud-B. Because the SS-23 has been banned, it would not be surprising to see the Soviets begin testing a new missile with a range just under the 500 km threshold. Indeed, the Soviets reportedly were developing, and may be about to test, a new shorter-range ballistic missile that could possibly be ready for deployment by the end of this decade or the early 1990s.[29] Although Soviet planners might lose coverage of certain deep targets in NATO's Central Region with the elimination of the SS-12 and SS-23, most critical airfields, nuclear storage sites, and air defense units could still be held at risk by an upgraded Scud-C or a new 450 km range ballistic missile.

The Soviet military is served well by an active research and advanced development program in the basic technologies supporting conventional munitions for shorter-range system delivery. In the area of conventional warhead technologies, the Soviets stand even with the United States. Equally important, in the area of missile-delivered weapons, the advocate within the Soviet military (the Missile Troops and Artillery) commands a powerful bureaucratic position (in contrast to the woeful state of conventional munitions advocacy within the U.S. military services).

Expressions of Soviet interest in developing tailored conventional munitions are not new. As long ago as 1968, when requirements were probably formulated and initial design work commenced for the new generation of dual-capable ballistic missiles, Soviet military specialists were discussing various ways missiles with 500 to 1,000 kg of payload could be more effectively employed using submunitions.[30] A full panoply of conventional submunitions is being examined and possibly developed and deployed, including high explosive, fragmentation, incendiary, shaped charge, and antiarmor bomblets and minelets, in both unguided and terminally guided packages.[31] An article in the Polish military literature notes the importance of "attacks by missile troops involving the use of cluster charges with conventional weapons."[32] Area submunitions of this sort appear ideally suited for attacks against soft targets, such as air defense batteries and handling and transport equipment at nuclear storage sites.

Soviet military authors have also closely followed Western progress in specialized munitions for airfield attack, and the Soviets may already possess specialized munitions for attacking airfields.[33] Although evidence is thin on the current availability of kinetic-energy penetrating munitions for aircraft or missile delivery, such weapons are likely to appear soon in the Soviet inventory, if they are not there already. But attacking runways is not the only method for suppressing airbase operations for short periods; the Soviet military has also investigated ways of temporarily limiting the maneuver capacity of targets (in this case aircraft) in cases when conventional munitions cannot meet optimal damage expectations.³⁴ An example might involve "pin down" precursor missile attacks against NATO airbases, with runway-busting submunitions or antivehicle and antipersonnel mines (both are already in the Soviet inventory³⁵), designed to prevent aircraft takeoffs for an hour or less, until mass waves of bombers can follow with more decisive attacks.

The Soviets also show growing interest in cruise missiles, though none are now dual-capable or appear destined for deployment with Soviet forces in Eastern Europe. The 3,000 km range air-launched AS-15, a clone of the U.S. Tomahawk, became operational in 1984 with the long-range Bear H aircraft. Its ground-mobile cousin, the SSC-X-4, will probably become operational soon; employment missions and deployment areas are expected to mirror those of the SS-20 intermediate-range missile force.³⁶ Even though the Soviets could eventually furnish these systems with sufficient accuracy to undertake conventional missions, it is doubtful that cruise missiles would supplant the role shorter-range ballistic missiles play in support of the air operation. Cruise missiles possess few of the attributes Soviet planners find so compelling with ballistic missiles—prompt, assured penetration to target, which enhances surprise, shock effect, and tight coordination with subsequent aircraft attacks. Rather, cruise missiles could supplement aircraft by increasing the weight and effectiveness of the air threat.

EXPLOITING NATO'S VULNERABILITIES

Clearly, Soviet planners view the opening stage of war as decisively important to strategic success. Exploiting the initial period need not depend on a "bolt from the blue" surprise attack. Soviet planners undoubtedly recognize the low probability of ever catching NATO completely by surprise. But NATO's decisionmaking process allows the Soviets much room to manipulate crisis circumstances. Once the Soviets reach a decision to go to war, their chief goal is to exploit NATO's severe vulnerabilities before the Alliance can complete mobilization and dispersal of its air, ground, and nuclear forces.

Increasing the weight of the initial preemptive blow could compound the inherent predilection of NATO airpower to operate with reduced efficiency in the initial stages of a war. As a consequence of NATO's lack of realistic pilot training, we may expect higher aircraft attrition and reduced sortie effectiveness during the critical first few days of conflict. Moreover, Western historical experience underscores the impact that a short-term but significant increase in aircraft attrition rates can have on the overall course of war. In World War II, for example, the attrition rate for B-17s and B-24s was an acceptable 2 percent but was so high for one particular day that strategic daylight bombing was suspended until enough escort fighters were available.[37] Of course, the reduced efficiency of air power during the initial period could cut both ways. But as noted in a recent Soviet historical account of the initial period,

> even when both opposing sides had considerable forces and means, but one of them preempted the other in deploying and launching an attack, the outcome of operations in the initial period placed the nation subjected to surprise attack in an extremely difficult situation.[38]

NATO's most worrisome airpower vulnerabilities are by no means diminishing. An especially adverse trend is the rising cost and complexity of high-performance aircraft.[39] Consequently, NATO procures fewer aircraft; moreover, system complexity encourages the concentration of aircraft, maintenance, and repair facilities at a small number of main operating bases (roughly twenty bases, supporting dual-capable and interceptor aircraft in NATO's Central Region). Given the fragile nature of aircraft, even modest levels of conventional attack could achieve disproportionate damage. Although future conventional weapon improvements could threaten the survivability of even hardened targets, aircraft protected in shelters will not necessarily represent the most tempting target for Soviet conventional missile attacks in the late 1980s. Generating sorties from an airbase requires a supporting infrastructure to prepare, launch, control, recover, rearm, refuel, and maintain aircraft. Missile and air attacks against the soft, vulnerable airbase infrastructure could severely tax NATO's ability to sustain aircraft sorties. The Soviets emphasize meticulous target planning, and the unique vulnerabilities of each individual airbase can be identified in advance so that aimpoints and weapons allocations can be tailored to each specific case.

Perhaps the most frequently discussed airfield attack technique is the closure of runways to preclude aircraft takeoff and landing. Preventing aircraft departure, or forcing already departed aircraft to land at bases without ready support facilities, could severely affect NATO's ability to cope with the initial air battle. As few as six to eight SS-23 missiles could, with a probability of 90 percent, temporarily close a typical NATO runway and parallel taxiway.[40] These calculations are sensitive to the attacker's damage criteria; not knowing these criteria, the general analytical tendency is to make offense-conservative assumptions. For instance, if the damage criterion is changed to a 90 percent probability of the runway being cut in three places (to prevent takeoff as well as landing), the number of SS-23s required rises by a factor of two to three. It is highly doubtful, however, that a Soviet planner would expend missile resources in this way. Even assuming that missiles alone were being counted on to close the runways, a Soviet planner would probably allocate the smaller number with the intent of pinning aircraft out (by preventing landing, which requires fewer cuts) from their primary means of support. In the Soviet view, success is to be judged by the temporary disruption of operations at the base, if only for a matter of minutes, pending the arrival of the follow-on attack, and this may result for various forms of damage.[41] In the few cases where the United States has tested airbase response to attack under quasi-wartime conditions, damage assessment and repair times have been significantly higher than anticipated.[42]

Growing target concentration also marks NATO's nuclear stockpile—the Warsaw Pact's highest priority target set. In the last decade, the number of nuclear storage sites has declined, the product of site consolidation and concern over peacetime terrorist threats. The vulnerability of NATO's diminishing nuclear stockpile is most sensitive to whether Western decisionmakers act in time to disperse nuclear weapons, aircraft, and missiles from their peacetime bases. Dispersal in the Central Region would render Soviet strike calculations dubious at best by multiplying the nuclear target set from eighty fixed installations to well over 300 mobile (and thus more survivable) field units. For this reason, many view rapid nuclear dispersal as the most sensible course for NATO decisionmakers; such an act would at once produce substantially greater survivability for nuclear forces and lessen pressures for early nuclear use. Other observers are not so sanguine. Critics maintain that nuclear dispersal provokes attack because the widespread distribution of nuclear warheads throughout NATO forces is fundamentally no different from a delegation of authority to lower-level military authorities to use such weapons.[43]

Regardless of whether or not one equates nuclear dispersal with loss of positive control, fewer incentives to preempt would exist were the dispersal process not so cumbersome a task. Because of its perceived sensitivity, NATO forces are not practiced in dispersal operations.

Preparing, outloading, and dispatching large numbers of nuclear weapons could take nearly a full day, and during the process the weapons, truck convoys, handling equipment, and personnel are exposed to attack. Even light conventional weapon attack would do enormous damage during this period. In this regard ATBM defenses could reduce the tension between prudent military response and fear of provocation during ambiguous crisis settings by decreasing decisionmakers' incentives to substitute military for diplomatic solutions.

Air defense suppression is another critical objective in Warsaw Pact targeting plans. If the Warsaw Pact is unable to carry out a "cheap shot" attack against the C^3 "head" of NATO's air defense system, it will need to open up several penetration corridors through the Patriot and Hawk air defense belts. NATO faces serious challenges in maintaining the integrity of its ground-based air defenses. The simplest means of complicating Soviet air defense suppression attacks lies in SAM battery mobility. Yet when SAMs move, they are more difficult to coordinate. Frequent movement creates lower battery availability rates, gaps in coverage, and airspace management problems. Moreover, the sheer size and limited off-road mobility of Patriot and Hawk batteries makes them insufficiently mobile to the extent needed for survivability.[44] And their radar sets and control vans are extremely susceptible to conventional area munitions. As Patriot deployment plans now stand for the 1990s (less than a one-for-one replacement of the existing air defense batteries), NATO air defenses will be so thin as to compel virtually all units to maintain high duty cycles during extended deep crisis and the first day of hostilities. Such high emission levels mean that even those batteries that manage to relocate (at the risk of creating gaps in coverage) will likely be found by Warsaw Pact preattack electronic reconnaissance. But as worrisome as these problems may appear, they do not represent the worst—though still plausible—case: a short warning contingency in which NATO's air defense batteries are attacked while they are still at their semipermanent (but well-known) peacetime locations.

Thus, despite NATO's sizable investment in upgrading air defenses (Patriot and AWACS being only the most notable examples), the Alliance has been barely able to keep pace with major quantitative and qualitative improvements in the Warsaw Pact air threat. Adding Soviet conventionally armed ballistic missiles to the picture makes the future viability of NATO air defenses even more questionable.

THE ROLE OF MISSILES IN THE AIR OPERATION

Many Western analysts are skeptical about Soviet ability to execute a conventionally oriented operation in the western theater. They question whether the Warsaw Pact could achieve the air superiority needed for deep raids behind NATO's forward lines and whether the Pact could locate and attack NATO nuclear forces once they have dispersed. At least two recent studies of the NATO-Warsaw Pact air campaign question the extent of Soviet confidence in the air operation's success.[45] But neither study considers the emerging contribution of Soviet shorter-range missiles. One, for example, concludes that *if* NATO surveillance radars were not severely degraded, *if* active and passive defense measures, including runway repair and aircraft dispersal could prevent recurring and extensive damage to NATO airbases, and *if* NATO interceptors and surface-to-air missiles could impose at least a two-to-one exchange ratio, then NATO might be able to defeat the Warsaw Pact air campaign. And it is not enough merely to nullify Warsaw Pact air forces; in addition to surviving the air operation, NATO air forces must sustain sortie generation to forestall the Warsaw Pact's ground offensive.[46]

Conservative Soviet planners share the skeptics' doubts over Warsaw Pact prospects under Western-preferred conditions. Despite recent long-war preparations (such as logistics stockpiling), Soviet military authorities acknowledge Warsaw Pact weaknesses, among them the questionable reliability of the USSR's allies, command and control inflexibility under rapidly changing circumstances, and shortcomings in theater reconnaissance capabilities. Such a combination of shortcomings would probably render any Soviet prospects for a sustained offensive against a prepared NATO highly dubious. Yet these vulnerabilities, coupled with the Soviet Union's emerging attack options, make the Warsaw Pact more — not less — worrisome an adversary in crises. One way for Soviet planners to reconcile Warsaw Pact weaknesses is through achieving decisive results preemptively in the air operation.

Warsaw Pact authors indicate various quantitative measures of success in the conduct of the air operation. One declassified Warsaw Pact account indicates that 60 percent of NATO aircraft must be destroyed in the air operation.[47] A figure of 50 to 60 percent of NATO's major fire support weapons (probably representing dual-capable aircraft and nuclear missiles) appears elsewhere in the literature.[48] Invariably, however, Soviet planners emphasize an equally important quantitative dimension: lengthening the time needed for NATO to reconstitute its capacity to retaliate. For example, recently declassified lecture materials from the Voroshilov General Staff Academy in Moscow stress that "subsequent massed strikes must be brought to bear on the enemy after the shortest of intervals following the initial mass strikes, so the enemy is denied the chance of restoring his airfields and regrouping his air forces."[49] Such a Warsaw Pact strategy seriously devalues NATO's reliance on rapid runway repair as a primary counter to conventional airfield attack.

Two to three mass strikes can be expected on the first day of the air operation, with one to two for a few days thereafter. The initial mass strike is the largest.[50] Soviet experience in air operations during World War II underscores the effectiveness in the initial mass strike: More than 40 percent of enemy aircraft losses occurred during the initial mass strike, 30 percent during the second, and 20 percent during the third.[51] Before the advent of highly accurate conventional ballistic missiles, Soviet planners were compelled to allocate a majority of their first-wave aircraft to air defense suppression. Roughly two-thirds of the typical Soviet air strike force in World War II had to neutralize air defenses, leaving only one-third to attack primary targets.[52] In a contemporary setting, Warsaw Pact aircraft would be expected to open three to six penetration corridors in the Central Region about 40 to 50 km wide and 150 to 200 km deep.[53] Aided by the massive use of standoff jammers and chaff, first-wave aircraft would disrupt an organized NATO air defense through attacks against warning and surveillance radars, air defense batteries, and interceptor airfields.

Although such an allocation strategy was conceived out of necessity (and substantially reinforced by the growing sophistication of NATO air defenses), it suffers from several important drawbacks. For one, it risks the loss of tactical surprise. Even under circumstances where Soviet decisionmakers decide to attack without reinforcing Eastern European airbases with aircraft from the Soviet Union, it would appear reasonably safe to assume that NATO could still track Warsaw Pact aircraft from takeoff. Successful tracking and quick response permit at least some NATO interceptors to take off and thereby increase Pact aircraft attrition rates during the initial mass strike. Moreover, by not being assured that NATO's medium- to high-altitude SAM defenses were effectively suppressed, Warsaw Pact pilots would fly less-preferred low-altitude penetration routes, at the risk of suffering losses from traditional yet effective low-altitude anti-aircraft guns and missiles.[54] Most important of all, however, suppressing enemy air defenses dissipates the weight of the initial blow on the primary target set—NATO nuclear weapon sites and airfields.

A precursor missile attack, executed minutes before the first-wave air strike, mitigates these drawbacks. The chances of achieving tactical surprise and catching NATO aircraft on the ground are materially improved by employing missiles first; their flight times range from thirty seconds to five minutes, in contrast to aircraft flight times of fifteen minutes or more. Moreover, because missiles have a high assurance of penetrating to suppress air defense targets, aircraft released from such missions can then fly to the primary target set using higher and deeper routes with heavier payloads. And if missiles succeed in pinning down the main body of aircraft at NATO airfields, fewer allied interceptors will rise to meet the first-wave airstrike. The Soviet attack will thus enjoy more favorable force ratios.

One rough measure of how missiles can free up aircraft for attacks on primary targets is illustrated by comparing an aircraft attack on a Hawk air defense battery to a missile attack. In the first case, two flights of four fighter-bombers or eight aircraft, are required to ensure multiple attack angles. And the maneuver is by no means simple; it entails low-altitude tactics in which Soviet pilots foresee considerable risks. Two aircraft armed with antiradiation missiles (ARMs) conduct low-altitude penetration runs, pop up, and fire their missiles. The ARM engagement is designed to force the Hawk radar to disengage or be destroyed. The remaining six aircraft then pop up, roll in, and deliver bombs on single passes of two aircraft, from three different directions.[55] In contrast, because missiles do not have to contend with active defenses (which accounts for the large number of aircraft required), only two are needed to meet the Soviet damage criterion (suppression or neutralization); three missiles would permanently incapacitate the targets.[56] Attacking twenty air defense batteries in the Central Region with missiles instead of fighter-bombers could free up nearly four and one-half air regiments (of thirty-six aircraft each); each regiment is suitably configured to attack a major NATO airbase, whose aircraft might be limited from taking off as a result of the precursor missile attack.[57]

The preceeding illustration naturally assumes that SAM battery location is precisely known. SAM vulnerability to missile attack logically might compel NATO commanders to move air defense batteries more frequently than would otherwise be the case if aircraft alone represented the dominant threat. But if the TBM threat provokes SAM batteries to move more frequently, the Warsaw Pact effectively achieves a degree of virtual SAM attrition, by forcing lower battery availability rates, gaps in air defense coverage, and complex command and control problems.

Allocating first-wave aircraft to the primary target set also has a leveraging effect on subsequent waves of aircraft in the first mass strike. In an unreinforced attack, the first mass strike today could conservatively entail around 1,200 aircraft from forward-based Frontal Aviation and the Legnica and Smolensk air armies. To maximize surprise, fighters and bombers from Frontal Aviation units in East Germany, Czechoslovakia, and Poland would form the first wave. Within minutes of the precursor missile and first-wave air strikes, a major strike force primarily composed of bombers from the Legnica and Smolensk air armies of the Supreme High Command would deliver the main blow of the first mass strike. Configured into squadrons of seven to eight bombers each, this wave (or waves) could attack around forty-five major airfields or nuclear targets. Its effectiveness would be materially aided by virtue of the air defense suppression and pin-down attacks by ballistic missiles and the first wave's shock effect against primary airfields and nuclear weapon sites. In effect, the preceding elements of the first mass strike have become increasingly capable of rendering the primary target set more vulnerable to decisive attrition by the main body of the first strike. Air reconnaissance will help determine the course of subsequent mass strikes. The primary strike force for the first and third strike would likely be the Soviet High Command's long-range aviation, while the main blow for the second strike would come from frontal fighter-bombers.

At least two to four hours would be needed for recovery and reconstitution between mass strikes. One to two mass strikes could be planned for each successive day. Refire times for new Soviet shorter-range missiles are such that launch units could readily support a second and third mass strike on the first day, spaced two to four hours apart.[58] For example, assuming that NATO's nuclear dispersal did not begin until the onset of the first-wave attack, by the second wave (say $H + 4$ hours), a substantial portion of NATO's nuclear stockpile sites and missiles garrisons would still be in the early stages of outload activity. During the dispersal period, these units are significantly more vulnerable to conventional attack. A portion of the second-wave missile attack might therefore be allocated to "pinning down" or disrupting dispersal, thereby making these targets more vulnerable to follow-on aircraft attack.

SOVIET ATBMS: STRATEGY, FORCES, AND TARGETS

Although Western analysts of Soviet strategy emphasize the offensive character of the strategic operation in the TVD, a substantial defensive component, under the guise of the "anti-air operation," exists to blunt NATO retaliatory responses that survive the air operation. The Soviets have a longstanding investment in overlapping defenses against NATO aircraft. Soviet ATBMs represent a new dimension, no doubt stimulated partly by the Alliance's 1979 decision to deploy Pershing II and cruise missiles.

At least on the surface, the Soviet Union would seem to be ahead of the West in ATBM development. The SA-10—now deployed at over eighty sites in the USSR, with twenty more under construction—furnishes a point-defense capability against low-altitude targets with small radar cross-sections such as cruise missiles. It also reportedly is capable of intercepting tactical ballistic missiles and possibly has potential against some types of strategic ballistic missiles. A mobile version is also being deployed.[59]

Moscow's best near-term ATBM option, however, appears to be the SA-12B. Operating like the dual-mode U.S. Patriot system, SA-12B has been tested against shorter-range ballistic reentry vehicles such as the SS-12 Scaleboard and medium-range SS-4. The system consists of a tracked vehicle-mounted radar and a missile launcher that can engage targets at altitudes as low as 100 meters and as high as 30,000 meters or more. The range of the interceptor is 100 km. According to the U.S. Department of Defense, the SA-12B has some capability to intercept the Lance tactical missile and the longer-range Pershing I and Pershing II missiles. Any point target protection against strategic missile attacks—including United Kingdom and French independent forces—would hinge on integrating the SA-12B into a net of early warning and battle management radars. The SA-12B would likely require a nuclear warhead to cope with high-speed reentry vehicles.

A rather widespread deployment of the SA-12B could occur if the Soviets intend to use it to replace at least a portion of the SA-2s and SA-4s at front and army levels.[60] The mobile SA-4 (configured as a brigade) currently furnishes high-altitude defense (5,000 to 24,000 meter engagement zone) for armies and fronts; the semimobile SA-2 protects critical command and control sites, rear airfields, and supply installations in the front's area of responsibility. A dual-mode SA-12B would at once extend the horizontal and vertical engagement ranges for front and army air defense and provide some level of point defense against tactical and longer-range ballistic missiles.

The purposeful imprecision of NATO's nuclear employment policy creates an interesting dilemma for Soviet decisionmakers in planning ATBM deployments—at least in contrast to NATO's ATBM choices. NATO planners can examine the military precision of the Warsaw Pact air operation and focus attention on enhancing the survivability of a small number of fixed installations (less than 100) to present the Warsaw Pact with serious targeting problems. Warsaw Pact planners, by contrast, are blessed with much territorial space within which to site hundreds of critical military installations. But furnishing point missile defense for each and every one of these sites (airfields, nuclear storage bunkers, command and control posts, transloading facilities along the USSR-Eastern European border, and so forth) would come only at enormous expense. Such a course might prove militarily significant, but it would not necessarily deny NATO the ability to employ nuclear forces, the objective of which is intentionally imprecise with respect to clearcut military objectives and targets. Only a successful Soviet air operation can deny NATO such options. It should, of course, be noted that, however much satisfaction some may derive from these asymmetrical politico-military circumstances, others nonetheless view growing Warsaw Pact offensive and defensive options as a direct challenge to the credibility of NATO's escalatory strategy.

THE WIDER GEOGRAPHIC CONTEXT

The Warsaw Pact-NATO context is not the only focus of ATBM attention. Shorter-range ballistic missiles are organic to Soviet divisions, armies, and fronts along the Sino-Soviet border and in the Soviet Far East. As such, the very same capabilities discussed above (albeit in different quantities) are relevant to U.S. friends and allies in the Pacific region. And Soviet shorter-range missiles have been and continue to be exported to Soviet Third World clients. Syria already has received the SS-21, which directly threatens critical military targets in Israel.

There are, however, important differences between the European and out-of-area threat contexts. Critical targets in South Korea and Japan are, for the most part, outside the range of all Soviet shorter-range missiles, save the SS-22. But only forty SS-22 launchers are currently deployed along the Sino-Soviet border and in the Far East.[61] From the area around Vladivostok in the Soviet Far East, parts of northern Japan and roughly two-thirds of South Korea are within range of the SS-22. Alternatively, missiles could be deployed on the disputed Kuril Island of Iturup, north of Hokkaido. China, by comparison, faces well over a hundred shorter-range launchers, but that country possesses strategic depth and relative target survivability, especially against conventional attacks.

Israel is not as fortunate. Several of its airfields could be struck by Syrian-based SS-21s; the introduction of the 500 km range SS-23 would endanger the entire country. Given Israel's grave dependence on airpower and the need to sustain sortie generation, legitimate cause for concern exists about Soviet missile exports to the Middle East. What is not known is whether the Soviets have exported the highly accurate or a less sophisticated version of the SS-21 to Syria. The same question holds for conventional munition payloads. Are the Soviets simply exporting unitary warheads, as furnished their client states in 1973, or do they and will they provide submunitions appropriate for runway closure or delay? Not knowing, Israel can only assume that they are.

On the other hand, Israel is in a much better position than NATO to undertake effective counterstrikes against an adversary's shorter-range missiles. Syrian missiles are close to a preemptively oriented Israeli Air Force. Moreover, Syria lacks the forested terrain of Eastern Europe, where mobile missiles can seek survival by hiding. Israel's counterstrike advantages, when considered in light of the preemptive qualities of ballistic missiles, raise obvious crisis stability problems. This reason, among others, may account for Israel's active interest in developing an ATBM system.

Deployments of shorter-range missiles by Moscow's Warsaw Pact allies are also a significant issue. As we shall discuss in more detail shortly, projected force sizes for Soviet shorter-range missile units in East Germany and Czechoslovakia may prove barely adequate for covering high-priority NATO targets in support of the air operation. There are projected to be around 330 forward-based Soviet missile launchers in East Germany and Czechoslovakia by 1990.[62] Non-Soviet

Warsaw Pact forces typically modernize their frontline units a few years after Soviet units do. Thus, by perhaps the mid-1990s one might expect to see Moscow's allies with a full complement of SS-21 and SS-23 missiles. A one-for-one replacement of the current generation of missiles would result in roughly 115 launchers (64 SS-21 and 51 SS-23) with East German and Czech forces, and over 200 more in the other allied states. Although the Kremlin may have had serious doubts about releasing nuclear warheads to East German or Czech missile units for the initial mass nuclear strike, contemporary Soviet strategy strongly encourages full Warsaw Pact participation in the conventional air operation. Moscow might therefore be tempted to pressure her allies toward modernizing more rapidly than otherwise might be the case.

But such pressure is not without its risks. New Soviet shorter-range missiles are dual-capable, and as Eastern European publics may view them, Moscow's new shorter-range missiles in Eastern Europe appear to transfer the burden of risk of NATO nuclear attack from Russian to Eastern European soil. This could exacerbate a longstanding but muted divergence of views within the Warsaw Pact over nuclear deployments in Eastern Europe, limited nuclear war, and Soviet security guarantees. In fact, during U.S.-Soviet SALT I negotiations in 1972, the Soviets proposed a bilateral renunciation of the use of nuclear weapons against each other, which suggested the confinement of nuclear warfare to allied territory.[63] Although the principal purpose of this blatant Soviet initiative was to drive a wedge between the United States and her European allies, its implications cut both ways for Eastern and Western Europeans. Thus, as the Western Alliance draws down the battlefield portion of its nuclear stockpile, the political costs of Moscow's growing shorter-range missile, air, and artillery arsenal in Eastern Europe may loom larger.

LOOKING TO THE FUTURE

Despite the significant accumulation of military power over the past thirty-five years, senior Soviet military officials have begun to doubt their ability to manage the future of military competition with the West.[64] Soviet planners express concern about the long-term implications of new weapon technologies. The West's current fascination with such doctrines as AirLand Battle, Follow-on Forces Attack or Deep Attack, and counterair initiatives impress and worry Soviet planners.

They respect these more offensively oriented strategies; in contrast to the seriousness with which AirLand Battle has been greeted, Soviet military specialists were virtually mute in their reaction to the U.S. Army's more defensively oriented "active defense" doctrine promulgated in the field manual FM 100-5 of 1976. They are especially impressed with the potential of the West's emerging conventional technologies to achieve decisive results early in any military campaign.

Perhaps the most worrisome development for the long-term military competition is the U.S. Strategic Defense Initiative. SDI's technological challenge cannot simply be dealt with by increases in military expenditures, which, in any event, are somewhat problematic. SDI raises the more fundamental issue of whether the Soviet technological base can keep pace with Western military developments. The Soviets evidently want to develop the necessary industrial potential to compete with the West, but a near-term and perhaps more effective approach for grappling with SDI lies in a political strategy of negotiations and detente with the West. In this sense, arms control (especially a dramatic abatement in SDI development) becomes a means of broadly controlling technological competition with the West.

Soviet politico-military strategists are probably displeased to see ATBM now being treated as an extension of air defense. A close coupling of European missile defense issues to SDI has several distinct advantages from a Soviet perspective. For one, skeptical European attitudes toward SDI have fostered equally negative views of ATBMs. Thus, should SDI be curtailed through negotiations or terminated after a change in U.S. administrations, ATBMs might be affected just as well. Another advantage is that linking ATBMs with SDI helps to obscure the true military significance of ATBMs. Viewed in the SDI context, ATBMs tend to be seen primarily as a nuclear defense. But Europeans can legitimately claim that NATO has successfully deterred the outbreak of war over the past three decades, despite dramatic improvements in the Soviet nuclear missile threat to Europe. The utility of ATBMs for thwarting the Soviet air operation below the nuclear threshold is thereby obscured.

What must prove particularly worrying for Moscow is that even modest point defenses like dual-mode Patriot could pose serious problems for the Pact conventional-only contingency and raise the entry price of limited nuclear and chemical attack options as well.[65] More robust NATO defenses, able to furnish substantial area protection or even eliminate the utility of Soviet theater ballistic missiles altogether, would be immensely troubling. A problem for Soviet planners — and a crucial consideration for NATO's ATBM decisions — is the availability of countermeasures to ATBMs.

If NATO were able to undercut TBM effectiveness through ATBMs, the Soviets could consider several alternatives. One would be a return to heavier reliance on aircraft, cruise missiles, or special operations forces. But none of these is wholly satisfactory in meeting the time-urgent requirements associated with the air operation and deep penetrations into NATO's rear areas. Each fails to replicate the more predictable leveraging effect of coordinated missile and air operations. Indeed, it may serve NATO well to steer the Soviet Union in the direction of slower reacting threats, given the Warsaw Pact's emphasis on a strategy that so strongly relies on speed of execution, pacing, and timing factors.

Conceivably, the Soviets might alter their missiles or tactics to cope with NATO ATBMs. Yet it is highly unlikely that the Soviets would modify the reentry payloads of shorter-range missiles to overwhelm ATBM defenses. Such modifications could include using multiple independently targetable reentry vehicles (MIRVs), and the installation of decoys. But MIRVs and decoys take weight from the payload, which is critical for conventional attack effectiveness. A shift in tactics might be considered, to strain the capacity of an upgraded Patriot to switch rapidly between its air defense and ATBM radar modes by having missiles and aircraft arriving simultaneously rather than sequentially, as is the preferred tactic. Besides losing the advantage of freeing up aircraft for other critical missions, such a modified tactic would also eliminate the element of surprise by forcing Soviet planners to marshall aircraft before shorter-range missiles are launched (rather than after, as would be the case in the preferred sequential tactic). If NATO detected the marshalling procedures, it could disperse forces and prepare for the first-wave air attack.

Perhaps more consistent with the Soviet style of warfare are brute-force measures to overwhelm ATBM defenses. Sheer firepower to exhaust ATBM interceptors and saturation attacks designed to overstress ATBM traffic handling are obvious choices. In the first case, it is probably safe to assume that the Warsaw Pact's stockpile of on-line and refire missiles will exceed NATO ATBM interceptors, especially in view of the large reserve of second-echelon launchers and missiles in the Soviet homeland. (Rather than building up interceptor inventories to cope with a large reserve of missiles, NATO would perhaps

THE SOVIET THEATER THREAT 85

benefit more by counting on offensive counterair to attack the Warsaw Pact's prolonged refire capability.) That ATBM exhaustion could eventually occur is likely, but this prospect is immaterial from the Soviet standpoint of decisively exploiting the weight of the initial blow in the first few days of the war. What is more, although its inventory of shorter-range missiles is clearly large, the Warsaw Pact's capacity to sustain the complex command, control, communications, and intelligence network needed to support prolonged missile use is highly dubious.

Saturation, on the other hand, has promise in principle, particularly against more modest defenses such as a dual-mode Patriot system. The idea is to employ several missiles against a fire battery simultaneously so as to saturate its radar's traffic-handling capability. This tactic allows some portion of missiles to "leak through" and destroy the target. But Soviet planners face a problem with saturation attacks: Projected launcher numbers leave little margin for error even without ATBM defenses. The requirements of saturation would draw a limited first-salvo missile population away from its primary attack objectives and, thereby, deny the leveraging effect that flows from close missile and aircraft interaction. The following attack option illustrates the Soviet dilemma.

Let us consider a short-warning attack contingency in which NATO has failed to exercise most of its alert options and is tactically surprised. No significant nuclear weapon and aircraft dispersal has occurred and air defense batteries are still in their semi-permanent peacetime locations. A plausible Soviet attack force for the 1990s drawn from front-line units in East Germany and Czechoslovakia could consist of ninety-six SS-21 launchers and 180 SS-23 launchers (or, under an INF agreement banning missiles with ranges greater than 500 km, an equivalent number of alternative missile launchers). The Soviet force could be supplemented by at least an additional sixty-four SS-21 launchers and fifty-one SS-23-class launchers in East German and Czech units. Warsaw Pact planners might choose to suppress perhaps one-third (or thirty) of the SAM batteries in NATO's air defense belts, by targeting two missiles on each battery to achieve the Soviet damage criterion for area targets called "neutralization." The first salvo might also include suppression attacks against the Central Region's twenty main operating airfields. Eight missiles per airfield could be assigned to temporarily disrupt (for fifteen to sixty minutes) damage assessment and repair operations long enough to permit direct and standoff attacks by the first wave of aircraft. An additional thirty missiles (or two per target) might be expended against the soft handling equipment and motor pools associated with fifteen nuclear storage sites, again to delay dispersal until the arrival of first-wave aircraft. Of the sixty-five targets in the attack, all but perhaps fifteen are beyond the range of the SS-21. Deeper targets require 220 missiles; 231 are available. Thus, a small number of SS-23-class missiles and nearly the entire SS-21 force could be available to stand on nuclear alert.

Imposing a need to saturate an ATBM system on top of non-ATBM attack requirements would clearly stretch Warsaw Pact attack resources. For example, Soviet planners might assign two TBMs against each Patriot air defense battery if Patriot lacked an ATBM capability, but they might have to allocate more than double that number to defeat a dual-mode Patriot battery.[66] Saturation attacks would therefore come only at the expense of freeing other critical NATO targets from the precursor missile attack. The Soviets do not have inexhaustible launcher capacity. Too often Western planners assume that all or nearly all of the total shorter-range missile inventory (1,600 launchers throughout the USSR and Eastern Europe) is available for the first salvo. But these launchers have an organic relationship to ground force divisions (SS-21), armies (SS-23), fronts (SS-23 and SS-22), and thus have geographic boundaries within which they operate. Just as Soviet ground formations are echeloned, so are their organically related missile units. Therefore, even in the case where the Soviets choose to reinforce the forward area (at a loss of surprise), it might add the missile forces of an additional front—perhaps thirty-two SS-21s and thirty-six SS-23s added to the precursor attack.

Arms control limitations on missile launchers would also be relevant to countering the Soviet shorter-range missile threat. An agreement that eliminated only those missiles with ranges greater than 500 km, however, would only marginally affect Soviet nonnuclear contingency planning. Indeed, in a perverse way, a ban on INF and longer-range TBMs would free up Soviet shorter-range missiles and aircraft that otherwise would be devoted to attacking NATO's Pershing II and cruise missiles. Most (over 80 percent) of the critical targets associated with the air operation (air defense batteries, interceptor and dual-capable airfields, and nuclear storage sites) are located within 300 and 350 km of the inter-German border—that is, within the Federal Republic of Germany. Moreover, an agreement that limits only the longer-range TBMs will do virtually nothing to control quantitative growth in the tactical and operational-tactical categories. As Soviet planners so frequently indicate, conventional effectiveness hinges on the volume of fire delivered within a narrow timeframe. Only by placing a cap on further launcher growth could the West limit the Warsaw Pact's capacity to support the demanding volume requirements discussed above.

Perhaps the most important military task before NATO now that an agreement limiting INF and TBM forces has been reached is to furnish NATO with enough conventional staying power to raise the prospects of a robust escalatory response. A combination of modest active and passive defense measures could clearly demonstrate NATO's capacity to survive the critical first few days of the Warsaw Pact air operation, thereby denying Soviet planners the early success they deem so important.

NOTES

1. This chapter expands on the author's "A New Dimension to Soviet Theater Strategy," *Orbis*, Fall 1985, pp. 537–569.
2. See, for example, Peter Petersen, "NATO's Need for Air Defense," *Air Force Magazine*, August 1986, pp. 74–76, and Warren Strobel, "Think-Tank Report Sees Soviets Able to Humble NATO," *Washington Times*, 5 August 1986.
3. For a recent discussion of likely contingencies, see Maj. Gen. M. M. Kir'yan, ed., *Military-Technological Progress and the USSR Armed Forces* (Moscow: Voyenizdat, 1982), pp. 312–313.
4. V. D. Sokolovskiy and M. Cherednichenko, "Military Strategy and Its Problems," *Voyennaya mysl'*, October 1968, p. 156.
5. Robert P. Berman, *Soviet Air Power in Transition* (Washington, D.C.: Brookings Institution, 1978), p. 54.
6. J. J. Martin, "How the Soviet Union Came to Gain Escalation Dominance—Trends and Asymmetries in the Theater Nuclear Balance," in Uwe Nerlich, ed., *Soviet Power and Western Negotiating Policies* (Cambridge, Mass.: Ballinger, 1983), vol. 1, pp. 110–111 and 114–115.
7. See the discussion in B. Samorukov, "Combat Operations Involving Conventional Means of Destruction," *Voyennaya mysl'*, August 1967.
8. James McConnell, "The Interacting Evolution of Soviet and American Military Doctrines," Center for Naval Analysis Memorandum no. 80-1313.00, (Washington, D.C.: Center for Naval Analysis, 17 September 1980), pp. 96–97.

9. For details on the POMCUS sites, see U.S. Congress, House, *Department of Defense Appropriations for FY85*, Hearings before a Subcommittee of the Committee on Appropriations, 98th Congress, 2d Session, p. 129.
10. Maj. Gen. M. M. Kir'yan, for instance, expressed confidence that the Soviet armed forces had perfected appropriate methods and a force structure capable of conducting warfare "both with the use of nuclear weapons and with the use only of conventional means." Kir'yan, pp. 312–313.
11. Capt. 1st Rank L. Ol'Shtynskiy, *Cooperation of the Army and Navy* (Moscow: Voyenizdat, 1983), p. 7.
12. Changes in the Warsaw Pact logistics structure are reported in U.S. Department of Defense, *Soviet Military Power 1985* (Washington, D.C.: U.S. Government Printing Office, 1985), pp. 65–66. The value of Warsaw Pact logistics activity as a warning indicator is discussed in William J. Lewis, *The Warsaw Pact: Arms, Doctrine, and Strategy* (Cambridge, Mass.: Institute for Foreign Policy Analysis, 1982), p. 234.
13. See D. F. Ustinov, *We Serve the Motherland and the Cause of Communism* (Moscow: Voyenizdat, 1982), p. 82, as cited in James McConnell, "The Soviet Shift in Emphasis from Nuclear to Conventional," (Washington, D.C.: Center for Naval Analyses, June 1983), CRC 490, vol. II, pp. 27–28. Reportedly a portion of Soviet nuclear forces in Eastern Europe has been placed on "quick alert" for the first time. See Jay Mallin, "Russia at High Level of Battle Readiness," *Washington Times*, 26 July 1984.
14. *Soviet Military Power 1985*, pp. 81–82. For a discussion of Soviet air reorganization, see Mark L. Urban, "Major Reorganization of Soviet Air Forces," *International Defense Review*, June 1983.
15. For a detailed discussion of allocating Soviet aircraft to an air operation, see Phillip A. Petersen and Maj. John R. Clark, "Soviet Air and Antiair Operations," *Air University Review*, March–April 1985, reprinted in *Current News*, Special Edition, 31 July 1985, pp. 8–9.
16. Reference to an improved Scud, designated as the KY-3, is made in Steven J. Zaloga, "Soviet Weapons Designations: Part 1," *Jane's Defense Weekly*, 2 May 1987, p. 837. The Scud-C is discussed in David C. Isby, *Weapons and Tactics in the Soviet Army* (New York: Jane's, 1981), p. 199.
17. Stephen M. Meyer, "Soviet Theatre Nuclear Forces, Part II: Capabilities and Implications," *Adelphi Papers*, no. 188 (London: International Institute for Strategic Studies, 1983/84), p. 54. Meyer reports CEP accuracies (averaged) of 200, 300, and 400 meters for the SS-21, SS-22, and SS-23, respectively.
18. Soviet improved conventional munitions for the SS-21, SS-22, and SS-23 are reported in *International Defense Review*, April 1984, p. 373. See also *Soviet Military Power 1985*, p. 38.

19. The defense official was Director of Defense Research and Engineering Richard D. DeLauer, as reported by Walter Andrews, "Allies' Weapons Said to be Inadequate to Threat of New Soviet Missile Power," *Washington Times*, 1 November 1984. An accuracy of 50 yards is reported for the SS-21 in "Missile Deployment Strains U.S.-European Alliance, Tass Claims," *Washington Times*, 30 May 1984.
20. A. Starostin, "Tactical Rockets," *Tekhnika i vooruzheniye*, November 1981, pp. 8–9.
21. Michael Getler, "New Generation of Soviet Arms Near Deployment," *Washington Post*, 11 October 1983. Getler notes that the Soviets were adding four new SS-21 missile launchers per month in East Germany, and that thirty to fifty were believed deployed at that time. Assuming that rate was continued, all units in the Group of Soviet Forces Germany should currently have SS-21 (*vice* Frog-7) launchers.
22. U.S. Department of Defense, *Soviet Military Power 1987* (Washington, D.C.: U.S. Government Printing Office, 1987), p. 66.
23. *Soviet Military Power 1987*, p. 41.
24. *International Defense Review*, April 1984, p. 373. Because of limited changes to the SS-12, the International Institute for Strategic Studies now refers to the SS-22 as the SS-12 Mod.
25. Kerry L. Hines, "Soviet Short-range Ballistic Missiles," *International Defense Review*, December 1985, p. 1913.
26. *Soviet Military Power 1985*, p. 38.
27. Caspar W. Weinberger, *Annual Report to Congress, Fiscal Year 1988* (Washington, D.C.: U.S. Government Printing Office, 1987), p. 30.
28. *Force Structure Summary—USSR, Eastern Europe, and Mongolia*, U.S. Defense Intelligence Agency, DDB-2680-170A-85, November 1985, p. 39.
29. *Soviet Military Power 1984* (Washington, D.C.: U.S. Government Printing Office, 1984), p. 53, and *Soviet Military Power 1987*, p. 42.
30. Marshal K. P. Kazahov, ed., *Artillery and Missiles* (Moscow: Voyenizdat, 1968), pp. 341–344.
31. Hines, p. 1911.
32. Col. (DPL) Pilot Aleksander Musial, "The Character and the Importance of Air Operations in Modern Warfare," *Polish Air Defense Review*, no. 2, 1982, translated by the Soviet Studies Research Centre, Royal Military Academy, Sandhurst, UKTRANS, no. 138.
33. Col. I. Karenin, "Aviation Weapons for Striking Airfields," *Zarubezhnoye Voyernoye oboyreniye*, December 1984, JPRS-UMA-85-031, 7 May 1985, pp.132–144. One Warsaw Pact author noted in 1982, "the Rocket Troops would conduct attacks using warheads with submunitions against enemy airbase targets." Cited in Musial.
34. Hines, p. 1911.
35. *Soviet Military Power 1987*, p. 64.

36. *Soviet Military Power 1986* (Washington, D.C.: U.S. Government Printing Office, 1986), pp. 33–34.
37. Lt. Col. D. J. Alberts, "Deterrence in the 1980s, Part II: The Role of Conventional Air Power," *Adelphi Papers*, no. 193 (London: International Institute for Strategic Studies, 1984), pp. 18–19. For a recent expression of concern about airpower survival on the first day of a future war, see Rick Atkinson and Fred Hiatt, "The Changing Blue Yonder," *Washington Post*, 7 June 1986.
38. Lt. Gen. A. I. Evseev, "On Certain Trends in Changes in the Content and Nature of the Initial Period of War," *Voenno-istoricheskii zhurnal*, November 1985, p. 15.
39. This point is made in Carl H. Builder, "The Prospects and Implications of Non-nuclear Means for Strategic Conflict," *Adelphi Papers*, no. 200 (London: International Institute for Strategic Studies, 1985), pp. 7–8. For a provocative indictment of the military's increasing complexity, see David Evans, "We Still Don't Have the Arms and Tactics for a Major War," *Washington Post*, 3 August 1986.
40. See Chapter 5 in this volume. The lower figure is based on a missile reliability of 0.9 and the higher is based on one of 0.75.
41. Perhaps the most serious damage mechanism, other than destruction of runways, would be the use of mines to delay airbase damage assessment and repair. Also of concern are the effects of near misses, secondary fires, and foreign object damage to aircraft forced to take off under adverse conditions. The notion of judging success on the basis of temporarily delaying aircraft departure (*vice* a specific level of damage to runways, for example) is discussed by Karenin, p. 134.
42. The Salty Demo series of exercises illustrates the excessive optimism associated with airbase response to attack. According to a former senior military official with NATO experience, even a simulated chemical attack with just a few missiles (using smokes) would have a paralytic effect on airbase response time.
43. Paul Bracken, *Command and Control of Nuclear Forces* (New Haven: Yale University Press, 1983), pp. 129–178.
44. Richard D. DeLauer, "Emerging Technologies and their Impact on the Conventional Deterrent," in Andrew J. Pierre, ed., *The Conventional Defense of Europe: New Technologies and New Strategies* (New York: Council on Foreign Relations, 1986), p. 54.
45. Joshua M. Epstein, *Measuring Military Power: The Soviet Air Threat to Europe* (Princeton: Princeton University Press, 1984), and Alberts, "The Role of Conventional Air Power."
46. Alberts, p. 30.
47. Lt. Col. Jan Blumenstein, "Frontal Aviation in an Air Operation," *Voyennaya mysl'*, August 1975, cited in Petersen and Clark, p. 7.

48. U.S. Defense Intelligence Agency, *The Soviet Conventional Offensive in Europe* (Washington, D.C.: U.S. Government Printing Office, 1982), pp. 41–43.
49. "Air Operations to Destroy Enemy Groupings," lecture materials from the Voroshilov General Staff Academy, quoted in Petersen and Clark, p. 10.
50. Blumenstein, cited in Petersen and Clark, p. 5.
51. John Erickson, Lynn Hansen, and William Schneider, *Soviet Ground Forces: An Operational Assessment* (Boulder, Colo.: Westview Press, 1986), p. 203.
52. Erickson, Hansen, and Schneider, p. 203.
53. Petersen and Clark, pp. 6–7.
54. Col. E. Tomilin, "What to Take from Combat Experience," no. 12, *Report: Military Affairs*, no. 1567, JPRS 77371, 11 February 1981, p. 33.
55. Petersen and Clark, pp. 6–7.
56. Soviet damage objectives and related weapon calculations are discussed in more detail in Gormley, "A New Dimension to Soviet Theater Strategy," pp. 561 and 563–564.
57. Of course, some of these "freed up" aircraft might have to compensate for any missile failures in air defense suppression, just as extra aircraft would have been allocated to account for aircraft failures prior to the advent of missiles. Alternatively, additional missiles could be assigned to retarget unsuppressed air defense batteries.
58. Meyer, p. 23, reports a half hour refire time for the SS-23.
59. Information on the technical characteristics and deployment status of Soviet ATBM are derived from *Soviet Military Power 1987*, pp. 60–61.
60. If a military system works reasonably well, the Soviets find it hard to discard it from their inventory. It may therefore be difficult to predict the extent and pace of the SA-12B deployment based on the status of SA-2 (first deployed in the 1950s) and SA-4 (1964) deployments.
61. *Soviet Military Power 1985*, p. 38.
62. All projections are the author's and are based on launcher expansion discussed in this chapter and on force data found in *The Military Balance 1986–87* (London: International Institute for Strategic Studies, 1986).
63. Henry A. Kissinger, *Years of Upheaval* (Boston: Little, Brown, 1982), p. 277.
64. See especially Col. Gen. M. A. Gareyev, *The Views of M. V. Frunze and Contemporary Military Theory* (Moscow: Voyenizdat, 1985).
65. Imperfect defenses raise the attacker's entry price by denying him a "free ride." If unopposed by defenses, the attacker can optimize nuclear warhead yield and height of burst in accord with target vulnerability, while minimizing unwanted collateral damage. Imperfect defenses like dual-mode Patriot are criticized because the intercept altitude against a nuclear-armed missile that is salvage fuzed would not be high enough to preclude collateral and perhaps even some target damage, and because Patriot's accuracy and warhead may not be sufficient to destroy the attacking warhead. Chemical warhead interception must also occur

at a very high altitude to prevent dissemination over the target. But in each of these cases, the attacker is forced to adapt to non-ideal conditions, whether by increasing nuclear yields, employing salvage fuzing, or subjecting dispersed chemicals to uncertain meteorological conditions. Each of these exacts an entry cost by increasing attack complexity and may thereby affect the decision to escalate. Finally, by furnishing Patriot with self-protection capability against TBMs, and clustering these dual-mode Patriot batteries around its highest-priority airfields, NATO could raise the Soviets' entry cost for a conventional TBM attack against airfields.

66. The *DMS Market Intelligence Report*, DMS Inc., 1986, reports that a Patriot fire unit can guide five interceptor missiles simultaneously. There is no technical reason why Patriot could not be improved to handle a larger number of simultaneous intercepts.

4 A TECHNICAL ASSESSMENT OF THE SOVIET TBM THREAT TO NATO

Benoit Morel and Theodore A. Postol

Prior to the most recent Alliance debate over antimissile defenses, Soviet tactical and theater ballistic missiles were thought to have roles that might well be described as that of super-heavy, long-range artillery. Armed with nuclear warheads, and having ranges from tens of kilometers to nearly a thousand kilometers, even the relatively primitive and inaccurate early Soviet TBMs have been a formidable nuclear threat to NATO since at least the mid-1960s.

The goals of a Soviet conventional attack would be, simply speaking, to degrade or destroy those NATO forces and functional capabilities that pose the greatest threat to Warsaw Pact forces, and hence the greatest threat of defeat. It is generally accepted that, in initiating an attack on NATO, the Soviet goals would be to disable or destroy NATO airbases, air defenses, nuclear storage sites, command and control facilities, and communications. These goals are often discussed in a context that suggests they are a peculiar byproduct of Soviet doctrine, but in reality they are dictated by the extraordinary firepower, range, and capabilities of modern weapon systems. These modern capabilities, not doctrine, impel the military planner toward a "strategic" vision of warfare.

Several modernized versions of Soviet TBMs—the SS-21, SS-23 and SS-22—have recently begun to replace their predecessors. There is almost no unambiguous public data yet available about these missiles. Nevertheless, what is known about improvements in Soviet guidance and propulsion technology over the past decades has led to speculation that these newest TBMs might be sufficiently accurate to pose a threat even when armed with conventional munitions. These speculations have fostered still more speculation that modern Soviet TBMs are uniquely suitable for certain critical, nonnuclear missions that would be part of a larger Soviet nonnuclear attack on NATO.

If the Soviet TBM threat proved to be both real and unique, the military implications if NATO failed to react are obvious. However, the military implications could be no less grave if NATO were drawn into an inappropriate commitment of its resources in response to a threat that proved to be improperly characterized, overstated, or fictitious.

This chapter presents a technical analysis of the threat from conventionally armed TBMs. In broad terms, what emerges from this analysis is an important set of conclusions. First, TBMs will have little or no capability to attack mobile targets such as air defense radars and divisional command posts, if mobility is properly exploited for protection. The greatest difficulty is finding these targets, not destroying them. Second, given their small payloads, TBMs cannot carry enough conventional explosives to damage properly hardened underground structures, hence, they should have little or no ability to damage or disrupt operations at fixed, hardened NATO command posts. Third, TBMs with submunitions will not be capable of doing significant damage to runways at NATO airbases unless they achieve accuracies on the order of 30 to 40 meters. Even with such accuracies, many hundreds and perhaps several thousand TBMs might be required for the Soviets to achieve a major impact on NATO tactical air operations during the early phases of a surprise attack. In our judgment, both cruise missiles and aircraft, not TBMs, will continue to be the most efficient means of delivering conventional munitions or chemical/biological weapons in a surprise attack against NATO targets.

CHARACTERISTICS OF TBMS

The ability of a specific conventional TBM to damage a specific target is affected by many factors, some determined by the properties of the TBM, others by properties of the target. The factors that affect a TBM's lethality are the accuracy of delivery; the weight of munitions that it can deliver; and the effectiveness of munitions that can be

Table 4–1. Surface-to-Surface Missile Characteristics.

	First Deployed	Nuclear Yield	Range in km	CEP in Meters IISS	CEP in Meters CRS
United States					
Honest John	1953	5–25 KT	40	830	—
Pershing I	1962	60–400 KT	840	370	400
Lance	1972	1–100 KT	130	460	400
Pershing II	1983	5–50 KT	1,800	40	40
GLCM	1983	200 KT	2,500	20	20
Soviet Union					
SS-1b Scud A	1957	40 KT	90	930	—
SS-4	1959	1 MT	2,000	2,300	2,000
SS-5	1961	1 MT	4,600	1,100	1,100
Frog	1965	200 KT	70	460	400
SS-1c Scud B	1965	1 KT	300	930	900
SS-12	1965	1 MT	900	740	—
SS-21	1977	100 KT	120	280	300
SS-22	1977	500 KT	900	370	300
SS-20	1978	3–150 KT	5,000	430	—
SS-23	1981	100 KT	500	370	350

Source: John M. Collins *United States/Soviet Military Balance* (Washington, D.C.: Government Printing Office, 1980–85); International Institute for Strategic Studies, *The Military Balance 1986–87* (London: IISS, 1986); Stockholm International Peace Research Institute, *1986 Yearbook* (Stockholm: SIPRI, 1986); U.S. Department of Defense, *Soviet Military Power 1987* (Washington, D.C.: Government Printing Office, 1987).

carried. The properties of the target that determine the likelihood of damage are the precision to which its location is known to the attacker; the dimensions of the target; and the "hardness" of the target to effects from munitions.

Publicly available information about the characteristics of Soviet TBMs remains limited and contradictory. Table 4–1 shows the accuracies, or CEPs, of currently deployed U.S. and Soviet ballistic and cruise missiles with ranges between 40 and 5,000 km, as reported by the International Institute for Strategic Studies (IISS) and the Congressional Research Service (CRS). These sources report accuracies of 250 to 350 meters for the new generation of Soviet TBMs. However, certain other sources have reported accuracies almost ten times better—that is, about 30 meters.[1] This suggests either uncertainty or confusion (or both) about Soviet TBM capabilities. A review of technical issues relevant to TBM guidance and control will therefore be useful as a foundation for assessing the TBM threat.

The index of a missile's accuracy or CEP (circle of equal probability) is the radius of an imaginary circle within which half the missiles would fall, if a large number were fired at a target. Modern TBMs employing inertial guidance systems (SS-21, SS-23, SS-22, Lance, Honest John, Pershing I), all have accuracies between 300 and 400 meters. Significant enhancements in accuracy, however, have been demonstrated by the Pershing II, using inertial guidance in combination with terminal guidance. In the final moments of flight, as the missile approaches its target, it scans the terrain around the target with a radar beam, and by correlating the radar scene with a digital map stored in its computer, it corrects any inertial guidance errors that have accumulated during launch and flight to the target. Because the Pershing II reentry vehicle also can make small trajectory corrections as it falls toward the target, it is able to achieve a greatly enhanced accuracy of between 30 and 40 meters. Although there are no public reports of this type of guidance on the new Soviet TBMs, the possibility of terminal guidance on a future generation of Soviets TBMs, or less likely, as an upgrade of current missiles, cannot be dismissed.

There are constraints on the TBM accuracies achievable in this way, we should note. Modern advances in *cruise missile* guidance have produced better results, with CEPs of 15 to 20 meters or less. But cruise missiles are fundamentally different weapons. Because they are aerodynamic craft and fly close to the ground, they can correct guidance errors far more frequently by scanning the terrain; as aircraft, they are quite maneuverable and can follow circuitous paths to targets, exploiting prominent terrain features; because their slower speed of approach to the target (less than 0.5 km/sec) facilitates maneuvering, the addition of even relatively short-range sensors can allow them to home on their targets in final seconds. Thus, they can in principle have near perfect accuracy.

In contrast, a terrain-sensing TBM like Pershing II is constrained over most of its flight path to a ballistically determined trajectory. Because its high speed of approach (1 to 3 km/sec) grants less time for final maneuvering, the missile must begin terrain measurements from high altitudes, where precise details of the target area are less discernible; as a practical matter, its sensor must confine its scanning to areas immediately below the trajectory and around the intended target, which may not contain prominent landmarks. Both constraints enlarge the room for error. So for our analysis we will assume that, in the immediate future, TBM accuracies will be no smaller than the 30 to 40 meters reported for Pershing II.

The second vital factor in determining a TBM's lethality is the weight of munitions that it can deliver. Our review of various public sources of data on Soviet TBMs suggests that the SS-21 could deliver about 800 to 900 kg to a range of about 100 km, while the SS-12/22 and SS-23 could deliver about 1,000 kg to ranges of 1,000 km and 500 km respectively.[2] Because small differences in payload size are irrelevant to our general analysis, we will assume that each missile is capable of delivering 1,000 kg of payload to its maximum range.

There are many types of conventional munitions that might be carried by a TBM. Among these might be warheads optimized to maximize damage from blast, or from fragments accelerated to high speed from a blast. Other munitions, like "shaped-charge warheads," might be designed to direct explosive effects so they penetrate deep into a target. Still other munitions, like "fuel-air explosives," are designed to spread the effects of an explosion, so that the largest possible area is covered with enough blast to destroy intended targets. Yet other types of warheads might utilize incendiary, chemical, or biological agents as means of damaging targets or disrupting military operations. The choice of munition for a TBM would depend on which munitions effects are most damaging to the class of targets being attacked.

The common blast or fragmentation munition derives its destructive power from high-explosives like TNT or RDX. When detonated, a rapid chemical reaction in the explosive converts it into a hot gas that expands violently, acting like a fast-moving piston on the surrounding air, compressing it and creating a high-pressure shock wave that propagates outward. These hot gases are also able to carry fragments to very high speeds, up to several kilometers per second, sufficient to penetrate light armor. However, the designer of munitions is faced with a choice: With each kilogram of payload, he can try to maximize damage from blast by using mostly high explosives or try to maximize damage from fragments by reducing explosive and increasing the weight and/or number of fragments.

The blast effects of an unconfined explosion fall off rapidly with range. A 1,000 kg charge of TNT/RDX type high-explosive, for instance, would cause a blast pressure of about 40 pounds per square inch (275 kPa) at a range of 16 meters, but only 15 psi (105 kPa) at about 30 meters and 5 psi (35 kPa) at about 60 meters. A 40 psi blast would completely demolish a typical unreinforced building, but it might be unable to destroy a properly hardened, above-ground bunker. Other types of targets, such as radars, trucks, and missile launchers are much "softer" and would be likely to suffer heavy damage from only 5 to 10 psi of blast. The deadly effects of a fragmentation munition also fall off with range—in part because the distance between fragments increases as they travel outward from the detonation, reducing the probability they will hit the target; in part because the speed of the fragments is diminished by atmospheric drag effects, reducing the probability they will pierce the target. Against targets such as trucks or radars, high-fragmention munitions offer no special advantages over high explosives.

Still another conventional munition are the various forms of "shaped charges." A shaped charge consists of a cylinder of high explosive that has a conical depression at the forward end and a fuze at the other. Because of the way in which the blast front propagates through the cylinder of explosive when the fuze is triggered, a very hot and highly focused jet of gas is created at a distance of three to four cone diameters from the forward end of the charge. The destructive efficiency of the jet can be enhanced if the conical depression is covered with a liner of metal, such as copper or aluminum. Because the pressure at the leading edge of the jet is well in excess of a 100,000 psi, it can penetrate deep into the interior of a target. Penetration distances of three to four cone diameters can be achieved through steel, and as much as 10 to 12 diameters can be achieved through concrete.

Shaped-charge munitions have a number of features that could make them difficult to use with TBMs, however. Because their destructive efficiency is achieved by a directed blast, they must essentially "hit" their intended target if they are to produce damage. As will be shown in discussion to follow, even a very accurate TBM will rarely make a direct hit on a target. Depending on the trajectory used by the attacker, a TBM also is likely to approach the target's surface at an angle. The jet from the shaped charge will therefore have to penetrate a distance 10 to 100 percent larger than the thickness of the barrier it is intended to pierce. If the munition is triggered prematurely by an overburden of extra soil, or by light structures that are above the target, the result will also be greatly reduced penetration of the target. Finally, damage to a target from a shaped charge is likely to be very severe but very localized. If, for instance, the target is a properly constructed large bunker, its interior may well be divided into many separate hardened rooms. Damage from a hit might then be localized to only those units at or near the point of penetration.

A fuel-air explosive (FAE) is another form of munition that might be considered for use on a TBM. The details of FAEs will vary, but the basic principle is that the munition disperses an explosive aerosol over its target. After a delay of several tenths to several seconds, during which the aerosol spreads to a wider area, a delayed-action fuze detonates the aerosol. Because they achieve destruction by spreading an explosive over a large area, FAEs generally do not achieve very high peak overpressures. For this reason, they are primarily useful against soft targets, and in appropriate tactical circumstances, can be very effective as antipersonnel weapons. The high speed of arrival for a TBM does complicate delivery. Mechanisms must be devised for the controlled dispersal of the aerosol and the detonation of the explosive mixture after a proper delay. Such dispersal and fuzing mechanisms may well be complex, heavy, and undependable, reducing the overall reliability of the TBM as well as the fraction of payload that can be devoted to explosive. If the munition must be deliberately slowed prior to impact, it may also require terminal guidance and maneuvering all the way to the ground, to offset potential miss errors due to winds. Such a technique, while technically feasible, would add weight to the reentry system, again reducing the payload fraction devoted to explosive.

Chemical or biological agents might also be carried by TBMs. Because the purpose would be to disperse an aerosol over the target, the mode of delivery—and attendant problems—might resemble in general terms those associated with FAEs. The U.S. Department of Defense has offered a graphic but hypothetical representation of a chemical/biological attack on a military airbase, using a Soviet TBM.[3] TBMs certainly could be used to deliver such agents. But in our judgment, they would lack the controllability and reliability that a military planner is likely to demand and could get by using other delivery modes, such as aircraft or cruise missiles. The direction and speed of local winds at the target are important in the dispersal of C/B agents, and a cruise missile could be designed from available technologies that would use data from its guidance system to determine local wind conditions, calculate an optimal cross-wind path for dispersal, and release the agents all at once or in a controlled pattern as it flies.

Yet another possibility for TBMs would involve submunitions, clusters of smaller munitions rather than a unitary warhead, which can

Figure 4–1. Comparison of Total Bombing Capabilities of Soviet/Pact TBMs and Ground-Attack Aircraft at Various Ranges.

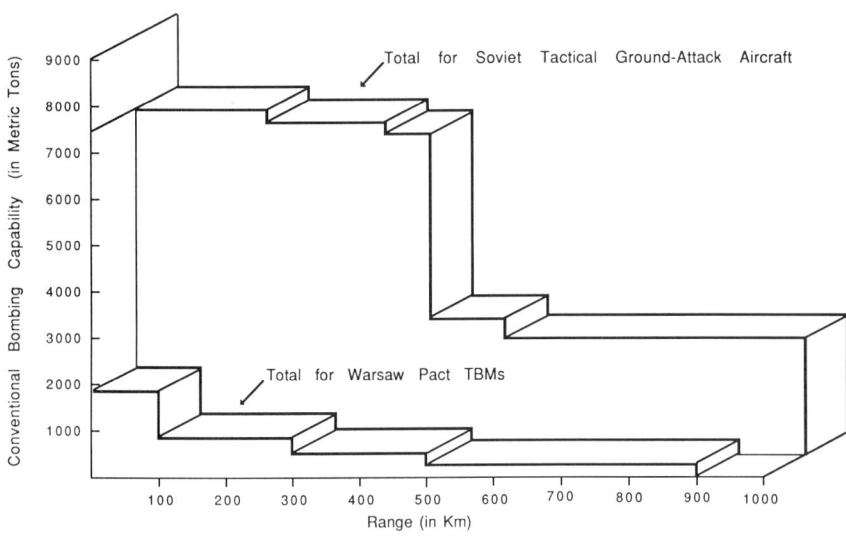

considerably increase the likelihood that a TBM will destroy or severely damage certain types of targets. The submunitions would generally be dispersed in a pattern designed to maximize destructive effects or impact with a target. The actual mode of destruction might be any of the mechanisms discussed above, perhaps a combination of them. Submunitions to be delivered by NATO aircraft, for instance, include varieties that use a shaped-charge to pierce a hole in the target (an aircraft shelter or runway, for example), through which the main charge is then propelled and detonated.

It is well worth bearing in mind that whatever the munition or submunition involved, the total payload capabilities of the Warsaw Pact TBM force are small in contrast to those of Soviet tactical ground-attack aircraft. Figure 4–1 shows a very rough comparison of the conventional bombing capabilities of the two forces, as measured in metric tons of ordnance that can be delivered. As the figure shows, a single sortie of Soviet tactical ground-attack aircraft could potentially deliver over 7 million kilograms (7,000 metric tons) of munitions up to 450+ km from operating bases, and about 2.5 million kilograms (2,500 metric tons) to ranges between 500 to 1000 km. In contrast, roughly 3,000 SS-23s would be needed to deliver a comparable load of munitions against targets at 500 km range, and about 2,500 SS-12/22s would be needed for similar missions at ranges between 500 and 1,000 km. Such numbers far exceed current Warsaw Pact TBM forces, or future projections of those forces. Put differently, whether the range of interest is less than 500 km or 500 to 1,000 km, current Pact TBM forces could deliver less than one-tenth the payload deliverable by a single sortie of tactical aviation. TBMs, of course, have certain advantages: They can arrive at targets within minutes, rather than tens of minutes for aircraft, and they do not have to contend with air defenses. But it is Soviet air forces that will determine whether any temporary advantage or element of surprise from TBMs becomes a decisive advantage for the Warsaw Pact.

The third factor that governs the lethality of TBMs is the effectiveness of their munitions against particular targets. This draws our attention from the properties of TBMs to the properties of targets. We cannot examine in detail each category of target in NATO, so we will focus on those categories that play most prominently in scenarios of TBM attack and look at some of the generic technical issues that arise.

OBJECTIVES OF TBM ATTACKS

It is widely recognized that in almost any circumstance (surprise attack or otherwise) that leads to warfare between the Warsaw Pact and NATO, the destruction of the enemy's airpower would have to be a major objective of both the adversaries. If NATO airpower were immediately available to answer a Warsaw Pact attack, it might be able to assert local superiority in firepower through direct support of forces on the ground, it might disrupt or prevent the movement of Warsaw Pact reinforcements and supplies to critical areas of combat, and it might deny Frontal Aviation the ability to carry out similar actions against NATO's forces. NATO could use its aircraft to assert superiority by destroying Warsaw Pact aircraft over the battle area, and possibly by directly attacking Warsaw Pact airfields, surveillance systems, and communications centers on Pact territory. Hence, the denial of airpower to NATO would be an overwhelmingly important objective of any Warsaw Pact surprise attack.

If Soviet TBMs were part of this assault on NATO airpower, they might be used against several categories of targets, including air defense units and their radars, which are mobile but soft targets;

aircraft in shelters at main operating bases, which are large, fixed, semihard, above-ground bunkers; airfield runways, which are large, fixed, semihard targets; and command and control facilities, which may be superhard, underground bunkers. We will review some general principles for determining the destructiveness of TBMs and then examine the vulnerability to TBMs of each of these generic types of targets.

The probability that a TBM will damage its target—that is, the "damage expectancy"—is itself the product of other probabilities, including: the probability that the TBM survives to be launched; the probability that all missile systems function reliably in flight; the probability that the missile penetrates opposing defenses; and the probability of its warhead killing the target. Because NATO currently has no defenses capable of engaging TBMs, the probability of penetrating defenses is one. Because in our scenario the Warsaw Pact executes a surprise attack, the prelaunch survivability of Soviet TBMs is also one. Thus, for the circumstances under consideration here, the damage expectancy against each target is merely the product of the probability of kill (P_k) and system reliability (P_{RE}). For example, if the probability that a target will be "killed" by a TBM that successfully functions is 0.7 and the TBM system reliability is 0.8, then the damage expectancy per TBM is $0.7 \times 0.8 = 0.56$.

The probability of kill (P_k) depends on the hardness of the target to weapons effects and the accuracy of TBM delivery. Because probability of kill is a very important quantity that can vary drastically with the properties of the target, it merits a careful explanation.

If a target is destroyed when subjected to a given intensity of weapons effects, then the range at which a detonating weapon creates such effects can be thought of as the "lethal" range. For example, a blast of 5 to 10 psi (35 to 70 kPa) is probably sufficient to destroy or damage a radar antenna. Such blast pressures occur at ranges of 38 to 55 meters from the detonation of a 1,000 kg high-explosive warhead, so the lethal range (or radius) of such a warhead against a radar is 38 to 55 meters. On the other hand, a lightly fortified above-ground bunker, its equipment, and occupants might not be seriously disrupted or destroyed unless subjected to blast effects in excess of 40 psi (275 kPa). The lethal range of a 1,000 kg warhead against this target would be only 16 to 17 meters.

The accuracy of a TBM, as noted earlier, is designated by its CEP, the radius of a circle within which half of the missiles would fall. If the area of the target is small relative to the area of circles with radii equal to the CEP or lethal radius, the probability of kill is well approximated by the following expression:

$$P_k = 1 - 0.5^{[(R_L/CEP)^2]}$$

where:

CEP = the distance within which half the missiles will fall and detonate;

R_L = the range at which the effects of the detonation result in the loss of the target as a militarily useful entity.

Suppose, however, that the target's location is not precisely known, as might be the case with a mobile target. Even a perfectly accurate missile will, on the average, miss the target by a distance equal to the uncertainty in target location. For missiles with either finite or perfect accuracy, this effect can be accounted for by assuming that the missile has an "effective CEP." The effective CEP (CEP_{eff}) is equal to the square root of the sum of the squares of the CEP and the average uncertainty of the target's location. That is:

$$CEP_{eff} = (CEP^2 + R_u^2)^{1/2}$$

where:

R_u = the radius of uncertainty, that is, the radius of a circle within which the target is presumed to reside.

The implications are several. The first is that uncertainty about the precise location of the target matters as much as missile accuracy in determining probability of kill. Second, even exceptional accuracy with a large warhead does not assure high damage expectancy against very hard targets. Consider our baseline TBM with a 1,000 kg warhead and a 30 meter CEP. Despite such accuracy, its probability of kill against a 40 psi target—a fixed, above ground, semihardened bunker, for instance—is no better than 0.2. If missile reliability is 0.8 or 0.9, then the damage expectancy per TBM fired against such targets drops below 0.2. If the target's location is not known to better than 20 or 30 meters, the damage expectancy drops to well below 0.1.

A radar, unlike a semihard bunker, would probably be hardened only to 5 or 10 psi. If its location were known, the probability of kill would be 0.9 and the damage expectancy per TBM would be 0.7 to 0.8.

For protection, radars, like many other military assets, are intentionally designed to be mobile — to make it hard for an enemy to locate and target them. If by moving about (perhaps in conjunction with other deceptive techniques, such as remaining silent or deploying decoy transmitters), the radar can increase the attacker's uncertainty about its location by 75 to 100 meters, the damage expectancy per TBM would be no better than against a semihard bunker. The attacker may be able to offset such measures through reconnaissance and tactics that provoke the air defense unit to turn on its radars. The Israelis did this very well against Syrian air defenses in 1982, using drones, aircraft, and air-launched antiradiation and homing missiles. But TBMs are not adaptable to tactics that could provoke a radar to reveal its location, and in that degree they are less threatening to radars and other mobile air defense elements than aircraft.

CAPABILITIES OF TBMS ARMED WITH SUBMUNITIONS

Because it is so difficult to damage some targets with a single high-yield warhead, it is relevant to ask how much the likelihood of success might be altered if the unitary TBM payload were exchanged for one of submunitions. The attractiveness of submunitions is that they can spread destructive effects over a larger area. The enlarged destructive area is evident by contrasting a unitary 1,000 kg munition with one hundred 10 kg submunitions. The unitary warhead, as we noted earlier, could produce a 40 psi blast at 16 meters and 5 psi at about 60 meters. A 10 kg submunition could produce 40 psi only out to 3.5 meters and 5 psi out to 12 meters. Nonetheless, if all 100 submunitions could be uniformly dispersed, a roughly circular area of radius 35 meters could be covered with blast pressures of 40 psi or more. If a less dense pattern of dispersal is instead chosen, a circular area of about 120 meters radius could be subjected to 5 psi or more. Thus, a TBM that can carry and disperse such submunitions could achieve more than twice the lethal range of a unitary warhead.[4]

However, because the radius of effects is so much smaller for each submunition, it is also possible that a hit with a submunition might not result in the complete destruction of a target or termination of its operation. In addition, the previous estimates of lethal range assume uniform dispersal of submunitions, which may be difficult to achieve from a TBM arriving at speeds between 1 to 3 km/sec. Nonuniformities in dispersal due to random motions of submunitions as they are deployed from a TBM will result in some zones in the impact area being hit more than once while others are not hit at all.

The dispersal pattern for submunitions does involve trade-offs. Because the impact point of an arriving missile, on average, will not be squarely on the target, the larger the area over which submunitions can be spread, the more likely the target will be encompassed within the area where they fall. However, the larger the submunition impact area, the lower will be the density of submunitions, and the less likely it will be that the target is hit by one or more them. For missiles of specific accuracy, and for targets of specific hardness, there is a well-defined value of submunition dispersal radius that results in a maximum probability of hit.

A simple probabilistic theory provides a good estimate of target hit probabilities for a submunition-armed TBM. Because the numerical results of the theory yield important insights about TBM effectiveness, we will describe the theory briefly.

We begin with the probability that at least one of N submunitions hits a target that is enclosed within the submunition dispersal pattern, which is assumed to be a circle of radius R_d. This radius is equal to the distance between the TBM's impact point and the outer edge of the circular area in which the submunitions uniformly fall. Next we look at the probability that the TBM itself lands close enough to a target for the target to be enclosed within the dispersal radius. The product of these two probabilities is then the probability that a target will be hit by at least one of N submunitions that have been dispersed over the circular area from a TBM with a given CEP.

If we assume for the moment that the TBM *does* land close enough to the target for it to lie within submunition dispersal radius (R_d), then the probability that a single submunition will hit the target is equal to the ratio of the area covered by the target to the area in which the submunition might land. If the area covered by the target is A, and the submunition falls within a circle of radius R_d surrounding the missile impact point, then the probability of a target hit is

$$\frac{A}{\pi R_d^2}$$

and the probability of a miss is simply

$$1 - \frac{A}{\pi R_d^2}$$

If N such submunitions all fall within the dispersal radius R_d, then the probability none of the submunitions will hit the target is

$$\left(1 - \frac{A}{\pi R_d^2}\right)^N$$

and the probability of at least one hit is

$$P_D = 1 - \left(1 - \frac{A}{\pi R_d^2}\right)^N$$

Next we turn to the probability that the TBM lands close enough to the target so that the distance between the TBM impact point and the target is equal to or smaller than the submunition dispersal radius (R_d). The probability (P_H) that a TBM impacts within a distance R_d from the target is as follows:

$$P_H = (1 - 0.5^{[(R_d/CEP)^2]})$$

Finally, the probability that at least one submunition will hit the target is the product of the probabilities P_D and P_H:

$$P_k = P_D P_H$$

$$P_k = \left[1 - \left(1 - \frac{A}{\pi R_d^2}\right)^N\right]\left[1 - 0.5^{[(R_d/CEP)^2]}\right]$$

If the lethal range of a submunition is R_L, and the critical components of the target that can be damaged by weapons effects can be thought of as all concentrated at a single point, then the area which is covered by weapons effects lethal to the target is

$$A = \pi R_L^2$$

This quantity can be thought of as the "effective area covered by a point target" because any weapon that "hits" within it will produce a target kill.

The effective target area can be modified to account for the finite size of critical target components. In circumstances where it is possible to designate an average "target radius" R_t for a target, and that radius is not very large relative to the lethal radius R_L, the effective area can be written as

$$A = \pi(R_t + R_L)^2$$

However, small differences in the choice of effective target area do not result in significant changes in predicted values for the probability of a hit—provided that R_t is not very large relative to R_L and a new optimized dispersal radius (R_d) is chosen for the new value of target effective area. Hence, a more detailed analysis that includes the finite size of such targets leads to nearly identical predictions of probability of kill. We will therefore avoid such unwarranted complications by considering soft, mobile units like radars to be point targets with an effective area

$$A = \pi R_L^2$$

After discussing targets that can be treated in this way, we will generalize the theory to include targets that have dimensions that are large compared to a submunition lethal radius R_L. A submunition hit on such large targets will damage only a small part of them. Treating them as point targets would therefore lead to misleadingly high damage predictions.

In Figure 4–2, we have shown the probability that at least one of 100 TBM submunitions would destroy an illustrative target—in this case a radar—plotted against effective CEP (that is, missile accuracy and target location uncertainty). Again, we assume a submunition with 10 kg of explosive, and hence a lethal radius (R_L) of 12.3 meters against a radar hardened to 5 psi, and a lethal radius of 8.1 meters against a 10 psi radar. We have assumed a near optimal submunition dispersal radius (R_d) of 70 meters.

The advantage of submunitions is quite evident. Above we noted that a radar might reduce the probability of kill for a unitary, 1,000 kg warhead to 0.2 by generating uncertainty about its location and thus raising CEP_{eff} to 100 meters. As Figure 4–2 shows, TBMs of similar "effective accuracy" will have a considerably larger probability of kill if they are armed with submunitions rather than unitary warheads. With submunitions, if the CEP_{eff} is 100 meters, the probability of kill against a radar can be increased to 0.6. To drive the P_k back down to 0.2, the radar would have to employ technical and tactical measures designed to obscure its position so it cannot be located to better than about 400 meters.

It is next of interest to ask how effective a TBM armed with submunitions might be against an above-ground, semihardened (40 psi) bunker. Figure 4–3 shows the probability of a TBM submunition hitting the roof of such a structure, which we assume to have a roof area of about 325 square meters (18 × 18 m). The dispersal radius (R_d = 60 meters) is chosen to maximize the probability that at least one submunition hits the shelter. Bunkers for warheads at nuclear weapons storage sites might be about this size. The hardened shelters for

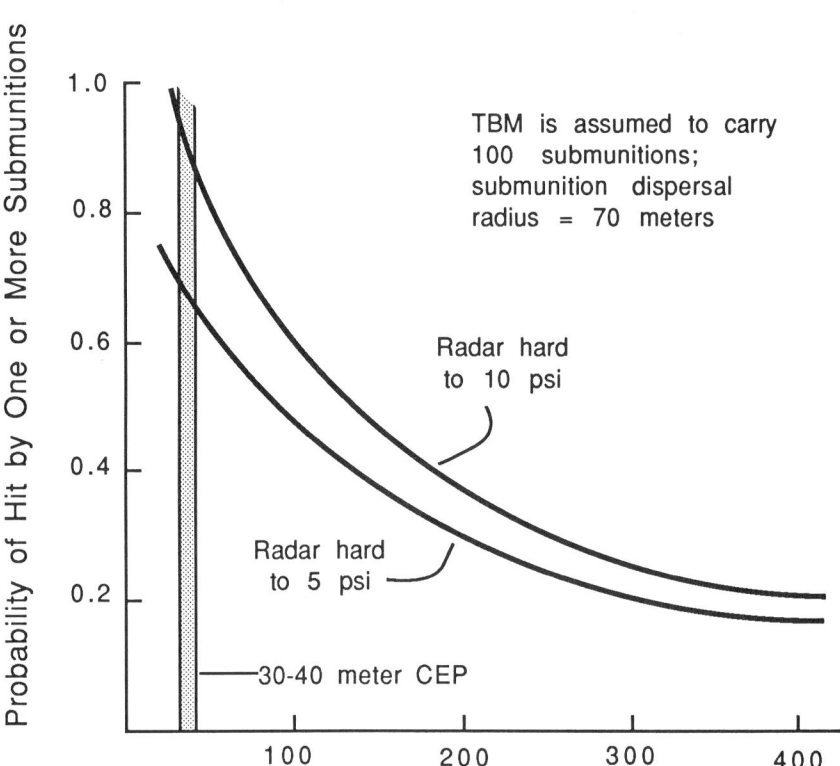

Figure 4-2. Probability That a TBM Destroys a Radar.

aircraft at main NATO airfields would be substantially larger, perhaps 15 × 20 meters or more. These shelters are fixed, and their locations undoubtedly known, so the probability of being hit by at least one submunition from our baseline TBM would be quite high, as Figure 4–3 suggests. On the other hand, if the shelters are sensibly spaced at the airfield, the attacker may be forced to allocate a TBM to each shelter for each aircraft—driving up the numbers of TBMs required very sharply. Also, if shelters are adequately hardened, a submunition hit may not result in damage to the sheltered aircraft.

In cases where individual submunition hits on a large semihardened bunker are able to inflict damage, each submunition hit might still only destroy a small section of the bunker. For this situation, it is also of

Figure 4-3. Probability of TBM Submunitions Hitting a Bunker.

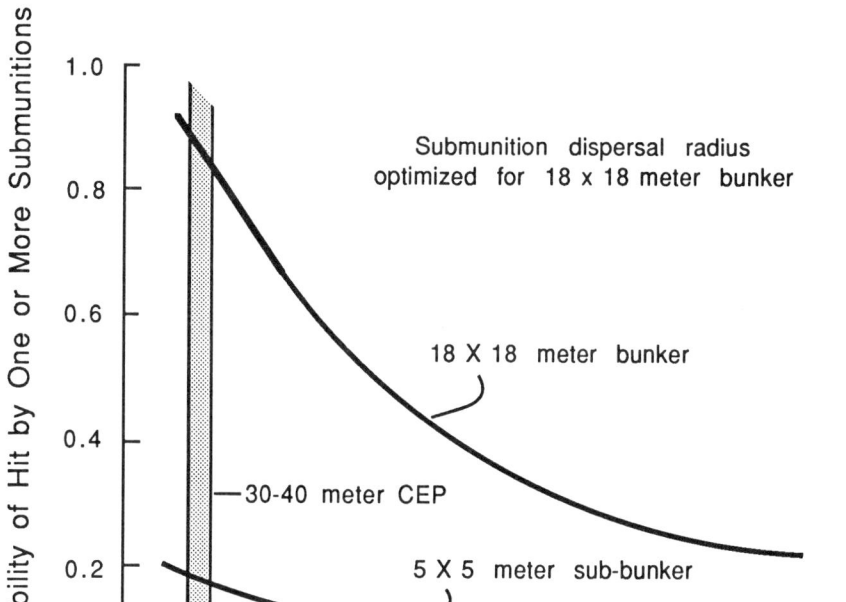

interest to have an assessment of the levels of damage that might be achieved with TBMs. It should be noted, however, that without detailed engineering data on relevant military installations, it is unclear what structures might fall into this category of susceptibility to damage. Such structures might be buildings needed for operations at airbases or modestly hardened command centers of perhaps minor importance.

In order to estimate damage from submunitions against such large semihardened targets, we will consider a single large bunker made up of perhaps twelve different "subbunkers" which are about 5 by 5 meters on a side. We will assume each subbunker will be completely destroyed if it is hit by a 10 kg submunition. The probability of at least one submunition hitting a subbunker is also plotted in Figure 4-3. As the figure shows, if the TBM has a 30 meter *CEP* and the attacker knows the target's location with certainty (CEP_{eff} = 30 meters), then the probability that the bunker will be hit with at least one submunition is 0.88, and the probability that a specified subbunker will be hit is 0.19. Since there are twelve such subbunkers, the average number of submunitions expected to hit the total bunker would therefore be 12 × 0.19 = 2.28 submunitions. Two TBMs, each carrying 100 submunitions, would raise the average number of hits to 2 × 2.28 = 4.56; three TBMs would result in 3 × 2.28 = 6.84 hits; and so on. However, even an attack that results in an average of twelve submunition hits does not mean a bunker has been totally destroyed because there is a significant probability that submunitions will hit some subbunkers more than once while other subbunkers are not hit at all.

If we assume that the attack must destroy 50 percent of the subbunkers to eliminate the target as an effective fighting unit, then about three TBMs would be needed to meet this objective on the average.[5] But these are averages. If three TBMs are used to attack such a target, some of the time more than 6.84 submunitions will hit the bunker, while at other times less than that number may hit. In addition, for a given number of hits on a bunker, some fraction of the submunitions will hit subbunkers that have already been destroyed. These redundant hits will therefore not inflict more damage on the bunker. It is of interest to know how much of the time the goal of 50 percent or higher damage is achieved.

The probability that k = 6 of the n = 12 subbunkers are hit is easily calculated. If p is the probability that a subbunker is hit, then the probability it will not be hit is $1 - p$, and the probability that k out of n subbunkers are hit is

$$P(k, n) = \binom{n}{k} p^k (1 - p)^{n-k}$$

where

$$\binom{n}{k} = \frac{n!}{k!(n-k)!}$$

The probability that *at least* N out of n subbunkers will be hit ($P_{cum}(N, k)$) is

$$P_{cum}(N, n) = \sum_{i=N}^{n} P(i, n)$$

Figure 4–4. Probability of Achieving Various Levels of Damage against a Target Composed of Twelve Sub-units.

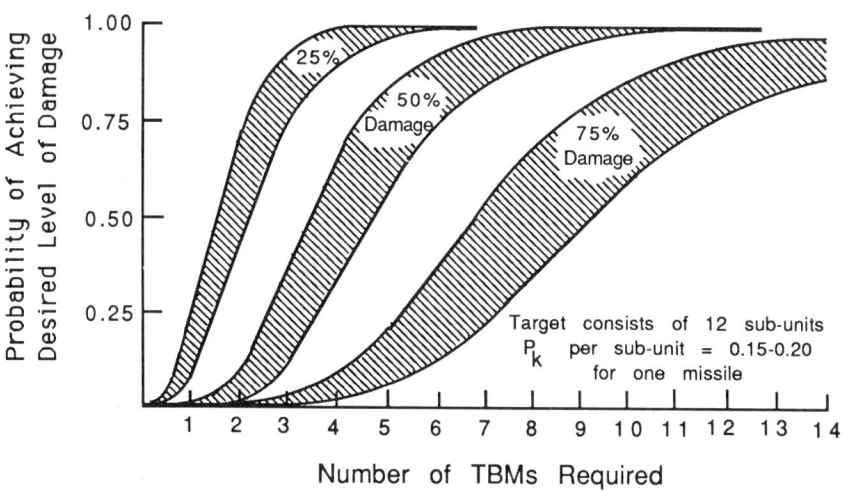

Each missile attack is a probabilistically independent event. Hence, the probability that any single subbunker will be destroyed after M missile attacks is

$$p = 1 - (1 - p_1)^M$$

where p_1 is the probability a subbunker will be destroyed per missile attack.

Figure 4–4 shows the probability that 25 percent, 50 percent, and 75 percent damage will be achieved as a function of the number of attacking TBMs with 30 or 60 meter CEP. As can be seen from the figure, although four attacking TBMs with 30 meter CEPs will result in more than 50 percent damage to the target more than half of the time, between four and five will be needed to achieve at least that level of damage more than 75 percent of the time. If the the CEP of attacking TBMs is 60 meters, then nearly five missiles will be required to achieve more than 50 percent damage more than half of the time, and six will be needed to achieve 50 percent damage more than 75 percent of the time. As can be clearly seen, if redundancy is built into the target bunker in such a manner that more than 50 percent of it must be destroyed before it ceases to be a threat, a large number of

Figure 4–5. Probability of TBM Submunitions Hitting a Sub-bunker.

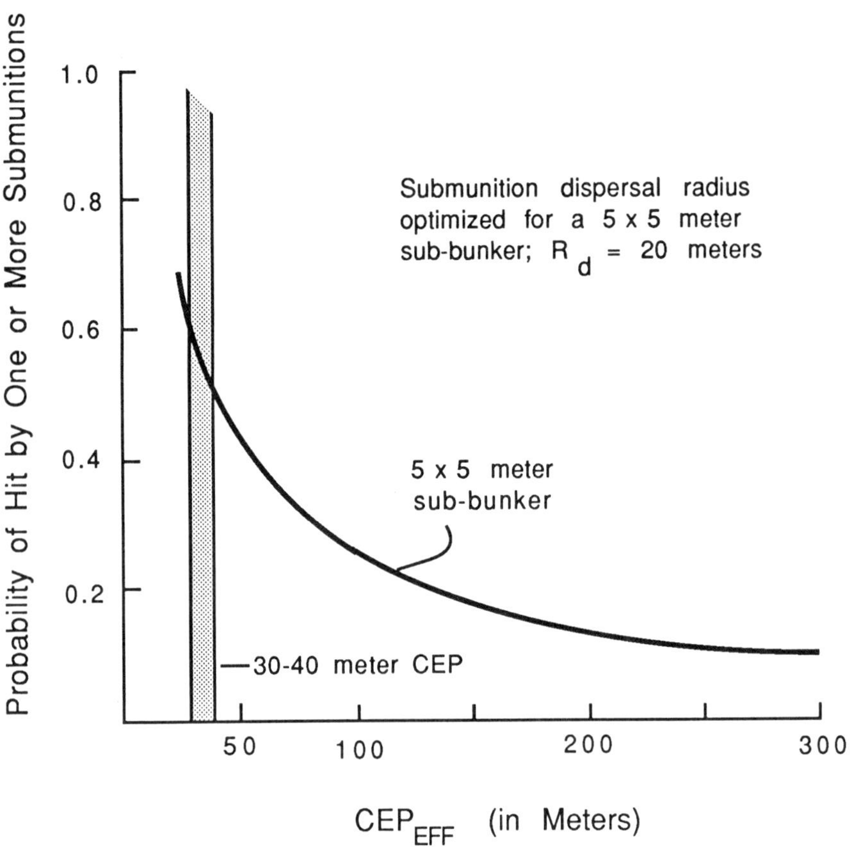

TBMs will be required to attack each such bunker before it is no longer able to continue functioning as a militarily useful unit.

The price of a TBM attack is driven still higher if the bunker facility is not only broken into twelve subbunkers, but each of these is then separated from the others by 20 to 30 meters. Against this semidispersed, semihard target, the optimal attack strategy requires that a TBM be used to attack each separate subbunker. Figure 4–5 shows the probability of a subbunker being hit, assuming TBMs use a submunition dispersal radius optimized to give the highest probability of a hit against the smaller dispersed subbunkers (R_d = 20 meters). In this case, nearly a dozen TBMs would be required to achieve the destruction of half the subbunkers on average, and two dozen would be required to destroy three-quarters of them.

This simple example serves to illustrate how effective dispersal in combination with redundancy and hardening can be as means of increasing the number of TBMs required to achieve the objectives of attack. Should a high-accuracy, submunition-armed TBM threat eventually emerge, it is clear that appropriate passive measures like dispersal and hardening should be considered as potentially cost-effective and robust counters to a TBM threat.

TBM EFFECTIVENESS AGAINST AIRBASE RUNWAYS

Because even very large numbers of accurate nonnuclear TBMs could not destroy a large fraction of hardened structures at an airbase, a TBM surprise attack might instead be aimed at damaging runways. The objective of a runway attack would be to deny — or sufficiently slow — the takeoff of NATO's fighter aircraft that would be used to defend the bases from massive follow-on attacks by Pact air forces.

This task could be quite demanding. Two characteristics of modern fighters that make them so suitable for air combat is their low wing loading and high thrust-to-weight ratio. These characteristics — which result in a high maneuver and acceleration capability in air combat — also result in an aircraft that can take off using very short sections of runway. An F-15 interceptor, for instance, needs only 275 meters of take-off run before its wheels are no longer in contact with the runway. A fully loaded ground-attack aircraft, on the other hand, generally needs a longer takeoff run and thus may be pinned in at airfields until longer sections of runways can be repaired. This fact emphasizes the importance both of rapid runway repair and of getting fighter/interceptors aloft to protect airfields from follow-on attacks by Warsaw Pact aircraft.

Because many NATO airbases are sized to handle the long takeoff and landing runs of large, heavy-lift aircraft in addition to interceptors and fighters, this type of TBM surprise attack would have to decisively deny NATO a very large fraction of its available runway space. A detailed evaluation of how many TBMs might ultimately be needed to achieve this objective requires consideration of the following factors: the length of runways available at NATO airbases; the average width of these runways; the length and width of runway required by interceptors for takeoff; the accessibility of the runway sections to aircraft (that is, the existence of pathways for ferrying aircraft to undamaged runway sections); and the number of TBMs required to deny a section of runway to NATO interceptors.

Runways at large military air facilities are typically 50 meters or more wide and 1,500 to 2,500 meters long. A large airbase will have one or more large main runways, plus secondary runways or taxiways that might also be used in emergencies. (Figure 4–6 shows the arrangement of runways and taxiways at a major NATO airbase in Bitburg, West Germany.) During normal peacetime operations, fighters can take off two abreast from a runway that is 50 meters wide, and with standard safety lapse times of about ten seconds between pairs of aircraft. Hence, if only a single section of runway is used for fighter launch, and there are no bottlenecks to prevent aircraft from assembling to take their turn taking off, launch rates of twelve aircraft per minute can be routinely achieved. In wartime operations, the standard safety lapse time might be reduced from ten seconds to perhaps six or eight, raising the launch rate to fifteen or twenty aircraft per minute in unimpeded operations.

Table 4–2 shows wheelbase, takeoff run, and landing run data for typical NATO air defense and fighter/ground attack aircraft currently in service.[6] Since the wheelbases of these aircraft are between 3 and 6 meters, the main impediment to takeoff and landing on a runway that is not totally blocked will be control of the aircraft in cross-winds. In wartime, faced with the choice of being caught on the ground and destroyed, or taking off to engage approaching Warsaw Pact air forces, it is reasonable to speculate that pilots would be willing to chance a takeoff if more than 15 meters of runway width is available along a straight line path the length of the aircraft's takeoff run (in contrast to the 25-meter width in side-by-side, peacetime takeoffs).

The size of a crater caused by a bomb or submunition that hits a runway can vary considerably with the nature of the runway, the subgrade, and the ground below. It can also vary considerably with the depth of penetration achieved by the munition before it explodes. We estimate that a unitary 1,000 kg warhead delivered by a TBM could create a crater of 12 to 17 meters diameter in a runway — assuming that the warhead can survive impact and penetrate one to two meters into a runway's pavement before detonating in the subgrade.[7] Because upheaval around the crater periphery can potentially extend its effective "blocking" diameter an additional 20 to 30 percent, a TBM armed with a unitary warhead could potentially deny more than 20 meters of

ATBMS AND WESTERN SECURITY 115

Figure 4-6. Main Runway, Taxiways, Aircraft Shelters, and Main Base Operations Buildings of Major NATO Airbase at Bitburg, West Germany.[a]

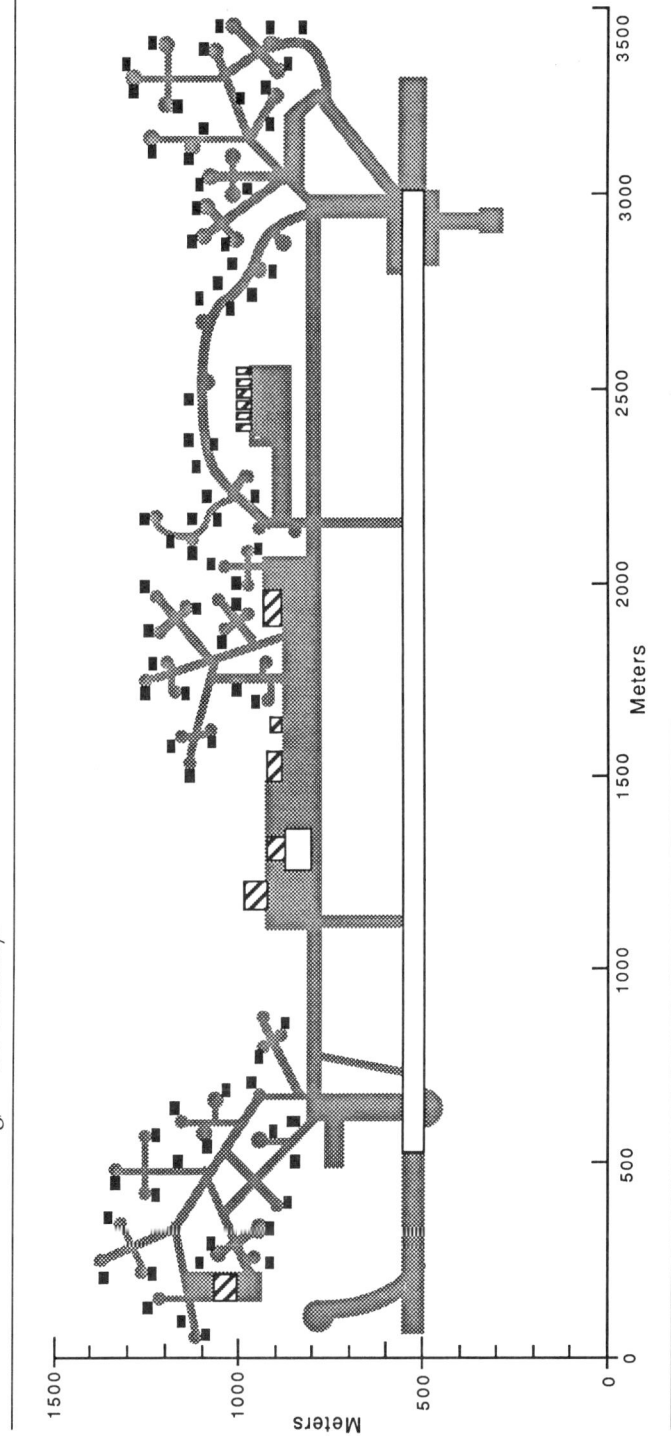

a. The main runway is 2,500 × 45 meters; the main taxiway is 2,400 × 25 meters; the unpaved area between the runway and taxiway is 2,300 × 180 meters.

Table 4–2. Take-off and Landing Runs for NATO Aircraft.

	Takeoff Weight	Takeoff Run	Landing Run	Wheel-base	Number Deployed[b]
F-4	26,600 kg	900–1,300 m	1,000 m[a]	—	284
F-5	7,000 kg	610–700 m	790 m[a]	4.3 m	89
F-15	18,800 kg	275 m	760 m	5.5 m	96
F-16	10,800 kg	320 m	—	4.0 m	319
F-18	15,700 kg	430 m	—	5.5 m	42
F-104	9,000 kg	—	—	3.0 m	90
Harrier	13,500 kg	350 m	10–20 m	0.5 m	36
Tornado	20,400 kg	900 m	370 m	6.2 m	211
Alphajet	—	—	—	—	126
Draken	—	—	—	—	16
Mirage 5	13,500 kg	—	—	2.7 m	52

Sources: *Jane's All the World's Aircraft* (London: Jane's, 1981–85); International Institute for Strategic Studies, *The Military Balance 1986-87* (London: IISS, 1986).

a. With brake parachute.

b. Air defense and fighter/ground attack aircraft, including operational conversion units, deployed with the air forces of the United States, West Germany, the Netherlands, Belgium, Denmark, Canada, and Great Britain in NATO's central region.

runway width to aircraft. If the crater were right on the centerline of a runway 50 meters wide, it could effectively cut it. Two craters on each half of the runway would certainly cut it, but the runway would have to be cut into lengths of less than 300 meters to deny F-15 and F-16 takeoffs, or sections less than 600 to 900 meters to deny F-4 and F-5 takeoffs.

Each TBM fired at an aimpoint on a runway will not necessarily impact at a location that results in optimal runway blockage. In order to determine the number of TBMs that might be required to cut the runway at chosen points, it is necessary to derive a mathematical relationship for the probability of TBM impact as a function of distance from the runway centerline.

If it is assumed that the distribution of TBM impact points around intended aimpoints can be represented as a normalized Gaussian probability function, then the probability that a target of area A (in this case, a runway) will be hit is given by

$$P_{\text{runway}} = \frac{1}{2\pi\sigma^2} \int_A dA \; e^{-(r^2/2\sigma^2)}$$

A TECHNICAL ASSESSMENT OF THE SOVIET TBM THREAT

Where r is the miss distance between an impact point and the intended aimpoint and sigma is the standard deviation of miss distances. Sigma is simply related to the CEP by the constant

$$\sigma = \frac{CEP}{[2\ln(2)]^{1/2}} = (0.849322)(CEP)$$

A missile will be very unlikely to hit a runway unless the magnitude of its CEP is roughly equal to the runway's width. Because runway lengths are very much larger than their widths, a runway target can be treated as if its length is infinite relative to the magnitude of the TBM's CEP. If the x-axis of integration is parallel to the runway length, the y-axis is parallel to its width, and the runway's width is w, then the probability of a runway hit (P_{runway}) can be written in the form of the following integral:

$$P_{\text{runway}} = \frac{1}{2\pi\sigma^2} \int_{-\infty}^{\infty} dx \int_{-w/2}^{w/2} dy \, e^{-[(x^2+y^2)/(2\sigma^2)]}$$

On integration this integral reduces to the Gaussian error function

$$P_{\text{runway}} = ERF\left(\frac{w/2}{\sqrt{2}\sigma}\right)$$

Where

$$ERF(x) = \frac{2}{\sqrt{\pi}} \int_0^x e^{-t^2} dt$$

Hence the probability of a TBM impact at a distance less than b from the runway centerline is

$$P_{\text{runway}} = ERF\left(\frac{b}{\sqrt{2}\sigma}\right)$$

and the probability of an impact at a distance *greater* than b is

$$1 - P_{\text{runway}}$$

Figure 4–7 is a plot of the probability that a missile will impact at a range *greater* than a distance R from the centerline of a runway. The distance R is expressed in units of missile *CEP* on the graph. If it is assumed that a TBM achieves a 30 meter CEP, and a runway is 50 meters wide, then the curve in Figure 4–7 indicates that more than 30 percent of the missiles fired at the runway will have impact points that are *not* on the runway (CEP = 30 meters, R = 25 meters or 0.83 CEP, results in a 0.33 probability of impact at a distance in excess of 0.83 CEP). For a TBM armed with a 1,000 kg warhead to block half the

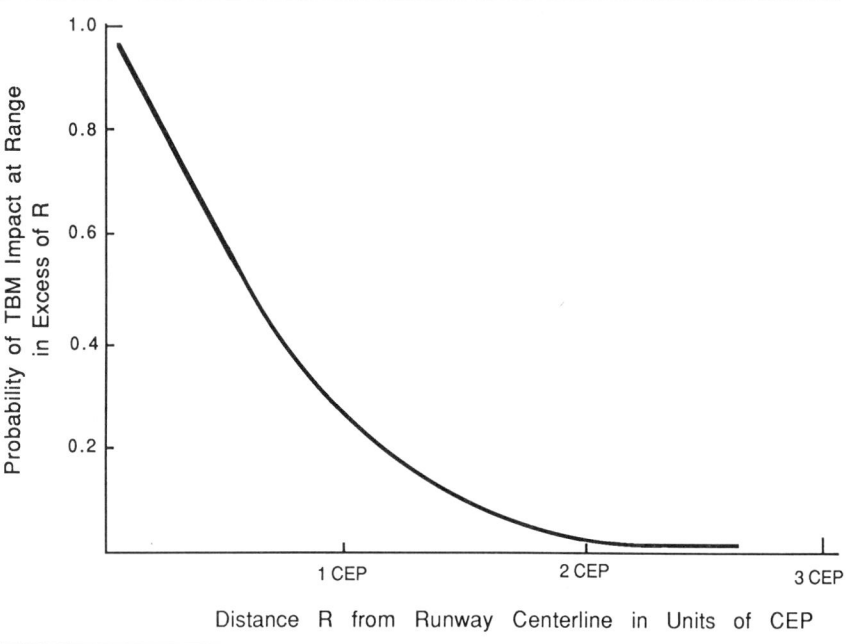

Figure 4–7. Probability that a TBM Will Impact at a Range in Excess of Distance R from a Runway Centerline.

runway, it might have to impact at a distance no more than perhaps 5 to 20 meters from either side of the runway centerline. The probability of landing in this band can be estimated using the curve plotted in Figure 4–7. It is simply the probability the missile will impact at a range in excess of 5 meters (that is, 0.17 CEP) from the centerline (about 0.85), subtracted from the probability it will impact at a range in excess of 20 meters (that is, 0.67 CEP) from the centerline (about 0.44) — that is 0.85 − 0.44 = 0.41. The probability that a second TBM will impact at the same distance from the centerline, but on the other side of it, is half the previously calculated probability. Hence the probability that two TBMs aimed at the same point on the runway will cut it so aircraft will not be able to use it is 0.41 × 0.205 = 0.08.[8] It is therefore clear that TBMs with unitary warheads cannot efficiently deny sections of runway to aircraft taking off, unless they are considerably more accurate than 30 meters CEP.

What if the TBMs are armed with submunitions rather than unitary warheads? We will assume each 10 kg submunition that hits a runway might block a width of 2 to 3 meters to aircraft. Hence, if 20 to 30 submunitions could be distributed over the width of each 200 to 300 meter section of runway, even F-15s and F-16s would not be able to use those sections for takeoff (see Figure 4–8).

Figure 4–9 shows a plot of the expected number of TBM submunitions that will hit a runway as a function of both missile accuracy and choice of dispersal radius. As can be seen from the plotted calculations, if a TBM has a both a dispersal radius R_d and CEP of 30 meters ($R_d = CEP = 30$ meters), then the average number of submunitions that will hit the runway is about sixty. Because the dispersal radius is so small, whenever a missile impacts on the runway, a very large fraction of its submunitions also hits the runway. However, an inspection of the probability curve in Figure 4–9 shows that more than 40 percent of the time the TBM will impact at twenty or more meters (that is, 0.67 CEP or more) from the centerline, leaving 15 or more meters of runway on the other side of the centerline undamaged, enough for aircraft to use when taking off.

This problem could be addressed by expanding the dispersal radius — but at a cost of decreasing the density of submunitions within the radius. As Figure 4–9 shows, the net result of enlarging the dispersal radius (R_d) to two or three CEPs is that only 30 to 40 submunitions hit the runway, even if a TBM with a 30 meter CEP is used. Moreover, even with a two-CEP dispersal radius, there is some probability that the TBM will land too far from the runway centerline. To ensure that more than 35 meters of a 50-meter wide runway are encompassed within a dispersal radius of two CEPs or 60 meters (so that aircraft are denied a 15 meter width), the TBM must impact closer than 50 meters (that is, 1.6 CEPs) from the centerline to effectively cut the runway. As the curve on Figure 4–7 shows, the probability that the TBM will impact at a greater distance than 50 meters is about 0.06. That may seem small. Yet if a runway must be cut in four places along its length, and each attempt to cut the runway has a 0.06 probability of failure, then the probability that at least one part of the runway will remain open is 0.22. If it must be cut in six or eight places, the probability of an open stretch will be 0.31 to 0.39.

It is therefore evident that since fighter/interceptor aircraft have such extraordinary abilities to take off from short stretches of runway, the objective of the attack cannot be met with confidence unless there is a relatively high probability of runway cut per TBM fired. This can only be achieved if the TBM submunition dispersal radius is more than two

Figure 4–8. Submunition-Armed TBM Attack on Runway and Taxiway of Major NATO Airbase at Bitburg, West Germany.[a]

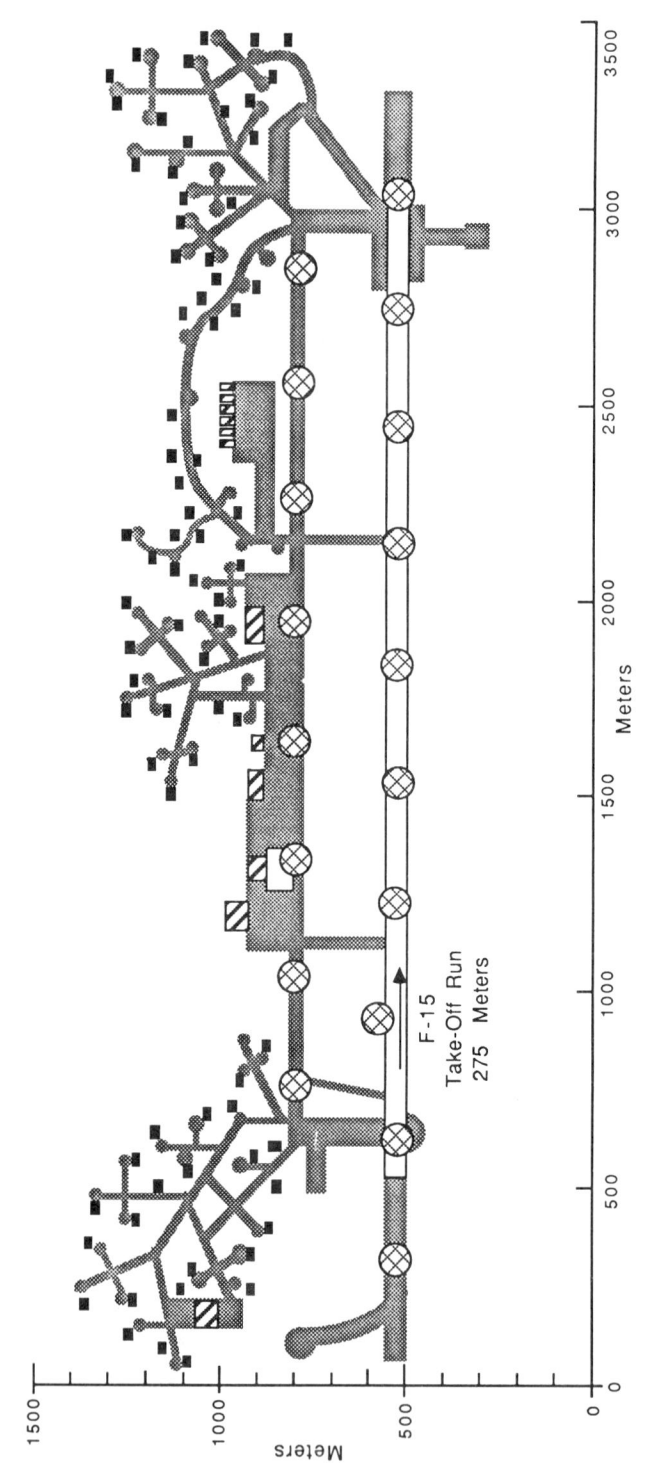

a. The figure also illustrates how a miss by one CEP (30–40 meters) might leave enough runway undestroyed for F-15 air defense aircraft to take off.

Figure 4–9. Expected Number of Submunitions Hitting a 50 Meter Wide Runway for Various Submunition Dispersal Radii.

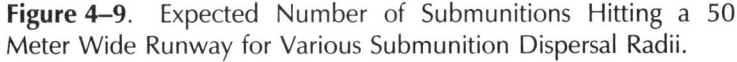

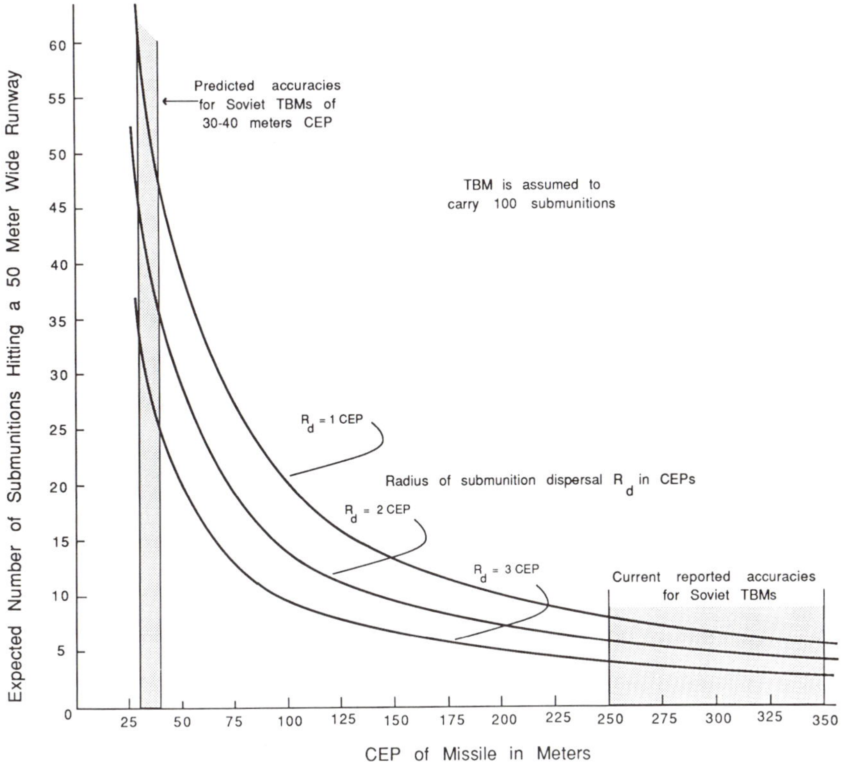

TBM CEPs—to offset miss effects due to the inaccuracy of the TBMs—and if the attacker fires at least two TBMs at each section of runway to be cut—to offset the effects of finite missile reliability (P_{RE}).[9]

Even if each TBM that is launched against a runway section could achieve a probability of runway blockage of one, missile in-flight reliabilities would likely result in one to two out of every ten missiles failing during flight, reentry, or submunition deployment. Where a high probability of runway blockage must be achieved to prevent fighter/interceptor takeoffs, two missiles would have to be assigned to each section of runway to be attacked, to improve the chance of success.

This means that more than 5 to 10 accurate TBMs ($CEP = 30$ meters) could be needed to close a runway to F-15/F16 takeoffs if the runway were 1,500 meters in length, 8 to 16 TBMs if the runway were

2,500 meters long. Each taxiway that could be used for takeoff might require the same number.[10] In excess of 15 to 48 TBMs could therefore be required if each base had two runways and a taxiway, with 300 to 1,000 TBMs needed just for the twenty or so main operating bases and 750 to 2,400 in total to cover the fifty major airbases in NATO's central region. If 30 percent of the Soviet TBM force are withheld for nuclear strikes (or counterstrikes) against NATO, or for later nonnuclear contingency missions that might require TBMs, a total force of 1,000 to 3,000 TBMs with accuracies equal to Pershing II would be necessary. Current public data on Soviet TBM forces suggest that perhaps only 200 to 300 of the Soviets' 750 TBM launchers have been equipped with modern SS-21s, SS-23s, and SS-12/22s, with TBM accuracies still on the order of 250 to 350 meters. Even with substantial enhancement of accuracy, a TBM force of this character appears marginal for an assault on no more than NATO's major airbases, without consideration of other targets that play prominently in scenarios of Soviet attack. It therefore appears that claims of an imminent Soviet nonnuclear TBM threat against NATO's airbases are overstated.

TBM EFFECTIVENESS AGAINST HARDENED UNDERGROUND C^3 FACILITIES

Because a very large number of nonnuclear TBMs are required to deny NATO interceptors the ability to defend their bases, a better strategy might be to attack NATO communications and command facilities with TBMs. If the Warsaw Pact could disrupt coordination and proper allocation of NATO's forces in this manner, it might hope to inflict heavy damage on NATO before communications and command functions could be reestablished.

The challenge in such an attack is that a well-constructed communications and command facility will have a heavily reinforced concrete and steel roof, covered with several meters of earth overburden. A direct hit with a unitary 1,000 kg warhead would produce a crater roughly 3 to 5 meters deep. Hence, if a command center has an earth overburden of more than 5 meters, and a reinforced roof beneath, a direct hit should not result in its destruction. A command center that has 6 or 7 meters of earth overburden on top of a 2 meter thick roof of concrete and steel could therefore be expected to survive many direct hits from such TBMs.

A gigantic shaped-charge warhead mounted on a TBM could penetrate to a greater depth. A 1 meter diameter shaped-charge warhead detonated at an optimal standoff distance above a bunker could create a hot penetrating jet that might pierce to a depth of 7 to 12 meters, depending on whether the shaped-charge arrived perpendicular to the target or (more likely, given TBM flight paths) at an angle. However, even if the command facility were shallow enough for such a jet to reach it, the shaped-charge warhead has to make a direct hit. Here we return to the probability that TBMs with different CEPs will hit the roof of a square bunker. Figure 4–10 graphs these probabilities, for square bunkers whose width and length vary from 0 to 100 meters. For example, if a square bunker is 50 meters on a side (for a total area roughly half that of a soccer field), a TBM with CEP of 30 meters will have a probability of hit of about 0.47; the probability of a hit on a command center of 20 meters on a side would only be 0.1.

One could imagine other forms of munitions—earth-penetrating warheads, for instance, that would plunge deeper into the earth overburden before detonating. But more exotic munitions are not themselves of much benefit unless the probability of hit can be improved. A dispersed pattern of submunitions might raise the probability of hit in the area over the target's roof, but smaller submunitions would lack sufficient lethal effects to pierce the bunker, even if they hit in the proper area. This is one case where even a modest degree of low-technology hardening would protect command and communications facilities from high-technology TBMs.

TBMS AGAINST ARMY DIVISION COMMAND-POSTS

Last, we consider the effectiveness of TBM attacks against somewhat softer command facilities, the division-level command posts that belong to NATO's twenty-nine or so ground-force divisions. Again, the objective would be to produce a collapse in coordination and command, long enough for Warsaw Pact forces to exploit the confusion.

It has long been recognized that in large-scale, coordinated military operations, chaos and confusion that can follow the loss of key command elements can spell defeat. Consequently, great efforts are made to reduce the likelihood and consequences of successful long-range strikes against key command elements. Figure 4–11 shows the approx-

Figure 4–10. Probability of a TBM Hitting a Square Bunker (for Various TBM Accuracies).

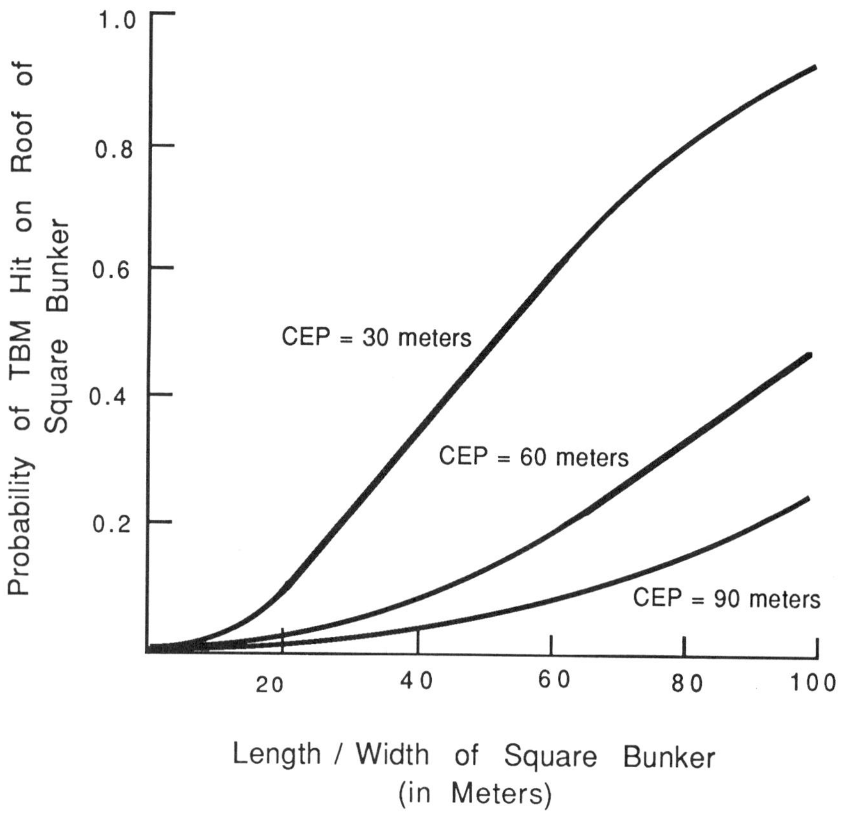

imate arrangement of the elements of a U.S. Army Main Divisional Command Post (DMAIN) deployed in the field. Because this is the most well staffed and equipped of three command posts associated with the division, the division commander — a two-star general — will usually be in residence when the command post is not in motion. The different elements of the command post are housed or dispersed around armored vehicles or trucks that transport personnel and equipment associated with each functional subunit of the post. The units are typically spread over an area that is about 300 meters on a side. Each of the subunits may make extensive use of natural cover and/or camouflage to make them difficult to observe from the air.

Figure 4–11. Approximate Arrangement of Trucks, Vans, and Armored Vehicles in Deployed Main Divisional Command Post (DMAIN)

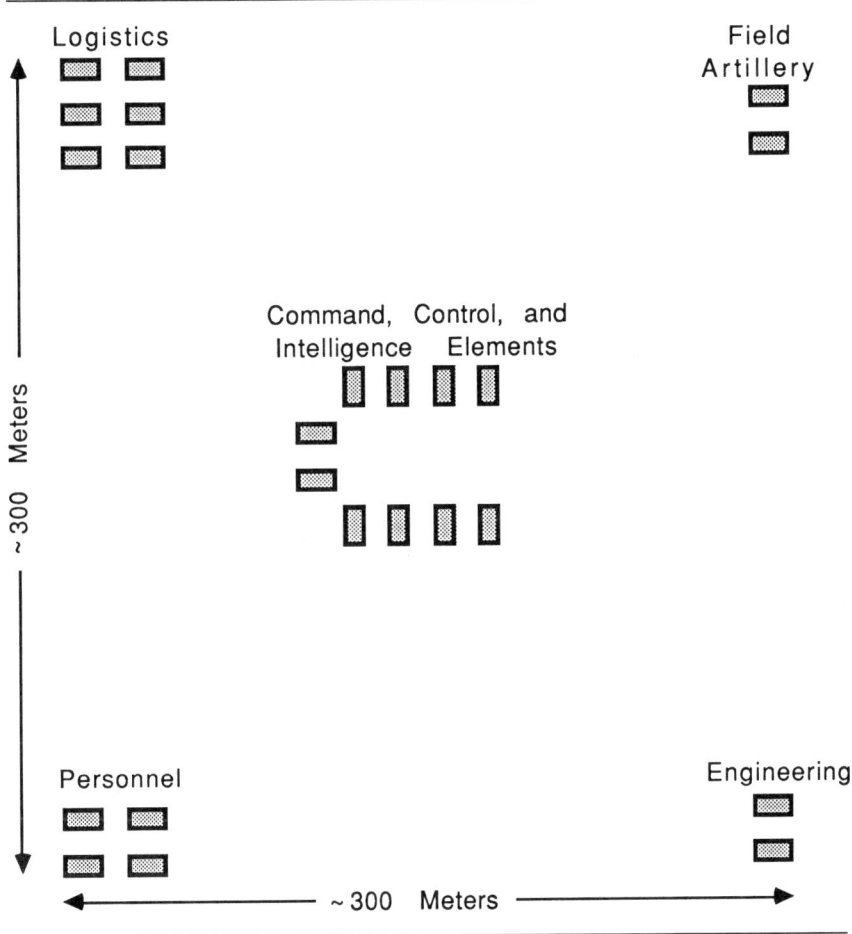

In Europe, communications between units in the field can be carried out over commercial phone lines rather than radio, to reduce the likelihood that enemy radio direction-finding will locate a command post. When radio communications cannot be avoided, remote radio transmitters that are connected to the command post by temporary land-lines are used. These transmitters would use directional, low-sidelobe microwave antennas, to reduce the likelihood of enemy cross-fixing on signals, and they would typically be displaced from 7 to 10 km from the command post.

The DMAIN is backed up by two other command posts, the Tactical Operations Command Post (DTOC) and Jump Command Post (JUMP). Each of these posts is commanded by a one-star general who, if circumstances dictate, can take over command of the division. During periods of combat—or perhaps crisis—one of the three posts will be performing command functions for the division, one will be passively monitoring the status of the active post in case it is successfully attacked, and the final unit will be in motion. It is therefore clear that divisional command functions could be very difficult to attack with TBMs, scattered as they are in numerous dispersed, hidden, and semimobile elements.

As with radars, elements of the command post are soft targets, so if their position became known, they are potentially subject to devastating levels of damage. It is of some interest to know how well the command post must be located for it to be endangered by TBMs.

Because the command post is both soft and dispersed, submunitions are the obvious choice of TBM armament, as they spread potentially lethal effects over a much larger area. As we noted previously, a 10 kg submunition will destroy a target that can only withstand a 5 to 10 psi blast (35 to 70 kPa) if the submunition lands within 8 to 12 meters of it. Because we can settle for a rough estimate here, we can consider each truck or armored vehicle to be a target of area equal to

$$A = \pi R_L^2$$

Where R_L is the lethal radius associated with an overpressure of 5 or 10 psi, that is, 8 or 12 meters.

Here we can use Figure 4–3 again. That figure plots the probability that a TBM submunition will hit an 18 by 18 meter bunker. Because the area of that bunker is nearly the same as the "effective" area swept out by a submunition that lands near a soft command vehicle, the calculated curve of probabilities for the 18 by 18 meter bunker is suitable for our rough estimates.

As Figure 4–3 shows, if the attacker knows the location of the vehicle precisely, and fires a TBM at it (with 30 meter CEP and radius of dispersal of submunitions of 60 meters), then the probability of the vehicle being within lethal range of at least one submunition is 0.9. Indeed, if the vehicle is one of several vehicles constituting an element of the command post and clustered close enough together to lie within the submunition dispersal pattern, the probability is high that all will be destroyed. Suppose, however, the attacker only knows the location of the 300 by 300 meter deployment area, not the location of any particular element or vehicle within it. In effect, the location of any particular command subunit is uncertain to 150 meters. This means that the effective CEP (CEP_{eff}) for a TBM with 30-meter accuracy is slightly more than 150 meters. And Figure 4-3 shows that a single TBM attack might destroy 40 percent of the vehicles in the command unit. Hence, it is clear that the unit must keep its location uncertain to many hundreds of meters if it is to be relatively safe from TBM attack.

It is perhaps worth reiterating that if the attacker can learn the location of these important, soft command units to the degree of accuracy noted above, he can bring many threats other than TBMs to bear on the unit and its personnel. For this reason, the use of multiple command posts with great mobility was devised to maintain continuity of command at the divisional level. Although TBMs could add to the threat, if measures already taken to protect such units are properly implemented, these same measures could also be more than adequate for countering TBMs armed with submunitions.

CONCLUDING REMARKS

In the analysis above, a wide variety of military-technical issues related to NATO's potential vulnerabilities to accurate conventionally armed Soviet TBMs have been presented. This analysis clearly demonstrates that many NATO assets can maintain a high degree of invulnerability to Warsaw Pact attack if mobility can be maintained in a crisis. The analysis also indicates that careful and determined efforts must be made to operate air defense radars in ways that make it so difficult and time-consuming for the enemy to locate them prior to attack as to be effectively impossible.

Airfields, unfortunately, are more problematic. The analysis of attacks on airfields assumes that there are no critical nodes that could be destroyed with a small attack and whose destruction would shut down airfield operations. In our judgment, this assumption is correct. But military experience is replete with examples of planning errors, neglect, or simply failures to recognize which problems create the greatest vulnerabilities and therefore require the most immediate attention. Hence, it should be recognized that while our estimates of Soviet TBM force size and capabilities indicate what *could* be required to shut down NATO airbases, they do not necessarily indicate what *is* required.

Of still greater importance are questions raised by our analysis about the future viability of NATO's air power, if it is dependent on relatively few runways in the European theater. Although TBMs are unlikely to emerge as a major threat in the near term, it appears that a wide variety of stand-off and cruise missiles, in combination with "smart" submunitions, could well play havoc with air operations in a future large-scale NATO-Warsaw Pact conflict. If NATO's air power is to offset Warsaw Pact numerical advantages, as some would argue, the question of continuing dependence on airfield runways within reach of Pact weapons must be addressed.

We stated our major conclusions regarding the conventional TBM threat at the outset of this paper, as a way of introducing our analysis. We reiterate them here. First, although there is no publicly available evidence that the Soviets have achieved spectacular improvements yet in TBM guidance, even if we assume that by the 1990s they will achieve 30 meter CEPs, TBMs will have little or no capability to attack mobile targets such as air defense radars and divisional command posts, if mobility is properly exploited for protection. The greatest difficulty is finding these targets, not destroying them. Second, given their small payloads, TBMs cannot carry enough conventional explosives to damage properly hardened underground structures, hence, they should have little or no ability to damage or disrupt operations at fixed, hardened NATO command posts. Third, TBMs with submunitions will not be capable of doing significant damage to runways at NATO airbases unless they achieve accuracies on the order of 30 to 40 meters. Even with such accuracies, many hundreds, and perhaps several thousand TBMs might be required for the Soviets to achieve a major impact on NATO tactical air operations during the early phases of a surprise attack. In our judgment, both cruise missiles and aircraft, not TBMs, will continue to be the most efficient means of delivering conventional munitions or chemical/biological weapons in a surprise attack against NATO targets. Finally, at the risk of stating the obvious, we do not want to end this discussion without making one additional point. It should be understood that diplomatic agreements limiting the number of TBMs can clearly have as real an impact on NATO's future military security as they can on its political security.

NOTES

1. Michael Feazel, "German Study Encourages Development of ATBM," *Aviation Week and Space Technology*, 7 July 1986, p. 84.
2. We are assuming that the SS-21 dimensions and launch weight are about the same as those of the Frog-7, which it is replacing. The SS-23 is replacing its 300 km range predecessor, the SS-1c Scud B, and the SS-22 is replacing the SS-12 Scaleboard. Various public sources suggest the SS-1c Scud B weighs around 6,000 kilograms, while the SS-12 is suggested to weigh more than 7,000 kilograms. In detail, we assume the following:

Table 4–3. Baseline Soviet TBM Characteristics.

	SS-21/Frog-7	SS-23	SS-12/22
Range (km)	100	500	1,000
Length (m)	9.0	7.4	11.5
Diameter (m)	0.55	1.1	1.1
Launch gross weight (kg)	2,000	5,130	8,000
Dry weight of missile frame (kg)	100	370	630
Motor specific impulse (sec)	250	250	250
Average thrust (newtons)	45,000	119,210	206,940
Payload/warhead/ guidance weight	900	1,086	1,086

3. U.S. Department of Defense, *Soviet Military Power 1986* (Washington, D.C.: Government Printing Office, 1987), p. 90.
4. For purposes of illustration and simplicity, we have assumed that a 1,000 kg TBM unitary warhead contains 1000 kg of high explosives and that this warhead can be replaced by one hundred 10 kg submunitions. These assumptions result in exaggerated estimates of improvements in the effectiveness of submunition-armed TBMs relative to those armed with unitary munitions. In reality individual submunitions would suffer losses in destructive capability due to packaging inefficiencies, and additional weight would be needed for a dispensing mechanism. Such a submunition-dispensing mechanism could well be as heavy as the munitions it dispenses. Our estimates of the amount of explosives carried by TBMs with unitary or submunition payloads are high — since

50 percent of the weight of a general purpose demolition warhead or submunition is generally metal casing. The 2,000 pound general purpose MK 84 bomb, for instance, contains 945 pounds of high-explosives in a casing that weighs 1,025 pounds (see Tom Gervasi, *Arsenal of Democracy III*, Grove Press, Inc., New York [1984], pages 246 to 253 for details on a wide variety of large and small conventional munitions). Each submunition can, of course, also contain 50 percent explosives by weight, but this depends on the mechanism chosen by designers to inflict damage. For example, the BKEP submunition under development by the U.S. Air Force is designed to inflict damage with a "kinetic energy projectile." This particular munition contains no seek or guidance devices. Since only a small amount of explosives is required to impart a high velocity to a projectile, only 3 kg of its 20 kg weight is high-explosive (See U.S. Office of Technology Assessment, *Technologies for NATO's Follow-On Forces Attack Concept — Special Report* [Washington, D.C.: Government Printing Office, July 1986], p. 35). We also note that each pound of inert material delivered by a 500 km range TBM impacts with the kinetic energy of its equivalent weight of high-explosives. Detailed untested comparisons of the damage-inflicting capabilities of various munition payloads carried by TBMs should therefore be regarded as highly speculative.

5. To simplify the illustration here, we are assuming perfect missile reliability, so that when we say three TBMs would be needed on average, we mean three TBMs that successfully complete launch, flight to the target, and munition dispersal. In fact, depending on how reliable Soviet TBMs are, they would have to allocate more than three TBMs to each such target, on average, to ensure that three actually arrive.

6. According to IISS figures for NATO air defense and fighter/ground attack aircraft in Central Europe, the United States has seventy-two F-16A/B, ninety-six F-4E, twenty-four F-4G, and seventy-two F-15C/Ds in West Germany, plus another twenty-four F-15C/Ds in the Netherlands; Great Britain has thirty-six F-4s, thirty-six Harriers, and 108 Tornadoes in West Germany; Canada has forty-two F-18s in West Germany; the Netherlands has 101 F-16s and eighty-nine F-5s; Belgium has seventy-two F-16A/B and fifty-two Mirage 5; Denmark has sixty-four F-16A/Bs and sixteen Saab Draken; West Germany has ninety F-104s, 128 F-4s, 101 Tornadoes, and 126 AlphaJets.

Hence, of roughly 1,300 NATO fighter and fighter/ground attack aircraft deployed in the Central Region, about 36 percent are Harriers and F-15/16/18s with takeoff runs of 300 meters or less, another 34 percent are F-4/5/104s that require 600 to 1,300 meter takeoff runs, and the remaining 30 percent are Tornado, Draken, Mirage, and AlphaJets with various takeoff runs. France could have available perhaps 400

Mirage and Jaguars from bases beyond the central region, and there are roughly 680 more such aircraft deployed in Great Britain with U.S. and British forces. By the 1990s, when Soviet TBM accuracies arguably will improve, the portion of newer NATO aircraft with shorter takeoff runs will undoubtedly increase.

In contrast, IISS figures suggest there are 1,550 Soviet and Pact fighters and fighter/ground attack aircraft in East Central Europe, and an additional 725 such aircraft in the Soviet Baltic, Carpathian, and Byelorussian military districts. See the International Institute for Strategic Studies, *The Military Balance 1986–1987* (London: IISS, 1986).

7. Our estimate is derived from data for a typical runway crater made by a 750 lb (340 kg) bomb, scaled to approximate a 1,000 kg munition. For more information on bomb craters, see Cecil Hudson and Peter Hass, "New Technologies: The Prospects," in Johan Holst and Uwe Nerlich, eds., *Beyond Nuclear Deterrence* (New York: Crane, Russak, 1977), Figure 16, pp. 114.

8. There is a small probability of the extreme case in our illustration here—that is, that the first TBM impacts 20 meters on one side of the runway centerline and the second TBM impacts 20 meters on the other side. The result would be an uncut section down the centerline of the runway. A more careful calculation of the runway blockage probability could account for such details by conceptualizing the runway as a series of narrower strips—in this case, perhaps four or six strips rather than two. Then by summing over all the relevant combinations of hits that would result in blockage, a more accurate estimate of the total probability of blockage would be obtained. However, our simpler calculation is only intended to provide an order of magnitude estimate, and a more detailed calculation would differ little from the result obtained with this simpler method.

9. Even under these conditions, only thirty to forty of the one hundred submunitions on each TBM will hit the runway. We assert our judgment that cruise missiles would offer a less expensive and more effective method of delivering the same number of submunitions to the runway. Unlike the TBM, the cruise missile might also be able to choose a dispersal path along the length of the runway, dropping submunitions as it flies. Submunitions delivered in this manner would not have to be heavily armored to survive the tremendous 1 to 3 km/sec impact with the runway, as they would if they are to be dispensed from a TBM.

Furthermore, cruise missiles would be a far more appropriate platform for delivering a wide variety of advanced "smart" submunitions against runways. These microprocessor-controlled submunitions could be designed to behave unpredictably, sometimes detonating when they are moved, and perhaps even detonating when they sense the presence of nearby aircraft. The result of such an attack would therefore be a "mined" runway that would be very hazardous for aircraft to use and time consuming for base personnel to clear. Unless they were decelerated during the final moments of flight, TBM submunitions would impact runways at speeds between 1 to 3 km/sec, and microprocessor-controlled submunitions would have to be very heavily armored to survive such an impact. Whether armored or decelerated, either mechanism would result in still a greater reduction in TBM delivery capacity relative to that of cruise missiles.

10. We note that in their chapter in this volume, Rubenson and Bonomo estimate that as few as 6 to 8 TBMs could close a base consisting of one 2,400 meter runway and a parallel taxiway, under certain assumptions. Applying different sets of assumptions, they suggest the number could be as high as 16 to 30 TBMs. Although our estimate here—that 8 to 16 TBMs would be needed for *each* runway and taxiway of 2,500 meters length—may seem sharply at odds, fundamentally it is not.

Rubenson and Bonomo arrive at their lowest estimate on the basis of two key assumptions: that a very large submunition dispersal radius allows each TBM to deliver munitions on both the runway and the taxiway; and that aircraft cannot take off unless undamaged sections of runway and taxiway are at least 1,100 meters in length. In contrast, we have assumed shorter runway sections more closely corresponding to F-15/16 takeoff runs (300 meters), and more tightly clustered submunition dispersal patterns that require each runway and taxiway to be targeted separately, giving us an estimate of 8 to 16 TBMs required for a 2,500 meter runway, 16 to 32 for a runway and separate taxiway. When Rubenson and Bonomo adopt assumptions closer to our own in their examples, they arrive at a figure of 16 to 30 TBMs for a runway and taxiway, essentially the same as our figure.

5 ALTERNATIVES TO ATBMS
David Rubenson and James Bonomo

The potential development of anti–tactical ballistic missile (ATBM) systems has become an important and confusing defense policy question. Widely differing ATBM systems have been discussed for widely different military missions: advanced systems as a European extension of SDI; more modest systems as a near-term method of demonstrating some SDI technology, while remaining within the Anti–Ballistic Missile Treaty; more recently, German Defense Minister Manfred Wörner's proposal for ATBMs as a counter to Soviet conventionally armed ballistic missiles (TBMs), giving ATBMs a role within NATO's conventional strategy.[1]

The potential military utility of a NATO-ATBM is an old issue that has coincidentally become more important during the current SDI debate.[2] Technological advances have increased the likelihood that short-range ballistic missiles can be made sufficiently accurate for efficient use with conventional warheads. Improved TBM accuracy could also allow the Soviets to implement theater nuclear options with reduced yields, thereby reducing collateral damage. Such developments could affect NATO's ability to implement its strategy and create a requirement for a NATO ATBM capability.

Accurate conventionally armed TBMs would pose a new and serious threat. However, the tendency to focus on a single accuracy parameter has obscured other factors relevant to determining the

133

utility and effectiveness of such a weapon system. An important distinction not captured by focusing on a single accuracy parameter is the difference between fixed and nonfixed targets. The high accuracies potentially achievable with a terrain-matching sensor pertain only to fixed targets, where detailed terrain maps can be developed.[3] Equally accurate guidance systems for use against mobile or transportable targets present additional technical challenges beyond simple improvements in missile accuracy—for instance, in sensing and computing, where the Soviets have traditionally lagged the United States by many years.[4] The most often discussed guidance approach, a terrain-matching sensor, would require that a detailed map of the area around the mobile target be supplied to the missile. This map can be generated only after the target is found, and it must be transmitted to the missile before the target moves again.

Using an inertial guidance system to avoid this difficulty is problematic. High-quality inertial guidance may produce errors of less than 50 meters, but reentry errors can be substantial when a bulky conventional warhead must be used. Inertial guidance without terminal corrections may be only marginally adequate for conventional missions. A purely inertial system also requires the use of previously surveyed launch sites. The Soviets might judge that scattering TBMs to prepared launch locations in preparation for a strike would raise NATO's ability to detect a surprise attack. Soviet reliance on inertial guidance might also be discouraged by the maintenance difficulties and high costs that a high-quality inertial system may imply, especially for mobile TBMs.

Both terrain-matching sensors and especially inertial systems place demanding requirements on Soviet reconnaissance. The target must be located in the same geodetic coordinate system used at the TBM launch site, and the target's location must be determined with great precision because the performance of the TBM is as sensitive to aimpoint errors as to guidance errors. The ability of a target to make even very small, but frequent location adjustments would stress the Soviet acquisition, data processing, data transfer, and missile targeting requirements and would probably eliminate the purely inertial guidance option from consideration.

A third alternative would be to use a less accurate TBM and to rely on "smart" submunitions to search out the target. This would ease reconnaissance requirements. Primitive versions of such submunitions were tested in the U.S. Assault Breaker program and may be part of NATO's Follow-On Forces Attack (FOFA). However, Soviet development of submunition systems that could overcome simple NATO countermeasures and locate targets in a variety of terrain conditions may be many years away.

Attacking nonfixed targets thus involves solving problems beyond that of simply improving missile accuracy. In addition to the issues mentioned above, simply finding nonfixed targets in NATO's rear areas will be a formidable problem. It will require advances in Soviet reconnaissance, surveillance, and data handling capabilities and will again challenge the Soviets in areas where they lag behind. Prior to the outbreak of conflict, the problem of locating targets could be compounded by the ability of many targets to remain silent or to use duping tactics in order to hide. Once conflict begins, the reconnaissance systems themselves will be vulnerable. Target detection, data processing for the guidance system, data transfer, and missile targeting all must be achieved before the target moves again. Attacking nonfixed targets will require progress in a broad range of technologies and could be made more difficult by a determined defender. Overcoming all of these problems would present major challenges for western technology and might be a distant goal for the Soviets.[5]

The difficulties of developing conventional TBM warheads are also a factor not captured by a narrow focus on missile accuracy alone. The dispersal of submunitions is a more complicated problem for TBMs than for aircraft, and the vulnerability of many targets to TBMs would be dependent on control of the submunition patterns that may emerge from the missile. An earlier study of conventionally armed TBMs that examined four submunition dispersal mechanisms found that simple mechanisms, such as gas bags or explosive foams, produced poor pattern control. Heavier mechanisms, using launch tubes, were judged to produce only "reasonably controlled patterns," to suffer from "mechanical complexity," and to entail an obvious loss in payload.[6]

Similarly, the development of earth-penetrating warheads for attacking hardened targets would result in significant payload reductions and only seem plausible with nuclear weapons, at least until TBM accuracies improve another order of magnitude.

These considerations are not intended to imply that conventionally armed TBMs cannot be made into militarily useful weapons, but the scope of the problems that must be solved, involving development of warheads, dispensing mechanisms, reconnaissance, and guidance systems, and integration of these subsystems, indicates that highly effective and flexible TBM systems are not likely to emerge suddenly.

Many years of testing all the elements of an integrated targeting and strike system will be needed. The authors concur that in the long run conventionally armed TBMs may provide great flexibility, but early generations of accurate conventionally armed TBMs will probably have many limitations. They are likely to be expensive and therefore limited in numbers. They also may lack a full array of warhead types and therefore will be restricted in the types of targets they can attack. They most likely will be limited to attacking fixed targets where guidance and acquisition problems can be minimized.

This does not suggest that the Soviets will abandon conventionally armed TBMs. Soviet military writings emphasize a continued interest in surprise and preemption. Conventionally armed TBMs would support this interest in unique ways. TBMs seem particularly suited to attacks on time-critical targets, particularly if such targets can be temporarily paralyzed by small quantities of munitions, allowing time for follow-on air attacks to disable the target permanently or at least for an extended period of time. Thus, for soft and fixed targets, and in cases where the advantages of speed and certain penetrability outweigh delivery inefficiencies, TBMs may offer the Soviets important advantages. The use of TBMs in this manner, and the protection of these types of targets, should be NATO's first concern.

NATO AIRFIELDS

Of all potential targets, NATO airfields may most closely match these vulnerability criteria. Airbases, and particularly the runways, are vulnerable, fixed, and highly time-critical targets. Destroying aircraft in their shelters would require direct hits from conventionally armed TBMs and is unlikely. Attacks on support equipment or personnel should be more efficiently executed by follow-on aircraft. Runways, however, are critical to the immediate operation of an airbase. Their fixed locations, and the large distances needed for aircraft take-off and landings, imply that TBMs might pin-in NATO aircraft by attacking runways, without the necessity of destroying the aircraft or the base infrastructure. Other targets on the base could then be attacked at a later time by Soviet aircraft. Thus TBMs and aircraft could work synergistically. Small quantities of runway-cratering submunitions or scatterable mines delivered by TBMs could have a military effect far greater than is indicated by the payloads delivered.

As an example of the advantages provided by TBMs, one could imagine a highly coordinated, preemptive, Soviet TBM strike against NATO Main Operating Bases (MOBs) at the onset of a war. Analytical modeling has shown that as few as six to eight SS-23 TBMs carrying runway-cratering submunitions could, with 90 percent probability, temporarily close an 8,000 ft (2,438 meter) runway and parallel taxiway.[7] Because TBMs carry only limited payloads, such attacks would produce only limited numbers of runway craters and result in only temporary base closure. However, NATO aircraft would be pinned-in, allowing Soviet aircraft to arrive within an hour, with greatly reduced air opposition. These aircraft could then close the base for an extended period. In this scenario, TBMs and aircraft work synergistically, and the distinctive TBM advantages of speed and penetrability outweigh the disadvantage of limited payload.

Although TBMs play a unique role in this scenario, aircraft still inflict the vast majority of damage. Thus, it is logical to first look toward defenses that simultaneously counter the aircraft, cruise missile, and TBM threat, rather than toward techniques that counter only TBMs. One such technique is to make the target less vulnerable through "passive defenses." Many such techniques have already been planned to counter the existing air threat. It is obviously desirable to consider the effectiveness of these techniques against TBMs before considering active defenses. The logic of first looking toward passive defenses is underscored by the potential costs of ATBM. A Patriot fire unit, a surface-to-air missile system, costs more than $72 million in FY 1986 dollars.[8] Any system capable of intercepting TBMs would cost at least as much because the higher speed of TBMs compared to aircraft implies greater stresses on the defensive system. Although Patriot has not been optimized for ATBM, these costs make it seem unlikely that dedicated ATBM will be a cost-effective answer to a coordinated attack unless significant cost reductions or performance improvements (relative to Patriot) are obtained.

PASSIVE DEFENSES OF AIRBASES

One passive defense option that is potentially cost effective against even a highly refined threat is the construction of redundant runways (see Figure 5-1). A second runway at an airbase might cost around $5 million and would more than double the number of TBMs needed to

Figure 5–1. Additional Runway and Taxiways That Could Be Constructed to Complicate Soviet TBM Attack on Major NATO Airbase at Bitburg, West Germany.[a]

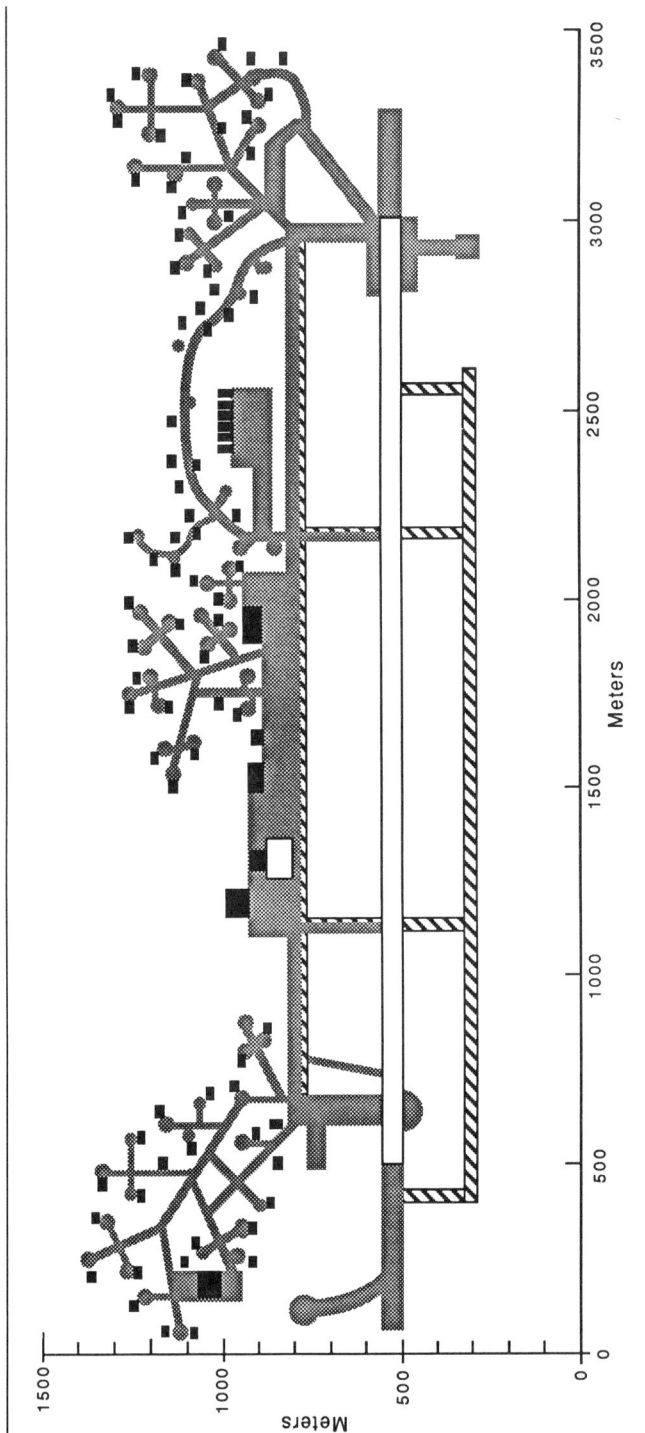

a. The added runway is 2,150 × 30 meters; taxiways widened to 30 meters. Figure provided by the editors, based on U.S. Air Force proposal, FY 1979.

close a base.⁹ Unfortunately, not all MOBs could accommodate even one additional air strip. Visual inspection of maps indicates that seventeen of twenty-five MOBs in the central front region might do so, but actual engineering and logistical constraints could lower this number. More land might be acquired, but one should not underestimate the difficulty in doing so in West Germany, where military land use is a sensitive political subject. However, even where no additional land can be obtained, simply paving over the region between the runway and the taxiway might increase Soviet TBM requirements by more than 50 percent.¹⁰ Thus, additional runways are an important and available mechanism for increasing the numbers of TBMs that might be needed to close an airfield.

Dispersal away from MOBs to other military airfields is another passive defense measure that might double or perhaps triple the number of targets and has obvious benefits. Effective dispersal would require that the air defense aircraft on alert be dispersed to as many bases as possible. (We would note, though, that dispersal beyond the limited set of designated military airfields strikes us as both politically and operationally questionable.) Ideally, the support equipment would also be dispersed. Failure to achieve this would allow the Soviets to concentrate their TBM forces on a smaller set of more valuable airfields. The true effectiveness of dispersal, however, is also highly dependent on the lethality of Soviet TBMs. If only six to eight TBMs are needed to close a base, then doubling the number of targets would imply that 300 to 400 TBMs would be needed to target the entire set of military airfields. Such numbers are not grossly inconsistent with projections concerning the number of launchers for TBMs the Soviets may have in the 1990s.¹¹ The military value of closing NATO airfields would surely encourage the Soviets to build an adequate number of TBMs, if they were as efficient as described above. Six to eight TBMs might cost $18 to $24 million (assuming a cost of $3 million per TBM) but could pin-in a far more valuable set of aircraft.

There are, however, several reasons to believe that Soviet TBMs will not be this efficient and that greater numbers will be needed to close an airbase. This will enhance the benefits of dispersal, particularly in relation to the numbers of conventional TBM launchers being predicted. A few airbases already have redundant air strips and a few have significantly longer strips than assumed in the above calculations.

In both cases, the number of TBMs needed for closure will be larger. In the calculations mentioned above, highly dispersed ring patterns of runway cratering submunitions were assumed. This allowed the runway and taxiway to be attacked simultaneously, and hence the base could be attacked with only two aimpoints, significantly reducing the importance of missile reliability.[12] However, the effectiveness and required weight for such a dispensing mechanism has not been demonstrated or studied, and estimates of payload penalty or dispensing system performance were not included in the analysis. The effectiveness of attacking the runway and taxiway simultaneously, and leaving large numbers of submunitions in between, is also highly sensitive to the numbers of submunitions and hence to the actual payload the TBM carries.[13]

A more conservative analysis would be to consider the more tightly bound cluster patterns of penetrators that the United States previously considered in its own conventional TBM studies. With such patterns, an airbase might be attacked using four aimpoints, two on the runway and two on the taxiway. RAND's TSARINA model has shown that a highly accurate arriving TBM could lay craters across the runway with a probability of near unity when such patterns are used.[14] Thus four arriving TBMs could close the base. However, the need for all four aimpoints to be struck implies that between eight and twelve TBMs would be needed to obtain a 90 percent closure probability.[15] This still assumes that NATO aircraft require a minimum operating runway length of more than 3,500 ft (1,067 m), a highly defense-conservative assumption. This should be the landing run for an F-15E without braking parachute, but other NATO aircraft do not require such long distances. Moreover, the F-15E take-off distance should be only 900 ft (275 m).[16] The Soviets will undoubtedly assume (and perhaps correctly) that such aircraft can still take-off from an airbase attacked in such a manner and recover at another base or at an Emergency Landing Strip on the German Autobahn, thus negating the initial pin-in effect.[17] A requirement to hit six or eight aimpoints would be a more realistic offense-conservative assumption for the Soviets to make, and this would dramatically increase the number of TBMs needed. For six aimpoints, between twelve and twenty-four TBMs would be required; for eight aimpoints, between sixteen and about thirty TBMs. (Again, the spread in numbers stems from different assumptions about missile reliability.) And of course, the number of

TBMs required would increase still further if additional runways were constructed or the region between the runway and taxiway were paved over, or both.

Obviously it is not possible to know the precise number of TBMs needed to close a base without a detailed description of a Soviet TBM. However, measures that can drive the numbers higher have important implications for the attractiveness of aircraft dispersal. If for example the number of TBMs needed to close an airbase is twelve to sixteen rather than six to eight, dispersal to fifty airbases would stretch Soviet TBM launcher requirements well beyond the 264 predicted by Gormley, to at least 600. The sensitivity of TBM requirements to the number of aimpoints also highlights the value of several other "passive defense" measures, including reducing the take-off and landing distances of NATO aircraft, purchasing arresting gear to cut landing distances, and increasing the number of Autobahn landing strips. All of these factors would increase the number of TBMs needed to pin NATO aircraft.

The uncertainties the Soviets would confront in executing a successful TBM attack also point to the value for NATO of implementing simple damage assessment measures, such as making helicopters available for estimating the condition of a runway. Given the demanding requirements, it is possible that Soviet TBM attacks will fail to do enough damage to prevent airbase operations. However, the shock of such an attack and the need for the base commander to verify that the attack failed, could delay operations. The implementation of shorter take-off distances also requires that the undamaged region of the strip be identified. Thus, there will be substantial benefits for rapid damage assessment—indeed, because no defense will be perfect, rapid damage assessment would be vital even with ATBMs.

Passive defense measures could also help counter munitions other than runway penetrators. For example, explosive mines delivered by TBMs might block key pathways between aircraft shelters and the runways. This would not close a base, but it could disrupt operations long enough to prevent NATO aircraft from contesting a follow-on Soviet air attack. Nonetheless, even this threat can be countered if enough effort is put into rapid damage assessment and the proliferation of aircraft pathways. Mine-sweeping equipment, such as the heavily armored ORACLE vehicle, would also be effective. These measures would be useful against mines delivered by aircraft or cruise missiles as well.

There are also good reasons to minimize runway repair times as a form of "passive defense." Runway crater repair will never be achieved before the arrival of the follow-on air attack in a perfectly coordinated aircraft/TBM assault. However, difficulties in obtaining this coordination, and the likelihood that only a few of NATO's airbases can be attacked on the first aircraft raid, imply that improved runway repair times will also aid in combating the TBM threat.[18] Thus there will be no substitute for training personnel to react optimally to a surprise TBM attack.

The above discussion is dominated by uncertainty, as is any discussion of emerging threats and war in Europe. Still, a few broad conclusions can be drawn. Airbases are vulnerable, fixed, and highly time critical targets, whose temporary paralysis would have a significant military effect. Despite the limitations on TBMs discussed in the proceeding section, airbases would seem to be inviting targets for conventional TBMs in the 1990s. The Soviets will probably need many more TBMs than "perfect" models indicate, but it is undoubtedly worth many TBMs to close even a few of NATO's bases, especially if air defense interceptors are concentrated on those bases. At the same time, there are a variety of passive defense techniques that may be very effective against the limited TBM threat that we expect in the 1990s and that have the benefit of simultaneously countering the traditional air threat to bases. Given their relatively low cost, and their capabilities against aircraft, it would seem logical to continue implementing the passive techniques before considering ATBM. However, all the passive defense techniques have definable limitations, particularly against a highly refined threat. These limitations are generally linked to political difficulties in obtaining land for military use in West Germany, and hence they might be overcome. Nonetheless, given this limitation, and the possible evolution of the Soviet TBM threat in time, the authors conclude that ATBM is an important, but longer-term, option for protecting air bases.

SAM SITES

Anti-aircraft defenses, or SAM sites, are also often discussed targets for TBMs. Like airbases, SAMs are time-critical targets, and if the Soviets could disable them even temporarily, it would aid all their air operations, particularly follow-on air attacks against NATO air fields. SAM radars are probably susceptible to damage by even lightweight submunitions, such as the Combined Effect Munitions.[19] A decision to protect SAMs is arguably made easier by the fact that, with upgrading, they may be able to protect themselves against TBMs (as the planned improvements to Patriot are intended to do). This would appear to be a logical way to develop ATBM technology without procuring systems that cannot also counter aircraft.

There are, however, arguments against upgrading SAMs. SAMs are vulnerable to a wide range of threats (HARM missiles, cruise missiles, drones, and aircraft), and to counter them, SAMs could use mobility, decoys, and radar silence. One must question whether active defenses against TBMs are really needed, when these techniques seem especially well suited for countering them. Even if air defense units are located, their transportability presents targeting and missile guidance problems for any TBM attack, as we noted earlier. The prospects of locating SAMs at the onset of the war, when TBMs offer the greatest advantage, seems particularly remote. NATO's command and control system would still be intact, and SAMs should be able to maintain silence at that stage. Thus, continued improvement of the passive defenses already used to help counter other threats is essential for SAM survival and will be even more effective against TBMs.

Providing SAMs with an ATBM self-defense capability can also become costly, depending on what improvements are actually implemented. Because SAMs are designed to cope with a slow-moving, low-altitude threat obscured in ground clutter, it would be surprising if the ATBM role, against high-speed, high-altitude threats, were completely compatible. Simple changes, such as in the computer software controlling the radar, might cost little, but might also buy little ATBM capability. If such small upgrades provide any credible capability, they would introduce uncertainty into Soviet plans and also help counter antiradiation missiles (ARM) whose terminal flight profiles resemble a slow TBM. More significant upgrades, including new or improved missiles and radars, will raise the cost of the system. To the extent that this occurs they will by definition decrease the cost-effectiveness against aircraft. Upgrades such as those now planned for Patriot may add little additional cost, may not penalize the air defense mission, and might provide some minimal ATBM capability. However, if more significant upgrades produce sharply increased procurement costs or decreased mobility, the trade-off between the upgrade and buying more, non-ATBM-capable Patriots should be carefully studied. Such trade-offs should also be considered for any follow-on to Hawk.

COMMAND AND CONTROL BUNKERS

There are a variety of other valuable NATO assets, but few seem to require active protection against TBM attacks. For most of these targets, attack by aircraft is likely to remain the major threat. The difficulties in finding and targeting mobile targets, such as command posts and missiles, imply they would be unlikely targets for conventionally armed TBMs. Fixed command and control bunkers are easily targeted, and many have important, time-critical functions. However, all important time-critical bunkers are hardened to some degree, making it unlikely that they can be attacked by lightweight munitions from a TBM. A unitary warhead would be required, but such a weapon deployed on a TBM would require a direct hit to be effective. Thus, even more demanding accuracy is needed. A very accurate, earth-penetrating warhead should be required to attack a well-designed bunker.[20] Additional hardening of the softer bunkers could be implemented to further increase the difficulties in attacking these targets, with the added benefit of providing protection against air attacks. Communication gear for command posts could also be attacked, but additional redundancy is probably a cost-effective answer and one that would also provide increased protection against the existing air threat.

NUCLEAR STORAGE SITES

With adequate warning of impending conflict, nuclear weapon storage sites will generally be empty, with the weapons dispersed, and will not be inviting targets for TBM attacks. Some argue, however, that NATO cannot count on dispersal. They argue that NATO may misread Soviet preparations for war and, given the obvious hesitancy to disperse nuclear weapons, will fail to do so before the war begins. Even if one accepts this argument and assumes the weapons are still present in storage sites at the time of the attack, a substantial portion of the nuclear weapons themselves might not be destroyed by conventionally armed TBMs. Instead, the weapon dispersal process might be delayed by attacks on mobile dispersal equipment. But this would require that the equipment be parked in vulnerable positions that the Soviets would know prior to the attack. Even if all these condition are met, the bulk of Soviet air power will likely be dedicated to the air battle during the first phase of the war. This brings us back to the question of whether the Soviets would be able to spare sufficient aircraft from the main air battle during the opening phases of the conflict, in time to prevent dispersal from resuming.

It should also be noted that the time criticality of attacking nuclear storage sites does not dictate the use of TBMs, even assuming that dispersal can be delayed by small payloads. Because dispersal of all stored weapons would take hours to complete, the short flight time of a TBM offers no significant advantage over subsonic attack by aircraft or cruise missile. Even if the Soviets could spare only a small number of aircraft from the main air battle, they would still be more appropriate for attacking nuclear storage sites than TBMs because they can more easily pinpoint the location of dispersal equipment. If aircraft cannot be spared, subsonic cruise missiles would offer at least the same capabilities as TBMs because the longer arrival time presents no significant disadvantage. Special forces might also be employed. Thus, were we to accept the argument that dispersal can be delayed by small payloads, it would only be an indication that the operations at nuclear storage sites are themselves far too fragile and must be made more resilient through redundancy and hardening.

OTHER TARGETS

There are other soft, area targets that could be attacked by TBMs, such as seaports, troops in the field, and POMCUS sites where weapons are stored awaiting arrival of U.S. reinforcements. However, these targets do not have the same time criticality as air defense assets and so can be more effectively targeted by Soviet aircraft, after suppression of NATO air defenses. It seems highly unlikely that the Soviets could use TBMs to attack these targets in a cost-effective manner. It can of course be argued that a target like a POMCUS site may have a special time criticality (though still not as critical as air defense) and therefore might be targeted by TBMs in order to effect some kind of delaying action. However, the precise mechanism by which delivery of small quantities of munitions could achieve this is unclear. Although the equipment at POMCUS sites may be relatively exposed and unprotected, the sites themselves are very large, and an attack with munitions on relatively few aimpoints would do limited damage. As with attacks on nuclear storage sites, TBM assaults on POMCUS sites might disrupt operations temporarily, but the important defense would be against the Soviet follow-on air attack that would be necessary to destroy the site.

TBMS AND THE NATO TARGET BASE

Our discussion thus far has provided only a brief description of how TBMs might be used against the NATO target base. Despite many uncertainties, a few general observations can be made. Based on the preceding analysis, the authors conclude that the number of targets vulnerable to TBMs in the 1990s is limited. Only for those targets that in the narrowest sense involve the air battle, such as SAMs, airbases, and certain command and control centers, does the speed of TBMs offer any real advantage over subsonic delivery. However, even for these targets, aircraft will inflict the greatest amount of damage, and passive defenses deployed against TBMs also help counter the air threat. Airbase defense by passive techniques alone could eventually reach its limits, so active defense must be kept open as a long-term option. Therefore, NATO's ATBM needs can best be met by research programs oriented toward providing defense of a limited number of point targets. The availability of passive defenses for responding to both the projected threat and for hedging against greater than expected TBM threats lead the authors to conclude that there is no need for ATBM deployment at this time. The authors conclude that ATBM research can proceed in an evolutionary manner, without the need to undertake undue risks in order to overcome any gaps in NATO preparedness.

ATBMS AND LIMITED NUCLEAR STRIKES

Thus far, we have discussed only conventionally armed TBM threats. A second NATO-ATBM military issue involves Soviet TBMs in nuclear roles. Considering the immensely more complex physical environment produced by nuclear explosions, and the opportunities for the attacker to suppress ATBM defenses, it would seem to be a distant goal for ATBM systems to function effectively against a massive employment of Soviet nuclear-armed TBMs. This threat is of course not new. Soviet nuclear-armed TBMs have threatened NATO for many years, and retaliation has long been the chosen means for deterring any initial Soviet use.

There has, however, been increased interest in using ATBMs to increase Soviet uncertainty in executing limited nuclear options. This has resulted from concern that the Soviets could use improved TBM accuracies to significantly reduce warhead yield requirements. Historical trends in accuracy and yield loosely support this argument.[21] Gormley argues that 70 percent of the NATO target base might be attacked with subkiloton yields if the Soviets can obtain a 50 meter CEP with their missiles. This would greatly reduce the predictable collateral damage and might encourage the Soviets to think about initial and limited nuclear use. Such possibilities have provoked interest in ATBMs for an antinuclear defense role. If ATBMs could perform both conventional and nuclear defense, it introduces the possibility that ATBMs might be justified by a combination of nuclear and conventional missions.

A number of logical steps must be traversed first, however, before one could conclude that the Soviet nuclear threat justified ATBMs. First, one must convincingly argue that limited strikes are an important part of Soviet nuclear strategy. Clearly, one aspect of Soviet nuclear strategy is to deter initial NATO nuclear use by the threat of a massive nuclear response. Arguments about Soviet limited options are less widely accepted. Second, one must argue that TBMs would play a critical role in any limited options, in preference to the large variety of other delivery mechanisms available to the Soviets. Third, one must argue that the Soviets would not simply overwhelm the uncertainties induced by ATBMs by enlarging their attack. It is not obvious, given 50 meter CEPs, that saturating particular aimpoints to overwhelm the defense would greatly increase the predictable collateral damage. Fourth, one must show that NATO's nuclear retaliatory capability is not adequate to deter Soviet nuclear use. Fifth, one must show that counteractions to scenarios satisfying the first four conditions have a higher priority than other NATO needs.

Undoubtedly, one can describe scenarios that fulfill the first two conditions. Many conclusions regarding Soviet doctrine can be reached, and TBMs would be the weapon of choice for time critical targets. Fulfilling the third condition, however, requires highly optimistic assumptions about ATBM performance in a nuclear burst environment. The fourth condition is even more difficult to fulfill. If the Soviets use very small numbers of TBMs—less than ten, for example—to supplement an otherwise conventional attack, NATO could respond with enough nuclear weapons to have an equalizing effect on the conventional battle. No conventional advantage would remain and doubts about NATO's resolve to cross the nuclear threshold would have been eliminated. A Soviet attack with larger numbers of nuclear weapons would seem to have extraordinary escalation risks, independent of weapon yield. NATO leadership is unlikely to know the extent of collateral damage, the yield of the weapons used, or the accuracy with which they were delivered. The Soviets would have no guarantee that NATO leadership would dispassionately consider the total weapon yield as a basis for a response. Thus, the threat of a second strike would seem to be a credible deterrent to larger attacks as well. It might be argued that even with a NATO response, the Soviets might emerge from such an exchange with a significant advantage in conventional forces.[22] However, such an advantage seems irrelevant given the resultant freedom to use large numbers of nuclear weapons.

Finally, it might be argued that even if the contribution of ATBMs to deterring a Soviet limited nuclear strike is marginal, its potential for a dual, nuclear/conventional role does increase the rationale for development. However, there are technical reasons to be skeptical about the dual-use argument. Although incoming conventional and nuclear warheads cannot be distinguished, engineering requirements for the defense are not similar. Operation of an ATBM in a nuclear environment implies vastly different performance requirements from the sensors and the communication links. Depending on the assumed weapon yield, and target hardness, greater intercept ranges may also be necessary, to defend larger keepout zones. Because the larger lethal radius of a nuclear warhead makes it appropriate for a rather different set of targets than a conventionally armed TBM, the configuration and area coverage requirements for an ATBM in a nuclear role would be correspondingly different. An ATBM designed for meeting NATO's conventional needs would only help deter nuclear options in the most limited and constrained cases.

It might still be argued that an ATBM designed for defense against conventional missiles could induce some minimal uncertainty in a Soviet plan for nuclear use, and thus provide a foundation for the evolutionary development of a more extensive antinuclear capability. However, the primary technical change needed to operate in the nuclear environment is in the surveillance sensors and communication links. Unfortunately, these are the most expensive portions of existing systems and thus the least likely to be changed. There may be little latitude for evolutionary improvement in such systems. In looking at an ATBM for conventional defense, NATO should avoid expensive upgrades in other components, such as interceptors. Such upgrades might siphon away large amounts of money, significant when compared to the pool of funds for air defense, but insignificant compared to the cost of any nuclear defense.

THE ROLE OF NATO-ATBM AND THE LINK TO SDI

The authors conclude that the foregoing analysis points to a limited role for ATBM. In the nuclear area, improved TBM accuracy will not in any obvious way undermine NATO nuclear strategy. Highly accurate, conventionally armed TBMs would provide the Soviets with new capabilities, but there are also technical and operational limitations. These limitations should restrict the use of these TBMs to targets strictly related to NATO's air defense. Most threatened are airbases. Passive defenses exist, will initially be cheaper than ATBMs, and would have the advantage of simultaneously protecting against other threats. However, identifiable limitations to passive techniques for air bases suggest that some ATBM could eventually be needed as a supplement. Thus, ATBM as a long-term option for air base protection is seen as the major reason for research. The availability of passive defenses to cope with even refined TBM threats lead the authors to conclude that there is no rationale for ATBM deployment at this time.[23]

REQUIREMENTS FOR A NATO-ATBM RESEARCH PROGRAM

If ATBMs should eventually prove necessary for air base protection, NATO would obviously prefer to have the most capable ATBM system possible. Greater capabilities generally imply greater costs and technical risks. It is undoubtedly logical to limit a research program in a way that is consistent with NATO's military needs. First, a capability to counter nuclear threats is not required. Second, the number of targets that will need protection by active ATBM defenses is relatively small. Because defense keepout zones as small as the size of an airstrip could provide important protection, there is little advantage to ATBM architectures that might protect a significant fraction of Western Europe over architectures intended to protect just these targets. NATO's general situation also implies that few technical risks need to be taken. Because the threat is only a developing one and passive defenses provide a hedge, the authors conclude that there is no need for NATO to undertake undue risks in order to overcome any gaps in preparedness. ATBM may be developed in an evolutionary manner, maximizing the probability that some demonstrated capability might be available for development in the 1990s.

These requirements imply a research program built largely on traditional ground-based radar and interceptor technologies. Excluding the nuclear threat eliminates the need to cope with a disturbed environment and implies that mobility may be adequate to ensure the survivability of the defenses themselves. Severely hardened defenses and air- or space-based components are probably unnecessary to protect against conventionally armed TBMs. Excluding the nuclear threat also allows for low intercept altitudes, and when combined with the small area coverage requirements, ensures that mobility can be easily obtained. For example, the Patriot system is mobile and has sufficient radar size and interceptor speed to provide intercepts at militarily useful distances. Although not necessarily the optimal choice, it does indicate that the first steps in ATBM development can be based on existing technologies. Because many of these technologies have already been developed, the focus of NATO research should be technology integration, so that a working ATBM prototype can be built, and the costs and performance better understood.

NATO's needs also imply little connection with the SDI program. Because there is no urgent need for ATBM deployment, NATO is not critically dependent on active defense technologies, nor do NATO's needs necessarily provide a basis for demonstrating SDI technologies. Any missile defense will benefit from progress in the basic technologies being pursued in SDI, but SDI system technologies do not strongly correspond with NATO's first-generation ATBM needs. Technologies such as a fast-scanning, boost-phase detection satellite, the Airborne Optical Adjunct (AOA), the Exoatmospheric Reentry Vehicle Interceptor Subsystem (ERIS), and the High Endoatmospheric Interceptor (HEDI) generally offer the possibility of intercepting missiles at significantly greater distances from the defense than do traditional technologies.[24] This offers the possibility of constructing a multilayer defense and eventually developing a highly efficient defense system.[25] Although high efficiency is obviously desirable, a research program on a multilayered system implies that scarce research dollars must be divided among the layers. Although there may be some elements of commonality, intercepts at different altitudes will require different interceptors, different homing mechanisms, and different surveillance sensors. Where research dollars are scarce, such an approach would imply that NATO must gamble on a sophisticated ATBM to overcome deficiencies. However, ATBM need only be a supplement to passive defenses, which provide a hedge against a threat that is still developing. Thus evolutionary ATBM development is acceptable. NATO can concentrate its research efforts on the lowest and technically simplest layer of the defense, so as to have some demonstrated capability in the 1990s should further development then be needed.

NOTES

This chapter is based on work sponsored by the U.S. Air Force. The views expressed are those of the authors and do not necessarily represent those of the RAND Corporation, the U.S. Air Force, other sponsors of RAND research, or any other U.S. government agency.

1. See Fred S. Hoffman, Study Director, *Ballistic Missile Defenses and U.S. National Security: Summary Report* prepared for the Future Security Strategy Study, (Washington, D.C.: October 1983); Manfred Wörner, "A Missile Defense for NATO Europe," *Strategic Review*, Winter 1986, p. 13.; and Senator Pete Wilson, "A Missile Defense for NATO: We Must Respond to the Challenge," *Strategic Review*, Spring 1986, p. 9.
2. The term NATO-ATBM will be used to indicate an ATBM system that would be developed to serve NATO's military needs within the context of current theater strategy. In terms of the military utility of such a system, it will refer only to its application in NATO and not its potential contribution to SDI. If such a system incorporated some SDI technology, it might incidentally benefit SDI research goals.
3. Thomas Cochran, William Arkin, and Milton Hoenig, *Nuclear Weapons Databook, Volume I, U.S. Nuclear Forces and Capabilities*, (Cambridge, Mass.: Ballinger, 1984), p. 295.

4. With regard to computing, the U.S. Department of Defense states: "Although the Soviets have a solid understanding of basic principles, they have lingering problems in applying this knowledge to computer production." *Soviet Military Power 1987* (Washington, D.C.: U.S. Government Printing Office, 1987), p. 112.
5. Some would argue that the Soviets could use SPETSNAZ forces to provide targeting information. The authors have no ability to determine whether or not the relevant NATO units could be infiltrated. If infiltration cannot be achieved, a massive number of SPETSNAZ forces would be required. In both cases, the forces would require the ability to locate precisely the target and transmit the target coordinates in a timely manner.
6. See "A Ballistic Approach to AXE for Airfield Attack Weapon AAW," unclassified briefing presented by Boeing Aerospace Company, Seattle, Washington, 1982. The payload loss from these more complex mechanisms was assessed to be as high as 700 lbs (320 kg) in the Boeing study. However, it should be remembered that the missile being considered carried about twice the payload of the SS-23. Advanced terminal guidance systems also exact a payload penalty. As an example, we estimate that the RADAG (Radar Area Correlation Guidance) system used on the Pershing II weighs at least 300 kg. This is based on the total Pershing II payload and the mass of the B61 bomb, both in Cochran, Arkin, and Hoenig, pp. 65 and 294. On the basis of these estimates of weights for guidance and munitions dispensing systems, we would judge that a missile such as the Soviet SS-23 might carry as little as 500 to 600 kg of munitions.
7. This is based on the authors' own calculations using RAND's TSARINA model. Closure is achieved when there are no 50 × 3,500 ft (15 × 1,067 m) runway strips available. The differences between six and eight represent the differences in missile flight reliability. The lower number is based on 0.90, which may be typical of U.S. systems and the higher number on 0.75, which the International Institute for Strategic Studies assigns to Soviet systems, see *The Military Balance 1981–82* (London: IISS, 1981), p. 128.
8. David Dreyfuss of the RAND Corporation has estimated this cost from the relevant Selective Acquisition Reports (SAR) (private communication).
9. The nonlinearity is due to the fact that we have assumed the same probability for overall base closure. Thus, to obtain a 90 percent probability of closing a base with two runways, each runway must be closed with approximately 95 percent probability.
10. The value of 50 percent was based on the following assumptions. Munitions from the TBMs used to target the runway and taxiway would also strike the region between these two strips with equal

density, if we assume the highly dispersed ring submunition patterns discussed subsequently in the text. The runway and taxiway constitute approximately one-fourth of the total width of the paved configuration and would still be closed with 90 percent probability. However, to maintain a 90 percent probability for closing the equivalent of four such widths, each must be closed with 97.5 percent probability. Our TSARINA results indicate that about 50 percent more TBMs would be needed to do this. For more confined patterns the effectiveness of this technique can be even greater.

11. Dennis Gormley provides an example. See Chapter 3 in this volume and Gormley, "A New Dimension to Soviet Theater Strategy," *Orbis*, Fall 1985, pp. 537–569.
12. The air base was assumed to consist of a runway 2,438 × 46 meters (8,000 × 150 ft) and a parallel taxiway 2,438 × 15 meters (8,000 × 50 ft) separated by 198 meters (650 ft). The two aimpoints were both located between the runway and taxiway, each 406 meters (1,333 ft) from the center of the configuration.
13. The number of submunitions is a critical assumption. The so-called BKEP penetrating munition designed by the United States weighs approximately 20 kg (see U.S. Office of Technology Assessment, *Technologies for NATO's Follow-on Forces Attack Concept — Special Report*, OTA-ISC-312 (Washington, D.C.: U.S. Government Printing Office, July 1986), p. 35). This weapon would require a modified design for use on a TBM. However, the 20 kg weight probably indicates that the illustrative assumption by Morel and Postol that a TBM of 1,000 kg payload might carry 100 submunitions of 10 kg each (Chapter 2 in this volume) is highly favorable to the offense.
14. This mode of attack has the advantage of not being sensitive to numbers of runway penetrating submunitions or the precise dispersal pattern. Its effectiveness is sensitive, however, to missile accuracy and the radius of submunition dispersion. If the radius of dispersion cannot be controlled, it would be better to implement a two-aimpoint attack. However, the number of TBMs needed to close the airbase in that case will be higher.
15. The lower number is again based on a 0.90 reliability figure, the higher number on 0.75 reliability.
16. Take-off and landing distances are from *Jane's All the World's Aircraft 1984–1985*, (New York: Jane's, 1985), p. 448.
17. The Autobahn landing strips are extremely valuable for avoiding the initial pin-in. However, if the aircraft are to continue to execute air defense sorties, they must return to a base with appropriate support equipment.
18. See Joshua Epstein, *Measuring Military Power: The Soviet Air Threat to Europe*, (Princeton, N.J.: Princeton University Press, 1984), for a discussion of limitations on Soviet air power.

19. The Combined Effect Munition is the principal new U.S. Air Force cluster munition. See U.S. Office of Technology Assessment, *Technologies for NATO's Follow-on Forces Attack Concept — Special Report*, OTA-ISC-312, July 1986, for details.
20. For example, a modern control center for air defense operations might be protected by as little as one and a half meters of concrete and five meters of overburden. See D. Boyle, "C^3 — The Essential Ingredient to Air Defense," *International Defense Review*, June 1978, p. 860–864.
21. See for example, Stephen Meyer, "Soviet Theatre Nuclear Forces Part II: Capabilities and Implications," *Adelphi Paper* no. 188 (London: The International Institute for Strategic Studies, 1983), p. 57.
22. This is argued in D. Blair and B. Chow, "European Ballistic Missile Defenses — Reducing the Danger of War," in Senator Dan Quayle, ed., *Strategic Defense and the Western Alliance*, Significant Issue Series, vol. VI, no. 6, The Center for Strategic and International Studies, Georgetown University, 1986.
23. In the interest of space, we have not discussed the potential of chemically armed TBMs. Based on analysis not presented in this chapter, however, the authors have reached the judgment that ATBM will not play an important role in countering or preventing chemical attacks. The authors base this judgment on the variety of delivery vehicles (most importantly aircraft) that could deliver chemicals and on the authors' assessment that the unique features of chemical attack by TBM do not provide significant advantages over attacks from other delivery vehicles. The authors believe that the best method for coping with the chemical threat involves a combination of passive defenses, arms control, and the threat of retaliation.
24. The SDI program also includes older and more traditional technologies, such as FLAGE (Flexible Light Weight Agile Guided Experiment) that would be relevant to the research program described here.
25. Multilayer in this context implies layers within what is often categorized as the terminal layer, in the context of defense against ICBMs.

6 TBMS, ATBMS, AND NATO DOCTRINE

Peter Volten

Should the NATO Alliance exploit new missile defense technologies to fulfill its military requirements? One might expect that the Alliance could answer such a question in a straightforward manner, by consulting its formal military doctrine and deciding whether ATBMs have a place within it.

Yet matters are never quite so simple. In theory, NATO's military doctrine serves as a body of guiding principles that is called on to promote unity of thought in the process of decisionmaking. But NATO is an alliance of diverse and sovereign nations. In practice, the complexity of the Alliance's decision process and the multitude of players interfere with this envisaged theoretical clarity in matching doctrine to technologies. In order to reduce complexity to manageable proportions, as well as to highlight his own considerations and interests, each player tends to simplify, even oversimplify, the issues in the course of Alliance discussion. Players lose sight of the total picture. Even on a matter as central to the Alliance as its military doctrine, fragmented and distorted views cloud theoretical clarity.

Consequently, whether and to what extent a new technology is likely to be, or ought to be exploited by the Alliance is dependent on a range of nontechnological factors. However important the strictly technological dimension of a weapons issue is, Alliance decisions are shaped by the combination of political, bureaucratic, and doctrinal inputs, and often in unexpected ways. The manner in which the Alliance has dealt with the ATBM issue thus far illustrates the point.

NATO'S FLEXIBLE RESPONSE STRATEGY

NATO's strategy of "forward defense and flexibility in response," formally adopted in December 1967, aims at avoiding war through deterrence. To fulfill this objective, the Alliance maintains a complementary array of conventional, theater nuclear, and strategic nuclear forces. Should any form of attack occur, Alliance forces must have the capability to respond directly at whatever level the aggression occurs—"direct defense." At the conventional level, this implies collective forward defense at the point of aggression, in order to minimize loss of allied territory in the opening stages of conflict. In a theater of operations where the distance from the inter-German border to the seaports and airfields where reinforcements must arrive is no more than 100 to 200 km, forward defense has an important military function. It also fosters political cohesion in the Alliance, by assuring each member that it is not being asked to sacrifice its own territory for the protection of others.

Also important for direct defense is the Alliance's ability to raise the costs and risks of aggression by selective use of nuclear weapons. Although the primary purpose of NATO's use of nuclear weapons would always be political—to persuade the aggressor to cease hostilities, and thus to restore deterrence—theater nuclear forces serve to deter the Warsaw Pact's use of nuclear forces. At the same time, theater nuclear forces provide a critical link between the Alliance's conventional forces and its strategic nuclear capabilities, the latter being the ultimate deterrent.

At precisely what point in response to aggression the Alliance would begin using nuclear weapons is not formally specified. In this sense, flexible response is a general strategy, not a detailed operational military doctrine. The uncertainty of NATO's response conceivably may help deter an aggressor, but the reason for uncertainty stems as much from the Alliance's concerns for its own political cohesion: The alliance members have historically held sharply different views about how much of the deterrence burden should be placed on nuclear rather than conventional forces. In earlier years, NATO's nuclear superiority compensated for the Pact's advantages in conventional forces, but now the changed ratio of nuclear capabilities in the Soviets' favor seriously complicates NATO's strategy and affects its credibility.

The Soviets' numeric superiority in nuclear-armed theater and tactical ballistic missiles has confronted NATO for some time and could conceivably be exploited by the Soviet Union for nuclear "blackmail." But the Soviets quite likely would do so only in the presence of conventional superiority or after significant conventional successes in a war. If the Soviets could apply their numerical superiority in TBMs to conventional advantage as well, it would thus place in their hands a two-edged sword. NATO must look to its own shield of conventional forces, not only to bolster direct defense but also to undermine the significance of Soviet nuclear preponderance.

NATO'S CONVENTIONAL FORCE PLANNING

The Alliance's most recent formulation of the link between its general strategy and its specific conventional forces requirements is to be found in its Conceptual Military Framework (CMF), prepared by the Military Committee (as document MC 299) and endorsed by NATO's defense ministers in the Defense Planning Committee (DPC) in December 1985. The immediate impulse for the CMF was a proposal from U.S. Defense Secretary Caspar Weinberger, in December 1982, that NATO offset its quantitative inferiority in the Central Region by jointly planning, developing, and deploying weapons that would exploit "emerging technologies." During the ministerial DPC meeting of December 1983, several countries expressed their reservations about adopting the U.S. approach without first clarifying the alliance's military-operational requirements. The Federal Republic, in particular, pointed out the need for a "conceptual military framework" before one could proceed to include new weapons systems in national defense plans. Furthermore, it was pointed out, the feasibility of "emerging technologies" had to be considered, along with the possibility of international cooperation, particularly a "two-way street" in which the United States would be willing to purchase weapons developed by Europeans. Because financial constraints would require a selective approach to the application of emerging technologies, there was a unanimous opinion that consultations within the Military Committee should yield not only a CMF but also an establishment of priorities.

The CMF that emerged was designed as a NATO-wide framework, in which all militarily essential tasks were identified, defined, and related to each other. The purpose was to establish a common foundation as a guide for long-term planning. The CMF took as its basis the goal of maintaining credible deterrence, and it specified the conventional measures required to achieve that goal. Even though nuclear missions were excluded from the CMF, its development took into account, as necessary, the relationships that exist between the conventional and nuclear elements of NATO strategy. The overarching strategic objectives of the Alliance were stated as:

- Preventing the occupation of NATO territory by the enemy;
- Ensuring free use of the sea by allies and friendly nations;
- Securing NATO airspace.

To achieve these strategic objectives, "forward defense" remained the most important principle. Within that context, the essential tasks for NATO forces were identified:

1. Defense against advancing enemy units, to prevent an enemy breakthrough and regain any territorial losses. A critical situation can develop in the initial phase of conflict when the enemy exploits surprise, massed attack, and air superiority, while NATO forces have not been fully mobilized or deployed, and reinforcements from overseas have not yet arrived. It is therefore necessary that the troops deployed forward in peace time possess high readiness and sufficient capabilities to withstand a short-warning, concentrated attack by Warsaw Pact ground forces.
2. Follow-On Forces Attack (FOFA), to attack and delay Warsaw Pact reinforcements that are arriving in the battle area to exploit any weaknesses generated by the initial attack. Thus, FOFA provides an indirect means to prevent breakthrough at the front. The concept was developed by SACEUR and applies to the entire Allied Command Europe (ACE).
3. Achievement of a favorable balance in the air, to protect both NATO territory and forces against air attacks by the Warsaw Pact. This task encompasses both offensive and defensive components: offensive counter air (OCA) and defensive counter air (DCA). Warsaw Pact air forces will perform an important mission, supporting their ground offensive and obtructing NATO's

mobilization and defense preparations. OCA is designed to deny air superiority to the Warsaw Pact, in spite of the Pact's numeric superiority in fighter aircraft, by putting Pact airbases out of operation and destroying any aircraft not yet airborne. The means for executing the OCA mission are the same as those planned for FOFA, that is, air-to-ground and surface-to-surface missiles. The Warsaw Pact will attempt to execute its own OCA against NATO air power. The aim of NATO's Defensive Counter Air is to limit the effects of such an attack by either passive or active measures. Passive measures include mobility of systems, concealment, dispersal, and hardening. Active measures would include anti-aircraft defenses and ATBMs.

4. Assurance of free use of the sea and protection for allied ships. These tasks, including the protection and defense of harbors, are vitally important for the supply of reinforcements and logistic support. Navy forces are also required to support the air defense (DCA) and ground operations.

5. Protection for rear areas, which includes all allied territory behind the forward army corps. This rear area is of high military significance because it includes the highest command and control centers, logistics facilities, and stations for receiving reinforcement units, building up reserve units, and reconstituting active units.

These key mission components are interrelated, but within each alliance region, the role and importance of each task would be different.[1] Hence, some judgment is necessary about which key mission components take precedence. Yet despite the initial request of the defense ministers, the CMF does *not* include a priority scheme. The recommendations are stated in general terms, focusing primarily on modernization of equipment and improvements in organization, readiness, and sustainablility. The CMF can only be viewed as a basis for further detailed planning efforts to identify operational requirements and priorities for each region and country.

In May 1985 the DPC also approved a report on short-term improvements to the conventional defense, including various recommendations regarding the most urgent shortfalls. Those recommendations are referred to as Conventional Defense Improvements (CDI) and were reviewed in the November 1985 meeting of NATO's Permanent Representatives and by the Assistant Secretaries for Materiel. General

Bernard Rogers pointed out the relationship between the "civilian" CDI Initiative and the CMF: "the conventional defense improvements identified by the CDI Initiative related directly to those capabilities and functions which must be performed to support the ACE key mission components inherent in NATO's strategy, and will be in consonance with the longer term capability requirements postulated in the Conceptual Military Framework."[2]

There are some telling observations to be made, parenthetically, from this example of NATO's way of doing business. First, it required a political challenge from the U.S. defense secretary and SACEUR to shake up the alliance bureaucracies and produce an overall picture of what needs to be done, now and in the long run. Over the years, hundreds of alliance committees, laboring uncounted hours on thousands of alliance problems, had nonetheless failed to produce anything resembling the more or less comprehensive view of alliance requirements that CDI and CMF together have provided. These two studies were provoked, quite simply, by the fears of ministers that they would have to foot the bill for too enthusiastic a course of action being pushed by the U.S. administration and General Rogers. Second, this episode has induced greater attention to long-term planning. In order to influence national planning, NATO has to go beyond national planning cycles. Long-term planning guidelines are a necessary, though not sufficient, means to attract the attention of the individual nations to the defense needs of the alliance as a whole and thus to reinforce international coordination of common strategic capabilities that no nation can or ought to do individually.

A third observation concerns the other side of the coin, the inability of the bureaucratic machinery in Brussels to assist the political masters and even the most involved military master, SACEUR. As one observer rightly put it: "there would seem to be an unresolved conceptual ambiguity with the CMF. It is intended to guide *conventional force planning* . . . over the longer term, and that is its organizing principle. It was not created as a guide to *operational* planning. . . . Yet its drafters viewed this document as an 'attempt to define more precisely how allied strategy should be implemented in the conventional field.' "[3]

ATBM, POLITICAL INTERVENTION, AND BUREAUCRATIC MUDDLING

Where precisely does ATBM fit in all this? Again, the answer is as much political as doctrinal. Until 1983–84 when the political impulse of President Reagan's SDI pushed the issue to the fore, NATO studies regarding ATBM had been inconclusive and vague. Bureaucratic muddling was as evident in this case as it was in the effort to provide overall recommendations for conventional force improvements. Already in 1979, NATO's military authorities had pointed to the need for an air defense program for the period 1980–94 and, in particular, to the anticipated threat from Soviet TBMs. In 1982 the U.S. Air Force presented its "CounterAir 90" study in NATO, which included a role for active defense against tactical ballistic missiles. In November 1983, NATO's Advisory Group for Aerospace Research and Development (AGARD) started its Aerospace Application Study (AAS-20) on ATBM system concepts. The study was completed in March 1986, but its purpose was essentially to review technology options, not to make specific recommendations. In the interim, both the Dutch Defense Minister De Ruiter and the German Defense Minister Wörner had stepped forward with proposals for ATBM defenses against Soviet conventionally armed TBMs. Moreover, General Rogers as SACEUR also threw his weight into the scale. In July 1986, he sent a Long-Term Planning Guideline entitled "Theater Ballistic Missile Defense" to the Military Committee, requesting that it be forwarded to the Defense Planning Committee for adoption by all the allies.[4] He ascribed—quite abruptly—a high priority to the proposal. In light of such events, the Military Committee asked AGARD for yet another study that would focus on C^3/battle management architecture for a missile defense, a study to be completed in 1988.

Two subgroups of the NATO Air Defense Committee (NADC) have also been involved in ATBM studies. The Panel on Air Defense Philosophy (PADP) was requested to develop "ACE Long-term Counter-Air Philosophy," to identify "OCA/DCA Relationships," and to suggest possible counterair reactions to attack options of the Warsaw Pact during the first phase of a conflict. The other subgroup, the Panel on Air Defense Weapons (PADW), started its more specific work on active measures to counter the TBM threat in January, 1986. The NADC panels consist of experts from capitals, so that a direct exchange of national views is possible. It is generally believed in NATO that these panels are the right fora for allied consultations on ATBM's at the working level because of their composition—all nations, including France—and their expertise.

The actual impact of this collective endeavor within NATO seems inevitably limited, however, given the fact that PADW has to wait for the advice of AGARD and for half a dozen other studies to be completed in 1987 before it can complete its own work. This may be welcomed by those who have doubts about the desirability or financial and technical feasibility of ATBMs. Requests for additional studies and demands for a consensus are tried-and-true tactics in delaying decisions. On the other hand, proponents of tactical or theater ballistic missile defense may not be willing to wait that long before taking action within their own governments. That is, one should be aware that national force planning processes in NATO can to a considerable extent shape and direct studies and affect operational doctrine.

THE SOVIET CHALLENGE TO NATO'S DOCTRINE

If weapons decisions in NATO are inevitably clouded with political and bureaucratic concerns, one can nonetheless ask whether NATO's doctrine and military-operational guidelines provide a key to the ATBM issue. Given the ambiguities and lack of specifics in the Conceptual Military Framework, it cannot give all the answers but it can help in formulating the criteria on which a decision should hinge.

Shortfalls in conventional defense preparations can be found in each of the key mission components of the CMF, but they are not equally important. The relative weight of each shortfall must be assessed by considering not only the military capabilities of the Warsaw Pact but also NATO's distinctive defensive posture. The fundamental shortcoming of much debate within the alliance on military preparations is the persistent neglect of the difference between the offensive character of Soviet military strategy and its implementation on the one hand, and its consequences for the defensive strategy and posture of NATO, on the other.

Failure to distinguish between offense and defense and the respective force structures leads to confusion in an number of ways and hampers the determination of priorities in strengthening NATO's conventional defense. Western governments and NATO officials might find it easier to reach consensus in matters of operational doctrine if they would delve into some basic tenets of strategy and the Soviet art of warfare. Political and parochial considerations, some of which have been mentioned earlier, often stand in the way of a conceptual approach to allied operational doctrine.

Soviet military doctrine makes a distinction between strategy, operations, and tactics.[5] This distinction is important because the approach to the question of war and peace and the problem of combat and warfare are very different for each concept. The difference between strategy and tactics makes itself felt on the level of policymaking and the responsibility of military commanders. The West does not have an equivalent counterpart to the Soviets' operational doctrine, which determines the methods of preparation for and execution of operations to achieve strategic objectives. Tactical successes must be exploited at the operational level to achieve the strategic objective, which is surrender by the enemy. Therefore, military forces must be mobile to pursue "operational gains" and they must be structured for maneuver warfare.

Implementation of Soviet operational doctrine is based on a command structure that consists of an "operational commander" who controls assigned units varying from an army (four to five divisions) to a front (three to five armies), depending on terrain and the opponent's deployment of forces. This concentration of military power under one operational commander at a high command level provides significant flexibility, including the ability to switch main axes of attack rapidly and to control the assignment of different units such as armor, infantry, and artillery. The air operation is an inseparable part of the Soviet combined arms concept and assumes at least operational significance in the land war.

In sharp contrast to this, NATO's "operational" doctrine and force structure is characterized by a tactical mindset. National corps commanders prepare their battle according to their own inclinations, and although NORTHAG has recently achieved some greater degree of coordination, in general the operational commanders lack significance because NORTHAG, CENTAG, and even SACEUR face a critical shortage of operational units, particularly in the early phase of a conflict. "The West still approaches operational art from below. Tactical concepts become the basic building blocks for operational art and operational success tends to be defined as the accumulation of tactical successes."[6] The Soviet air operation and the emerging technologies enabling dramatic improvements in that operation significantly enlarge this asymmetry between military strategies and structures in East and West.

The recognition that rapidity is essential for a decisive offensive, and is reflected in the operational doctrine and organization of Soviet military forces, compels NATO to consider very carefully the factor of *time* in war. The strategy of flexible response itself requires answers to the question how NATO can postpone the decisive moment. In the conventional phase of war or in "classical" strategy, "time which is allowed to pass unused accumulates to the credit of the defender. He reaps where he did not sow. Any omission of attack—whether from bad judgment, fear, or indolence—accrues to the defender's benefit."[7] Time is one of the main factors that makes the defense the stronger form of war. In order to avoid surrender, the defender must gain time and in the first phase of conflict try to nullify the attacker's advantage of surprise. Nuclear deterrence adds another decisive moment the defender must avoid: the decision forced on him to employ nuclear weapons first, with all the associated risks. That possibly fatal decision for state and society—not merely the armed forces—should be forced on the leaders in Moscow.

NATO is not dealing with a tactical battle in which it may be advantageous to trade space for time in order to be better prepared for the defense and the counterattack. On the strategic—or Soviet operational—level there is little or no time to be had in trade. "Nonprovocative defense" schemes that one hears proposed for NATO confuse tactics with strategy.[8] A purely defensive posture can only lead to defeat or surrender, since there is no counteroffensive capability. One needs, to use Raymond Aron's words, a "defensive strategy and offensive tactics [to] create a progressive reversal of the relation of forces up to the annihilation of the enemy by the defender who passes over to attack."[9] Soviet operational art and technology, which grant speed and accuracy, have drastically shortened the distance, measured in time and space, that von Clausewitz saw between tactics and strategy in a war. Now, much more than in his day, the rule applies that "all forces intended and available for a strategic purpose should be applied simultaneously."[10] The center of gravity is seen by the Soviet generals at the operational level and goes beyond tactical calculations. Success in a defensive posture today critically depends on the ability to frustrate the attacker's tempo right from the start and to force on him as soon as possible the "culmination point" beyond which "the scale turns and the reaction follows with a force that is usually much stronger than that of the original attack."[11] NATO quite likely cannot deny the speed and mobility of the Warsaw Pact forces everywhere on the local level, but it can or should deny tempo and maneuver in the theater of operations as a whole, Western Europe.

The unavoidable conclusion from such considerations is that the highest priority in NATO's Central Region is the prevention of a breakthrough of the forward defense line. Under no circumstances should Warsaw Pact maneuver units be permitted to conduct raids behind the forward line and disrupt rear area defense during the initial phase of the conflict. Debate among Western observers over whether the Pact would be favored in the net balance of conventional forces in the event of war in the Central Region has been perennial, vigorous, and ultimately indecisive. What is clear is that given sufficient time to mobilize and prepare, NATO's capabilities in the aggregate would not be so obviously inferior that the Pact could anticipate easy victory. The Soviets have therefore drawn the appropriate conclusion: The best prospect of success lies in an initial blow that is heavy and decisive in spreading confusion within NATO, disrupting mobilization and reinforcement, and preventing the efficient allocation of available forces. In this context, the importance of the Pact air threat can hardly be overstated, in particular the offensive counter air (OCA) capability of the Pact against C^3 centers and other critical air defense installations, the Achilles heel of NATO.

The core of NATO's air defenses in the Central Region are the roughly fifteen sites for air defense control, several of which jointly share facilities with nine or ten major C^3 headquarters. A network of fixed and mobile surveillance radars would provide attack early warning. The NATO Air Defense Ground Environment (NADGE) surveillance system consists of at least five 412 L fixed radar sites, sixteen mobile 407 L radar Control and Reporting Posts, and perhaps eighty other radars. In some instances, these sites are composed of many elements and, depending on how they were attacked, might have to be regarded as several separate targets.[12] On the other hand, when in operation they can be located by their emitted signals. The vulnerability of these assets can partially be offset by NATO's squadron of Airborne Warning and Control System (AWACS) aircraft, which can keep up to four aircraft aloft at all times.

If the Warsaw Pact cannot disable NATO's air defense system by attacking vital C^3 sites, it will have to assault the Patriot and Hawk air defense belts directly, in order to open up several penetration corridors to other targets. These air defense batteries have limited mobility and are extremely soft. Moreover, they cannot move and perform their mission simultaneously. On the other hand, once in position and "silent," the SAM units are very difficult to locate. And they are quite numerous. The United States began deploying Patriot as replacement for the nuclear-armed Nike Hercules in 1984, with plans for the eventual deployment of eighty-one batteries, including fifty-four with U.S. forces in West Germany. The United States anticipates that another sixty-four to seventy-two batteries may eventually be deployed by other allies, including thirty-six by West Germany and perhaps four each by the Netherlands and Belgium. The Hawk system has been deployed since 1972, thirty batteries with U.S. forces in Germany, twelve batteries with the German Air Force, twelve batteries with the Netherlands Air Force (eight of them in Germany), and four batteries with the Belgian Army. There are an additional eleven batteries of Hawk with the French Army, six batteries with the Danish Air Force, and a variety of other SAM systems deployed among the allies. Each Patriot battery will be equipped with twenty-four to thirty-two missiles mounted on launchers (plus roughly as many reloads), each Hawk battery with eighteen to twenty-seven missiles. SAM batteries are "soft," but in general each must regarded as a separate target; indeed, if the elements of a battery are scattered, a single battery may represent several separate targets.

Successful missile and air attacks against the soft, vulnerable infrastructure of airbases could severely tax NATO's ability to sustain aircraft sorties. A "heavy" Soviet TBM threat against NATO's air assets could mean a reduction of more than 50 percent of aircraft sorties during the first two days, dropping from, say 10,000 to under 5,000 sorties for the total available aircraft.

The growing target concentration of NATO's nuclear weapons stockpile is another concern. The last decade has seen a shrinkage in the overall number of nuclear storage facilities. Of course, dispersal would render Soviet surprise attack calculations dubious at best by multiplying the nuclear target set from about eighty fixed installations to well over 300 mobile, more survivable field units. But some see nuclear dispersal as risky or even provocative and doubt whether NATO's governments would act in time to disperse nuclear weapons.

Thus, the target set of NATO's main air defense capabilities, including major C^3 headquarters, lower-level communication centers, warning and surveillance assets, and aircraft main operating bases totals only some forty-five. Taking into account other target categories—theater nuclear weapons storage (eighty), reinforcement facilities (twenty-five), and the roughly 132 targets formed by SAM batteries in West Germany — Dennis Gormley arrives at the conclusion that "suppressing half (or sixty-six) of these targets would materially aid establishment of perhaps five penetration corridors. Overall, then, some 225 targets (of which sixty-two are within range of seventy-six SS-21 missiles and 163 are within range of 180 SS-23 and SS-22 missiles) constitute the maximum target set."[13] The crippling effect of a Warsaw Pact superiority in the air, and a NATO loss of communications, mandate a serious effort by NATO in the area of Defensive Counter Air.

The Soviet air operation, however, is not just an anti-air mission but is aimed against NATO's overall defense effort. Indeed, securing a favorable balance in the air in the first phase of a conflict is essential for the course of the ground offensive because the success of operational maneuver groups (OMGs) is largely dependent on achieving air superiority. NATO's task will be to stem the Pact offensive from the start and to trap any breakthroughs in the rear area. This priority scheme is in accordance with the political requirement of "forward defense," but it also points to the Alliance's need for a mobile defense in depth. Unfortunately, the lack of sufficient maneuver units in the rear area during the first phase of a conflict is a most serious shortcoming in NATO's current defense organization.[14] If Soviet and Warsaw Pact TBMs were capable of reducing the number of aircraft sorties to one-half or even one-third during the first two days of a conflict, NATO's ground forces would find themselves in a very precarious, if not hopeless, position.

An additional aim of the Warsaw Pact air operation could be to cripple NATO's reinforcement potential. NATO has a significant initial surge capability for mobilizing ground forces within Europe — perhaps twenty to twenty-five division equivalents within the first three to five days of mobilization. A total of some 1,500 aircraft could also arrive as reinforcements within the first ten days, with maintenance personnel and equipment airlifted in separately. After that, the bulk of reinforcements — another twenty division equivalents or so — must come from the United States, the first units by airlift and later ones with their equipment by sealift.[15] NATO's reinforcement process presents the Pact with an attractive and lucrative target. The POMCUS sites where equipment awaits arrival of U.S. reinforcements, for instance, are few in number and relatively "soft," consisting of large warehouses with stored equipment. Moreover, massive airlifting of troops and distribution of their prepositioned equipment are complex and time-consuming activities.[16] The sites where reinforcement takes place may be less time-urgent as targets for this reason, yet if Pact forces could disrupt and delay the process, it could have an impact on both the ground offensive and on NATO's will to continue resisting.

Once one paints the picture in these grim terms, it is difficult to resist the conclusion that ATBMs for NATO would be nice to have. But one comes back to a point of reality stated earlier: Shortfalls exist in the forces necessary for *all* key mission components identified in the Conceptual Military Framework. The initial force proposals put forward by the major NATO military commanders for 1985–90 would have required an average 7 percent real increase in military spending for member nations. The defense ministers in May 1984 agreed to less than half that request (3.2 percent). For some members, even half of that reduced goal may be unachievable; it proved unattainable by the European allies throughout the early 1980s.

Even though nobody knows exactly what the cost for any ATBM system would be, mere guesses are already frightening enough to temper enthusiasm.[17] The current Patriot system, for instance, costs about $80 million for each fire unit (battery), and the total cost for all U.S. and European purchases may come to about $11 billion. Upgrading Patriot for an ATBM role, with a new interceptor and new radars, might be the least expensive course. The unit cost of each Patriot missile appears to be about $300,000 at present, and each battery is equipped with sixty-four interceptor missiles (fewer for the Dutch Patriot units). If a new high-performance interceptor for the ATBM task were to cost two to three times as much, and if each battery were equipped with no more than thirty-two such interceptors, the R&D and procurement cost for this upgrade to all NATO batteries could be $3 to $5 billion for missiles alone. Similarly, the current cost of the radar, power plant, and engagement control center for each battery is about $57 million. If an upgraded system required replacement of much of this equipment, the additional cost could be $5 to $8 billion. Even these simple calculations suggest that an ATBM capability would cost NATO at least as much as Patriot itself—and one can doubt whether a full ATBM system would prove as inexpensive as these rough calculations.

One is forced back to a sober assessment of whether the TBM problem is so bad for NATO that ATBMs are an indispensable response and ought to have high priority.

It would be easier to assess the potential impact of a Soviet offensive counter air attack if NATO had an agreed doctrine for the use of air power, and mission priorities within that doctrine, against which the loss of aircraft sorties could be weighed. Unfortunately, although NATO stands closer to such agreement now than before, it still has distance to go.[18] If NATO had ample time to mobilize, the air forces it could bring to bear in the Central Region would probably still trail those of the Warsaw Pact in simple numbers; but ample opportunity for mobilization is not the contingency often assumed, and simple numbers don't tell all. Warsaw Pact air forces themselves may be stretched thin in the opening phase of conflict. As Gormley argues, a precursor attack with TBMs can perhaps disable but not destroy crucial targets. Destruction will require follow-up attacks by Pact aviation. Although the target set identified by Gormley is not large (225), neither is it small in comparison to the total aircraft the Pact may have available—perhaps 1,400 fighter/ground attack aircraft and bombers, another 2,000 fighter/interceptors.[19]

And many of the NATO targets are quite resilient. Perhaps the most resilient are the SAM belts, which may force heavy attrition on attacking aircraft and may be very difficult to disable with precursor TBM assaults.[20] The Soviets may choose to throw their forces at the entire target set simultaneously, or focus their attack at a few places — to form corridors in the SAM belts, for instance. One approach stretches resources taut, the other offers the unattacked targets an opportunity to prepare, disperse, and so forth. Unless Soviet reconnaissance and damage assessment are quite good out to the far reaches of the precursor TBM attack, follow-on aircraft will have to approach targets with caution, perhaps as carefully as if the TBM attack had not taken place. Again, this means either stretching air resources thin or concentrating them at fewer points.

Nor will the assault on this target set be the only demand on Pact air resources. In the past, Pact aircraft and weapons appear not to have been well adapted for close air support missions in conjunction with ground forces, although the appearance of the Su-25/Frogfoot and its extensive use in Afghanistan may signal an institutional change. Nonetheless, one would expect at least some allocation of Pact aircraft to ground attack and battlefield counter air missions.

Clearly, it would be unreasonable for NATO to assume that it could carry out air operations unimpeded in the opening phases of conflict, with or without a Soviet TBM threat. NATO's ground forces must be, and are, prepared to mobilize and fend for themselves under conditions of degraded air operations. Attack and transport helicopter forces should not be ignored as sources of integral air support and airlift for NATO ground forces.[21] To judge by the composition of NATO air forces, training, and allocation of resources, close air support and battlefield air interdiction are missions for which NATO is well prepared, so whatever air elements survive an initial Soviet assault may function with unusual effectiveness. Certainly NATO air forces train more than their Pact counterparts and may well train more realistically. If historical precedent counts, the heaviest losses in the air battle will occur in the first days on both sides and then will decline for the side that learns and adapts most quickly. One would expect that for deep-seated institutional and cultural reasons, NATO forces will have clear advantage in adaptability.

One must also take into account that the most dire TBM scenarios cannot occur unless the Warsaw Pact catches NATO forces unprepared — that is, either NATO has no expectation of war or is too paralyzed to respond to warning. Some steps of preparation perhaps NATO will hesitate to take because they are judged as too provocative — dispersal of nuclear weapons, for instance. But other actions that would make the Soviet air operation far more difficult are not so problematic: bringing air defense batteries up to combat status, dispersing aircraft to other bases, and raising alert status of aircrews, ground support crews, and airfield damage repair personnel. Much has been made of recent improvements in the combat readiness of, and logistics support for forward deployed Warsaw Pact forces, reducing the signs of Pact preparation for war that NATO in the past could use as warning of attack. Yet even if the Warsaw Pact acquired the technical capacity for its troops to attack "from a standing start," one could certainly doubt the Soviets would attack from a *political* "standing start." The profound risks in an assault on NATO, especially one that might rapidly push NATO to nuclear desperation, are not ones the Soviets could regard lightly. They are risks the Soviets would surely embrace only when confronted with an equally profound political crisis, a crisis that itself would give NATO warning and time for preparation. One can always debate whether NATO, with its democratic and decentralized decisionmaking structures, would respond promptly and sensibly in time of crisis. It would be wise for the Alliance to give some priority to missions and forces that would help buy time for NATO's ponderous decision process. Although ATBMs might help buy time, they are not the only method of doing this, nor necessarily the most cost effective.

ATBMS AND NATO'S ESCALATION OPTIONS

If it proved possible for the Warsaw Pact to surprise NATO and essentially to neutralize NATO air operations through the combined effects of TBMs, aircraft, and air defenses, NATO ground forces could find themselves in an untenable position, bordering on collapse. At that stage, NATO's flexible response strategy envisions escalation to nuclear warfare. At this juncture, the Alliance would have to view the ATBM issue from a different perspective: How will NATO's nuclear missions fare, if NATO lacks ATBMs and/or the Warsaw Pact possesses them?

Again what one needs for sound analysis is a clear specification of NATO's nuclear employment doctrine, against which to weigh the factor of ATBMs. NATO does have a nuclear operations plan, and a Nuclear Activities Branch of SHAPE with responsibility for developing targeting plans against Pact military forces and support facilities. Reportedly SHAPE has identified some 18,500 targets at short and medium range, with roughly 1,800 designated as "priority targets."[22] The guidelines for which, if any of these targets would be attacked in wartime are formally to be found in NATO's "Provisional Political Guidelines," first drafted in 1969, and the general political guidelines agreed upon at Gleneagles in 1986.[23] The size of NATO's nuclear response could range from a general release involving virtually all available warheads to very selective employment of a few weapons.

As with many things in NATO, ambiguity serves as a useful device to avert fractious debates over contingencies that may never arise. There are those who argue that the size, character, and use of nuclear weapons by the Alliance ought to stem principally from military considerations. The title of NATO's guidance document, Provisional *Political* Guidelines, and its formulation of *Selective* Employment Plans (SEPs) reflect another view that NATO's purpose in nuclear strikes should be fundamentally political—to alter the decisions and behavior of Soviet leaders. The debate is not always sharply divided. One can argue that nuclear use will not have political effect on Soviet leaders unless it alters the military situation, and that in using nuclear weapons for political effect, NATO's leaders could not be indifferent to the dire military situation that presumably was forcing the Alliance to escalate.

ATBMs have bearing on this matter because the Soviets are more likely to establish ATBM defenses around military targets, and because high-performance ATBM defenses might interfere with the selective strike plans of NATO, Europe's independent nuclear states, or even those of the United States. As German Defense Minister Manfred Wörner has remarked, "If the Soviets were able to put around the European part of Russia an anti-ballistic defense system of even limited effectiveness, NATO's capacity for exercising even its limited nuclear options could be substantially compromised — and the credibility of the Alliance's nuclear deterrent would thereby be seriously weakened."[24] One has no assurance that the Soviets will prove interested in mutual limitations on ATBM systems, but NATO must at least ask itself whether, on balance, its fundamental strategic purpose — deterrence of all war — would be better served through restricted or unrestricted ATBM deployments on both sides (taking into account the political, economic, and technological asymmetries between the Pact and NATO).

The answer is obscured by many uncertainties. If no agreement banning theater and longer-range tactical ballistic missiles had been made, and the continuity of NATO's extended deterrence pivoted on the Alliance's own theater ballistic missiles, then extensive Soviet deployments of ATBMs with some antinuclear capability would erode NATO deterrence — according to the arguments originally made on behalf of INF deployments. But a negotiated agreement that permits only tactical ballistic missiles with ranges under 500 km shifts the burden of theater nuclear deterrence and missions to NATO's shorter-range nuclear systems, its aircraft, the 400 or so U.S. SLBM warheads designated to SACEUR, and the IRBM and SLBM forces of its European members. The shortest-ranged systems could likely evade Soviet ATBMs, but they also confront the allies with the prospect of using nuclear weapons on their own territory. NATO aircraft could reach deeper into Pact territory, although relying on them for nuclear strike missions would reverse the trend of the past decade, of shifting scarce aircraft from nuclear to conventional missions. NATO's tactical and strategic ballistic missiles could also reach deeper — provided they are not susceptible to Soviet ATBMs.

One cannot know for sure how extensive Soviet ATBM defenses might become, if constrained only by Soviet budgets, technology, and doctrines. Gormley argues that if the Soviets continue with current practices of deploying ATBM-potential systems for point defense and with military forces, it would leave largely unprotected a great number of Soviet targets, both political and military. One may not view with comfort (as Gormley notes) the fact that so far the Soviets are placing the SA-10 SAM system, with its asserted ATBM potential, only around their *vital* political-military sites. Moreover, NATO must consider the import of ATBM capabilities that might be incorporated in modernization of the 1,200 SAM sites deployed throughout the Soviet Union, including systems such as the SA-5 with its area defense capability.

Against a well-developed ATBM network, NATO would no doubt still be able to destroy Soviet or Pact targets by saturating local defenses with larger numbers of missiles or by using longer-range strategic ballistic missiles. And depending on how good Soviet air defenses become, cruise missiles might also get through. One must recognize, however, that these are very different strike plans from what many in NATO have thought appropriate in the past. Indeed, by the logic of those who argue that the *Soviets* would be deterred from selective nuclear strikes if NATO ATBMs forced them to enlarge nuclear strikes and raise collateral damage, so too would NATO presumably be deterred from its own selective strike options by comparable Soviet defenses. NATO's nuclear use plans in part embody deterrence theories, of which there are many, and in part the delicate political balance among allies with differing sensitivities and sensibilities. Vigorous debate has occurred over whether "limited" nuclear conflict is feasible or desirable. Nevertheless, the ability to carry out selective strikes is important to the political cohesion of NATO, and certainly more than it is to the Soviets or the Warsaw Pact. Even with the spread of ATBMs across Soviet and Pact territory, undoubtedly some targets will remain lightly protected or unprotected. But NATO's nuclear escalation choices could be increasingly dictated by Soviet ATBM decisions, not by NATO's preferences.

THE CRITERION OF COST-EFFECTIVENESS

The foregoing shows that questions regarding TBMs and ATBMs cannot be answered in isolation but must be addressed in the context of the overall defense of NATO. Allowing these matters to be "decided" through the accretion of the national planning decisions of sixteen separate alliance members will not be a rational solution, geared to the needs of the Alliance as a whole. In the case of ATBM, significant differences in the perception of the air threat among member nations also hamper common decisionmaking. Great Britain, for example, is not—and has never been—keen about ATBM, and in the Netherlands, an initial attitude favorable to ATBM has gradually given way to reluctance and reservation as the financial implications have tempered enthusiasm.

Budgetary implications and uncertainties about whether and when the TBM threat will emerge are likely to result in only modest ATBM investments, if any, in the short run. It seems unwise in any case to spend much on technologies that cope only with one particular threat. A variety of relatively cheap measures such as dispersal, rapid repair, hardening, or redundancy offer for the time being an effective answer to different kind of threats. The vulnerability of aircraft on the ground, the burden of operations at damaged airfields, and the efficiency of air defense missions could also be tackled by the acquisition of more air-refueling tankers.[25] Because the bulk of the air threat consists of the follow-on attack by aircraft, expansion and modernization of "conventional" air defenses will remain high on any list of priorities. Such an effort will reduce the effects of Soviet TBMs, as well.

Assuming that the Soviet Union wants to force the West to spend money on a variety of defensive measures rather than on other things, ballistic missiles will continue to be a part of the Soviet air operation.[26] It is wrong to state this part of the total air threat in percentages, say 5 or 10 percent as is sometimes heard. Rather, the question is how many time-sensitive, high value targets NATO must defend under all circumstances. If other methods are insufficient at some point in the future, an ATBM capability, however expensive it may be, can become a cost-effective way to safeguard those absolute operational needs.

Exploiting the West's technological superiority over the Soviet Union is unquestionably one way to redress the Alliance's shortcomings in conventional forces. Technology is a "force multiplier." But too often, advanced technologies have been introduced without a thorough, prior analysis of their impact in a military-operational sense. The utility of new weapons system technology cannot and should not be taken as self-evident. A new technology can be decisive only if one (but not both) of the opponents possesses the know-how. Such a condition is rare in the military-technical race between East and West; the advantage is temporary at most. In addition, the improvements in weapons that result from incorporating new technologies in them tend to exhibit a declining return on investment: The marginal operational improvements become ever smaller while the costs of further technological refinement rise sharply. New technologies must be adopted selectively, not simply because they are technologically feasible or available.

For the time being, a prudent, gradual approach limited to ATBM research and testing seems reasonable. What NATO should not do is to produce an endless list of so-called key targets and then ask for thousands and thousands of ATBM systems. Such an enormous capability NATO cannot afford, and it could be justified only on the unrealistic, worst-case scenario of an attack-out-of-the-blue. In all likelihood, NATO will have warning time, and alerted critical targets will be dispersed, protected, and made combat ready. From a European perspective one might add that such great numbers of ATBMs may give rise to thought of "conventionalizing" the war by denying "selective" nuclear options to the Soviets. This would be a very unattractive course, one that gives a false sense of security and that could never be justified on grounds of cost-effectiveness.

All this being said, one must come back to a central fact about NATO. However solid an "objective" analysis of the military-operational and organizational-financial aspects of ATBM for the alliance may be, it is not international but national planning that prevails in Brussels. The individual nations determine which force proposals from the major NATO commanders they are willing to accept as force goals. National views and national interests—political, industrial, interservice—will ultimately shape the outcome. In that sense, the influence of SACEUR as allied operational commander and the possibility of international funding by means of the infrastructure fund are limited. Some member states will be more, others less inclined to see the need for ATBM or to pay for it. Smaller countries are not likely to take the lead; they might support an initiative taken by medium-powers and the United States, but quite likely in a modest and reluctant way. For the Alliance, the case of ATBM still seems to be very open.

NOTES

1. General Bernard W. Rogers, "NATO's Conventional Defense Improvement Initiative—A New Approach to an Old Challenge," *NATO's Sixteen Nations*, July 1986, pp. 14–22.

2. Rogers, p. 20.
3. International Institute for Strategic Studies, *Strategic Survey 1985–86* (London: IISS, 1986), p. 39.
4. *The Times* (London), 12 August 1986; *Strengthening Conventional Defense and Emerging Technologies*, Report to Parliament by Minister of Defense Job De Ruiter (in Dutch), 26 June 1985; Manfred Wörner, "A Missile Defense for NATO Europe," *Strategic Review*, Winter 1986, pp. 13–20.
5. See Christopher Donnelly, "The Soviet Operational Maneuver Group, A New Challenge for NATO," *International Defense Review*, September 1982, pp. 1177–1186.
6. John Hines and Phillip A. Petersen, "Changing the Soviet System of Control," *International Defense Review*, March 1986, p. 568.
7. Karl von Clausewitz, *On War*, edited and translated by Michael Howard and Peter Paret (Princeton: Princeton University Press, 1984), p. 357.
8. H. Afheldt, *Verteidigung und Frieden* (Munich: 1976), and *Defensive Verteidigung* (Hamburg: 1983); E. Spannocchi and G. Brossolet, *Verteidigung ohne Schlacht* (Munich: 1976); Frank Barnaby and Egbert Boeker, *Defense Without Offense: Non-Nuclear Defense for Europe*, Peace Studies Paper no. 8 (London: University of Bradford, 1982); Lutz Unterseher, *Strukturwander der Verteidigung* (Opladen: Studiengruppe für Sicherheitspolitik, SAS, 1984); A. Weinstein, *Frankfurter Allgemeine Zeitung*, 28 April, 25 June, 4 July 1977; H.J. Löser, "Raumdeckende Verteidigung," *Osterreichische Militärische Zeitschrift*, no. 4, 1977; Norbert Hannig, *Abschreckung durch konventionelle Waffen, das David-Goliath Prinzip* (Berlin: 1984); "The Defense of Western Europe with Conventional Weapons," *International Defense Review*, November 1986, pp. 1435–1443.
9. Raymond Aron, *Clausewitz, Philosopher of War* (London: Routledge and Kegan Paul, 1983), p. 171.
10. Clausewitz, *On War*, p. 209.
11. Clausewitz, p. 528.
12. See Joshua Epstein, *Measuring Military Power: The Soviet Air Threat to Europe* (Princeton: Princeton University Press, 1984), pp. 196–197.
13. Dennis M. Gormley, "A New Dimension to Soviet Theater Strategy," *Orbis*, Fall 1985, p. 560. See also Gormley, Chapter 2 in this volume, for a different attack configuration.
14. Of roughly thirty-two division equivalents of ground forces deployed in West Germany, the Netherlands, and Belgium, thirteen or 40 percent are stationed in rear areas during peacetime. An additional five divisions or so of French troops are stationed in northern France. Not all of these units are in fact fully manned in peacetime.

NATO apparently plans to hold roughly one-fourth of the forces deployed after two weeks or more of mobilization as operational reserves in rear areas. The forces designated as operational reserves in the

Central Region, however, will be provided principally by the United States. U.S. reinforcements in the first several weeks of mobilization must arrive by airlift, underscoring the importance of NATO airfields and air superiority. See William P. Mako *U.S. Ground Forces and the Defense of Central Europe* (Washington, D.C.: Brookings Institution, 1983), pp. 37–38 and 52–53.

15. For discussions of NATO's reinforcement and mobilization plans, see the report of General Bernard Rogers's testimony to the U.S. Congress, Senate Committee on Armed Services, *New York Times*, 2 March 1985; the International Institute for Strategic Studies, *The Military Balance 1986–87* (London: IISS, 1986), pp. 223–227; and William P. Mako *U.S. Ground Forces and the Defense of Central Europe* (Washington, D.C.: Brookings Institution, 1983), Appendix C.

16. The U.S. Department of Defense plan is to provide six U.S. reinforcement divisions within ten days of a decision to mobilize, by airlifting them to Europe and uniting them with prepositioned equipment (U.S. Department of Defense, *Annual Report to the Congress FY 1987*, p. 235). Reportedly, each unit would require one to two days of preparation in the United States, one day of travel, and four to five days after arrival to draw equipment from storage and reach assembly areas. Although NATO's annual *Reforger* exercises practice this procedure, they have never involved more than one division. See William P. Mako, *U.S. Ground Forces and the Defense of Central Europe* (Washington, D.C.: Brookings Institution, 1983), pp. 52 and 68–71.

17. See *Defense Estimates 1987*, Summary in English, Netherlands Ministry of Defense, The Hague, 1986, pp. 6–7.

18. See Lt. Col. D.J. Alberts, USAF, "Deterrence in the 1980s: The Role of Conventional Air Power," *Adelphi Paper* no. 193 (London: International Institute for Strategic Studies, 1984), pp. 14–15.

19. See Alberts, Table 2, p. 56. William Kaufmann gives air order of battle figures for the Pact of 1,200 fighter/ground attack and 1,480 fighter aircraft on M-Day, rising to 1,780 FGA and 1,850 fighter aircraft on M+14, "Nonnuclear Deterrence," in John Steinbruner and Leon Sigal, eds., *Alliance Security. NATO and the No-First-Use Question* (Washington, DC: Brookings Institution, 1983), p. 77. The U.S. Department of Defense reports 2,000 Soviet "tactical aircraft" in the Western TVD and an additional 1,600 with non-Soviet Warsaw Pact forces (*Soviet Military Power 1987*, p. 17).

20. In estimating Soviet losses against NATO air defenses, one can look to historical precedents. The problem is determining which precedent to give attention to: U.S. bomber raids against Hanoi in December 1972 and the worst days of Allied bomber missions in World War II, for instance, or Israel's air operation against Syrian forces in the Beka'a

Valley in 1982. For an interesting argument that the Syrians' catastrophe in 1982 stemmed in part from Soviet institutional rigidities that prevented their Soviet advisers from absorbing available information on the adversary's counterair capabilities, and adapting procedures accordingly, see Benjamin Lambeth, *Moscow's Lessons from the 1982 Lebanon Air War*, RAND Report no. 3000 (Santa Monica, CA: RAND Corporation, September 1984).

Two analysts of Soviet air power have suggested that Soviet Frontal Aviation might exhaust itself within the first three to five days of conflict, simply carrying out its counterairfield and counternuclear missions — leaving perhaps 50 to 70 percent of the targets undestroyed. See Joshua Epstein, *Measuring Military Power: The Soviet Air Threat to Europe* (Princeton: Princeton University Press, 1984), Appendix C, pp. 243–245, and William Kaufmann, "Non-Nuclear Deterrence," in John Steinbruner and Leon Sigal, eds., *Alliance Security: NATO and the No-First-Use Question* (Washington, D.C.: Brookings Institution, 1983), pp. 76–77.

21. U.S. Department of Defense, *Soviet Military Power 1986*, p. 91.
22. See Catherine McArdle Kelleher, "NATO Nuclear Operations," in Ashton Carter, John Steinbruner, and Charles Zraket, eds., *Managing Nuclear Operations* (Washington, D.C.: Brookings Institution, 1987), p. 450.
23. J. Michael Legge, *Theater Nuclear Weapons and the NATO Strategy of Flexible Response* (Santa Monica, CA: RAND Corporation, 1983), pp. 17–23.
24. Manfred Wörner, "A Missile Defense for NATO Europe," *Strategic Review*, Winter 1986, p. 16.
25. The United States currently deploys a squadron of KC-135 tanker aircraft in Great Britain, which presumably could arrive over Germany within an hour. With midair refueling, aircraft could stay aloft until their weapons were used, and once the tankers arrived, could possibly get aloft from damaged airfields with shorter takeoff runs on reduced fuel loads. However, the U.S. tankers are assigned to the Strategic Air Command (SAC), and argument might be made that they should be held in reserve during conflict for possible strategic nuclear strikes by SAC aircraft. And although basing the tankers in Britain puts them farther from Soviet TBMs, it also means they may not arrive in time to help against the initial follow-on attack by Soviet Frontal Aviation. NATO might consider a mix of large and smaller tanker aircraft and perhaps dispersed basing to civil airfields.
26. NATO's decision in December 1979 to deploy both cruise missiles and ballistic missiles, for instance, was in part intended to complicate Soviet defense tasks and force Moscow to spend more money on diversifying its defense capabilities.

7 TBMS AND ATBMS
Arms Control Considerations
Ivo H. Daalder and Jeffrey Boutwell

The ATBM issue has become entangled in the arms control process in a number of ways. In the course of the Alliance debate over President Reagan's SDI—of which the ATBM matter has inevitably become a part—European governments have made it abundantly clear that they regard the survival of the ABM Treaty regime as vital. Left utterly uncontrolled, ATBMs could advance to the threshold of ABM capabilities, and at the same time depart from ABM Treaty limitations in significant ways, with mobile deployments, rapid-reload and multiple-warhead interceptors, or new technologies based on "other physical principles." At the least, ATBMs of this sort could grant a substantial R&D base in missile defense technologies that were deliberately restrained in 1972; at worst, they could establish a deployment base for strategic "breakout" from the ABM Treaty. Verifying that the treaty's limits on strategic defenses were still being honored could become exceedingly complicated—and perhaps pointless.

The pace at which ATBM technologies march is, of course, not independent of the threat they are intended to counter—tactical and theater ballistic missiles. One of the many surprises in the hectic period of U.S.-Soviet arms control talks following the Reykjavik summit in October 1986 was the growing possibility that arms control might prove an effective way of constraining the TBM threat. Yet at each step there was no assurance that a bargain on TBMs would be struck, even after Gorbachev's acceptance in July 1987 of a global ban on INF weapons and TBMs with ranges greater than 500 km. And certainly there was no assurance that the bargain that emerged would make sense from the perspective of the ATBM question. For instance, adoption of the "global double zero" proposal would still leave hundreds of shorter-range ballistic missiles in central Europe, with corresponding pressures for development and deployment of ATBMs.

What we undertake here is a clarification of ATBM issues, the ABM Treaty, and emerging limitations on INF and TBM systems. Although the development, testing, and/or deployment of *some* types of tactical missile defenses can clearly be accommodated by the ABM Treaty, others would obviously violate the treaty's terms. This conclusion, however, leaves a substantial gray area. In order to strengthen both the treaty and military stability in Europe, we propose a number of candidate limitations on both ATBMs and the ballistic missiles they are to counter.

THE ABM TREATY AND DISTINCTIONS BETWEEN ABM AND NON-ABM SYSTEMS

The ABM Treaty defines an antiballistic missile system as a system "to counter strategic ballistic missiles or their elements in flight trajectory" (Article II.1). By linking the definition of an ABM system to *strategic* ballistic missiles, the ABM Treaty leaves open the matter of defense systems capable of intercepting tactical or theater ballistic missiles. There were two reasons for this omission. First, at the time the treaty was negotiated, the U.S. Army was developing a new air defense system, the SAM-D, which was intended to intercept TBMs. So U.S. negotiators consciously sought to avoid limits on such ATBM systems.[1] Second, even if the United States had sought such limits, negotiating them would have been exceedingly difficult. All surface-to-air (SAM) defense systems have some inherent capability against ballistic missile warheads, particularly against shorter-range missile warheads that have a low reentry speed. Because neither the United States nor the Soviet Union was about to limit the deployment of SAMs, any negotiated limits on ATBM systems would have been difficult to verify. This is not to say that SAMs were not discussed during the ABM Treaty's negotiation. Quite the contrary. The United

States, for one, was concerned about the widespread Soviet deployment of air defenses, including some 10,000 SAMs. The military services and the Director of Defense Research and Engineering (DDR&E), John Foster, expressed apprehension about Soviet high-altitude SAMs, most notably the SA-5, believing that these systems could be upgraded to perform an ABM role.[2]

The ABM Treaty negotiations dealt with this "SAM-upgrade" problem by limiting the capabilities and testing of non-ABM systems and components.[3] At the insistence of the United States, the Soviet Union agreed to include Article VI in the treaty, which states in part that each party undertakes "not to give missiles, launchers, or radars, other than ABM interceptor missiles, ABM launchers, or ABM radars, capabilities to counter strategic ballistic missiles or their elements in flight trajectory and not to test them in an ABM mode." Moreover, specific limitations on radars were agreed on, to prevent the development of a possible base for nationwide ABM defense. These included limits on the number of engagement and large phased-array radars (LPARs) that could be deployed at specific ABM sites, as well as upper limits on their emitting power (Article III, Agreed Statements A, B, and F). And in recognition of the inherent ABM potential of ballistic missile early warning radars (BMEWs), each side agreed to not deploy such radars in the future, "except on locations along the periphery of its national territory and oriented outward" (Article VI).

Despite these provisions, the United States remained concerned that Soviet actions and emerging SAM capabilities might provide Moscow with a base for a nationwide ABM system. Not surprisingly, therefore, a number of compliance issues concerning the distinction between ABM and non-ABM systems were raised following the treaty's signing.

The first controversy involved Soviet use of an SA-5 air defense radar in conjunction with flight tests of strategic ballistic missiles during 1973 and 1974. In 1975 then-Secretary of Defense James Schlesinger argued before Congress that three explanations were possible for such concurrent testing: "(1) use of the radar in an instrumentation role to collect diagnostic data on reentry vehicles, (2) collection of data for use in modifying the SA-5 to achieve an ABM intercept capability, or (3) collection of data for use in developing a new, perhaps dual-role SAM and ABM system."[4] In a unilateral statement made during negotiations, shortly before the treaty was signed, the U.S. delegation had explicitly stated that the use of non-ABM radars for instrumentation and air safety purposes during strategic ballistic missile flight tests would be allowed (Unilateral Statement B). When the United States raised the matter of the SA-5 radar in the Standing Consultative Commission (SCC) in February 1975, the Soviet Union argued that the radar had indeed been used for range safety and that therefore the activity was permitted under the treaty. Nevertheless, within three weeks of the SCC meeting, the Soviet Union ceased the practice.[5] Notwithstanding this cessation, the Reagan administration, in its various reports on Soviet noncompliance, has argued that Soviet testing of various non-ABM radars means that "the USSR probably has violated the prohibition on testing SAM components in an ABM mode."[6]

The second compliance controversy concerned the development and testing of a new Soviet air defense system, designated the SA-X-12 by NATO. Within Congress and the Pentagon, assertions have been made that the Soviet Union has violated Article VI of the ABM Treaty by testing the SA-X-12 against both longer-range (the SS-4) and shorter-range (the SS-12) ballistic missiles.[7] The Reagan administration, however, while expressing concern, has not formally claimed a treaty violation. Instead it has argued that since the SA-X-12 can engage tactical ballistic missiles, it may have the capability "to intercept some types of strategic ballistic missiles." Nevertheless, the Reagan administration, which in other circumstances has seldom been reluctant to charge the Soviet Union with violating arms control agreements, concedes that current "evidence is insufficient to assess compliance with the Soviet Union's obligations under the ABM Treaty."[8] One reason for this reluctance might be that the SA-X-12, while tested against TBMs, apparently has little antimissile capability. As one administration official remarked of the SA-X-12's test record, "it hit once in about twenty times."[9]

In the summer of 1987 various reports concerning the SA-X-12 revived the compliance issue. In the 1987 edition of *Soviet Military Power*, the U.S. Department of Defense asserted that there are in fact not one but two new air defense systems, the SA-X-12A/Gladiator and the SA-X-12B/Giant. The Pentagon claimed that only the latter system "may have the potential to intercept some types of strategic ballistic missiles." According to other reports, the Soviet Union began deploying "several hundred" SA-X-12B systems in the western USSR near Mukachevo, Baranovichi, and Skrunda, the sites of three large phased-array early warning radars. Such deployments near LPARs pose compliance concerns identical to those raised by the SA-5 in the 1970s.[10]

Whatever the veracity of these various reports, the continuing development and deployment of new SAM systems with ATBM capabilities do point to the difficulties confronted in specifying and verifying distinctions between ABM and non-ABM systems. If, however, distinguishing between these two types of systems is difficult, it is not impossible. Indeed, the treaty was negotiated with the full knowledge that verifying these distinctions would not be easy. On the other hand, at the time of the ratification hearings before Congress, all administration officials, including Secretary of Defense Melvin Laird and the head of the U.S. SALT Delegation Gerard Smith, testified that the provisions in Article VI could be verified.[11]

Two different ways of differentiating between ABM-capable and non-ABM systems have been suggested: One would extract the distinction from the letter of the treaty and the other from its intent. As to the former, because ABM systems are defined as systems capable of countering *strategic* ballistic missiles or their elements in flight trajectory, defining the term *strategic* in a manner that distinguishes it from *tactical* or *theater* would be one way of dealing with the problem. As to the intent of the ABM Treaty, because the treaty intended to prevent the development of a base from which a defense of the national territory could rapidly evolve, distinguishing between systems on the basis of where they would be employed (that is, between Europe on the one hand, and the homelands of the United States and the Soviet Union on the other) is an alternative formulation.

Defining "Strategic Ballistic Missile"

There exist various legal and other definitions for the term *strategic* missile.[12] The Soviet Union has traditionally insisted on a functional definition: A strategic ballistic missile is any missile that can reach the other side's territory, including missiles based on allied territory. Strictly applied, however, this definition would prohibit the Soviets from deploying a defense to counter the Pershing II because the Pershing can reach Soviet territory and thus would be "strategic." Yet Western Europe could deploy a defense against the SS-20 because the SS-20 cannot reach the United States. This, at least from the Soviet viewpoint, as William Durch has pointed out, is a "political absurdity."[13]

In practice, in all strategic arms control agreements, the Soviet Union has accepted definitions of a strategic ballistic missile that more closely correspond to the U.S. view. One of the most explicit definitions is pegged to a missile's range capability: A land-based strategic ballistic missile is one that is capable of traveling an intercontinental distance. In the SALT I Interim Agreement, negotiated and signed at the same time as the ABM Treaty, that distance is specified as a range "in excess of the shortest distance between the northeastern border of the continental U.S. and the northwestern border of the continental USSR" (Agreed Statement A). Article II of the SALT II Treaty employs the same definition and adds more explicitly: "that is, a range in excess of 5,500 km." It is to this definition of "strategic" that Reagan Administration officials point when they argue that deployment of ATBMs, even those capable of intercepting a Soviet SS-20 (a land-based, "non-strategic" missile with a range of 5,000 km) is allowed under the terms of the treaty. Thus, in congressional hearings on ATBMs, Undersecretary of Defense Fred Iklé told Representative Duncan Hunter that "the SS-20 is not considered a strategic missile." And in answer to Representative Hunter's question, "So it is okay to take down [that is, intercept] the 20?", Iklé argued, "From that point of view, it is."[14]

The issue of defining the term *strategic ballistic missile* is, however, not as clear-cut as this statement and argument imply. In its limits on "strategic ballistic missiles," the SALT I Interim Agreement also swept in all submarine-launched ballistic missiles (SLBMs), including Soviet SLBMs with ranges no greater than 1,400 km (the SS-N-5). The later SALT II provisions on SLBMs added further complexities by defining strategic missiles according to test dates (all SLBMs flight tested after 1965) and deployment mode (all SLBMs on nuclear-powered submarines). As a practical effect, this excluded most SS-N-5s but included the SS-N-6, which had a range of 2,400 km.[15]

Although such complexities muddy the definition of a strategic missile, it must be recalled that these SALT definitions were devised in order to limit offensive missiles, not to establish fine lines of distinction among defensive systems. Appealing to such treaty provisions, or asserting range as the sole criterion for defining a strategic ballistic missile almost certainly misrepresents the intentions of the negotiating parties and would seem to be less than useful for the purpose of determining whether a missile defense system is or is not governed by the ABM Treaty.

A second place where one might appeal to the letter of the treaty in distinguishing permissible and regulated missile defenses is to use the

ABM Treaty's concept of systems "tested in an ABM mode" (Articles II and VI). The phrase "tested in an ABM mode" was not itself defined in the treaty, but the United States asserted a definition in unilateral statements during negotiations. Although avoiding specifics, the United States offered three examples of non-ABM component tests that it would consider to be in violation of the treaty (Unilateral Statement B):

- A launcher is used to launch an ABM interceptor missile;
- An interceptor missile is flight tested against a target vehicle that has a flight trajectory with characteristics of a strategic ballistic missile flight trajectory, or is flight tested in conjunction with the test of an ABM interceptor or an ABM radar at the same test range, or is flight tested to an altitude inconsistent with interception of targets against which air defenses are deployed;
- A radar makes measurements on a cooperative target vehicle with the characteristics of a strategic ballistic missile during the reentry portion of its trajectory or makes measurements in conjunction with the test of an ABM interceptor or an ABM radar at the same test range. Radars used for purposes such as range safety or instrumentation would be exempt from application of these criteria.

These standards, among others, were applied by the United States in judging Soviet test practices with the SA-5 radar and SA-X-12 air defense system.

To cope with the ambiguities of Soviet practices, the United States eventually sought clarification of the "tested in an ABM mode" provision. Pursuing the issue within the SCC, the United States negotiated two formal Agreed Statements with the Soviets, the first signed in November 1978, the second in June 1985.[16] Although both Agreed Statements remain classified, their contents can be gleaned from various public statements and reports. The June 1985 Agreed Statement is said to concern operations of non-ABM radars in conjunction with ABM radar and/or interceptor tests. In principle, the statement bans concurrent operations of air defense radars at ABM test sites, although it allows the deployment and even the operation of such radars for purposes of range air safety in order to detect errant aircraft.[17]

The November 1978 Agreed Statement is perhaps more interesting. According to a Defense Department report, the statement includes the stipulation that an interceptor missile is tested in an ABM mode once it is tested (successfully or not) against a strategic ballistic missile or its elements in flight trajectory, it being understood that this includes "ballistic target-missiles with the flight trajectory characteristics of strategic ballistic missiles or their elements in flight trajectory."[18] Hence, the 1978 Agreed Statement appears to include at least part of Unilateral Statement B made by the United States at the time of the ABM treaty negotiations. Other parts of that Unilateral Statement are, however, omitted. Most important is the absence of any reference to an interceptor missile being tested in an ABM mode if it is flight tested to an altitude inconsistent with targets against which air defenses are deployed. The reason for this omission, according to Paul Nitze, was that the treaty should not prohibit the testing of ground-based, anti-satellite interceptors. As Nitze argued, "neither the United States nor the Soviet Union considers 'flight trajectory' to include an orbit in space or 'tested in an ABM mode' to encompass tests against targets in space that do not follow a ballistic missile trajectory."[19]

Where does all this leaves us? It is clear that at the time of the treaty's signing, at least the United States believed that focussing on differences in flight characteristics between strategic and tactical missile warheads would provide verifiable distinctions between systems tested in an ABM mode and non-ABM mode. Thus, John Foster testified before Congress with respect to SAM-D that "we could test it against a tactical ballistic missile. The distinction here has to do with the *characteristics* of the ballistic flight trajectory."[20] The characteristics that Foster presumably had in mind would include such aspects of the ballistic flight trajectory as the reentry speed, reentry angle, and the altitude of the warhead at intercept (see Table 7–1). Among these, differences in reentry speed are particularly significant in defining the capabilities of a defense. The speed of an incoming target has bearing on the performance demanded of a defense system's interceptor missiles and search radar: The higher the speed of the reentry vehicle (RV), the greater the distance at which radar detection must occur and the more swiftly the interceptor must fly to the edge of its keepout zone (see Chapter Two in this volume for detailed discussion).

Unfortunately, as the data in Table 7–1 suggest, because reentry speed and missile range are related, the overlapping range capabilities of longer-range theater missiles and shorter-range strategic missiles precludes fine distinctions. The reentry speed of an SS-20 may approach that of an ICBM and may exceed that of a shorter-range SLBM. Hence, a defensive system capable of intercepting an SS-20 might be

Table 7-1. Missile and Reentry Vehicle Characteristics.[a]

Range in km	Reentry Speed km/sec	Reentry Angle degs	Apogee in km	Missile
10,000	7.2	22.6	1,325	Minuteman II
5,000	5.9	33.8	988	SS-20
4,000	5.4	36.0	813	Poseidon
2,500	4.5	39.4	560	SS-N-6
1,800	3.9	40.9	409	Pershing II
900	2.9	43.0	222	SS-12
500	2.2	43.9	120	SS-23
120	1.1	44.7	30	SS-21/Lance[b]

Source: Herbert Lin, "New Weapons Technologies and the ABM Treaty" (Cambridge, Mass.: Center for International Studies Working Paper, forthcoming), p. 64.

a. These figures assume minimum-energy trajectories in a vacuum. Atmospheric drag encountered on reentry will reduce a missile reentry vehicle's speed to a greater or lesser degree, depending on its aerodynamic characteristics.

b. The missile's trajectory is so low that it does not exit the atmosphere.

indistinguishable from a true ABM system.[21] Even at the extremes, a missile defense designed to counter the shortest range TBMs will still have some inherent capability of countering strategic missiles. There exist no specific guidelines that would determine that missile defense system X is a fully effective defense against SS-21s and SS-23s, yet utterly ineffective in countering an SS-25, let alone an SS-N-6. Indeed, any weapon system that can shoot up into the sky will have some ABM capability. Hence, in the absence of unambiguous technical distinctions between ABM and non-ABM systems, murky boundaries will persist.

Examining the ABM Treaty's Intent

If the ABM Treaty's terms do not themselves provide a clear distinction between ABM and non-ABM systems, perhaps the treaty's intent might. In this regard, it is important to note that the ABM Treaty was signed only by the United States and the Soviet Union and not by the West European allies. The treaty therefore did not intend to affect, indeed, it has no force over, the Europeans, and should any West European country feel obliged to build a missile defense—whether an ABM or an ATBM system—it can do so. Third parties are mentioned only in connection with the treaty's provision prohibiting the United

States and the Soviet Union from transferring ABM systems and components, including technology and blueprints, to third parties, and from deploying ABM systems outside their national territory (Article IX and Agreed Statement G).

What the United States and the Soviet Union did intend to do in the treaty is clearly stated in Article I.2: "Each party undertakes not to deploy ABM systems for a defense of the territory of its country and not to provide a base for such a defense." On this reading of the treaty's intent, a distinction can be made, according to an analysis by Thomas Enders, between defenses against missiles aimed at the national territory of the United States or the Soviet Union on the one hand, and defenses against missiles aimed at the territory of West European states on the other: "The ABM Treaty only imposes constraints on defense against strategic ballistic missiles targeted against U.S. or Soviet territory.... A problem would only arise [under the nontransfer clause of Article IX] if ATBM systems in Western Europe were technically capable of intercepting Soviet missiles aimed at targets in the U.S."[22]

If one accepts this interpretation of the treaty's intent quite literally, it apparently follows that the United States would be allowed to transfer to Western Europe defensive components, technologies, blueprints, and even whole systems that, if deployed in the United States, would be defined as ABM systems, but that, if deployed in Western Europe, would be incapable of defending U.S. territory against Soviet strategic ballistic missiles.

Enders's argument is, however, faulty on a number of counts. First, the ABM Treaty's provisions are categorical rather than conditional. The treaty defines an ABM system categorically as "as a system to counter strategic ballistic missiles or their elements in flight trajectory"—not conditionally as "a system to counter strategic ballistic missiles *if* headed toward the U.S. or Soviet Union." The prohibition on deploying ABM systems in Article III is equally categorical: "Each party undertakes not to deploy ABM systems or their components" except at the two regional sites (later reduced to one) and in the numerical configuration delineated in the same Article. The nontransfer provision of Article IX once again is categorical: "each party undertakes not to transfer to other States, and not to deploy outside its national territory, ABM systems or their components limited by this Treaty." Nowhere in the treaty are ABM-capable systems exempted from regulation on the condition that they not be able to intercept strategic ballistic missiles that are headed for U.S. or Soviet national territory. At the time of the ABM Treaty's ratification, U.S. spokesmen acknowledged that all missile defense systems still had to conform to treaty provisions, even if they were deployed elsewhere. In answer to a question concerning the potential deployment of SAM-D in Western Europe, for instance, Director of Defense Research John Foster stated, "If we ship it overseas to our allies, it is still within the provisions of the treaty *because* it is a non-ABM system."[23]

The categorical rather than conditional nature of the ABM Treaty provisions are important for a second reason, one that Enders ignores — that is, the geographical asymmetry of the homeland/theater distinction. The Soviet Union, as a Eurasian power, is both the homeland of one of the ABM Treaty's signatories and part of the European theater of potential conflict. The United States on the other hand is not a geographical part of the European theater. Therefore, under Enders's definition of ABM systems as defense systems that only defend U.S. or Soviet territory against a strategic ballistic missile, the United States could develop and test any ABM system or component, whether fixed or mobile land-based, air-based, sea-based, or space-based and deploy it anywhere outside of the United States, including within the European theater, as long as that system, once deployed, could not defend the United States itself against strategic ballistic missiles. The Soviet Union, on the other hand, would be banned from such actions even if it intended to deploy the system in Eastern Europe because any ABM system deployed in Eastern Europe might still be capable of defending Soviet national territory against strategic missiles.

It is improbable, to say the least, that either at the time of the treaty's signing or today the Soviet Union would accept such an asymmetrical application. This is particularly true once one examines the core intention of the ABM Treaty from which Enders's argument is derived. As noted, Article I of the treaty seeks to prevent either party from developing a base for the defense of its national territory. Yet if Enders is right, the United States, but not the Soviet Union, would be allowed to develop, test, and even manufacture and store large numbers of air-, sea-, space-, and mobile land-based ABM systems that could provide such a base, as long as the United States claimed that the systems were to be deployed only in Western Europe. Clearly this is absurd.

Surely the fundamental intent of the ABM Treaty must be kept squarely in view. Yet taken alone, the basic intent or spirit of the treaty is an insufficient guide for finding one's way through the particulars of the ATBM issue. The treaty's intent was to establish a threshold somewhere between regulated ABM activities and permissible non-ABM programs. That is the point of Article IV. But precisely where the threshold was to be, and how it was to be sustained, are not specified. Even though the maximum defensive capability of such systems is hard to define, some form of ATBM development, testing, and deployment is therefore possible under the terms of the ABM Treaty. Hence, if clear distinctions are desired in order to sustain the present ABM arms control regime, then further elaboration of the treaty's provisions is needed.

CANDIDATE LIMITATIONS ON NON-ABM SYSTEMS

In proposing specific elaborations of the treaty, we believe any new limitations on non-ABM systems should serve at least two objectives. First, candidate limitations must strengthen the treaty itself, while not forbidding currently allowable ABM development, testing, and deployment. Second, limitations on non-ABM systems should not prevent NATO from carrying out non-ABM military missions that are deemed vital to the Alliance's security.

Two such missions, in particular, should not be thwarted by candidate limitations. First, the air defense mission must remain a legitimate objective of military planning and force development. Second, in order for air defense systems to carry out their primary mission, they must first be able to protect themselves against a potential TBM threat. Hence, candidate limitations on non-ABM systems should at a minimum allow air defenses to intercept shorter-range, conventionally armed TBMs. Limitations on such defense systems could, however, be designed to preclude a defensive capability against nuclear TBMs, for the air defense mission exists principally to strengthen conventional defense, not to counter nuclear threats. The latter, as in the past, must continue to be deterred by the threat of offensive retaliation.

Of course, air defenses able to defend themselves against shorter-range TBMs could still be attacked by conventionally armed INF systems (such as the SS-20) or even by strategic ballistic missiles. Yet given the relative inaccuracy of such missiles and their importance for nuclear deterrence, it seems improbable they would be used with conventional warheads against NATO air defenses. In order to prevent erosion of the ABM Treaty regime, then, ceilings on non-ABM systems will have to be set just above what is minimally necessary for defense against shorter-range TBMs, even if that precludes defenses against longer-range TBMs.

If our objective is to buttress the ABM Treaty by banning ATBM systems that would have incidental effectiveness as ABMs, while permitting ATBMs that would be effective against shorter-range TBMs, one challenge we face is defining a standard of "effectiveness." A highly restrictive standard—banning all ATBMs that are even marginally effective as ABM systems—would in effect ban ATBMs altogether. Indeed, it would even ban modern air defense systems because almost any interceptor system will have at least *some* capability against *some* imaginable strategic ballistic missile targets, under *some* conceivable circumstances. On the other hand, a very nonrestrictive standard, allowing highly advanced ATBMs that were effective against the most sophisticated imaginable TBM threat, would permit systems with more than an incidental ABM capability. So the performance threshold must be set somewhere in between these extremes.

A standard proposed by Ashton Carter would set thresholds at the point where a defense system was able to counter the current, nonresponsive threat posed by the offensive weapons in question.[24] That is, any missile defense able to intercept a warhead from a current strategic ballistic missile, when the warhead is unaccompanied by decoys or other counterdefense measures, should be considered an effective ABM system. (For this purpose, a strategic ballistic missile would be any missile regulated by a strategic offensive arms control treaty.) Similarly, any air defense system able to intercept a TBM warhead, when that warhead is unaccompanied by decoys or counterdefense measures, should be regarded as an effective ATBM system. This is a fairly rigorous standard, but it would respect the original purpose of the ABM Treaty.

The problem posed by standards of effectiveness is rendered more difficult, and therefore more important, by the fact that effectiveness is not only related to the technical capability of the defense, but also to the desired mission of the offense. That is to say, the effectiveness of the defense is in part related to what the offense seeks to accomplish. For example, to those who believe that nuclear attacks must fulfill specific military missions, including the destruction of a few vital military facilities, even a small defensive posture with marginal ABM capability could pose severe problems for the offense if deployed around these vital targets. Such defensive systems would therefore be deemed effective. On the other hand, if all one wants to accomplish with nuclear weapons is to signal a determination to use nuclear weapons or, alternatively, to destroy the essential functioning of the opponent's society, then limited defenses will not impede the execution of those missions. In this case, such defensive deployments may be judged to be ineffective. Hence, the effectiveness of the defense, even with a given offensive capability, is very much dependent on what the desired offensive mission is.[25]

Having set out the criteria against which possible candidate limitations ought to be judged, we can now turn to proposing some possible limitations. Two complementary avenues exist for designing such limitations on defensive systems. The first would specify what is meant by "testing in an ABM mode," by exactly defining the testing parameters for defensive systems. The key to these parameters is the nature of the target vehicle used in tests. The second avenue would specify the permissible characteristics of defensive systems in a way that limits their capability to well below what is required for intercepting strategic ballistic missile RVs.

Testing in an ABM Mode

An appropriate limit on testing in an ABM mode would be linked to two characteristics of the target vehicle: its reentry speed and the altitude at which it is intercepted. As we noted earlier, the flight trajectories of TBMs differ in important respects from those of strategic ballistic missiles, including shorter-range SLBMs. The reentry speed of all current TBMs is equal to or less than 3 km/sec, while all IRBMs, SLBMs, and ICBMs have reentry speeds in excess of 4 km/sec. The 3 km/sec parameter would therefore provide us with one useful baseline.

The second characteristic of importance concerns the altitude at which the target vehicle is intercepted. Because aircraft do not generally fly at altitudes above about 30 km, testing an interceptor missile in excess of that altitude would indicate an interest in intercepting a ballistic missile (or a satellite). A 40 km altitude limit would therefore provide us with a second useful baseline. Accordingly, we propose to define *testing in an ABM mode* for interceptors as follows: *Any interceptor that is flight tested against a target vehicle flying above 40 km or at a speed in excess of 3 km/sec in any portion of its flight will be considered to have been tested in an ABM mode.*[26]

Parameter limitations on target vehicles are not, however, sufficient. Even a true ABM system could be tested against a target vehicle within these parameters, yet be capable of intercepting an RV at 80 km, flying at a speed of 7 km/sec. Hence, candidate limitations must address not only testing in an ABM mode but also the nature of the defensive system itself. The ABM Treaty sets a precedent for this: It limits characteristics of ABM launchers (by forbidding reloading), of ABM interceptors (by prohibiting multiple warheads), and of ABM radars (by limiting the power-aperture product).

Limitations on Defensive Systems

Two limitations on defensive systems suggest themselves, one on the nature of the interceptor and the other on the capability of the radar. The key determinant of a missile's ability to intercept an incoming RV is its flyout capability, a function primarily of its boost acceleration and speed at burnout. Limits on either or both of these interceptor characteristics will thus affect an interceptor's range at which, and the speed with which, it can reach an intercept point. In order to enforce a meaningful keepout zone against a nuclear-armed RV from a strategic ballistic missile reentering at a speed of 7 km/sec, an interceptor's range and/or speed must be greater than when attempting to intercept a conventionally armed TBM arriving at 1 to 3 km/sec.

We can find an appropriate baseline parameter by looking at the present capabilities of NATO's Patriot system. As the current Alliance debate on ATBMs indicates, a slightly modified Patriot has at least some ATBM capability against the current Soviet TBM threat. The Patriot interceptor's maximum burnout speed has been variously reported at Mach 3 (1 km/sec) to Mach 6 (2 km/sec), and its acceleration potential at 10 G to 30 G. Current or soon-to-be deployed Soviet SAMs are reportedly somewhat more capable, particularly in terms of their acceleration potential. An appropriate candidate limitation for non-ABM interceptors might therefore be set at the capability of these Soviet SAMs. Accordingly, *any interceptor missile with a burnout speed exceeding 2 km/sec or an acceleration capability greater than 100 G will be considered to be an ABM interceptor.*[27]

The second characteristic of defensive systems appropriate for limitation concerns the radar. The ABM Treaty limited ABM radars according to their power-aperture (PA) product; non-ABM radars might be limited in the same fashion. Again, a useful baseline would be current SAM capabilities. The Patriot radar has a PA product of 45,000 watt-meters-squared, which would provide us with an approximate boundary for the PA product of non-ABM systems.[28] A slightly higher boundary can be set, although as a practical matter, a SAM/ATBM radar that must be mobile (to assure its own survival and protect mobile targets) cannot have an excessively large antenna anyway. In order to ensure a common definition of the non-ABM/ABM radar threshold, however, a precise parameter is desirable. Accordingly, *a mobile radar with a power-aperture product in excess of 50,000 watt-meters-squared will be considered to be an ABM radar.*[29]

Yet limiting the capability of mobile radars still leaves open the possibility that the SAM/ATBM unit might be provided with relevant data from much larger radars that can detect and track the incoming missile or RV at much greater distance, calculate its approximate impact point and time of arrival, and "hand off" the data to the smaller radar located at the interceptor site, which would then guide the interceptor to the target. The provision of such "cues" to the SAM/ATBM unit would significantly enhance the defense system's overall capability, even to a point where it could possibly engage shorter-range SLBMs or ICBM RVs with low reentry speeds. The cueing problem was recognized at the time of the ABM treaty's negotiation and led the United States to declare that it would consider the deployment of air defense interceptors near early warning radars to be an indication of an intent to use these SAMs in an ABM mode.[30]

In the future, cues might be provided by space- or air-based sensors of types envisioned for the SDI, and this would make the problem more difficult still. Under the ABM Treaty regime, large, fixed, land-based surveillance radars are generally vulnerable to attack in the early stages of a nuclear conflict (hence the value of the Treaty requirement that early-warning radars be located "along the periphery . . . and oriented outward") and thus are not reliable components of an ABM network, so long as they remain unprotected by interceptors. Air- or space-based sensors might not have such vulnerabilities. Their deployment would therefore undermine the very candidate limitations we are proposing.

The potential problem of cueing is, however, not as severe as the above might imply. The ABM Treaty, in Article IX prohibits the deployment of ABM-capable radars outside of the national territory of the United States or the Soviet Union. Similarly, Article V prohibits the deployment of mobile land-, sea-, air-, or space-based ABM-capable radars. Hence, an ATBM system could only be cued by existing land-based radars, which are too far removed from the potential trajectory of the incoming TBMs to be of much use, or by existing space-based early-warning sensors, which are not likely to be able to track TBMs even if they could detect their launch.[31] As a result, the cueing problem virtually disappears as long as current restrictions on ABM radars are maintained. Our proposals for candidate limitations of ATBM systems, of course, are predicated on the assumption that the current ABM regime will be upheld. Should the treaty instead be abandoned, amended, or modified in such a way as to allow limited or more expansive ABM deployments, then efforts at limiting the potential ABM capability of non-ABM systems would be devoid of purpose.

LIMITATIONS ON THE TBM THREAT

Limitations on ATBMs will be much easier to justify and sustain if they are complemented by constraints on theater and tactical ballistic missiles. Prior to 1987, when the Soviets agreed in principle to a treaty linking limitations on shorter-range missiles with those being discussed for intermediate-range missiles (INF), there seemed little chance that arms control would address the broader span of TBM threats. Subsequent progress on an INF/TBM agreement banning all ballistic missiles with ranges between 500 and 5,000 km has clearly extended the boundaries of what now seems possible with arms control.

This is not the place to dwell at length on the military and political merits of first reaching agreement on systems with ranges of 500 to 5,000 km, while Soviet advantages continue to exist in other TBMs and conventional forces. In the best of all possible worlds, agreements on conventional forces that reduced the ability of Soviet forces to mount massive offensive operations against NATO would have been implemented simultaneously with large reductions in theater nuclear forces. And it would have been preferable for agreements on nuclear forces to have dealt at least as much with militarily less useful nuclear artillery as with TBMs. Yet too often "the best is enemy of the good," and a U.S.-Soviet agreement that reverses thirty-five years of nuclear buildup in Europe by eliminating two major weapons categories is no small achievement.

More than that, the INF agreement will help in one of the most important ATBM problems—that is, enforcing distinctions between ATBM and ABM capabilities. The more demanding performance requirements for intercept of longer-range INF and TBM weapons invites the deployment of defenses that would overlap, in some respects, systems appropriate for strategic missile defense. With such missiles banned and dismantled under an INF accord, that provocation for ATBMs will be removed. Again, this is no small achievement.

At the same time, however, the INF treaty, by allowing the Soviets to deploy unbounded numbers of shorter-range TBMs, is surely a mixed blessing for NATO, fueling the Alliance's anxieties about the strategy of flexible response, the Alliance's ability to field a credible conventional deterrent, and the need for defenses against the shortest-range missiles. Accordingly, we propose that limits be applied as well to these shortest-ranged TBMs, which for clarity here we will label as SRBMs—that is, ground-based ballistic missiles with ranges under 500 km. Our proposals for limits on SRBMs are attentive to the effects not only on the Soviet TBM threat but also on NATO's own SRBM options and the impact on incentives for ATBM deployments. As should be the case generally with arms control agreements, the primary goal of our candidate SRBM regime is that of promoting stability and reducing pressures and opportunities for surprise attack in a time of crisis.

Specifically, we propose that the sides limit SRBMs in the following ways:

- Each side would be allowed to deploy a total of only 300 SRBM launchers and missiles with ranges between 100 and 300 km in Europe and the European USSR. This limit could be extended to cover all of the Soviet Union and North America. However, NATO's purposes would be served if the limit applied to Europe and the Soviet Union West of the Urals.
- All SRBMs with ranges greater than 300 km, and their launchers, would be banned. The term range here would generally refer to

maximum range on a minimum energy trajectory, although it would be sensible to adopt the definition of range agreed on between the sides in the context of the INF treaty (plus accompanying limits on deployed or tested missile throw-weight and launch-weight that might improve verification).
- Deployment of permitted SRBM launchers and missiles with ranges between 100 and 300 km would be banned in the region lying 100 km on either side of the border separating West Germany from East Germany and Czechoslovakia (see Figure 7–1).
- Within these limits, modernization and replacement of SRBMs could take place.

The rationale for these particular limits can be set out briefly. First, with respect to the 300 km SRBM range limit, if TBMs with ranges greater than 500 km are to be banned under an INF/TBM accord, it is obviously desirable to establish a range buffer between permitted and prohibited TBMs. Restricting permitted SRBMs to a 300 km range does that. At the same time, it is desirable within NATO's flexible response strategy for the Alliance to have forces that can convincingly threaten selective nuclear strikes at Warsaw Pact targets. SRBMs have the appropriate combination of accuracy, penetrability, secure command-and-control, target flexibility, and survivability to do this. And with a secure SRBM force, the Alliance could hold fewer aircraft and battlefield artillery units in reserve for nuclear missions, freeing them instead to bolster conventional strength. A 300 km SRBM range would enable strikes launched from permitted deployment areas in West Germany to reach as far as the Polish border. NATO would, of course, retain longer-range forces in the U.S. SLBMs assigned to SACEUR, in British and French independent nuclear forces, and in tactical aircraft.

Second, with respect to the ban on deployment within 100 km of the border between the blocs, the purpose is to impede a Warsaw Pact surprise SRBM attack against NATO rear areas. To reach the deepest targets with SRBMs, the Pact would have to move its forces forward prior to attack, risking NATO detection and warning. NATO, as the defender in a conflict, would be well advised in any case to keep its own SRBMs well back from the battlefield area to assure their survival, whether they are assigned to conventional or nuclear missions. So a 100 km buffer zone demands little from NATO.

Third, with respect to the limit of 300 on SRBM launchers and missiles, the purpose is to constrain the Warsaw Pact's capacity for

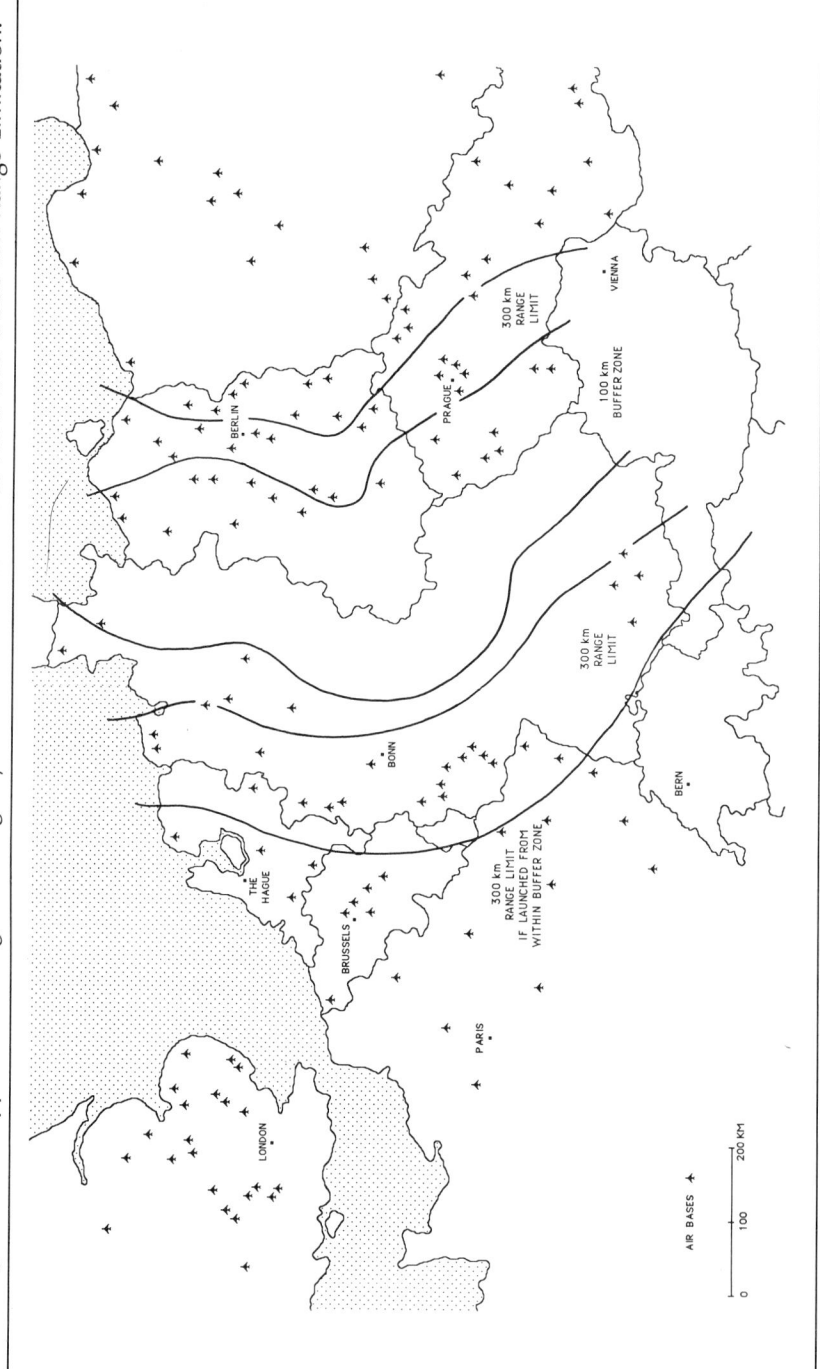

Figure 7-1. Approximate Target Coverage by NATO and Warsaw Pact TBMs with a 300 Km Range Limitation.

surprise barrage attack against the whole list of NATO targets, without at the same time cutting so deeply into SRBM forces that either side is denied an acceptable in-theater nuclear deterrent capability.

At present, the NATO SRBM force consists of 108 Lance missile launchers deployed in central Europe with U.S. forces, and an added fifty-five Lance launchers deployed by the European allies. The United States has another thirty-two Lance launchers deployed with its forces outside of Europe. Lance has a range of 120 km, and each mobile launcher carries one missile and is accompanied in the field by a support vehicle with two additional reload missiles. The Lance first entered NATO service in 1976 and is currently undergoing modernization that will keep it in service until the mid-1990s. The United States has initiated development of a successor for Lance, to be ready for deployment by the late 1990s. The total stock of Lance missiles currently held by the United States is about 1,450; the European allies originally purchased about 550 Lance missiles. Under the limitations being proposed here, NATO countries could expand the number of Lance launchers or follow-ons from the current 163 to 300 but would have to reduce the available stocks of reload missiles in Europe.

On the Warsaw Pact side, the Soviets currently have about 460 launchers for the SS-21/Frog missiles in Eastern Europe and the Soviet theater commands (TVDs) opposite NATO; its Warsaw Pact allies deploy another 120 launchers. The Soviets have an additional 340 Frog launchers in the Southern and Far Eastern TVDs. The Frog launchers would be exempt from SRBM limits (as would any similar NATO system) because the Frogs have a range of only 70 km. Thus far the Soviets have replaced about 130 Frog launchers with the 120 km range SS-21, presumably with several reload missiles per launcher. As with NATO, under the limits proposed here, the Soviets could continue these conversions up to 300 launchers but would have to eliminate reload missile stocks.

The utility for NATO in a 300 launcher and missile limit is evident from the TBM inventory requirements for a massive attack on prime NATO targets. If one takes as an example Dennis Gormley's hypothetical TBM scenario, the Soviets would allocate eight missiles each to NATO's twenty-five main airfields, another two missiles each to some thirty (or one-third) of NATO's SAM batteries, and two missiles each against the vulnerable dispersal equipment at fifteen of NATO's eighty-plus nuclear storage sites (see Chapter 3 in this volume). This is a rather limited attack. It would leave a substantial portion of NATO targets uncovered, and if NATO were to undertake a variety of passive defense measures, the missiles needed to disrupt operations at even these limited targets could easily double. Nonetheless, this limited scenario requires 290 missiles, which means—given the time evidently required to reload launchers—a prompt attack on all these targets essentially requires 290 launchers. Holding Warsaw Pact SRBMs to 300 launchers and missiles, therefore, would substantially confine the threat, even if all 300 were allocated to conventional attack.[32]

There is some likelihood that the Soviets would instead hold a significant portion of their permitted SRBMs as an in-theater nuclear reserve. Under the INF treaty, the Soviets are prepared to destroy all their SS-20 launchers, including some 270 deployed in the European USSR. With three warheads per missile and perhaps two to three missiles per launcher, the SS-20 force represents a substantial theater nuclear reserve. The Soviets can reallocate some NATO targets to ICBMs, once the SS-20s are dismantled. But presumably they will still want an in-theater nuclear reserve, in part for institutional reasons (to give theater commanders nuclear missiles under their own authority), and in part because launching strategic missiles at Europe from Soviet territory risks rapid escalation. A ceiling of 300 SRBM launchers and missiles would force a hard choice on the Soviets between nuclear and conventional missions, one that works to NATO's benefit.

In proposing these limits, we acknowledge several potential difficulties. One is the disposition of French SRBMs. France currently deploys forty-four Pluton launchers, with a range of 120 km, and has plans for a replacement missile, the Hades, with a range of 350 km. Although the Soviet Union dropped its traditional demand for taking French and British long-range nuclear forces "into account" in its INF and long-range TBM proposals, it may not be so willing in the context of an SRBM accord to exempt French missiles (as the Soviet posture on West Germany's Pershing IAs perhaps showed). This problem is not intractable, however. France would have to limit the range of the Hades, but the other Allies could either reduce their own launchers to accommodate French systems within the 300 limit, or grant an additional forty-four launchers to *non-Soviet* Pact forces in compensation. A ceiling on total Pact SRBMs is worth having, even at 344 rather than 300 launchers.

A second difficulty is verification. Whether or not monitoring of Warsaw Pact SRBM activities is (or could be) sufficiently exact to enforce limits on numbers and deployment areas of SRBM launchers and missiles involves details of intelligence methods about which we are uncertain. We can think of a variety of verification provisions that might help, including exchange of data bases on missile and launcher characteristics and on launcher deployment areas; dismantling and destruction of all support vehicles for carrying missile reloads; tests of permitted SRBMs only at designated test ranges; and prior notification of tests. But it must be conceded that an arms control regime that limits rather than bans weapons, especially mobile and concealable systems such as SRBM launchers, is problematic.[33] If the Soviets were able to deploy rapidly reloadable launchers and significant numbers of reload missiles plus their transport vehicles without detection, it obviously would nullify the merits of a formal agreement on SRBM limits.

A third difficulty is that constraints on SRBM deployments might appear to improve the potential effectiveness of ATBM defenses against nuclear-armed SRBMs, thus reinforcing rather than undercutting the incentives for vast ATBM programs. Unlike the current situation, where NATO faces over a thousand SRBMs, it might be argued that ATBMs could make a decisive difference when facing a "limited" threat of 300 SRBMs. Such arguments seem unpersuasive, however. Even if ATBMs could be effective against nuclear-armed SRBMs, such arguments would have force only if intercepting just this one form of nuclear weapon, SRBMs, made a crucial difference in NATO's security. Otherwise, an effective NATO ATBM would only compel the Soviets to use other in-theater delivery modes. For the same reason, it would be hard to justify constructing an ATBM network so that it could survive and operate in the rigors of a nuclear conflict, unless it would make a decisive contribution.

A final difficulty is that these SRBM constraints may be overtaken by emerging technologies. For instance, in formulating SRBM limits, we have distinguished between ground-launched ballistic missiles and other missile threats because our principal concern is to constrain the *ballistic* threat in order to support distinctions between ATBM and ABM defenses and diminish NATO's need for expensive investment in ATBMs. The Soviets might respond to SRBM limits by substituting ground- or air-launched cruise missiles for the conventional mission. In turn, this would force NATO into heavier investment in air defenses, yet this is a preferable focus for NATO resources because air defenses cope with more than one threat. But we recognize that future defenses against sophisticated aircraft and cruise missiles may impinge on distinctions among SAMs, ATBMs, and ABMs that we wish to encourage. As technologies evolve, therefore, the adequacy of SRBM limitations will have to be reassessed.

NON-EUROPEAN DEPLOYMENT OF TBMS

Both the United States and USSR have provided SRBM systems to a number of third countries. Moscow has transferred at least twelve SS-21 launchers to Syria, and a number of states in addition to Syria have older Frog and Scud launchers (North Korea, Egypt, Iran, Iraq, Libya, and South Yemen). The United States, for its part, has transferred perhaps twenty to thirty Lance launchers to Israel, and Israel has its own Ze'ev (Wolf) TBM and is in the process of extending the range of its Jericho missile from 480 km to 1,400 km. Also, U.S. forces in South Korea have twelve aging Honest John launchers, with a range of 40 km.

There are two potential problems posed by non-European SRBM forces. One is the extent to which such forces might be rapidly reintroduced into the European theater with decisive military effect. We would judge this to be highly improbable, risking loss of strategic surprise and granting the opponent increased opportunity for dispersal and other responses. The second problem is that widespread availability of SRBMs outside of Europe could add pressures for development and deployment of ATBM systems, both for transfer to non-European allies and for protection of home territory (the Soviets, for example, have already protested the potential threat posed by Israel's Jericho missile to southern regions of the USSR).[34] Again, we think it improbable that either alliance would develop ATBM programs merely for third parties or against such remote third-party threats. Reaching agreement on SRBM forces in Europe need not be postponed, therefore, until the limits can be made "global."

CONCLUDING REMARKS

Over the past fifteen years, the ABM Treaty regime has served the Alliance's strategy of flexible response well. ATBM systems pose a potential challenge to the treaty, unless specific limitations can be devised to strengthen the distinctions between ABM and non-ABM capable systems. By proposing what we judge are verifiable distinctions of such systems, by putting forward specific limits on allowable non-ABM system testing and by suggesting collateral limitations on TBM forces, we have pointed out ways in which the ABM treaty regime could be reinforced. Yet proposing measures is one thing, enacting them quite another. The latter will depend on a process to implement the measures and, more important, on a willingness to do so. As to the process, constraints on ATBMs and SRBMs could be incorporated into other agreements. A specific definition of what would constitute "testing in an ABM mode" could be worked out within the Standing Consultative Commission, established by Article XIII of the ABM Treaty. Limits on the characteristics of non-ABM systems could be written into the treaty as an amendment, a process described in Article XIV. Alternatively, a protocol could be adopted, along the lines of the 1974 Protocol that limited each party to one ABM site. The limitations on SRBMs could be appended to an INF/TBM agreement.

Above all, a political willingness to strengthen the foundations of flexible response, of which the ABM Treaty has become an important part, is needed. Without such a willingness, there is little hope. And this leaves us with the final thought that the vigorous pursuit of strategic defenses that marks the efforts of the Reagan administration cannot be divorced from the issue of ATBMs and the flexible response strategy of which ATBMs would be a part. The pursuit of SDI conveys a political desire to weaken rather than strengthen the ABM Treaty. In light of the heavy political investment the Alliance has in flexible response, and the absence of clear alternatives that could command broad European support, it is doubtful whether the Alliance's political cohesion can be sustained without vigorous arms control efforts to preserve the ABM Treaty.

NOTES

1. See the testimony of John B. Rhinelander in U.S. Congress, Senate, *Strategic Defense Initiative*, Hearings before the Subcommittee on Strategic and Theater Nuclear Forces, Committee on Armed Services, 99th Congress, 1st Session, 21 November 1985, pp. 250-51.
2. DDR&E John D. Foster expressed this concern even after the treaty was signed. See his testimony in U.S. Congress, Senate, *Military Implications of the Treaty on the Limitations of Anti-Ballistic Missile Systems and the Interim Agreement on Limitations of Strategic Offensive Arms*, Hearings,

Committee on Armed Services, 92nd Congress, 2nd Session, June-July 1972, pp. 259–60. On the debate over the SA-5 system, see Lawrence Freedman, *U.S. Intelligence and the Soviet Strategic Threat* (Princeton: Princeton University Press, 1986), pp. 91–94, and John D. Prados, *The Soviet Estimate: U.S. Intelligence Analysis and Russian Military Strength* (New York: Dial Press, 1982), pp. 155–171.

3. See Gerard Smith, *Doubletalk: The Story of the First Strategic Arms Limitation Talks* (Garden City, NJ: Doubleday, 1980), pp. 269 and 301–318.
4. See Schlesinger's testimony in U.S. Congress, Senate, *Soviet Compliance with Certain Provisions of the 1972 SALT I Agreements*, Hearings before the Subcommittee on Arms Control, Committee on Armed Services, 94th Congress, 1st Session, 6 March 1975, p. 4.
5. See Sidney Graybeal and Michael Krepon, "Making Better Use of the Standing Consultative Commission" *International Security*, Fall 1985, p. 191, and Gloria Duffy, et al., *Compliance and the Future of Arms Control*, Report of a Working Group, Center for International Security and Arms Control, Stanford University, 12 February 1987, pp. II–27ff.
6. This is repeated in the Administration's recent report, *The President's Unclassified Report on Soviet Noncompliance with Arms Control Agreements* (Washington, D.C.: Office of the Press Secretary, the White House, 10 March 1987), p. 9.
7. Both Senator Dan Quayle and Richard Cooper, then director of the Defense Advanced Research Projects Agency (DARPA), have claimed that the SA-X-12 was "tested in an ABM mode." For Quayle's statement, see U.S. Congress, Senate, *Strategic Defense Initiative*, p. 258. Cooper is cited in *Can America Catch Up?* (Washington, D.C.: Committee on the Present Danger, 1984), p. 25. See also U.S. Arms Control and Disarmament Agency, *Soviet Noncompliance* (Washington, D.C.: Arms Control and Disarmament Agency, 1 February 1986), p. 5; U.S. Department of Defense and Department of State, *Soviet Strategic Defense Programs* (Washington, D.C.: Departments of Defense and State, October 1985), p. 20; Thomas Longstreth, John Pike, and John Rhinelander, *The Impact of U.S. and Soviet Ballistic Missile Defense Programs on the ABM Treaty* (Washington, D.C.: National Campaign to Save the ABM Treaty, March 1985), pp. 55–56; and George Schneiter, "The ABM Treaty Today," in Ashton Carter and David Schwartz, eds. *Ballistic Missile Defense*, (Washington, DC: Brookings Institution, 1984), p. 239.
8. *The President's Unclassified Report on Soviet Noncompliance*, p. 10.
9. Cited by Michael Gordon, "Defense Dept. Is Rebuffed on Soviet ABM Threat" *New York Times* 5 March 1987, p. A10.
10. See Steven Zaloga, "Giant Strides for the SA-12 Air Defense System," *Jane's Defense Weekly*, 8 August 1987, pp. 226–227; U.S. Department of

Defense, *Soviet Military Power 1987*, p. 61; and Bill Gertz, "New Soviet Deployment May Breach ABM Treaty," *Washington Times*, 31 July 1987, p. 10.

11. See for example the assurances by Laird and Smith in U.S. Congress, Senate, *Military Implications of the Treaty on the Limitation of Anti- Ballistic Missile Systems*, pp. 53, 153, and 287.
12. See also Jim Steinberg, "ATBM and the ABM Treaty" Paper presented at a workshop on "The Role of ATBMs in NATO Strategy," International Institute for Strategic Studies, London, 5 December 1986, and Michael Rühle, "Anti-Missile Defense in Europe and the ABM Treaty," *Strategic Review*, Spring 1987, pp. 51–52.
13. William J. Durch, *The ABM Treaty and Western Security* (Cambridge, Mass.: Ballinger, 1987), pp. 121.
14. U.S. Congress, House, *U.S. Nuclear Forces and Arms Control Policy*, Hearings before the Defense Policy Panel of the Committee on Armed Services, 99th Congress, 2nd Session, 4 June 1986, p. 49.
15. The SALT II limitations excluded all SLBMs that were then deployed on diesel-powered submarines (SSBs) and only counted SLBMs deployed on nuclear-powered submarines (SSBNs). At the time of the treaty's signing, some SS-N-5s were deployed on SSBNs and thus counted, while the remainder were deployed in SSBs and thus excluded. Today, however, all remaining SS-N-5s are deployed in SSBs. All range figures are from International Institute for Strategic Studies, *The Military Balance 1986–87* (London: IISS, 1986), p. 205.
16. See Graybeal and Krepon, "Making Better Use of the Standing Consultative Commission," p. 190, and John B. Rhinelander, "Specific Proposals to Strengthen the ABM Treaty," paper presented at a meeting of U.S. and Soviet legal experts sponsored by the Lawyer's Alliance for Nuclear Arms Control, Moscow, 24–30 March 1986, p. 2.
17. See Richard N. Haass, "Verification and Compliance" in Albert Carnesale and Richard N. Haass, eds. *Superpower Arms Control* (Cambridge: Ballinger, 1987), p. 325, note 17. A more generous interpretation of the understanding is provided in R. Jeffrey Smith, "Arms Agreement Breathes New Life into SCC," *Science*, 9 August 1985, pp. 535–36.
18. On the contents of the 1978 Agreed Statement of the SCC, see U.S. Department of Defense, *Report to Congress on the Strategic Defense Initiative* (Washington, D.C.: Department of Defense, June 1986), p. C–7, and Paul H. Nitze, "Permitted and Prohibited Activities Under the ABM Treaty," speech before the International Law Weekend Group, New York, 31 October 1986, *Current Policy* no. 866 (Washington, D.C.: U.S. Department of State, 1986), p. 2.
19. Nitze, "Permitted and Prohibited Activities Under the ABM Treaty," p. 2.

20. U.S. Congress, Senate, *Military Implications of the Treaty on the Limitations of Anti-Ballistic Missile Systems*, p. 259.
21. See also Steven Weiner, "Systems and Technology," in Carter and Schwartz, eds., *Ballistic Missile Defense*, pp. 73–75.
22. See Thomas Enders, *Missile Defense as Part of a NATO Extended Air Defense* (Bonn: Konrad Adenauer Stiftung, Interne Studien 2, 1986), pp. 56–64. Passages quoted here are from pp. 58 and 61.
23. U.S. Congress, Senate, *Military Implications of the Treaty on the Limitations of Anti-Ballistic Missile Systems*, p. 259, emphasis added.
24. Ashton B. Carter, "The Structure of Possible U.S.-Soviet Agreements Regarding Missile Defense," revised draft (dated 17 February 1987) of a paper presented at the Aspen Strategy Group workshop on "The SDI and American Security," Aspen, CO., 10–15 August 1986, pp. 6–7.
25. For an elaboration of this argument in the context of the European theater, see Ivo H. Daalder, "The Implication of Soviet Defenses for NATO's Nuclear Escalation Strategy," paper presented at an International Institute for Strategic Studies' workshop on "The Role of ATBMs in NATO's Strategy," London, 5 December 1986.
26. These two baselines were at one time proposed by the U.S. Department of Defense as a way of judging compliance with Article VI of the ABM Treaty. See Longstreth, Pike, and Rhinelander, *The Impact of U.S. and Soviet BMD Programs*, p. 56. A number of analysts have proposed similar baselines. See for example, Longstreth, Pike and Rhinelander, p. 75 (although they would limit target speed to 2 km/sec); Carter, "The Structure of Possible U.S.-Soviet Agreements Regarding Missile Defense," p. 30 (with 40 to 80 km and 2 to 3 km/sec); and John Pike, "Limitations on Space Weapons: A Preliminary Assessment," (Washington, D.C.: Federation of American Scientists, 22 February 1987), p. 24 (with 4 km/sec).

    As noted, tests of a ground-based antisatellite system (ASAT) might also involve intercepting a target vehicle above 40 km in altitude, with a speed in excess of 3 km/sec. If ASAT tests are to be exempted, the burden of proof should clearly lie with the side claiming to have conducted a ground-based ASAT test rather than a SAM/ATBM interceptor missile test in a prohibited ABM mode. Evidence that the side performing the test could present to the other side could include the fact that the interceptor was never tested or deployed in conjunction with any air defense or ATBM radars, launchers, or other components; tested or deployed in a mobile mode; tested or deployed on a rapid-reload launcher; tested or deployed outside of national territory; tested or deployed at an ABM or ATBM test range.
27. See Wim A. Smit, "The Patriot Missile—An Arms Control Impact Assessment" in Frank Barnaby and Marlies ter Borg, eds., *Emerging*

Technologies and Military Doctrine (New York: St. Martin's Press, 1986), p. 161, and John W. R. Taylor, "Gallery of Soviet Aerospace Weapons," *Air Force Magazine*, March 1986, p. 98. Taylor cites performance figures for the SA-10 of Mach 6 for burnout speed and 100 G for acceleration capacity.

Our candidate limitations here are signficantly less than the fly-out capabilities of ABM interceptors from the 1970s, such as the U.S. Sprint missile. Ashton Carter suggests a similar limit for the burnout speed and the acceleration potential (Carter, "The Structure of Possible U.S.-Soviet Agreements regarding Missile Defense," p. 30). Herbert Lin suggests tighter limits of Mach 4 (1.3 km/sec) for burnout speed and 50 G for acceleration potential (Lin, "New Weapons Technologies and the ABM Treaty," Cambridge, Mass.: Center for International Studies Working Paper, forthcoming, p. 32).

28. On Patriot's power-aperture product, see Chapter Two in this volume; John Pike, "Limitations on Space Weapons," p. 34; and Wim Smit, "The Patriot Missile," p. 162. Herbert Lin, however, arrives at a figure of 100,000 watt-meters-squared. See Lin, "New Weapons Technologies and the ABM Treaty," p. 33.

29. There is a potential conflict between the limits we are proposing here and the emerging technologies for naval air defense, such as the U.S. *Aegis* system. The interceptor missile associated with *Aegis* (the SM-2, in conventional and nuclear warhead versions) apparently has a peak speed of about Mach 2.5 and thus conforms to our proposed limit, but the *Aegis* shipboard, phased-array radar might not. The United States reviewed the *Aegis* system for its compliance with the ABM Treaty before it was deployed and concluded that "the *Aegis*/nuclear SM-2 would have essentially no capability against strategic ballistic missiles. This is due to [deleted]. The system also would not be tested in an 'ABM mode.'" The heavily-censored public account of this review, however, does not reveal the basis for the official judgment, nor does it reveal the power-aperture product of the *Aegis* radar. See U.S. Congress, Senate, Committee on Foreign Relations, *Fiscal Year 1980 Arms Control Impact Statements*, 96th Congress, 1st Session, March 1979, pp. 184–193. Other sources indicate that each *Aegis* radar antenna has an area of about 13.32 square meters. See Bernard Blake, ed., *Jane's Weapons Systems 1987–88* (London: Jane's, 1987), pp. 510 and 689.

In our judgment, shipboard air defenses that marginally exceed the candidate limits we are proposing here are unlikely to provide a base for a strategic missile defense network that would challenge the ABM Treaty regime. If circumstances and technologies in naval air defense systems change in the future, it would be appropriate to consider additional limitations.

30. See Unilateral Statement D of the ABM Treaty, and Gerard Smith, *Doubletalk*, pp. 303 and 307.
31. See, John C. Toomay, "Warning and Assessment," in Ashton Carter, John Steinbruner, and Charles Zracket, eds. *Managing Nuclear Operations* (Washington, D.C.: Brookings Institution, 1987), pp. 299–306.
32. The total number of missiles and launchers required for some targets, such as airfields, might be reduced if the payload of each missile were increased. For instance, studies by the U.S. Department of Defense reportedly concluded that as few as three arriving TBMs might be sufficient to disrupt operations at Warsaw Pact main airfields. The various hypothetical TBMs on which these estimates were based, however, had payloads of 6,400 kg and used modified Pershing II and Trident I boosters. Unless constraints on numbers of SRBM launchers and missiles were coupled with throw-weight and launch-weight limits, the sides might simply build larger SRBMs. On the other hand, increasing the size of permitted SRBMs in order to use fewer against each target would impose penalties: higher expense per missile; reduced mobility and survivability; higher probability that the target would remain undamaged due to missile malfunction.
33. Our proposal might appear additionally problematic because it would permit the Soviets to retain SRBM launchers and missiles deployed in Central Asia and the Far East, systems that arguably could be transported to Europe. However, NATO has alert procedures that can significantly undermine a Soviet surprise TBM attack, if NATO acts on strategic or tactical warning. Movement of large numbers of Soviet SRBM forces from elsewhere in the USSR would presumably give that warning.
34. See "Israel Reported to Test New, Longer Range Missile," *New York Times*, 22 July 1987, and "Soviet Cautions Israel Against New Missile," *New York Times*, 30 July 1987.

8 THE POLITICS OF ATBMS
The United States and the Alliance
Catherine McArdle Kelleher

Discussions in Washington about ATBMs and the NATO alliance are remarkably reminiscent of earlier times and debates. It is not only that familiar questions have resurfaced: What should be defended, who should fund which systems, and what are the implications for transfer within the Alliance? It is also not just the obvious parallels with earlier considerations of the role of air defense in NATO Central Front strategy, notably those debates of the late 1950s and again in the late 1960s. More significant are the familiar patterns in the discussions themselves—in the timing and interplay of statements, in the evolution of technical and political assessments, and in the line-up of organizational support both within and across national debates. At issue is the tug and pull of differing interpretations of what are separable U.S. and European concerns, and what are common to the Alliance as a whole. Involved are U.S. interpretations of European security requirements and political needs, viewed through a lens defined by the decisionmaking habits of the present U.S. leadership, the perceived NATO commitment for collective risk-sharing, and the seeming dictates of congressional political agendas.

From this perspective, the ATBM issue is simply the latest in a long line of Washington's alliance "cases"—to cite the more dramatic examples, the debates over INF, the NATO conventional improvement initiatives of the mid-1970s, and even the Multi-Lateral Force

(MLF) arabesque of the mid-1960s. Involved in each was a Washington effort to set the NATO agenda given the existence of a newly defined military threat or political opportunity and the promises of emerging technology.

But there is also much that is new in the structure of the ATBM debate, reflecting major changes in the United States, within the Alliance, and within the supporting allied political arenas. Even the emergence of the issue itself mirrors a changing security agenda under conditions of strategic nuclear parity, superpower arms control, and renewed questioning of the viability of extended deterrence. The strands of European and U.S. debate are more clearly visible, in part because of the obvious linkage to the high drama of SDI, in part because of the positions taken by newly articulate, allied audiences.

This chapter will attempt to distinguish between what is new and what is familiar in the present alliance discussions about ATBM issues. Quite deliberately, the perspective will be on the development of the U.S. debate, with particular emphasis on points central to the U.S. policy of coalition building and U.S. vantage points on European developments. Its goal is not to predict a specific outcome but rather to delineate the factors that affect the range of U.S. choice and to assess the ATBM debate as both symptom and determinant of the new U.S. agenda for the alliance.

GOOD REASONS AND REAL REASONS: THE LINK TO SDI

The questions to be asked are "Why this debate? Why now?" A strict constructionist would answer with a familiar NATO litany: a new, impressive Soviet capability to threaten Western Europe by the early 1990s with increasingly accurate conventionally armed missiles, a set of emerged Western technologies with near-term applications to counter this new Soviet threat, and new sensitivities to trade-offs in theater offense and defense in an era of both strategic parity and increasing economic and political constraints.

Expanded air defense — against ballistic or cruise missiles, perhaps against all attacks from the air — is simply an idea whose time has come in technological, doctrinal, and political terms. From this perspective, ATBM is best understood as, broadly, "Son of SAM" or what proponents of an expanded, intensified air defense for the European Central Front have fought for since the end of the 1950s.

For the U.S. ATBM debate, at least equal causal weight must be given to the March 1983 launching of the Reagan Strategic Defense Initiative. ATBM as "Son of SDI" has been proclaimed in several quite different ways. In one form, ATBM is the essence of a European Defense Initiative (EDI), perhaps growing out of the French-proposed Eureka or another European advanced technology, cooperative, space-related effort but clearly to be designed, produced, and satisfying for European interests. Alternatively, ATBM is nothing more than an element of the broader, more ambitious SDI program, with goals and technologies directed toward the far future. Yet a third formulation posits ATBM as a separable alternative to SDI, one that secures many of the same technological benefits but with costs, risks, and benefits more appropriate to European requirements and concerns. The last and most cynical view posits ATBM as a short-run sop to European fears that SDI development means the end of existing alliance defense arrangements and the transatlantic bargain.

Both "Son of" perspectives have some claim on historical accuracy; both describe views heard often in the past and expectable in the future. The more important point, however, for analysts as for political leaders, is the familiar task posed: how to disentangle good reasons from real reasons behind the support of particular policy options. And the critical factors, particularly for the U.S. side of the ATBM debate, seem to result from the interplay of bureaucratic and partisan politics over the SDI program.

THE SDI SUPPORTERS

Certainly, the most visible, early support in Washington for ATBM came from those who saw an integral link—political and technical—between ATBM and SDI. The roots of this position stretched back to the earlier ABM discussions from 1967–69, when those then in the civilian Office of the Secretary of Defense and among the military saw the deployment even of a thin Sentinel system in the United States as requiring a compensating BMD-like area defense for Western Europe. Various schemes for the type and scope of a European defense, for the mode of deployment and mechanism of control were discussed. One example was the Sea-based Anti-Ballistic Missile Intercept System, or SABMIS. The debate in the Nuclear Planning Group (NPG) from April 1967 through April 1968, however, focused on ground-based systems equipped (as the earlier Nike Hercules) with nuclear warheads, to provide coverage for some but not all of the heavily populated areas in Western Europe in the initial stages.[1]

Then, as now, the principal interest of ATBM advocates seemed to lie in the Alliance's political requirements that follow from the unilateral U.S. decision to pursue BMD. The arguments were about shoring up alliance cohesion and about offsetting the impact on extended deterrence, should the United States and the Soviet Union pursue even light BMD programs. A European-based system would demonstrate the indivisibility of alliance defense; even a thin area defense would provide reassurance against the type of political blackmail practiced against Europe during the Suez crisis or conceivable during the recurring Berlin deadlock of the late 1950s and early 1960s.

Europeans reacted to these proposals also primarily in political terms. A U.S. BMD system that covered only the United States, it was argued, would be both ineffective and provocative: It would involve virtual decoupling and impose on Europe a status of continuing political inferiority. Even more clearly, a European system would, the NPG decided in April 1968, be too costly, not totally effective, and might compromise arms limitation discussions between the United States and the Soviet Union. The few European supporters of this concept also emphasized the political signals involved—as Johan Holst's worry that it would further perpetuate postwar division and confrontation between the two halves of Europe.[2] Official and even unofficial U.S. support in the face of these criticisms was relatively weak and unquestionably secondary to the main ABM debate. It dwindled off in response first to the transformation of the Sentinel area defense system into the Safeguard point defense system in 1969 and then to the formulation and ratification of the ABM Treaty in 1972.

The more recent stimulus to ATBM linked with BMD came in the 1983 report of a presidential advisory panel (the Hoffman report), which recommended ATBM as an intermediate option on the way to a system of comprehensive strategic defense.[3] Its direct value was instrumental and tied to SDI: ATBM was a system of near-term availability, with advanced midcourse and terminal components exploitable later for U.S. defense, yet still researchable within ABM Treaty restrictions. Its significance for European defense was partly political reassurance but also a step toward "the pressing military need to protect allied forces as well as our own . . . from either non-nuclear or nuclear attack."

Most statements from SDI supporters during the noisy transatlantic debates on SDI merely reiterated this view of ATBM—technically instrumental, almost immediately accessible, and politically significant. A few technical supporters, located largely within the weapons laboratories, went further in emphasizing the direct benefits of an ATBM-SDI link.[4] Strategic defense concepts could be applied to theater defense, often with "greatly improved performance" and allowing the integration of space-based and ground-based lasers for boost-phase intercept. Edward Teller—virtually alone—argued that this would be even more effective in the European theater and that it would be "relatively easy" to destroy missiles even of SS-20 range.

In the 1984–85 U.S. and transatlantic debates, the ATBM-SDI link remained a constant but secondary theme. In the face of European doubts and criticisms of SDI, the SDI organization (SDIO) under General James Abrahamson undertook a broad selling strategy, with support for ATBM as one element. The SDIO arguments stressed the general benefits of shared technology and the new U.S. and European confidence resulting from SDI, rather than the benefits of European theater defense or of a definable ATBM system. As Ivo Daalder has pointed out, SDIO took almost two years before taking more than rhetorical steps to include ATBMs in its ongoing research program.[5] The system architecture contracts that were let did not explicitly address the need to consider system extension to Europe until September 1985. Indeed, it was not until the spring of 1986 that plans were laid for a major research study competition to develop system architecture requirements for theater missile defenses. The seven contracts that were finally awarded in December 1986, totaling only $14 million, were preliminary in nature, and were considerably smaller in both scope and funding than European or U.S. supporters had hoped.[6]

As will be discussed below, the motive forces behind this late 1985–86 push were European and NATO concerns and especially congressional pressures, rather than any shift in SDIO's technical assessment or research priorities. Abrahamson argued that defensive systems against shorter-range missiles faced different, significantly more difficult problems than did the SDI; that formulation of an ATBM requirement beyond an upgrade of existing defensive systems was only beginning and would take the next several years; and that the threat to Europe was already a consideration in long-term SDIO research. As with SDI, he stated in 1985, firm decisions on ATBM would have to await technological feasibility studies; the earliest decision point would be in the early 1990s.[7]

SDIO reluctance to fund ATBM projects before 1986 stemmed in part from a broader administration political strategy. Actors as diverse as Defense Secretary Caspar Weinberger and George Keyworth, President Reagan's first science advisor, insisted that SDI would emphasize only long-term, high-technology, comprehensive space-based systems with implementation in a defense-dominant environment in the twenty-first century. This, and only this, was SDIO's presidential mandate.[8] Near-term, clearly accessible, limited projects or terminal defense programs reduced SDI's visionary symbolism and the political payoffs to be garnered, nationally and internationally, from the president's revolutionary initiative. The goals were drawn from the Fletcher Panel, not the Hoffman Report; without that, SDI was just a third postwar effort to achieve continental air defense—and the other two had ended in spectacular failure. For many allies, too, SDI's most valuable technological payoffs were to come in the later stages; present commitments involved sharing in an unknowable, evolving future. ATBMs or any ground-based defensive systems against current Soviet capabilities did not and would not provide the necessary incentives for either allied cooperation or arms limitation regimes with the Soviets.

The push for early deployment of "ready" SDI technologies in late 1986 saw a reversal of these arguments. Ground-based defenses as well as some initial space-based assets were characterized as leading, testable components that could be in place by at least the early 1990s, if not immediately. ATBMs were clearly an available "framework" for testing and deployment—within the broad or the narrow interpretation of the ABM Treaty. In any case, funding flowed toward research of greater relevance for ATBM-like point defense purposes.

A number of important SDI supporters, especially in OSD, gave a somewhat different twist to the SDI-ATBM link. ATBM in essence became the European channel to SDI in terms both of sharing relevant technology and of demonstrating/maintaining European support for SDI. On some occasions, Department of Defense spokesmen paralleled the arguments of supporters of a simultaneous European Defense Initiative.[9] ATBM would be an adjunct system, capitalizing on the latest developments (especially in France and West Germany) and addressing the specific character of "through the air" threats, nuclear and nonnuclear, aircraft as well as shorter-range missiles of all types, perhaps even surface threats. This theme became particularly marked in the fall of 1985 when SDI's implications for European security became the focus of growing European public debate and a source of disaffection among congressional supporters.

Others, particularly then Assistant Secretary of Defense Richard Perle, suggested a different approach: a more separable European effort to develop a comprehensive air defense system, including but not limited to an ATBM. The design and concept would be European. It would be the first effort to meet a significant Soviet threat that did not bear the "made in America" stamp that had caused criticism in INF, and the first effort to specify the nature and funding consequences of European decisions from the outset. SDI would be the U.S. priority; its ultimate aim would still be to protect the broader security of the United States and its allies by overcoming U.S. strategic vulnerability.

For this group, the ATBM effort belongs within a European, or NATO, research context. The United States has a role to play in encouraging ATBM research within or alongside of SDI (as incorporated in the FY 1986 Defense Guidance or the 1986 and 1987 SDIO Research Programs) or through U.S. support for an ATBM component in NATO's "Conceptual Military Framework." But ATBM capabilities would remain expanded versions of existing air defense systems under NATO direction and control; transition to SDI-related weapons would take place only when justifiable.[10]

Throughout each of these arguments, SDI supporters clearly saw the problems of ATBM as derivative and instrumental to the main debate, that over SDI. A European ATBM project was defined in political terms — to enhance alliance cohesion behind the SDI program, to provide an outlet for European concerns, to constitute a limitable vehicle for European technological sharing, and, above all, to demonstrate to allies and U.S. audiences alike that, in Jonathan Dean's formulation, NATO will survive ballistic missile defense.[11] The aims were primarily psychopolitical; ATBM was as political in conception as the original MLF proposals of the 1960s or even as the thrust behind the various IRBM/MRBM theater offense schemes of the late 1950s. The military needs addressed were important and perhaps even desirable in their own rights. But they were neither sufficient nor even necessary to the long-term goal of a defensive transition or to U.S. political acceptance of SDI itself. The ATBM initiatives could be expanded or contracted in size or status to meet the changing requirements of the SDI program—for domestic or European political legitimacy, for continuity in the face of arms control limitations, or even for protection against congressional budget cutting.

The specific kind of initiatives to be taken, however, were still very preliminary and politically tinged. One example, seemingly launched at the time of increasing pressures from congressional activists and early SDI employment discussions, was a program in SDIO called IST, colloquially referred to as "Invite-Show-Test," designed to explore the availability/suitability of European technologies for ATBM incorporation. But the amount of money involved in IST was low (around $50 million) and the deadline far too short (reportedly by the end of December 1988) to regard this as a serious attempt to stimulate technology sharing.[12] And the net political effect, especially within the European political leadership and the somewhat bemused bureaucracies, seems to have been limited.

By late 1986, in the aftermath of European anxiety over Reykjavik, and early 1987, in the face of European grumbling over an INF regime, the political requirements for an SDI-ATBM link were far clearer than they had been in the past. But the effective forces were relatively unspecific European and congressional concerns, and the ratio of SDIO rhetorical support to actual research and budgetary implementation was still high. For some, especially in a dawning era of domestic budget-balancing and in the face of probable U.S.-Soviet agreement on theater arms limitations, the ATBM initiatives are clearly more expendable than funds for SDI or even for a number of more pressing U.S. or alliance programs.

Congressional Advocates

From almost the outset, there has been steady, if limited, congressional pressure on SDIO to broaden its research agenda. Perhaps the strongest push has come from the Armed Services committees of the House and Senate, and particularly from a small group of pro-SDI and pro-ATBM activist members.[13] In the Senate, these are Republicans Dan Quayle of Indiana and Pete Wilson of California, with help from such conventional advocates as Sam Nunn of Georgia and William Cohen of Maine. In the House, Duncan Hunter (Republican, California) has been perhaps the most active; in the fall of 1985 he led a congressional delegation on a relatively aggressive European ATBM study tour that produced a well-publicized trip report, citing French and German support for increased research and development on ATBM.[14]

The broad goal of these varied congressional efforts is the same: prod SDIO to fund more research on ATBMs. Their good, if not real, reasons seem to turn on ATBMs potential for (1) immediate technological exploration and development without immediate ABM Treaty violations—a virtual precondition for any significant European support of SDI, even in Britain; (2) immediate payoffs for European-U.S. coordination that will be binding in the future; and (3) beneficial applications in interlocking issues of U.S. regional commitments—for Quayle and Wilson particularly, the urgent need for Israeli defenses against Soviet SS-21s in Syria, and future Japanese defense against Soviet offensive missiles in Asia, as well as Central Front contingencies.[15]

Of growing importance in 1986 was the attempt by these supporters to shape but also protect SDI funding from attack, at home and in NATO. Congressional discussions of the FY 1987 Department of Defense budget authorization showed clearly the tug-of-war between two camps: the far more numerous SDI critics and others unwilling to authorize funding toward an unknown future, pitted against those attempting to nail down critical support for present funding in order to preempt possible changes after the 1988 election or to assure eventual SDI technology sharing. Accordingly, the Senate and House Armed Services Committees' authorization reports for FY 1987 "identified" up to $50 million within the SDI program that could go to ATBM-related projects. The intent of this measure (loosely called the Quayle amendment) was to accelerate ATBM technology development, with full-scale engineering development in FY 1988 and projected deployment in the early 1990s.[16] The program would be a "cooperative" venture with "substantial" allied contributions. Actual funding would not occur until a Memorandum of Understanding was signed between the United States and the allied government, delineating the participants and their funding responsibilities.[17]

By early 1987 congressional supporters of ATBMs also emphasized a set of emerging military requirements, should an INF agreement be reached. The imbalance posed by Soviet shorter-range missiles armed with either conventional or chemical warheads would assume greater significance in an INF-free Europe. Without an ATBM system and passive defense to buttress the INF agreement, the West would truly have only a hollow victory.[18]

But these arguments met little resonance either within the Congress or among the attentive publics of lobbyists and activists. The principal effect seemed to be a change only in the rhetoric of the SDIO; the SDIO budget changes continued to reflect executive branch choices, not congressional influence.[19] At most, what had been purchased was time — to allow allied interest in ATBM designs and projects to mature and to allow the ripening of bureaucratic coalitions, in Washington and in transatlantic talks. But even in these discussions, the status and political requirements of SDI remained paramount.

GOOD REASONS AND REAL REASONS: ATBM ADVOCATES

The motives of U.S. ATBM advocates represent a similar mixture of good and real reasons. These have been less exposed to public debates; few have been subjected to rigorous questioning or the sustained attention that SDI supporters have received in all their activities. ATBM advocates are probably greater in number than SDI supporters, but their views show less ideological fervor and reflect at least three separate categories of argument.

Conventionalization Supporters: The Bottom-Up Approach

Perhaps the most visible group of ATBM advocates are those who have been engaged in the NATO debate that began in the early 1980s over increased emphasis on conventional forces. They represent a mix of policy constituencies — no-first-use analysts, "emerging technology" enthusiasts, long-time supporters of effective conventional options for NATO, military reformers on the Hill, and military critics especially within the operational Army at home and the NATO command structure abroad, to identify only the largest groups. For these groups, ATBM itself is a secondary issue. Their common starting point is significant concern about the role of nuclear weapons, especially tactical nuclear weapons, in Central Front defense. Their advocated solution is the exploitation of new conventional technologies both to substitute for missions formerly assigned to nuclear weapons and to counter growing, increasingly sophisticated Soviet conventional capabilities. Air defense of the European theater is simply high on the substitution list.

A significant part of this interest developed through the U.S. and NATO studies during the late 1970s of the growing Soviet air threat in the European theater. Their conclusions paralleled those of the later European-U.S. ESECS studies: important new aircraft and conventional missile technologies were available that could reduce Pact sortie rates and ensure early command of the air through deep interdiction against fixed bases and command centers, and could disrupt Soviet reinforcement through selective attacks on second echelon forces.[20] Only slowly did these advocates see the implications of similar Soviet conventional capabilities for the West, and thus the need for at least extended, nonnuclear point defense of vulnerable NATO targets (airfields, C^3I, supply depots, missile sites). Secondary themes throughout were the West's vulnerability to chemical attack and the new requirements of active defense for INF storage and launch sites.

These requirements were both military and political. Without these new technologies, NATO would find itself worse off than before—mired in its chosen conventional inferiority relative to the East and reliant on the increasingly less credible and less politically acceptable threat of tactical nuclear use. By exploiting these technologies, the Alliance would achieve political reassurance and demonstrate both new capabilities for defense and deterrence and new political resolve.

In a very real sense, therefore, this represented the latest restatement of the classic position of pro-NATO support. For a Senator Nunn, as for the Bundy-Kennan-McNamara-Smith "Gang of Four" supporting no-first-use, the issue was greater conventional capability at acceptable political and economic cost. Expanded air defense was an obvious candidate, too long neglected, for which advanced conventional weapons would be the necessary and probably sufficient conditions for effective defense and deterrence. Given the increasingly contested role of tactical nuclear use and European nuclear anxieties, a conventional, comprehensive air defense system that might protect against both missiles and aircraft would be major step forward.

ATBM, however, is not necessarily a first priority of those favoring increased emphasis on conventional forces. Most of this group supports the upgrade of the existing Patriot air defense system, as long as it does not detract from the more significant counterforce conventional options—things such as the the Multiple Launch Rocket System (MLRS), standoff weapons, and other smart munitions.[21] As in the

ESECS II study, many question the need to give high priority to expanded ATBM or air defense efforts given the attractiveness, politically and economically, of passive defense measures. Undertaking hardening, concealment, and dispersal is also easier than elaborate technical solutions for what seems the intractable problem of assured active defense in Europe's narrow battlefield. Moreover, opinions divide significantly on the wisdom of attempting defense against conventionally or chemically armed missiles. Only a very few allow any option for defense against nuclear TBMs or for developing a nuclear-armed Patriot interceptor.

The Rogers Factor

General Bernard Rogers, as NATO SACEUR, took many of the same positions over the past four years. The parallels between his thinking and that of the ESECS groups are close, not surprisingly, given the origins of the ESECS groups and their overt concern with safeguarding NATO cohesion in the face of new Soviet threats and domestic political divisions. Enhanced conventional capabilities has also been Rogers's central theme and the hallmark of the major NATO studies in his term as SACEUR, including: CounterAir 90, stressing the need to integrate offensive and defensive forces; Follow-on Forces Attack (FOFA), stressing strikes against the Warsaw Pact's front line and second echelon forces in the event of attack; and recently, the Conceptual Military Framework (CMF) embodied in MC-299, the long-term integrative guidance on NATO's military requirements.[22] Support for ATBMs or expanded air defense derives then from this general framework — as in the accelerated activities of the Advisory Group for Aerospace Research and Development (AGARD) leading to the AAS-20 study specifically on ATBM in 1985–86.[23]

Rogers's statements on ATBM, however, reflect the necessary ambiguities inherent in his positions as both a principal U.S. commander and a military leader responsive to all sixteen NATO states. His increasingly positive statements during 1985 and 1986 echoed the momentum he perceived in increased German and Dutch interest. An obvious reference was the concept advanced in 1985 and again in 1986 by Manfred Wörner for an autonomous (if still coordinated) comprehensive European defense system.[24] Rogers was thus able to stress simultaneously both independence from the SDIO, whose concepts and research directions are still politically unacceptable to many NATO publics and elites, and the benefits of SDI-derived technologies developed by the United States and through contracts with European firms and state programs.[25]

Rogers's political role in NATO led him to emphasize some unique approaches to ATBM, not all reflected in the official NATO Council endorsement of ATBM as a concept in May 1986. His argument was that a Europe-based ATBM must be designed, researched, and funded collectively, principally by Europeans themselves.[26] Coordination should come through the Independent European Program Group (IEPG) but surely with "some links" to the SDI effort. Present SDI research funds for ATBM should be for international programs; individual national developments tied bilaterally to the United States are inefficient and ultimately distorting. The United States may now be taking the lead in developing ATBM technology, but with the development of NATO planning guidelines by the Conference of National Armaments Directors (CNAD), and European assumption of funding leadership, European interests and control will be assured.

To what extent this position reflected Rogers's effort to balance good reasons and real reasons for ATBM support is less clear. His most frequent emphasis was on the vulnerability of NATO's air assets (including airfields and command and control, C^2) and the need to develop a direct engagement, counterforce capability (such as MLRS, JSTARS, JTACMs). He did not dwell on the merit of active over passive defense, nor on the defense of anti-air systems or port and storage areas.[27] He stressed the present Soviet ballistic missile threat rather than an evolving Soviet air attack capability. He clearly saw a requirement for selected nuclear capabilities, say, in the FOFA mission (such as short-range offensive missiles), but he also recognized the political difficulties in Europe in securing post-INF approval for either new nuclear elements or new offensive missiles to put new Soviet capabilities at risk.

Several Rogers supporters within U.S. political and military circles pointed to an underlying motivation: the desire to contain the possible centrifugal forces that ATBM poses for both the short- and the long-term. A failure to respond positively to any issue that attracts strong European interest is impossible, given both post-INF alliance history and the potential for domestic political turbulence once again. The trick is to encourage "European initiative" without directly broaching the problems of integration under a broader SDI program or opening the way to simplistic political conceptions of restructuring NATO toward defensive defense, as are heard particularly from the left in Germany. A secondary, more traditional concern is how to maintain and expand collective alliance programs in the face of both more attractive bilateral arrangements with the United States and the potential dominance of exclusively German-French cooperation in European research and development. These are concerns that will affect Rogers's successor and that reflect tensions endemic to the post of SACEUR.

Extended Air Defense Advocates: Willing and Unwilling

In some significant dimensions, therefore, Rogers's position contrasts with those ATBM supporters who come with a long-established vision of an air defense for Europe. The experience of this group—a minority in the U.S. Army, a small group in the U.S. Air Force—is one of limited success in the last decade. However, the roots of conflict over the priority air defense programs involve a series of conflicts between the Army and Air Force dating back to the 1950s, as well as within the Army itself, and between the services and SDIO. The present Patriot system is a lineal descendant of the original SAM-D project of the mid-1960s that foresaw both ATBM and comprehensive anti-air capabilities. The Army's Low Altitude Defense System (LoAD, later Sentry D), which was developed up to the stage of prototype demonstration as a point defense for MX, also was clearly one of the current SDI building blocks. And the need for a replacement of the present Hawk anti-aircraft system, expected to be fully obsolescent in the mid-1990s, is at least a proximate cause for a number of U.S. and NATO technical studies.

Renewed emphasis on extended air defense first was linked to INF and concerns about Pershing and GLCM vulnerabilities.[28] Arguing that with limited tactical warning, passive defense measures for INF (dispersal from bases) would be inadequate, some within Pentagon technical circles, centered primarily around the Patriot and Hawk programs, advocated ATBMs as an active defense against Soviet TBMs, including the SS-20. The limited public debate saw stress on the possibility of a nuclear warhead for the new Patriot system, but with a conventional armament option that would avoid delays in obtaining presidential release authority for nuclear use. Interest continued within the air defense bureaus of the Army and was carried into the special air defense studies of 1980 and 1981. The Air Defense Program Plan 90 (ADPP 90) provides a good example of this interest, calling for top-to-bottom improvements in the Army's air defense capabilities.[29] But the interest of the political leadership in both the Carter and initial Reagan years remained low, swayed in part by what seemed to be technical constraints and Soviet saturation capabilities. The purported necessity of a nuclear warhead for the Patriot system was a major stumbling block and explicitly rejected in all but a few of the responsible European and U.S. circles.

Central to present ATBM discussions is the continuing debate and significant ambivalence within the Army itself over European air defense. In significant respects, this reflects the traditional postwar battle over the Army's role in offense and defense—a battle that defense has almost always lost, because of Army tradition, the weak bureaucratic base of the defense proponents, and the vagaries of the various defense mission responsibilities. Current proponents are those who have been associated with the Army's Strategic Defense Command and with the specialized Patriot program office. But even between these two, there has been bureaucratic wrangling. Those within the Army's strategic BMD programs see the ATBM mission as a potential "catalyst" or budgetary can-opener that could attract support for their own programs. The Patriot office, on the other hand, wishes to appropriate the "self-defense" and ATBM missions as a way of expanding the role of both the current and a possible follow-on Patriot. In budgetary terms, the Patriot program has enjoyed only mixed success in its competition for Army allocations, for funds won against SDIO requests within the Department of Defense budget, and for congressional protection against appropriation slashes.[30] The challenges are indeed a Catch-22 set of questions: Is an upgraded Patriot equal to the Soviet aircraft/missile challenge of the mid-1990s? Is it, given its 1960s basic design, truly equal to new defensive systems available in either the United States or Europe in the 1990s? And if the answer to both questions is yes, does Patriot then still conform to the prohibitions of the ABM Treaty?

The Army's principal competitors in the defense mission, however congenial, are two: the Air Force and the SDIO. The debate between the Army and Air Force over ATBM has generally taken place within the framework of the Wickham-Gabriel Memorandum of Agreement signed in May 1984.[31] The agreement sought to encourage greater and more rationalized cooperation between the two services by revising the assignment of roles and missions worldwide, including the air defense mission. One of the first initiatives, now no longer active, was a proposal to transfer all programs for area defense against high-altitude aircraft—such as Patriot and all follow-ons—to the Air Force. This reflected the Army's continuing effort to shed responsibility for joint roles, especially expensive ones.[32] ATBM, or what some within the Army now call Theater Missile Defense, is still being discussed under Wickham-Gabriel's Joint Development Initiatives 2 and 4, which called for the establishment of a Joint Anti-Tactical Missile program.

Discussions are further complicated by the fact that among NATO's Central Front nations, the U.S. Army has a unique role in air defense, the result of the interservice treaty of peace on missiles signed at Key West in 1948 and later revised. The original agreement left open the question of responsibility for air defense: the Army was tasked with fielding air defense artillery units; the Air Force was given the job of land-based air defense. This apparent overlap was later corrected in 1956 with a clarifying Memorandum of Agreement, separating area and point air defense missions and assigning them to the Air Force and Army, respectively. This agreement made the Army responsible for defending Air Force bases, an assignment with which the Air Force has never been comfortable.[33] The Army later also assumed the additional role of ground-based area air defense. Many in the "traditional" Army do not view either of these roles as natural or particularly desirable missions for the Army, emphasizing instead divisional or broadly framed air defense as well as offensive firepower.

The Air Force (and especially U.S. Air Forces Europe) until recently saw any new ATBM initiatives as of secondary importance, despite the major increases in Soviet counterair capability. Broadly stated, they argued for a simpler, more cost-effective combination of available counterforce offensive weapons and passive defenses (such as building supplemental airfields, rapid runway repair, more aircraft sheltering, greater concealment, and dispersal). To most Air Force observers, ATBM appears to degrade further the present European air defense "misorganization" where the Air Force now controls the air space, but it is the Army that must actually fire SAMs. At the operational level, ATBM would leave the Air Force even more dependent on Army units for the active defense of its assets and airfields, and shift significantly the traditional postwar offense-defense ratio toward defense, in both funding and programmatic terms (that is, away from fighter aircraft and direct counterair munitions). Without an agreed operational concept, under a redivision of roles and missions, the Army's claim for priority would be a strong one within U.S. and NATO circles. And by most insider estimates, constrained resources will mean hard choices, rather than simply the stretch-out or minimum funding of competing programs—new tactical fighters, stand-off missiles, or even passive defense.

The Army's debate with the SDIO over BMD roles is less concerned with the requirements or specifics of even the ATBM concept than with SDIO's observed reluctance to grant the military services a broader share of its program or to fund terminal defense initiatives. ATBM thus becomes the latest instrument to crack open the BMD interservice disputes of the past, especially of the late 1960s.[34] For the Army leadership, the desirable ATBM timetable is medium-term—a system deployable first in 1995 would be "responsive"; the approach should be the most sophisticated possible with accessible future technologies and maximum attention now to all-service, all-ally, ground-based, space-assisted solutions. Thus, so long as the bulk of SDIO-sponsored research focused on long-range, space-based systems, the Army BMD program was an issue with which to push its claim for greater funding. Under the new directives issued by Undersecretary of Defense William Howard Taft IV, the Army now has the lead on ATBM. It has, however, retained its flexibility and is not tied down to expensive, overwhelming projects.

PERCEIVED CONSTRAINTS ON ATBM

As complex and intriguing as they are, the motivations of the various players in the ATBM debate are viewed by many Washington actors as secondary to the real constraints that are stalling or prohibiting ATBM deployments. There are major differences in the assessment of the significance of these constraints for U.S. and European security— and, not surprisingly, in the probability of their occurrence. But there is also surprising agreement among ATBM skeptics, in Congress and in the executive branch, on the four constraints highlighted here.

Money: Available and Shared

Virtually every commentary on ATBM in the last half-decade and every interview conducted in 1986–87 on this topic ended with a discussion of the bleak financial prospect ATBM faces. Whatever the rhetoric, no one expects major increases in real NATO defense spending. Inflation may have been tamed in the 1980s, but rising unit costs for weapons and demographic squeezes in the Federal Republic and (later) in the United States will ensure lowered real spending.[35] ATBMs therefore pose not only opportunity costs, but what almost every commentator argues are hard choices about costs and benefits relative both to alternative defenses (passive measures, compensatory offensive actions) and to other European security requirements. Only the most committed in the technical and contractor communities, as in the pro-ATBM group of SDI supporters, see the resulting calculations as overwhelmingly pro-ATBM. Most advocates find they must rest their case on asserted synergistic effects (multiplier effects for later SDI use or other applications) or on the less-tangible values of prompt investment for foreseeable returns.

The numbers themselves are still remarkably vague. Costs for the current Patriot program appear to be running at about $78 million per defense unit (in FY 1987 dollars). The full Patriot upgrade option has been estimated at $30 billion by 2010, with $10 billion for the research and development phase.[36] The Quayle identification of $50 million (which indeed had already been programmed in this way by the SDIO) seems minuscule in comparison; even Senator Nunn's specification of $200 million for U.S.-Europe collaboration on conventional modernization in FY 1987 seems barely a first step.

Even these sums seem insupportable, given the magnitude of the present NATO modernization and conventionalization agendas, and the huge effort needed just to maintain national expenditures at their present rates. Prospects for new funding initiatives seem even bleaker when attention turns to the rising tides of trade protectionism on both sides of the Atlantic, the mutual irritation over failures at collective management of interest rates and deficits, and the perennial congressional gambit of threats about burden-sharing. Since mid-1986, the cost of ATBM has been the subject of increasing European elite concern; U.S. criticism has been several steps behind.

Perhaps the obvious point for debate about money is the question of who pays the separable, assignable ATBM costs. Air defense supporters in the United States see a clear U.S. role, not perhaps as large as that foreseen by Manfred Wörner but still central to research and development and to initial production. SDI enthusiasts unquestionably apply tougher criteria: The lion's share, if not all, must be paid by Europeans and with as little interference as possible in SDI priorities. The amounts involved are not huge but are still of troublesome magnitude. As one observer has remarked, the present Patriot purchases by Europeans had to be directly offset by U.S. buys of Roland for European deployment. How will it be possible to immediately fund a substantial upgrade program, let alone the development of a new complex system? The free ride of INF, all agree, will not happen again.

Compatibility with Arms Limitation, Present and Future

One of the severest tests an extensive ATBM program will face is its compatibility with existing and desirable arms limitation in Europe. At issue particularly will be the prohibitions laid down in the present ABM Treaty or its extension and in agreements on constraints in Europe. The latter would include restraints on the numbers, types, and deployments of nonstrategic missile systems, as well as those imposed in the interest of crisis management or confidence building measures.

U.S. SDI supporters generally see the issue as clear cut. European elite commitment to the ABM Treaty as the core of the present arms limitation regime is obviously of great importance. Constraints on the emerging Soviet nuclear and conventional air and short-range missile threat or related capabilities (an INF freeze) will therefore be welcome and will actually ease the defensive transition. Adequate verification, however, will remain a difficult hurdle—and will be the ultimate constraint on effective strategic defensive limitation.

Air defense supporters seem somewhat more divided. For most, especially in the Army and among the congressional conventionalization supporters, an INF agreement would only accentuate the Soviet conventional air threat and compel attention to active and passive defenses against nonnuclear and chemical attack. European and continental air defense systems would increase, not decrease, in importance. For all but a few, however, extended Patriot would be the choice rather than ATBM because of its nearer-term availability and the fact that it is being sold as an "evolutionary system." Some, more on the left of the political spectrum, seemingly would be willing to forgo advanced air defense under a comprehensive European security agreement, one that featured deep cuts in nuclear and nonnuclear capabilities and positive/negative measures to ensure adequate warning and real-time surveillance and verification. Range limitations, a maximum number of launchers, a freeze or observable constraint on the testing of relevant technologies would all fit and be approved within such a framework. The gain would be a quick end to both an ATBM and extended air defense race in Europe—and the resulting gains in assuring theater stability.

A harder problem, especially for those basically interested in safeguarding alliance cohesion, would be the trade-off between global and regional arms limitations or constraints. The hurdles could be many, including the initial challenge of devising new constraints to bolster the ABM Treaty, and then the difficulties of distinguishing ATBM technologies or research on nonnuclear systems from activities constrained under the new limits. U.S. concerns and European commitment to the lodestone ABM Treaty all suggest caution.

Alliance Turbulence: Self-Fulfilling Prophecies

One of the clearest constraints on ATBM is concern that predictions of calamities that supposedly will be triggered by an ATBM program may well be self-fulfilling prophecies. The one calamity most often predicted in discussions is that ATBM will be a catalyst/cover for U.S. decoupling. The argument is a variant on the theme that any SDI effort will trigger a "retreat to Fortress America." If an ATBM program were begun, it would quickly become a palliative and, if ultimately effective for some substantial measure of population defense, a proximate cause for gradual U.S. withdrawal from Europe.

A prophecy that is substantively opposite, yet very similar, is that ATBM will become the occasion for Europeans to adopt a defensive defense posture—that is, a shedding of offensive military forces.

Effective area defense coverage—even at perhaps the 50 percent effectiveness level—would, it is argued, restore effective deterrence and reinforce actual defense. At present, most defensive defense supporters oppose ATBM—or see it simply as an SDI extension or foil. Yet an attractive option would still seem to be the combination of a comprehensive counterair system with the type of conventional "defensive entanglement" posture proposed by Andreas von Bülow of the German Social Democrats.[37] Stability with a progressive build-down of offensive capabilities in Europe appears to be an election-winning program and one with obvious implications for the continuation of an effective transatlantic relationship.

The Premature Demise of SDI: No More Technological Quick Fix?

The last constraint would seem to arise from the very point of attraction for SDI supporters: ATBM as "Son of SDI" may share the SDI's fate. A number of U.S. observers friendly to SDI fear for the program's future. The cumulative impact of a president other than Ronald Reagan, of a yawning federal deficit that can no longer be ignored, and of an accommodating Soviet posture on arms restraint would seemingly be to stop or significantly slow even the SDI research program. A string of technical failures or near misses under conditions of constrained resources would then be the final straw.

Some Americans, and many Europeans, doubt that support for any specific SDI program can be sustained. The cause will be the U.S. obsession with technological fixes—the lure of tomorrow's bells and whistles seems inevitably more appealing than whatever is at hand today. An ATBM achievable in the near term will always be at least one technological step behind, especially if it is only an upgrade of Patriot, a system born in the 1960s. ATBM may become doomed along with SDI to the attraction of a better idea.

Lessons from the Past

What, on balance, are the implications for the future of U.S.-European relationships in this fractured Washington debate? The simple and obvious answer would seem to be, none. ATBM appears to be an idea whose time has not yet come, an idea for which there as yet is no obvious set of powerful Washington patrons. Supporters of the ATBM concept per se are few, particularly if costs or trade-offs with other U.S. or NATO priorities become salient issues. In objective terms, the division between those who see primary identification with the SDI program and those favoring extended air defense solutions seems almost unbridgeable. In the end, logic would suggest, real reasons always count more than good reasons.

The recent Taft directive, which indeed combines these two arguments, suggests however that logic may not be relevant in this case. It is worth remembering the earlier historical parallels. The ATBM debate is only another case of Washington actors, working perhaps in tandem with European actors but also alone, attempting to define both the problem of and the solution for future European security requirements. The critical links are forged: specification of a new Soviet challenge or threat, identification of new or almost available technologies toward solution, and promotion of a new political-organizational framework for European-U.S. sharing of the costs and risks involved. Simple bureaucratic momentum, thus, may carry such a project along for a considerable distance.

It seems therefore prudent to briefly explore the parallels and the lessons to be learned if only because in many significant respects, NATO's past has been a reliable guide to the probabilities of the future. If the present seems to echo the past, the cause may be the reflection within the alliance of enduring structural interests, often obscured by the political rhetoric of the day or the exigencies of electoral politics. This comes as a surprise particularly to U.S. political leaders (but not to policy analysts) who tend to view the present as the measure of Western possibilities and the sure sign that things once were better.

Three model solutions or sets of lessons emerge from NATO's past, each involving costs and risks for peacetime and conflict. Each directly depends on the nature and direction of the domestic U.S. coalition, and its perception of European requirements and stakes. Each involves a different mix of political and technical instruments and a different range of expectations about the possibilities for compromise and the flexibility of the NATO bargaining process.

The first is the Multi-Lateral Force maneuver, especially observable in its last phases in 1964–65. Those with a memory for the Alliance's history will remember MLF as a U.S. scheme for a shared NATO nuclear missile force, manned by multinational crews drawn from the whole alliance. Broadly described, MLF was a political invention. But it was also an attempt to use an important (but not top-drawer) technical fix on an enduring transatlantic political problem, the differential European and U.S. interests in the timing and specifics of nuclear weapons control and use. The technical problems were solvable, but they were also complex and ultimately involved no particularly compelling technical logic. Yet the surrounding political agenda stimulated by U.S. neglect, mutual irritation, and an occasionally accommodating Soviet leadership, was seen as critical and demanding of solution. Thus, a cabal of Washington enthusiasts triumphed, with the grudging support of the technicians and the continuing amazement of politicians and military men. European briefings followed in series and technical planning became a NATO-sanctioned activity.

In the end, however, the technical fix would not hold. The sharing in second-order technologies (Polaris missiles on surface ships, in one formulation) and in second-order control without real payoffs (ultimately, only the U.S. president could authorize use of the missiles) was not worth the struggles and disincentives that the political context in the United States and in the major European allied states ensured. And a changing U.S. leadership, preoccupied with an Asian war and domestic change, was pleased to move to a new, less visible organizational solution — continuing consultation within a Nuclear Planning Group.

A somewhat different and perhaps closer parallel is to be found in another historical case: the Thor-Jupiter program for U.S. deployment of IRBMs in Europe in the late 1950s, provoked by the launch of Sputnik and Soviet IRBM deployments (the SS-4s and SS-5s, predecessors of the SS-20s). The parallels are striking. Still seeking an intercontinental missile capability but mindful of special European vulnerability, the United States proposed as a first-step solution the Thor and Jupiter deployments. A long-term solution would have to wait for the maturation of conceivable ICBM technologies; IRBMs would then be integrated into a final overarching system. In the meantime, these missiles would meet particular European security needs at an "acceptable" level. Those European states that accepted stationing would be offered political and technical incentives, and a channel of control over any final system solution. U.S. technicians were convinced and enthusiastic. Washington politicians saw a clear way home, and the military leadership was divided and generally silent, beset by interservice disagreements.

The denouement was quite different and ultimately somewhat surprising. A new combination of available technologies delivered up Polaris; reliable, relatively stable ICBM technologies were only somewhat behind. U.S. ICBMs became the centerpiece of the deterrence system, and the European stake in control was necessarily somewhat diminished. The problems posed by the Soviet SS-4s and SS-5s were perhaps offset, but not solved, by this counterdeployment of U.S. offensive missiles. European political and military leaders remained ambivalent. And whatever the military judgment of the threat, the alliance settled for a coping strategy.

A third, perhaps more hopeful, set of lessons emerges from U.S. efforts to promote European conventional modernization and expansion during the early 1970s. A loose Washington coalition of diverse interests supported a set of NATO modernization initiatives—most observable in the attempts by Defense Secretary James Schlesinger and Secretary of State Henry Kissinger to bring about new NATO conventional planning and the evaluation and specification of needed technologies. The pace of achievement was frustratingly slow and often barely observable in the noise of other events: parallel programs on strategic modernization, the waning phases of the Vietnam War, Watergate, and the irritation felt by virtually every major alliance partner toward an increasingly unilateralist United States. Perhaps the only major achievement was initiation of a set of comprehensive studies assessing the critical growth in Soviet conventional and theater nuclear capabilities.

The results came later in the complex of NATO initiatives during the early Carter years. The base conditions for Washington coalition-building had been laid; the successive study efforts narrowed the range of disagreement and set the limits within which the major actors might at least agree to disagree. The lines for discussion, for specifying costs and benefits, for delineating the range of needed and acceptable arms limitation were known and broadly accepted as legitimate. The final political agreement was still not smooth. The trauma of the neutron bomb fiasco and the fervor and pressure of the anti-INF movement were disruptive and costly. Yet the coalition held and these problems could at least be managed within the framework of known assumptions about future directions as well as present costs and risks.

The manner in which this third case was handled would seem preferable under most conceivable conditions, despite the changes in the objective and political bounds of the NATO consensus. The lessons are that if the ATBM issue is to be taken seriously and handled sensibly, a coalition must be built within the Alliance generally, and within the U.S. bureaucratic arena first and most particularly, that will buoy the issue along through the turbulence of other events. Unless such a coalition is constructed, the diversity of present motivations in Washington offers little hope for a stable, enduring outcome, one that would be calibrated to meet serious military requirements or to achieve major long-term political gains toward the transformation of alliance reliance on nuclear weapons and deterrence by risk.

NOTES

The author gratefully acknowledges the helpful comments and criticisms of the editors, Ivo Daalder, Dennis Gormley, Herbert Harrison, and Thomas Risse-Kappen. Steven McKay, along with Dwight Raymond and Margaret Sullivan, provided skilled research assistance supported by the Maryland International Security Project.

1. See, for example, David Yost's seminal "Ballistic Missile Defense and the Atlantic Alliance," *International Security*, Fall 1982, pp. 144–145.
2. See Yost, pp. 145–146.
3. Fred S. Hoffman, Study Director, *Ballistic Missile Defense and U.S. National Security Strategy: Summary Report* prepared for the Future Security Strategy Study (Washington, D.C.: October 1983), pp. 2 ff. One of the best initial treatments of this and other ATBM issues is Thomas Enders, *Missile Defense as Part of an Extended NATO Air Defense* (Bonn: Konrad Adenauer Stiftung, Interne Studien, 1986).
4. See, for example, Gregory H. Canavan, "Theater Applications of Strategic Defense Concepts," Los Alamos National Laboratory, 4 June 1985; and Edward Teller at the February 1986 Wehrkunde Conference.
5. Ivo Daalder, "Defense for Europe?" (Cambridge, Mass.: unpublished paper, June 1986), pp. 7–8.
6. *Announcement by Secretary of Defense Caspar W. Weinberger on Theater Ballistic Missile Defense Architectural Studies*, Brussels, Belgium, on 4 December 1986. See also, *Aviation Week and Space Technology*, 30 June 1986, p. 24, and 14 July 1986, p. 30. Seven contracts were awarded, each for $2 million. Only three of the seven consortia were led by European firms: Messerschmidt-Bölkow-Blohm from West Germany; CoSyDe from France; and SNIA from Italy. Of a total of fifty-one firms, twenty-nine were European.
7. See, for example, Abrahamson's remarks and written responses to questions posed by Senators Dan Quayle and Pete Wilson in U.S. Congress, Senate, Committee on Armed Services, *Department of Defense*

Authorization for Appropriations for FY 1986, 99th Congress, 1st Session, February–March, 1985, pp. 4001 and 4401–4403.

8. See the various statements handily published as "The SDI: Program and Rationale," *Survival*, March/April 1985, pp. 75–83, as well as the contrasting interpretative articles by Harold Brown and Colin Grey, pp. 50–64.

9. The parallels are most direct with the European High Frontier Group: Kai-Uwe von Hassell, Robert Close, Pierre Gallois, and Stewart Menaul. See, for example, Menaul's summary statement, "A European Defense Initiative," *Journal of Defense and Diplomacy*, February 1986, pp. 18–21. Manfred Wörner, the German Defense Minister, on the other hand, has explicitly rejected the label "EDI" for his concept of an extended air defense system in Europe, "independent" of the SDI. He has argued, however, that U.S. willingness to include defense against short- and intermediate-range missiles, in response to European pressures, means a new alliance dialogue within the SDI. See Wörner's comments in a *Westdeutscher Rundfunk* interview of 22 March 1986, reprinted in *Foreign Broadcast Information Service, West Europe*, 25 March 1986, pp. J1–J3.

10. See the report on parallel NATO developments, "NATO Planners Drafting Guideline on Europe-Based ATBM Development," *Aviation Week and Space Technology*, 14 July 1986, p. 30.

11. Jonathan Dean, "Will NATO Survive Ballistic Missile Defense?" *Journal of International Affairs*, Summer 1985, pp. 95–114.

12. Information taken from a personal interview.

13. The first full hearings on ATBM were not held until the spring of 1986, before the Strategic and Theater Nuclear Forces Subcommittee of the Senate Committee on Armed Services on 24 April 1986, and before the Defense Policy Subcommittee of the House Committee on Armed Services on 4 June 1986. Specific questions about ATBMs were asked in hearings before both committees on the Defense Department authorization bills for FY 1985, 1986, and 1987. See also Daalder, "Defense for Europe?" unpublished paper, pp. 31–33.

14. See, for example, Pete Wilson, "A Missile Defense for NATO: We Must Respond to the Challenge," *Strategic Review*, Spring 1986, pp. 9–15, and the remarks in David C. Morrison, "Army Fights for NATO Missile Shield," *National Journal*, 14 December 1985, p. 2870.

15. Senator Quayle, for example, asked the Congressional Research Service in the spring of 1986 to prepare a study on the potential for ballistic missile proliferation in the Third World (the Manfredi Study).

16. U.S. Congress, Senate, Committee on Armed Services, *Report on FY 1987 National Defense Authorization Act*, 99th Congress, 2nd Session, 23 June 1986, pp. 184–185.

17. By early 1987, active negotiations with at least two allied governments were underway. See "Harsh Facts Temper NATO Response to Moscow Talks," *Christian Science Monitor*, 17 April 1987.
18. See Senator Quayle, "Make It a Real Zero-Zero Option," *Christian Science Monitor*, 9 April 1987.
19. See Douglas C. Waller and James T. Bruce, *SDI: Progress and Challenges, Part Two*, Staff Report submitted to Senator William Proxmire and Senator J. Bennet Johnston, March 1987, pp. 3–5.
20. European Security Study (ESECS) Report, *Strengthening Conventional Deterrence in Europe* (London: Macmillan, 1983). See also the follow-up study by a rump group, *ESECS II: Strengthening Conventional Deterrence in Europe* (Boulder, Colo.: Westview, 1985).
21. Prominent among these proposed systems are the Army Tactical Missile (ATACM) and the joint Army/Air Force program, the Joint Tactical Missile (JTACM). Each would be launched from the existing and planned Multiple Launch Rocket System (MLRS) for deep strike missions. Each is intended primarily for dispensing conventional submunitions, but would be nuclear-capable as well.
22. On the Conceptual Military Framework, see Chapter 6 in this volume, and *Strategic Survey 1985–1986* (London: International Institute for Strategic Studies, 1986), pp. 36–42.
23. See Chapter 6 in this volume, and Enders, pp. 12–16.
24. See Wörner, "A Missile Defense for NATO Europe," *Strategic Review* Winter 1986, pp. 13–19.
25. See, for example, Rogers's comments in an interview with *Aviation Week and Space Technology*, 14 July 1986, pp. 30–31.
26. "NATO Planners Drafting Guidelines," *Aviation Week and Space Technology*, 14 July 1986, p. 31. This contrasts clearly with Wörner's view that the United States must take a major role in ATBM funding as well as in research. Rogers explicitly differentiated the ATBM funding imperative from U.S. funding of INF.
27. Hugh De Santis reaches a similar conclusion. See "A Theater Missile Defense for Europe," *SAIS Review* Summer-Fall 1986. pp. 99–116.
28. The account here relies primarily on Yost, "Ballistic Missile Defense and the Atlantic Alliance," *International Security*, Fall 1982, pp. 157 ff., and Enders, pp. 73 ff.
29. David Harvey, "Play It Again, SAM," *Defense and Foreign Affairs*, September 1980, pp. 12–19.
30. Daalder reports, for example, that until FY 1986 funding, Congress repeatedly cut the Patriot upgrade program request by fifty percent or more ("Defense for Europe?" unpublished paper, p. 19). In FY 1987, funding levels seem more secure, though still vulnerable.

31. "Air Force, Army Chiefs Sign 31-Point Agreement," *Air Force Times*, 4 June 1984, pp. 1, 14, and 18.
32. Arthur Downey, *The Emerging Role of the U.S. Army in Space* (Washington, D.C.: National Defense University Press, 1985), p. 74. Downey also mentions the frequent rumor in 1983–84 that the Army was willing to give up its residual BMD program as well. Patriot at the time was the second largest line item in the Army's 5-year budget plan, with 10,000 personnel slots and a total of $11.6 billion in projected program costs.
33. The U.S. Air Force provides its own air defense for its bases in the United Kingdom, using the Rapier system.
34. For background, see David N. Schwartz, "Past and Present: The Historical Legacy," in Ashton B. Carter and David N. Schwartz, eds., *Ballistic Missile Defense* (Washington, D.C.: Brookings Institution, 1984), pp. 330–349.
35. See generally the essays in Andrew Pierre, ed., *The Conventional Defense of Europe* (New York: Council on Foreign Relations, 1986), and especially the essay by Gen. Sir Hugh Beach, "On Improving NATO Strategy," pp. 152–185.
36. Quoted in De Santis, in his endnote 22.
37. Andreas von Bülow, "Defensive Entanglement: An Alternative Strategy for NATO" in Andrew Pierre, ed., *The Conventional Defense of Europe*, pp. 112–151.

9 ATBMS AND ALLIANCE POLITICS IN EUROPE
Phil Williams

The debate in Western Europe over ATBMs is still in embryonic form. Consequently, it bears within it not only great potential and promise but also the risk that development will go awry.

What the Europeans would like to find in the ATBM issue is an occasion for a common European voice, an opportunity for collaboration on a distinctive European solution to a European security problem, and a strengthened foundation for a more commanding European role within the Atlantic alliance. The incentives for West European cooperation, after all, have increased markedly as a result of a series of transatlantic differences over policy and strategy. In the early 1980s the problems centered around divergent assessments of the Soviet threat. The Reagan administration adopted a hardline stance toward Moscow and aroused considerable consternation in Western Europe, where there was still a strong desire to retain the benefits of detente. More recently, the SDI, the Reykjavik Summit, and the INF treaty have provoked a different set of worries. President Reagan's apparent desire to downgrade the role of nuclear weapons—by rendering them "impotent and obsolete" or by eliminating whole categories through arms control—casts new doubt on the U.S. nuclear guarantee to Western Europe, and thus on the viability of NATO's flexible response strategy. In an atmosphere characterized by European suspicions that U.S. policy might prejudice their security, greater cooperation both to strengthen allied influence in Washington and to act as a hedge against a future weakening of the U.S. security commitment might be anticipated.

The risk, however, is that the ATBM issue will prove to be yet another episode in which Europe finds neither common voice, nor common interests, nor an appropriate forum for addressing a new challenge. The harm done by such episodes is considerable. By setting back the development of a common European defense identity, they help to perpetuate the imbalance of power and responsibility within the Atlantic Alliance, which is becoming increasingly irksome to many Americans. Indeed, if the Europeans fail to come to grips with the ATBM issue, this can only provide ammunition for those in Washington who complain that the burdens of alliance are inequitable and that the Europeans have become a liability rather than an asset in the continued geopolitical competition with the Soviet Union. The result could be the worst of all worlds — continued divisions within Western Europe and a gradual but inexorable weakening of the U.S. commitment to European security.

Though it is difficult, at such an embryonic stage, to predict how the ATBM issue will be resolved in Europe, at the moment it seems unlikely that it will provide the occasion for a major and successful exercise in West European defense cooperation. The main reason for this is the number of factors that complicate the politics of ATBMs.

The first is the continuing ability of the United States to set the agenda for NATO and to complicate the ATBM issue by casting it in its own terms. Although ATBMs had been discussed in both the United States and the Alliance prior to President Reagan's speech of March 1983, the Strategic Defense Initiative changed the context within which the issue would be considered and gave it a salience and a symbolism that would otherwise have been lacking. European reactions to SDI, which have ranged from outright hostility to lukewarm support, led the United States to suggest that any defensive shield that might be created would be extended to Europe. Among the other means devised by the United States to obtain European support was the promise that participation in the research project would elicit a significant share of SDI contracts. Similarly, U.S. support for a European Defense Initiative was another means of bringing the allies on board. From this perspective, ATBM is simply "SDI with a human face for Europe." President Reagan's deep commitment to a world in which the defense is dominant was underlined in his discussions with

Mr. Gorbachev at Reykjavik and Washington. What remains uncertain is whether his successor will have the same commitment or will instead revert to the traditional reliance on deterrence through threats of retaliation. Whatever the case, it is clear that what the United States does or does not do in relation to ATBM will have a major impact.

A second factor that complicates the ATBM issue is that it has arrived on NATO's agenda at a time when the domestic consensus in Europe on defense matters is not what it used to be—to say the least. The peace movement may have become less visible since the mass rallies of the early 1980s, but the INF debate has left an important legacy. Antinuclear policies have become key elements in the platforms of opposition parties in Britain and West Germany, and although such policies have not won wide approval among the electorate, this development will ensure that in the later 1980s and the early 1990s, there will be unprecedented scrutiny of both national defense policies and NATO strategy. Although certain kinds of ATBM need not be particularly controversial because they have missions that are clearly defensive, if they are seen as having a close connection with the SDI and being part of another U.S. design for Europe, then their deployment could well arouse opposition. There is still considerable sensitivity in Europe to nuclear issues, not only at the public level but also within governments. Furthermore, if individual governments find it hard to establish a consensus, the problems of European-wide collaboration will be formidable.

A third factor is that history is not on Europe's side. Defense cooperation is an area in which European aspirations have considerably outmatched achievements. There are several very obvious reasons for this, most of which stem from the differing preoccupations and policies of the three leading West European nations. Although Britain, France, and the Federal Republic of Germany have much in common, on so many issues one of them seems always to be the odd man out. These "triangular asymmetries" are both substantive and procedural. France's absence from NATO's integrated military command complicates the development of a common European position within the Alliance, while on substantive matters, West Germany's nonnuclear status means that Bonn does not always appreciate the concerns which animate Paris and London. These differences could have important implications for the ATBM issue when it comes to questions of resource allocation within national defense budgets.

A fourth factor that complicates the ATBM issue is the ambiguity of the concept itself. Two things are often confused under the heading of ATBMs. The first is defense against a Warsaw Pact conventional threat. Here the emphasis is on maintaining the integrity of NATO's strategy of flexible response. Air defense has always been a crucial part of that strategy, and ATBMs merely pose the question whether or not to upgrade NATO's defense capabilities to deal with a new threat "through the air" from Soviet missiles. In this notion of ATBM, no conceptual or doctrinal change is required, and ATBM has nothing to do with President Reagan's Strategic Defense Initiative. Indeed, even if the SDI had never existed, there would still be discussion about the need to extend NATO's air defense.

The other conception of ATBMs, however, is more closely related to the SDI and sees ATBMs as part of the overall architecture of a multilayered defense against Soviet ballistic missiles. From this perspective, ATBMs, like the U.S. SDI program, would be designed to deal with a nuclear threat and would support a conceptual and doctrinal shift from deterrence through retaliation to deterrence through denial. This second conception of ATBMs, therefore, is both more radical and more visionary than the first. With one or two exceptions, the discussion of ATBMs in Europe has eschewed this visionary goal and has concentrated predominantly on the emerging conventional missile threat rather than the existing nuclear threat. For the most part the debate has been cast in relatively modest terms, with the focus very much on the protection of critical military assets such as airfields, command and control centers, reinforcement areas, and nuclear forces. Nonetheless, one difficulty in the emerging European debate is that these two separate and very different conceptions of ATBMs are not always clearly distinguished from one another—a difficulty that is compounded by the use of terms such as European Defense Initiative to cover projects that have different origins, rationales, and implications.

A final complicating factor is the impact of arms control achievements at Geneva. There are obvious technical uncertainties about whether the INF agreement eliminating the Soviet SS-20s, SS-22s, and SS-23s but leaving behind the SS-21s (and their modernized replacements) will diminish or enhance the importance of ATBMs for NATO's strategy. There are additional uncertainties about how progress at Geneva will shape political perceptions about Europe's position between the superpowers and the contribution that future arms control arrangements could make to security in Europe. The main effect of progress on arms control, however, could well be to undermine the rationale for ATBM and effectively remove the issue from the agenda.

So again, one hesitates to characterize the European debate on ATBMs, partly because the debate has not yet matured sufficiently for us to discern clearly the likely outcomes. With this caveat in mind, this chapter explores the topography of European opinion on ATBMs, the merits and drawbacks of alternative approaches to the ATBM and their resource implications, and finally, the likelihood of a concerted West European decision on the ATBM issue.

EUROPEAN OPINION ON ATBMS

The most striking aspect of the European debate over ATBMs thus far is the way in which the salience of the issue has varied from one country to another. In the Federal Republic of Germany, ATBMs have been the focus of more explicit and more public debate than anywhere else in Europe. In part this grows directly out of German concerns that the SDI might undermine the uniformity or equality of risk among the allies by protecting the United States while leaving Europe vulnerable. It is this that led to the strong German fear, spread across much of the German political spectrum, that SDI would have a decoupling rather than a recoupling effect. Moreover, it was in response to this fear that some Germans emphasized the need for at least some protection akin to what would be available for the United States, if an SDI system works.

It is clear, therefore, that Germany will play a pivotal role in the ATBM debate. This is not surprising because the Federal Republic is simultaneously the leading West European power and the most vulnerable, the strongest and the most dependent. History and geography combine to give Bonn a degree of sensitivity to security issues and to Soviet and U.S. policies and capabilities that is rarely matched elsewhere in Western Europe. The result is that West Germany, feeling more exposed than its allies, is often out in front on issues but is uncomfortable with such a prominent position—and makes strenuous efforts to persuade other European states to stand along side it. Something like this seems to have happened with the ATBM issue.

If there is a demand in West Germany for defenses in Europe to accompany SDI, however, it is a demand that has been created in part by the United States. Immediately after his March 23, 1983, speech,

President Reagan appointed three panels of experts to examine the technical and policy questions raised by his startling defense proposal. One of those groups—the so-called Hoffman panel—advised the president that:

> Deployment of an anti-tactical missile (ATM) system is an intermediate option that might be available relatively early. The system might combine some advanced midcourse and terminal components . . . with a terminal underlay. . . . Such an option addresses the pressing military need to protect allied forces as well as our own in theaters of operations from either nonnuclear or nuclear attack. It would directly benefit our allies as well as ourselves.[1]

This theme of defending the United States' allies was echoed in many subsequent statements, and it formed a key element in the attempt by the Reagan administration to mobilize support for an initiative that was greeted in Europe with considerable antipathy.

This mixture of U.S. salesmanship and German anxieties has meant that discussion of ATBMs has not only been more advanced in the Federal Republic than elsewhere in Europe but also more varied. One analyst has identified three distinct groups within Germany: the SDI supporters on the right; the Kohl government itself, which has exhibited considerable ambivalence; and the critics in the Social Democratic Party (SPD), the media, and the scientific community.[2]

The SDI supporters on the right of German politics, such as the Christian Social Union (CSU) chairman Franz-Josef Strauss, have advocated a European Defense Initiative (EDI) that would be a direct counterpart to the SDI program in the United States. The basis for this recommendation is partly technological enthusiasm, partly a desire to share in the economic bonanza that it is argued will spin off from SDI and partly a concern that Germany's vulnerability be reduced. CDU/CSU spokesmen in the Bundestag have claimed that the United States would strongly support an initiative of this kind designed to complement strategic defenses developed by the United States. Former Defense Minister Kai-Uwe von Hassel, who in 1984 had helped to found "High Frontier Europe," suggested in 1985 that the Western European Union should sponsor a European Defense Initiative that would complement the SDI and would concentrate on directed energy weapons. The enthusiasm of the German proponents of an EDI, however, was not matched by their influence—and the debate has in fact been dominated by more sober and more critical assessments.

The Kohl government itself, partly because of its internal divisions, has been more ambivalent about both SDI and similar European efforts, whether EDI or ATBM. There have been differences of emphasis within the ruling coalition, with Chancellor Kohl placing the emphasis on the maintenance of good relations with the United States and Foreign Minister Hans-Dietrich Genscher of the Free Democrats, evincing unhappiness about any measures that threaten to jeopardize East-West relations in Europe.[3] To some extent the issue also became bound up with the old question of whether Bonn should look primarily to Washington or to Paris for cooperation, with Genscher taking a stance more compatible with that of the French.[4] Gradually, though, the Federal Republic concluded that additional strains in the transatlantic relationship were best avoided and that participation in the research project might bring with it both economic benefits and political influence over the final shape of the SDI program.

This desire for participation in part explains a shift in emphasis by Defense Minister Manfred Wörner. Initially Wörner was one of the most outspoken skeptics about the SDI, arguing that perfect missile defenses were unachievable, that partial defenses were destabilizing, and that defenses that protected the United States but not Europe would dissolve the sense of shared risk that bound the Alliance together. In late 1985, however, Wörner began to change his position. Although still unenthusiastic about the U.S. initiative, he began to argue for European efforts to establish an "extended air defense" to deal with Soviet short-range missiles—an idea that was endorsed by General Bernard Rogers, then the Supreme Allied Commander Europe (SACEUR). Wörner's proposal was sometimes described as a European Defense Initiative, implying an affiliation with both the proposals by von Hassel and others on the German Right, and with the SDI. But the Minister of Defense himself argued that it was a distinct enterprise and one that should be kept separate from SDI. Furthermore, his position was very different from that of the von Hassel group. Rather than emphasizing exotic and space-based technologies to counter both the nuclear and conventional threat to the Federal Republic, Wörner focused primarily on terminal defense technologies to deal with the potential threat from Soviet missiles with conventional warheads. He advocated a "process of incremental steps proceeding from existing air defense capabilities. Relevant technologies could be harnessed to this process in complete conformity with current NATO guidelines covering the exploitation of new technologies for strengthening the conventional defenses of the Alliance."[5]

It is clear from this and other similar statements that Wörner was following a track far removed from SDI. As one commentator has observed, "West German interest in tactical BMD predates SDI and derives from some of the emerging military problems in the European theater."[6] These problems had already been been the focus of two recent studies by NATO's Advisory Group for Aerospace Research and Development (AGARD), one as early as 1980 (AAR-162) and another following Reagan's March 1983 speech (AAS-20), and of analyses done for the German Ministry of Defense and the Bundestag at the Stiftung für Wissenshaft und Politik at Ebenhausen.[7] The results of these assessments seem to have fed into Wörner's own view and encouraged his emphasis on a nonnuclear point defense for priority targets, to be tied in with NATO's air defense network. As Wörner stated it, "The overall defense need neither be impenetrable, nor cover Western Europe comprehensively in order to have strategic effect. Even limited defense capabilities would fulfill the objective of introducing the needed inhibiting uncertainties into Soviet calculations regarding the likely success of their offensive options."[8] Furthermore, Wörner suggested that the initiative should be a common European one, albeit with U.S. involvement. This idea of a common European approach was once again endorsed by General Rogers, who argued that "the West European nations ought to pool their resources and, working together, research such a weapon system, with an exchange across the Atlantic of research information."[9]

Wörner's enthusiasm for an extended air defense has an intellectual basis and a potential strategic rationale, neither of which has anything to do with SDI. Yet the Strategic Defense Initiative may have been relevant to Wörner's stance in a political sense. As noted above, the Kohl government of the mid-1980s was a coalition made up of the majority Christian Democrats and the more liberal Free Democrats. The Free Democrats, under Foreign Minister Genscher, were much more outspoken about SDI and opposed to participation in the research. To some extent, therefore, Wörner's emphasis on ATBMs may have been a way of legitimizing German involvement in SDI—an involvement that the minister of defense deemed necessary on industrial, technological, and scientific grounds. This would also explain why, once the Bonn-Washington Agreement on German participation was signed, Wörner's advocacy of ATBM became slightly muted. Yet it was not abandoned because it remained useful for the defense minister in personal political terms. With the German right supporting an ambitious European initiative to parallel that of the United States, and the left hostile to SDI, ATBM was a useful compromise which enabled Wörner to distance himself from the Reagan administration while lessening his vulnerability to charges from the right that he was oblivious either to new Soviet dangers or to new opportunities for countering them.

If the ATBM issue had political advantages for Wörner, it posed problems and dilemmas for the opposition Social Democrats. On the one hand, the SPD has increasingly favored military postures for NATO that are exclusively defensive and cannot be mistaken by the Soviets as offensive and provocative. On the other, the party is extremely hostile to the SDI because of its potential impact on East-West relations and the threat it poses to the ABM Treaty. Given the defensive role of ATBMs, it is difficult for the SPD to condemn the idea of development and deployment outright. Nevertheless, the antipathy of the Social Democrats toward the SDI has colored their response to Wörner's ATBM proposal. SPD members have questioned both the cost and the feasibility of a European program along the lines proposed by the minister of defense. One might have expected the SPD to move back toward the center on defense issues, perhaps with some tempering of its attitude on ATBMs, following the party's failure in the German elections of January 1987. But Gorbachev intervened with his offer to eliminate both intermediate and shorter-range missiles in Europe. And in the ensuing German debate over whether Gorbachev's "double zero" offer should be accepted or rejected, the ATBM issue was largely lost.

If Wörner failed to win unanimous domestic support for his ideas, the initial reaction of other European governments was also rather mixed. Certainly there was a less enthusiastic reaction from other European countries than Wörner had hoped for. The one exception was the Netherlands, which had become concerned over the threat from the shorter-range Soviet missiles for obvious geographical reasons. In June 1985 the Dutch Minister of Defense Job De Ruiter sent a report to Parliament, calling generally for qualitative improvements in NATO's conventional forces and asserting that "a defense of airfields, command centers, means of communication, etc. by Anti-Tactical Ballistic Missiles (ATBM) seems to be inevitable in the future." The impulse for this report was apparently not President

Reagan's SDI speech but Defense Secretary Weinberger's proposal in 1982 that the Alliance harness "emerging technologies" to NATO's conventional defense. Once again, a deliberate effort was made to differentiate this ATBM proposal from the SDI in origin as well as in concept. As was the case with Wörner, the main concern expressed in De Ruiter's report was the threat from Soviet conventional missiles. Although it was acknowledged that some of the technologies developed as part of SDI research would also be relevant to ATBMs, the rationale for ATBM was much more modest than that for SDI: to preserve NATO's existing strategy, not to embark on a wholly new defense-dominant strategy.[10] Considerable Dutch interest has also been expressed in the possibility of European research and initiative in this field — something in which the Dutch electronics company Philips would almost certainly make a significant contribution.

Neither Britain nor France has shown the same degree of interest in ATBMs as the Netherlands. Yet both the British and French positions have evolved in ways that conceivably could lead to greater support for some form of ATBM development and deployment.

As in the case of Germany, the official British reaction to ATBMs has been complicated by its ambivalent attitude toward the SDI.[11] Although there has been official support for the research program, it has been hedged around with the conditions established at the Camp David meeting between Prime Minister Thatcher and President Reagan in December 1984, where Mrs. Thatcher gained a U.S. promise to respect the ABM Treaty constraints on research and to explore negotiated limits on new ABM systems before deployment. Mrs. Thatcher's approach here reflects traditional British practice in managing its relationship with the United States. The French may choose open confrontation when they have doubts about U.S. policy, but successive British governments have believed that their influence is maximized by a more subtle approach that tries to influence the direction of U.S. policy from within. Yet this should not disguise the fact that British policymakers and officials have been anxious about the effect of SDI and the Soviet responses it may provoke on East-West relations and arms control, on strategic stability, and on the NATO strategy of flexible response.

At the same time that British participation in SDI research has been deemed an important way of shaping the U.S. program, it has also been viewed as a means of obtaining significant research contracts and staying in the forefront of technology. Moreover, it is hoped that participation will prevent an outflow of expertise and initiative to the United States, by ensuring that the "best and the brightest" will conduct their research in Britain, even if it is done at Washington's behest. Apprehension about the dangers that an exclusively U.S. SDI would pose for the technological gap between Western Europe and the United States has gone hand in hand with exaggerated expectations about the possible technological spinoffs from participation in the research program.

Another part of the rationale for participation is related to the British independent nuclear deterrent. Reagan's announcement of the SDI came at a politically inopportune moment for Mrs. Thatcher, following a divisive debate within Britain over a $16 billion program to upgrade the British deterrent by purchasing U.S. Trident II missiles. As in the case of France, nuclear modernization for Britain has been purchased in some degree at the expense of conventional forces. Participation in SDI research is therefore important to the survival—political and technical—of Britain's deterrent: Only if Britain is involved in such research will it have clear idea of the problems that may have to be overcome if Trident is to remain viable in the face of Soviet defenses.

Concerns over the strategic and political implications of SDI, however, are not easily reconciled with participation. To cope with the inherent tensions, there has been a tendency to compartmentalize the policy debate on the one side and involvement in the research program on the other. At some point in the future, this disjunction may no longer be feasible. If the U.S. program develops in ways that undermine the Camp David understanding, Britain will face difficult dilemmas—and could well find that participation has compromised its position and given it less, rather than more influence over United States policy.

Britain, as part of its participation in SDI research, has been undertaking a so-called architecture study of what an SDI for Europe might look like. With the focus primarily on the Soviet nuclear threat, this study is much closer in spirit to U.S. ideas than to Wörner's or De Ruiter's more modest schemes. Nevertheless, it is conceivable that, at the very lowest end of any European architecture for SDI, there could be some overlap with Wörner's idea of ATBM as extended air defense. Yet a focused debate on the ATBM issue is one in which Britain has lagged well behind West Germany. Although there was almost certainly some analysis of the ATBM issue within the British Ministry of

Defense in 1985 and 1986, there was little public discussion of the issue. Indeed, it was not until early 1987 that the House of Commons, through evidence before its Defense Committee, began to give even the most minimal attention to the question of ATBMs. This is not entirely surprising — only one of the three Soviet missiles the Germans are so worried about (the SS-22) could reach the United Kingdom.

It was inevitable, therefore, that although London naturally must be attentive to the protection of British forces and bases in Germany, the ATBM problem has been treated as one that primarily concerned Bonn. Furthermore, there remains a certain degree of caution, if not to say skepticism, within official circles about the seriousness of the Soviet conventional ballistic missile threat. Although it is accepted that there is a potential threat, its scale and intensity are far from clear. There are also worries about the resource implications of ATBMs, concerns that go hand-in-hand with the belief that other ways of dealing with the Soviet missile challenge may be preferable to active defenses. The implication of all this is that there could be some resistance in Britain, largely on cost grounds, to the idea of embarking on an ATBM program of the kind outlined by Wörner. The possibilities of greater convergence, of course, cannot be excluded. But there is a considerable way to go before there is a common assessment, let alone a concerted response from London and Bonn.

France, like Britain, has given far more attention to the SDI than to the ATBM issue. Nevertheless, there have been some signs of French interest in the Wörner proposal. Indeed, France in recent years has displayed far greater sensitivity toward the security problems of the Federal Republic, and this trend could influence the French stance on ATBMs. France, of course, also has an interest — as does Britain — in developing antimissile capabilities for its maritime forces and might see opportunities to extend the scope of its programs in conjunction with Britain and possibly other European states. This would have the added virtue for France of strengthening the European industrial base, thereby enabling the Europeans to go further toward the development of a two-way street in armaments cooperation between Europe and the United States.

Again, what complicates the ATBM issue for France is the shadow of the SDI. For France, in particular, the SDI has raised all the old anxieties about U.S. domination of Europe — a technological Yalta, as it were.[12] Some of the arguments in fact have been reminiscent of De Gaulle's concerns of the 1960s about the U.S. challenge to French sovereignty and status. Reagan's initiative has also provoked concerns that in a world where both superpowers deploy strategic defenses, serious decoupling could occur and Europe could be made safe for conventional war. In a sense this simply represents an additional twist to the traditional French argument that U.S. vulnerability casts doubt on the credibility of extended deterrence: In a world of strategic defenses, Soviet *invulnerability* would cast doubt on U.S. extended deterrence.

On top of these concerns there has been the inevitable anxiety in Paris about the implications of SDI and Soviet defenses for the French strategic nuclear deterrent capabilities, in which France has invested heavily in financial, political, and doctrinal terms. This anxiety is all the more intense because the rationale for the French deterrent has rested on doubts over the U.S. guarantee. Moreover, France's modernization of its conventional forces has lagged over the past decade, at least in part because the view has prevailed that "to develop them in an exaggerated fashion would be to behave as if nuclear weapons did not exist, to raise doubts about our will to use them."[13] If French nuclear capabilities and the backbone of French doctrine are called into question at the same time as there is a further weakening of the U.S. nuclear umbrella, then the implications for French security and the structure of French military forces could be far-reaching.

At the formal level, therefore, the response to SDI of the French government has been very different from that of Bonn and London. Not only was France more outspoken in its criticism of the SDI than any other European country, but it also refused to participate formally in the research program or to seek a government to government agreement of the kind Washington has reached with Britain and the Federal Republic. Indeed, the French response has had several distinct elements, each designed to cope with what is seen as both a technological and strategic challenge. One element has been the modernization of French strategic nuclear forces to make them capable of penetrating any Soviet defenses, through warhead hardening and improved penetration aids, as well as MIRVs. A second element was the introduction at the Geneva Conference on Disarmament in June 1984, of proposals for the demilitarization of space — in effect, a proposal to ban the SDI. Although the French in early 1984 briefly flirted with the idea of a European BMD program, this rapidly gave way to what may be taken as a third element: an emphasis on the need for a European space program that would help in surveillance and arms control verification and in these areas make Western Europe less dependent on the United States.

The fourth element in the French response was the launching of the Eureka project, designed to ensure that Western Europe would not become an economic and technological backwater if the SDI were to provide the kind of technological boost to the U.S. economy that its proponents hope. Eureka had its origins in a report on European participation in SDI prepared by the Forecasting and Analysis Center of the Ministry of External Relations:

> This report was especially critical of the argument that participation in SDI would be an effective way to meet the technological challenge posed by the U.S. program. It pointed out that SDI work would primarily be military, with little immediate civilian application—and this was in addition to the dual problem of America's obsession with technology transfer and the need to protect work labeled industrial-defense secret. Furthermore, it would make sense for the SDIO to seek out Europeans only in areas where Europe already has a lead, yet the key areas of SDI work—lasers, micro-computers, space— are exactly those where the American predominance is overwhelming.[14]

Eureka was intended as an attempt to overcome these problems and set European priorities for technological advancement.

Nevertheless, there have been signs of some modification of the French position, especially since Monsieur Chirac became prime minister in 1986. Chirac in opposition had warned that superpower defenses offered possibilities of a U.S.-Soviet condominium that could reduce Europe to a hostage role. He had also suggested, however, that this could be prevented by development, in cooperation with the United States, of a European antimissile system. After the election of March 1986, he became even more positive about the SDI and suggested that France could not afford to remain aloof from the program. In June 1986, Defense Minister Giraud also stated that he could envisage cooperation with allies to defend against the adversary, a remark that *Le Monde* claimed was his first public allusion to the idea of a European Defense Initiative.[15] Subsequently, the government gave up efforts to inhibit participation by French industry in SDI research. French companies are keen for contracts since, as one industrialist put it: "In Eureka we pay the bill. In SDI, the U.S. government pays."[16] Indeed, some industrialists are not only anxious to participate in the U.S. project but would also like a "military Eureka" with an emphasis on ATBMs and air defense systems.[17] The implication of this is that the French position on SDI — and perhaps ATBMs — is not as far removed from that of Britain and West Germany as it first appears.

The turbulence that the SDI has caused in the ATBM debate should not be underestimated. Reagan's proposal has raised fundamental questions about security arrangements in Europe. What is revealed in the French, British, and West German government positions on SDI is a pervasive conservatism on security issues. The French government, reflecting what appears to be an enduring national consensus in favor of nuclear weapons, has long opposed antinuclear policies, whether they come from the European left or the U.S. right. The British and West German governments, although they face more strident domestic opposition to nuclear weapons, have adopted a similar stance and see their security as dependent on a continuation of the U.S. nuclear guarantee, buttressed in Britain's case by the additional insurance of the independent deterrent.

This pervasive conservatism has manifested itself in a variety of forms. Perhaps most important, it has led to a mixed reaction from the European governments to the arms control position of the United States. On the one side, the European governments (supported by opposition parties) have opposed U.S. abrogation of the SALT II limits and the ABM Treaty; on the other they (unlike the opposition parties) have been unenthusiastic about the removal of U.S. long-range theater nuclear missiles from Europe and dislike the idea of the elimination of ICBMs from the arsenals of the two superpowers. The ABM Treaty has become particularly important and is something on which there is widespread agreement in Europe. The right supports it as a symbol of the existing strategic order in which nuclear weapons play a key role, while the left sees it as a constraint on SDI and therefore as a means of heading off an intensified arms race.

Although left, right, and center view the matter from very different perspectives, the spectrum of opinion on the SDI in France, Britain, and West Germany is surprisingly narrow. The opposition parties in Britain and the Federal Republic are rather more sympathetic to efforts to downgrade nuclear weapons, but they believe the SDI is an inappropriate means to this end. They contend that SDI will have the opposite effect and see in it little more than a badly disguised attempt by the United States to reestablish nuclear superiority, with profoundly destabilizing consequences.

Differences between governments and oppositions became more marked in the aftermath of the Reykjavik Summit of October 1986, where the Soviets insisted that agreement on a range of arms proposals was within reach, if only the United States would abandon the SDI. The major European governments found themselves in the awkward position of being grateful for Reagan's unyielding commitment to the SDI because the impasse at Reykjavik saved them, if only temporarily, from radical arms reduction agreements that many believed to be inimical to West European security. The opposition parties were much more openly critical. They saw President Reagan's desire to minimize the constraints on the SDI as the major reason for the impasse and therefore as an obstacle to progress on arms reduction. Real as they are, however, these differences should not be exaggerated. The debate is not so much between champions of SDI and critics; rather is it between those who give what is at best qualified support to the SDI research program—and believe that Europeans can benefit from participation—and those who are more publicly critical. The main European reaction is one of skepticism, if not hostility. Even the Thatcher and Kohl governments do not like SDI very much; center and left-wing opposition parties like it even less.

Where does all this leave the ATBM issue?

It is clear that Wörner has succeeded in placing ATBM on the public agenda in Germany and on the official agenda in NATO. What remains unclear, however, is how the alliance members are likely to proceed. Although an increasing convergence of attitudes and policies in London, Paris, and Bonn is conceivable, at the moment the differences of assessment and priorities are substantial. Even the position of the Federal Republic seems ambivalent. On the one hand, it has thrown in its lot in with SDI; on the other, it has argued that Europe has distinctive defense needs of its own that might best be dealt with through a cooperative European effort. In view of this disarray, it is pertinent to examine the merits and drawbacks of various approaches to the ATBM issue that the Europeans might plausibly take.

APPROACHES TO THE ATBM ISSUE

One path open to the Europeans is to involve themselves more deeply in the SDI and seek to adapt it to European purposes. Such an approach would address the ambivalence Europeans have felt from the beginning about the technological and industrial implications of SDI, seeing the SDI both as a threat to be contained and an opportunity to be exploited. And it would respond to an expressed fear that association with the SDI is the only way of preventing an exodus of scientific talent and expertise from Europe.

The problem with this approach is that, at least so far, it has yielded little to those who have tried it. Admittedly, the earliest expectations about lucrative research contracts flowing to Europe from the SDI were wildly optimistic. Nonetheless, the peculiarities of the U.S. contracting system, the concerns of the Congress with protecting U.S. defense industries, as well as the competitive edge enjoyed by these industries, will all serve to limit the European share of SDI research work. This has already become apparent and in June 1987 the Defense Committee of the British House of Commons, expressed serious disappointment at the limited amount of research funding that had been obtained by British firms.[18] Furthermore, even the contracts that are forthcoming to Britain and its allies are likely to be double-edged. As David Greenwood has argued, these contracts will generally be in areas where European technology is clearly ahead and where the United States has its own well-defined need. In a sense, the United States will simply be coopting European technological expertise to help in its own programs. The technology transfer is likely to be a one-way valve, which actually drains away European achievements in areas such as fiber optics and advanced computing, while offering little in return. The result is that participation, far from enhancing the European technological base and making Europe more competitive, could have the opposite effect.[19] Unless Europe can command a prominent technological role in the SDI, therefore, it seems unlikely it could wield the political influence necessary to shape the program to European needs.

The implication is that for economic, technological, and political reasons, there might be merit in a European program that runs in parallel with the SDI but is essentially independent of it. Such an effort, with a focus on ATBMs might provide a military counterpart to Eureka and could also be closely coordinated with the Esprit program, which attempts to coordinate European efforts in the area of information technology. Judicious exploitation of new technologies such as sensors that would be of importance to defense against Soviet missiles could help to strengthen Western Europe's technical and industrial base and enhance European competitiveness. Skeptics, of course, will argue that there is already a disproportionate amount of research into military applications, and that a European initiative on ATBMs, by diverting further resources into the military sector, would actually have a negative effect on European economies. In this view, the need for a European technological initiative is already met by Eureka, which has the great virtue of being primarily nonmilitary in character. Such an appraisal of the likely benefits of ATBM development seems rather negative, however. Indeed, for European governments that are anxious to compete more effectively with the United States in the military industrial field, ATBM might provide an important opportunity. This would not necessarily preclude cooperation in selected areas with the United States. Such cooperation, however, would be in areas of mutual benefit and would not involve Washington simply coopting European efforts to its own purposes.

The strategic rationale for this approach is that the focus on European requirements would be at the forefront of the research effort and would not simply be a by-product of U.S. activities. Western Europe would define the requirement and play the major role in fulfilling it, thereby going some way toward disarming U.S. critics who claim that the allies are unwilling either intellectually or economically to share the burdens of Western defense. But even if this rationale is persuasive, there are several factors inhibiting the development of a European ATBM.

One of the difficulties is that the leading countries of Western Europe may already be so far down the road of participation in SDI that they will be unable or unwilling to embark on an independent initiative. Although collaboration with other European governments is not excluded by participation in SDI research, there could be sensitivities about the transfer of information. Furthermore, the divergent security and national priorities of the three leading European states might prove a barrier to collaboration. The triangular asymmetries that have traditionally inhibited European defense cooperation could come to the fore once again. Both Britain and France are concerned less about the Soviet conventional missile threat that alarms Germany and the Netherlands than they are about the challenge to their own strategic nuclear forces, for instance. A research collaboration between allies who wish to build ATBMs and others whose primary concern is with devising ways of defeating them is far from ideal.

In spite of this, the ATBM issue could be the occasion for a major exercise in triangular collaboration between London, Paris, and Bonn, yielding at least a common appreciation of the defense problem and the best way to deal with it. This would have several advantages. Not only would it be an important extension of the bilateral consultation and cooperation increasingly taking place among the three capitals, thereby thickening the network of collaboration, but it would also allow the major European powers to identify areas of agreement and disagreement on the ATBM issue without being diverted by the concerns of others.

The difficulties of establishing a tripartite agreement on ATBMs remain formidable, however, and could be exacerbated by budgetary restrictions. In the late 1970s and the early 1980s, defense ministries in Europe could count on receiving fairly steady shares of their respective national budgets. The period ahead, in contrast, is likely to be one of considerable stringency in which the battle for budget shares will be acute. Unless there is either a substantial improvement in economic growth rates in Western Europe, or a marked deterioration in East-West relations, few governments are likely to devote substantially more resources to military spending.[20] Money for ATBMs, therefore, would mean less for other things.

Several consequences can be expected from this. One is that ATBMs are likely to have few champions in the uniformed military services. ATBMs do not fit naturally into traditional service roles and missions and, because of their resource implications, could be seen as a threat by the services. Compelled to make a choice between buying new aircraft and buying ATBMs to protect existing aircraft, most air force commanders will do what comes naturally—especially if the ATBMs would belong to the army. A second consequence is that the budgetary squeeze is likely to widen the differences of priority attached to ATBMs in Bonn, on the one side, and London and Paris on the other. Both Britain and France are giving high priority to the modernization of their strategic nuclear forces, and unless there are major changes in political climate, nuclear modernization will probably have to be done at the expense of conventional capabilities. In such a situation, enthusiasm for the development of ATBMs is unlikely to be high.

Yet another difficulty with triangular cooperation on ATBMs, however, is that it is too exclusive. Even if the obstacles to establishing a common approach by the "big three" were overcome, there would still be the problem of how the other European countries would be integrated into the project. It would be essential, for example, to have the Netherlands involved in a European project, not only in view of Dutch concerns about the Soviet ballistic missile threat but also because of the potential technological contribution of Dutch firms such as Philips. European-wide collaboration, however, would be even more complicated to arrange than triangular cooperation. Moreover, if the point is to make the project genuinely European-wide, it is not at all clear how allies for whom the ATBM issue is at best a peripheral concern are to be drawn into collaboration.

The problem of who is to be involved in European defense cooperation has implications for where such collaboration is arranged. An endemic problem in developing a common West European position on security issues has been the lack of an appropriate institutional framework. Certainly, the absence of a forum is sometimes used merely as an excuse for disarray, when the real difficulty is that there are substantive differences among the European allies. Nonetheless, the lack of an institutional setting is not an insignificant problem.

The Western European Union is sometimes mooted as a possibility. Symbolically, the WEU can claim to be the European heart of the Alliance, tracing its origins back to the Brussels Treaty of 1948, the precursor of NATO. But the WEU, composed of Britain, France, Germany, Italy, and the Benelux countries, has rarely been successful at such coordination in the past. The problem with the WEU is that it tends to be regarded in Washington as a vehicle for the Europeans, inspired by France, to gang up on the United States and present it with a fait accompli. Consequently, the United States has sometimes protested at the activities of WEU. It complained in particular that it was an inappropriate forum for the Europeans to develop a concerted response to SDI. Largely because of French and German sensitivity to U.S. attitudes, this protest helped to derail what appeared to be a promising attempt to work out a common European response to the president's initiative. Nevertheless, in the aftermath of Reykjavik, there have been attempts to revitalize the WEU and to thrash out a common European position on the requirements of European security. U.S. misgivings about European cooperation outside the NATO framework may command less regard in European capitals to the extent that U.S. arms control policy appears insensitive to European concerns. It is possible therefore that the WEU might provide a forum in which the conceptual, political, and arms control aspects of ATBM could be considered.

An alternative is the Independent European Program Group (IEPG), which was established in 1976 to serve as the principal institution through which the European members of NATO could develop greater cooperation in arms acquisition. The IEPG has in fact been suggested by French industrialists as a possible forum for cooperation on a "military Eureka." The attraction of the IEPG is that it is already concerned with the next generation of surface-to-air missiles (SAMs) that will themselves have some limited ATBM capability. The difficulty, however, is that although IEPG is the most coherent framework, it is essentially hardware-oriented. Although it could be an important vehicle for the second phase of a European ATBM project, the initial political, military, and economic assessments and decisions would almost certainly have to be hammered out elsewhere. There does appear to be some scope, however, for a "variable geometry" approach in which the WEU would provide the framework for political cooperation and the IEPG would offer the framework for industrial collaboration.

Another alternative is to use NATO itself as the forum. In this connection, the absence of France from the integrated military command is not necessarily a serious problem because France is deeply involved in the whole question of air defense and remains a participant in the NADGE. Furthermore, the emerging Soviet threat and the appropriate NATO response have already been addressed in several Alliance studies. One advantage of keeping the ATBM issue within the Alliance forum is that it would help ensure that potential European requirements for defense against conventionally armed missiles are given a proper priority in relation to the U.S. focus on nuclear missiles. The United States has already demonstrated its interest in ensuring that its bases and forces in Europe are given maximum protection in any hostilities on the Central Front. One often discussed possibility is that enhanced Patriot anti-aircraft missiles might be one of the most appropriate bases for an ATBM system in Europe, perhaps to be replaced later by terminal defense systems developed under the SDI.

The difficulty is that a "made in America" solution is unlikely to recommend itself to European governments increasingly anxious about U.S. technological dominance. Either an enhanced Patriot deployment or an SDI-related solution would merely underscore Western Europe's dependence on the United States for its security and would make no contribution either to the two-way street or to the European industrial base. Equally if not more important, at some stage the United States would almost certainly request that the Europeans pick up some of the costs of any extension of SDI to Europe, something that the Europeans will not find easy.

The other complication in all this is, of course, the ABM Treaty. As suggested above, the desirability of maintaining the integrity of the ABM Treaty is one of the few propositions that can command widespread support from both ends of the political spectrum in Europe. Although the ABM Treaty formally restricts only defenses against strategic ballistic missiles, there is an inevitable gray area: A system deployed to deal with theater ballistic missiles might also have some capability against strategic systems, particularly some of the older submarine-launched ballistic missiles, and thus run afoul of the Treaty's Article VI. Another set of issues relates to the noncircumvention provisions in Article IX of the treaty and Agreed Statement G. The United States and Soviet Union are prohibited from transferring not only ABM systems but also ABM components, technical descriptions, or blueprints to other states. There are two major implications of this. The first is that although ATBM as "son of SAM" is far less likely to contravene the ABM Treaty than an ATBM system which is SDI related, there could still be some gray area problems. The second is that a European initiative on ATBMs—although it might be criticized as contrary to the spirit of the ABM Treaty—may be a less direct threat to the treaty than a U.S.-dominated initiative. Even if this is the case, concerns over the ABM Treaty could provide additional political inhibitions against undertaking what will obviously be a costly and difficult project. Yet these anxieties might not be prohibitive, for in the final analysis, the fate of the ABM Treaty will be decided between the superpowers themselves. Although not irrelevant, it seems unlikely that European actions will be the decisive factor in determining the fate of the ABM Treaty.

The implication of all this is that there is a large gap between placing ATBM on the agenda and devising a coherent European response to the Soviet military challenge or to the U.S. doctrinal and technological challenge. Although it is far from certain that the opportunity will be grasped—the various inhibitions could prove overwhelming—the ATBM issue does provide an opportunity for the West Europeans to collaborate in ways that could prove of enduring importance in the Atlantic relationship, not only at the level of technology and strategy but also politically. The problems they face and the constraints they labor under, however, are formidable and unless there is a greater degree of convergence in the attitudes and policies of Britain, France, and the Federal Republic, a concerted West European approach will prove unattainable. On the other hand, with U.S. strategic and arms control policies moving in directions that the Europeans find disturbing, the incentives for increasing cooperation and self-reliance are probably greater than ever. The gap between incentives and the actual performance of the European allies, however, seems likely to remain large. Perhaps the best that can be hoped for, therefore, is that arms control will effectively remove ATBM from the agenda of European security issues. Although this would remove a possible occasion for cooperation, it would also remove an issue with the potential for very considerable mischief.

NOTES

1. Fred S. Hoffman, Study Director, *Ballistic Missile Defense and U.S. National Security: Summary Report*, prepared for the Future Security Strategy Study (Washington, D.C.: October 1983), pp. 2–3.
2. See Hans-Gunther Brauch, "Anti-Tactical Missile Defense — Will the European Version of SDI Undermine the ABM Treaty," paper presented at the 26th International Studies Association Convention, Washington, D.C., 5–9 March 1985, p. 3.
3. Brauch, "Anti-Tactical Missile Defense." See also Christopher Bluth, "SDI: The Challenge to West Germany," *International Affairs*, Spring 1986, pp. 247–264.
4. Ivo Daalder and Lynn P. Whittaker, "SDI's Implication for Europe: Strategy, Politics, and Technology," in Stephen Flanagan and Fen Hampson, eds., *Securing Europe's Future* (London: Croom Helm, 1986), p. 49.
5. Manfred Wörner, "A Missile Defense for NATO Europe," *Strategic Review*, Winter 1986, p. 16.
6. Bluth, p. 258.
7. Thomas Enders, *Missile Defense as Part of an Extended NATO Air Defense*, (Bonn: Konrad Adenauer Stiftung, Interne Studien 2, 1986), p. 14.
8. Wörner, p. 16.
9. Bob Furlong and Macha Levinson, "SACEUR Calls for Research On A European ABM System," *International Defense Review*, February 1986, p. 149.
10. See Job De Ruiter, report to Parliament on *Strengthening Conventional Defense and Emerging Technologies*, The Hague, 26 June 1985. Similar sentiments have been expressed outside parliament, with Brigadier-General G. C. Berkhof of the Netherlands Institute of International Affairs, Clingendael, proposing a European Aerospace Defense Initia-

tive which would parallel SDI but be European in origin and effort. See *The American Strategic Defense Initiative: Implications for West European Security*, Report on a Workshop, The Hague, 26–27 April 1985, The Netherlands Institute of International Relations, pp. 251–253.

11. For a good discussion of the British reaction, see Trevor Taylor, "Britain's Response to the Strategic Defense Initiative," *International Affairs*, Spring 1986, pp. 217–230.
12. For a good analysis of French concerns, see John Fenske, "France and the Strategic Defense Initiative," *International Affairs*, Spring 1986, pp. 231–246.
13. Former French Defense Minister Charles Hernu, "La politique et la volonté de défense," *Politique International*, Summer 1982, p. 13.
14. Fenske, p. 235.
15. See "M. Giraud évoque le projet de construction par l'Europe d'une défense antimissiles," *Le Monde*, 19 June 1986.
16. See David Marsh, "French High-tech Groups Seek To Win SDI Contracts," *Financial Times*, 8 January, 1986.
17. Fenske, p. 244.
18. Martin Fletcher, "Boom in SDI Work Fails to Appear" *The Times* (London) 19 June 1987.
19. See David Greenwood, *The SDI and Europe* (Aberdeen: Center for Defense Studies, 1986).
20. See Timothy Stanley, *Western and Eastern Economic Constraints on Defense*, (Washington, D.C.: Atlantic Council of the United States), Occasional Paper, Fall 1986.

10 PERSPECTIVE AND COMMENTARY
ATBMs and the Middle East
Shahram Chubin

The Middle East has been characterized by deep antagonisms, a high level of armaments, and a durable conflict of several rounds, with considerable involvement by the superpowers in each round. Even when conflict is not actually underway, the threat of war and the possibility of resort to arms compels states in the region to measure their military capabilities against each other carefully and constantly. The prospect of war can be made more likely or more tempting by changes at various levels, including shifts in the assessment of the military balance, actual or perceived; changes in the domestic orientation of the antagonist states; regional trends that encourage bellicosity and a false or real sense of unity, whether in the name of Arab nationalism or Islamic solidarity; and superpower policies and regional perceptions of the superpowers' commitments.

Changes in military technology do not drive the animosities among states in the Middle East. But arms acquisitions do tend to reflect the state of relations between regional actors and the superpowers and to determine whether there is a real or notional military "balance." Similarly, relations with the superpowers have become a critical and all-absorbing challenge as superpower involvement has grown from war to war, and as the United States and the Soviet Union have shifted from being bystanders to becoming arms suppliers, diplomatic shapers, and even defenders of last resort.

The current situation in the Middle East is one of unchallenged Israeli predominance. Only Syria makes any attempt to keep pace with Israel militarily. At the same time, the Arab world is fragmented not only on ideological issues and on reactions to the Iran-Iraq war but more profoundly by the great differences in resources and domestic political situations that place correspondingly different demands on individual states. In regional politics, these situational differences weaken the prospect of a broad coalition of states collectively threatening Israel. At the same time, however, another regional trend, Islamic fundamentalism, contains the seeds of a more serious threat, which might mobilize large and implacable forces against Israel.

It is against this general background that Middle Eastern states would look at the deployment of ABM/ATBM systems in Europe and the United States and ask themselves what the implications are for the relationship of the United States and Europe with third areas, for the relationship between the two blocs, and for the impact that the introduction of such technologies might have on Middle East politics and strategy.

Although the relationship between Israel and the United States is stronger and more organic than that between any Arab state and the USSR, there is always concern in Israel that it may come to be seen by the United States as a burden. There is also a recognition that the European states neither view Israel as sympathetically nor see Middle Eastern politics in the same way as Israel and the United States do. Although Israel is less concerned that the superpowers might strike a deal at its expense, it is far more concerned that new technologies might be introduced into the region that would undermine its military supremacy, which is based largely on Israel's maintenance of unrivaled qualitative superiority.

The Arab states in general would be interested in anything that might exploit differences between the United States and Israel on the one hand and the United States and Europe on the subject of Israel on the other. Aware (in the main) that they do not possess the political leverage of the 1970s, and lacking a credible military option, the Arab states would be eager to demonstrate their interest in maintaining a stable military balance that did not concede to Israel the right to permanent superiority or depend on their own continuing vulnerability and inferiority for its stability. At the same time, any technology that held open the possibility of enhancing their own defense would be doubly attractive, both for its own features and for the political relations it might help foster, particularly with European states.

Before turning to the likely reactions of the Middle Eastern states to the deployment of ABM/ATBM in Europe and the United States, it is important to put into context those aspects of the Middle Eastern military situation that have a bearing on this subject. For the sake of brevity these are stated as propositions, and their specific relevance is discussed more fully subsequently.

- Although Israel has depended heavily on its air superiority, the Arab states have since 1973 sought to offset this by reliance on short-range ballistic missiles and SAM defenses.
- The Arab states have in the past sought shortcuts in their competition with Israel — for instance, Egypt's missile program under Nasser, or Libya's efforts to purchase nuclear bombs and its cooperation with the German firm, Otrag, on a missile program. This quest for a wonder weapon or equalizer may recur. Chemical weapons have been used in the Gulf War between Iran and Iraq, and with adequate delivery they could be an "intermediate option" between conventional and nuclear weapons.
- Israel, with a sense of a slim margin for error, has hedged against the possibility of a sudden technological breakthrough by its adversaries by developing an ambitious nuclear capability married to an ambiguous nuclear doctrine.
- Both Israel and the Arab states currently possess short-range ballistic missiles in their inventory. Israel has the Lance and Jericho, with ranges of 120 and 480 km respectively. In 1975–76 the U.S. government refused to supply Israel with the Pershing missile (partly on the grounds that it could be used as a first strike weapon). Syria, Egypt and Iraq all have the Soviet-made Frog 7 and Scud B (with ranges of 70 and 300 km). In addition, Iraq and Libya have the SS-12 (900 km), and Syria has the SS-21 (120 km).
- Short distances to targets in the Arab-Israel and the Persian Gulf theaters, and the proliferation of advanced air defenses that increasingly make penetration to targets with aircraft difficult, may increase the incentives for development of alternate forms of delivery, such as short-range ballistic missiles.
- In the confined geographic space of the Middle East theater, distinctions between strategic and tactical, or civilian and military

targets would tend to be eroded, as there would be an overlap of categories. This would of course apply equally to air and missile defenses, where there could be no hard and fast distinction between point and area defense.
- Although conventionally armed short-range ballistic missiles have not yet proven effective in war, improvements in accuracy and payload could change this. On the other hand, vulnerable or unreliable missile systems could increase dangers by inviting preemption, or by necessitating launch-on-warning postures. Unless these missile systems are mobile and/or hardened and equipped with early warning and defense capabilities, they will not be very useful weapons.

ISRAEL'S VIEW OF ABM/ATBM

The deployment of ABM/ATBM systems in both Europe and the United States, possibly through a general upgrading of air defense systems, would raise a number of anxieties in Israel, anxieties not necessarily assuaged by the prospect of opportunities that ATBM deployments might also present. The move toward greater emphasis on defensive systems would be less worrisome to Israel if it occurs *within* the current context of nuclear deterrence and the mutual hostage relationship, rather than signaling a move toward an entirely different concept of security. Nevertheless, residual Israeli doubts would remain (analogous to those in Europe) about the effect such a move would have on the continuing viability of U.S. extended deterrence. Would the United States be as keen to take on commitments and risks in crises in third areas? Could it do so credibly? Would there not be the beginnings of a decoupling from more exposed allies, as the United States settled into a "fortress America"?

Given the practical and psychological importance of the U.S. link, Israel's concern on the political level would be to seek a ringing affirmation that these ties were in no way affected by the deployments in Europe of ABM/ATBM systems. The clearest indication the United States could give that it did not wish to differentiate among its important allies or start a category of second-class ally would be to extend an ABM/ATBM system to Israel as well. Or so Israel would be tempted to argue. More concretely, it could be pointed out that the provision of such systems would be beneficial to the United States because it would reduce the need for any active involvement in crises.

That is, the United States could reduce its own exposure, to the extent that it enabled the Israelis to take care of their own defense concerns.

On the military side, Israel would have a number of concerns about assuring the continuation of her military superiority and guarding against anything that might undermine it. An ABM/ATBM system would be useful to Israel both as a hedge against accelerated emphasis by the Arab states on short-range ballistic missiles or cruise missiles and as a counter if the Arab states were to gain access to equivalent defensive systems.

From Israel's perspective, anything undermining her dominance of the air would be profoundly destabilizing. Future acquisitions by several Arab states of large numbers of short-range missiles (perhaps the SS-21, SS-22, or SS-23) could threaten to saturate and overwhelm Israel's air defenses and assure a certain amount of penetration. Given Israel's sensitivity to casualties, such an attack would be especially damaging. At the same time, the use of short-range missiles as substitutes for aircraft would compensate for traditional Arab weakness in airpower and free up aircraft for other missions.

To the extent that Israeli airpower were neutralized by Arab air defenses, while Arab short-range missile capability remained intact, the effect would be to encourage probing on the ground — to test Israel without much fear of sanction. From Israel's point of view anything weakening its deterrent capability, such as an appreciable increase in the number and effectiveness of Arab ballistic missiles, would need to be countered. And the most effective counter would be an upgraded air defense system including an ATBM system.

In this connection, Israel would be interested in the development of upgraded air defense systems like the Patriot, which is intended to counter the SS-21, SS-22, and SS-23 and perhaps the SS-20. The German-sponsored European Defense Initiative (EDI), which is to look at air-defenses for shooting down aircraft, cruise missiles, and short- and long-range theater ballistic missiles, is precisely the sort of program that Israel would try to become associated with. The similarity of needs in the face of a common set of weapons systems (admittedly still only potential in the Middle East case) would argue for a strong Israeli interest in European developments. Israel's interest in associating with the United States in the development of the Strategic Defense Initiative, in part to assure access to U.S. technology and in part to demonstrate loyalty to its superpower ally, is likely to be paralleled by comparable interest in a European association—

especially if there are signs that the Europeans are on the road to developing effective indigenous air defense capabilities.

Another consideration for Israel would be the potential acquisition by any Arab state of upgraded air defense systems, including a limited ABM or ATBM system. Already the steady improvement of air defense capabilities in Syria has had the effect of inhibiting aggressive aerial reconnaissance by Israel. If these improvements continue, it could make the execution of air strikes too costly to contemplate, leaving Israel with the choice between no reaction and all-out war. Such a development would weaken Israel's air advantage and her deterrent, requiring a heavier investment in airpower to assure penetration while allowing for greater attrition. In this context Israel would want to gain access to advanced air defense technology, particularly to reduce any confidence the Arab states might have of launching a preemptive air and missile attack and following it up with ground assaults, under the umbrella of their own defense capabilities. Israel would want to offset this by limiting her own casualties and damage through air defenses and by reducing the confidence of her adversaries in their use of missiles as a screen or prelude to a more general attack.

For at least the last decade, Israel has kept in reserve the possibility of resorting to nuclear weapons as a final, desperate measure in her own defense. Generally her references to the conditions of use have been clear: The weapons would be used for the ultimate defense of Israel—a last resort. Voices have been raised from time to time advocating that Israel lower this nuclear threshold (on the argument that Israel could then ease the economic burden of conventional forces), and there has been some debate about the value of having a more explicit nuclear doctrine and a less ambiguous posture. Nonetheless, the official policy remains one of ambiguity, while making clear that a capability exists to assemble and deliver nuclear—and possibly thermonuclear—weapons rapidly.

Although there is no clear evidence for this, it is at least plausible to argue that Israel's possession of a nuclear capability, together with strong conventional forces, has gone a long way toward convincing many Arab leaders that the old aim of destroying Israel is no longer a viable one and that some form of accommodation is therefore necessary. The possession of a nuclear capability, however latent, has served as a guarantee of an ultimate deterrent in the defense of the homeland—an insurance policy in case there should be a breakdown on the conventional level and a reminder to the Arab states of the folly of framing their war aims in unrealistic terms. All this could change if the Arab states were to gain a significant ABM/ATBM system that might cast doubt on the ability of Israel to deliver its weapons or that might encourage Arab miscalculations. From Israel's viewpoint, anything that weakened its deterrent or retaliatory capability (particularly its airpower and nuclear lead) is likely to encourage conflict by reducing its qualitative advantage, thus increasing the importance of ground forces and sheer numbers, which are the Arab states' strong suit.

Lastly, quite apart from any possible Arab reaction, Israel would be interested in ABM/ATBM technology for the possible protection it could give not just its military forces but also its civilian population. Given the small geographic size of Israel, advanced defenses deployed to ensure the survival of Israeli military facilities would presumably also grant some protection to Israeli cities.

ARAB STATES' VIEWS OF ABM/ATBMS

Analyzing the probable reactions of the Arab states to future events is made difficult by the fact that the objectives and priorities of each state are heavily influenced by the nature of the individual leader of the day. Assuming, however, that rivalry with Israel will remain a dominant concern for most of these states, and that this will find continuing expression in an arms race in which each side's acquisitions are studied carefully and made the basis for subsequent decisions, then the question of upgraded air defense and ABM/ATBM are likely to figure prominently in the future.

Egypt in particular would be sensitive to any U.S. policy that differentiated to a significant degree between itself and Israel with respect to defense needs. Most Arab states would see any U.S.-Israel or U.S.-Europe-Israel cooperation in this field as only the concrete manifestation of a long and informal alliance. They would see this as a collusive enterprise to assure that Israel retains complete military superiority, with the freedom to dictate its own terms at will. The transfer of such technology to Israel would thus be seen in terms of freezing the military balance in Israel's favor while raising obstacles for other states wishing to challenge it.

The Arab states could seek to offset this by convincing the European states that they should also receive ABM/ATBM technology. (I do not consider it likely that the Arab states would be given this technology by Europe before Israel receives it.) Their arguments could revolve around the need for equivalent security and the flexibility that this would give them in their approach to Israel. They could point to the essentially "defensive" utility of this technology and argue for its stabilizing effect: It could counteract Israel's unchallenged air superiority without threatening her cities or population. Conversely, they could point to the fact that an Israeli ability to dominate the air and to blunt any Arab retaliatory response would be conducive neither to compromise nor to moderation.

If these arguments were insufficient to convince the United States or Europe, the Arab states could resort to the Soviet Union. Here, in theory, they would have two options. One would be to acquire comparable advanced defenses, to nullify Israeli advantages. The other would be to increase the number and quality of their short-range ballistic missiles in order to saturate Israeli defenses, thereby undermining Israel's confidence in its own defenses and exploiting Israel's extreme sensitivity to casualties. Alternatively, or perhaps in parallel, ballistic missiles could be explicitly targeted on Israeli civilian centers rather than military installations, to hold the cities hostage. Further measures could include embarking on a crash program to acquire an equalizer, however crude—possibly some form of chemical weapon deliverable by missile. And the Arab states would always retain the option for an increased emphasis on terrorism and subconventional actions, which could circumvent Israel's military strengths.

We can extrapolate from a concrete, contemporary case for purposes of illustration—namely, that of Israel and Syria. Israel's airpower has served to put limits on Syria's actions in Lebanon and the Golan Heights. Yet improved Syrian air defenses raise the prospect that Israel will become increasingly inhibited in the use of its airpower in the future, thus removing one of the restraints on a more active Syrian policy. Raising the price of Israeli air attacks while improving Syria's defenses to the extent of making parts of Syria a sanctuary, for instance, could favor Syria by allowing it to use its advantage in ground forces and artillery. From the Israeli view, the transfer of effective advanced defenses to Syria might encourage a Syrian attitude of "having a bash" on the expectation that whatever the numerical exchange rate, the attrition of Israeli forces would so weaken Israel that it could not withstand another Arab assault. Again from Israel's view, effective air defenses might encourage the Arab states to withhold their own aircraft in a future conflict, for use after Israel had exhausted itself in suppressing their air defenses. From the Arab standpoint, however, the acquisition of advanced defenses could be the beginning of a capability to neutralize the realm in which Israel has traditionally excelled, with implications for good and evil.

THE PERSIAN GULF AND ATBMS

The Iran-Iraq war, now in its seventh year of often intense fighting, is likely to whet appetites for enhanced air defenses. And indeed the Persian Gulf states do have several characteristics that would make the quest for better air defenses and ABM/ATBM capabilities logical and possibly even pressing. The vulnerability of critical installations, the short distances to targets measured in aircraft flight times, and the possiblity of attack from more than one quarter—all these could encourage reliance on such technologies. The fact that the air defense networks in the region have been relatively untested in combat—the Saudis' AWACS notwithstanding—may also encourage optimistic views of the value of advanced systems. And it could be persuasively argued that the transfer of such technology to the oil-producing Gulf states would be in the interest of the European states themselves. However, while a thicker air defense system would be prudent and useful against any missiles that go astray from the current fighting, or from future threats in subsequent rounds of fighting, internal subversion rather than external attack by ballistic missiles is probably the major form of threat confronting the Gulf states.

The Iran-Iraq war, whatever its other peculiarities, has again demonstrated the difficulty that Third World states have in mounting coordinated and large-scale aerial operations. In this war, air power has played a less than decisive role, tactically or strategically. In part this is due to Iraq's reluctance to risk losses of aircraft and pilots and thus leave itself exposed to Iran's superior numbers. In part it is due to Iraq's recognition that a sustained bombing of Iranian installations could elicit an Iranian response in the form of shelling of its own installations by artillery.

The experience of the war is thus equivocal with respect to the value of an ABM/ATBM capability. The mutual hostage situation that currently obtains has encouraged a degree of restraint by the adversaries. If one or the other were to obtain comprehensive defense against air attack from the other, the situation would change. This is particularly true for Iraq, which could then feel freer about hazarding its aircraft without risk of a devastating Iranian response by missile or air. However, it is striking in this case that Iran's air force has not been very active over Iraq and that Iran has not relied on missiles to threaten Baghdad, except in retaliation for Iraqi attacks. It has been Iran's long-range artillery that has caused the most damage, and it would remain free to do so even if Iraq had an ATBM capability.

So rather than having their appetites for ATBMs whetted, the two belligerents are not likely to come away from the Gulf War with a marked urgency in the quest for such weapons systems. And neither belligerent, even if they could afford it, would expect to get ATBM technologies from Europe, the United States or even the USSR.

THE IMPLICATIONS OF ATBMS FOR MIDDLE EAST SECURITY

The introduction of enhanced and upgraded air defense capabilities including ATBM/ABM could work in favor of peace or conflict depending on the context. An ABTM could stabilize situations in crises by enhancing the survivability and hence assuring the retaliatory capability necessary for deterrence. Alternatively, this capability could increase instability by inviting first-use and preemption. Given only to Israel to add to its present military dominance, ATBM capabilities would ratify the hegemony of that state and protect it from any increased acquisition of short range missiles by its adversaries. Whether it would make Israel any more confident or willing to be flexible vis-à-vis the Arab states is open to doubt. It would undoubtedly stimulate the Arab states into making greater efforts to prevent an increase in Israel's lead, not necessarily by seeking the same capability but perhaps by means of some putative shortcut.

If both Israel and its adversaries were to obtain equivalent upgraded air and missile defense coverage at the same time, the net effect would be mixed. Israel would gain greater means to protect itself, but at the price of reduced effectiveness in its air superiority. The Arab states might find that the result played to their strength in ground forces, but at the price of nullifying their current missile and aircraft threats against Israeli population centers.

Whichever case emerges, there seems little doubt that the introduction of improved air defenses would only constitute a new round in a qualitative arms race that would continue until the two sides muster the will to put aside their political differences. In this respect ABM/ATBM is neither the panacea nor the primary problem in the region.

11 PERSPECTIVE AND COMMENTARY
China, Japan, and ATBMS

Gerald Segal

ATBMs may be a topic of lively interest among Americans and Europeans, but finding references to ATBMs in East Asia is largely a fruitless enterprise. To be sure, both Japanese and Chinese officials understand the meaning of the term, but few of the concerns that animate NATO's interest in ATBMs are articulated or even felt by the East Asians because they perceive their security policies to be based on different principles. China and Japan perceive the likelihood of war, the amount of defense that is necessary, the linkage of conventional and nuclear war, and the SDI in very different ways than the Europeans do. In almost every respect, these divergent perceptions lead to an indifference toward the ATBM issue.

HOW LIKELY IS WAR?

The decision to acquire the most modern of military hardware is usually the outcome of interaction among an active military-industrial sector, a powerful armed forces, and an assessment by policymakers that war is likely. In the case of China, none of these ingredients is present. Certainly China is interested in new technology as part of its general commitment to the "four modernizations." But China approaches the ATBM issue from the base of a poor, peasant economy, and it has discovered that there are few shortcuts from "barefoot technologies" to the space age.

To be sure, parts of China are fully *au fait* with new technology, and many of these are in the military sector. New weapons systems acquired in the past five years have propelled China into the military technology of the 1970s: not quite first rate but not third rate either. Yet China's military policy retains many legacies of the "people's war" tradition, and Beijing has adopted an approach to new technology characteristic of developing states: China seeks modern equipment that is rugged and inexpensive as much as it is sophisticated. The new strategy of "people's war under modern conditions" sees a greater role for new technology as China proceeds to reduce its armed forces. But modernization does not necessarily bring unquestioned imitation of modern Western defense policies. China is likely to remain deeply skeptical about the utility of ATBM.

What is principally absent in China is an emphasis on imminent threat from its neighbor to the north. One of the major reforms in Chinese foreign policy in the 1980s has been to discount the chances of war.[1] China has embarked on its military modernization program on the assumption that, in the current period, war is "preventable or postponable" rather than "inevitable" and that China has a breathing space to concentrate on economic modernization, free from external worry. Moreover, from the Chinese perspective, war is unlikely because the things worth attacking — Chinese cities and troops deployed well back from the border — would require a major rather than minor strike. Such a strike from the Soviets has become less probable because of changes in Moscow's circumstances, including the new preoccupation with domestic reform, the burdens of the Afghan quagmire, and the greater U.S. challenge to Soviet power.

In part China's diminished anxiety over war is an act of faith: It is the Chinese assessment that changed, not necessarily the objective Soviet threat. But to a large extent, the reassessment has become self-fulfilling.

As part of its new policy, China has begun cutting its armed forces by one-quarter. One million men were demobilized by the spring of 1987, and several hundred thousand troops have been withdrawn from various frontiers. China's military industry has been reorganized and transferred in part to the civil sector. It is now turning out fewer weapons but is benefitting from greater long-term investment.

Coincident with these changes, China has been engaged in a far-reaching process of tacit arms control with the Soviet Union. More than 100,000 Chinese troops have been removed from the Sino-Soviet frontier, and the troops that remain are now based several hundred miles further back from the border. The Soviet Union has quietly thinned out its own divisions, removing some 80,000 to 90,000 troops while leaving the official number of divisions constant. In January 1987 the Soviet Union announced that more than a division of troops would be pulled out of Mongolia by the summer.[2] This far-reaching, tacit arms control by China is hardly the action of a country in fear of imminent war or concerned with the need to keep pace with the latest military threat.

At the same time, China has also been raising the cost of any Soviet strike by modernizing its armed forces: A new model weapon has been tested or deployed in every major category during the past four years; the navy has increasingly become a blue-water force; in-flight refueling has been discussed for the air force; and training in combined arms operations has been conducted in China over the past five years.[3] In the nuclear field, China deployed a new model ICBM in 1981 and a new SLBM in 1983. Nonetheless, despite these signs of ferment and innovation, there has been scant Chinese discussion of tactical nuclear weapons issues generally, not even in the context of NATO-Warsaw Pact conflict. And there is not a single sign of a special concern with the ATBM issue.[4]

Unquestionably, China is quite vulnerable to a Soviet attack. No sensible Chinese strategist doubts that Soviet troops could strike deep into China's territory and could do so relatively unopposed. Prudent Chinese planners would concede that their airfields and troops are vulnerable to attack by Soviet tactical missiles, but they will point out these have always been vulnerable, even in the age of the venerable bomber. Yet like any poor state, China must see defense as a matter of priorities. Perfect defense against its superpower neighbor is impossible. If China cannot afford all the defense it might want, it needs to choose what is most essential. It has little time for the obsessions of European planners who have money to burn. In any case, the very size of China, and the great distance from its frontiers to any significant target, makes China relatively unconcerned with Soviet SS-21s, SS-22s, and SS-23s. The real threat is not shorter-range Soviet missiles but the longer-range SS-20s and Backfire bombers, weapons that have now been deployed for more than a decade in East Asia. Even if China wanted to defend against SS-20s, it is not in the technological league to do so.

Japan, in contrast, is far from being a poor, peasant, continental power like China. It can be considered a Western state, especially in technology and economic development, and thus one might expect the Japanese to understand the merit of ATBMs, especially if there were a possible technological spin-off to be exploited. Also, like many West European countries, Japan is a highly urban society with concentrated, high-value targets in need of air defense. Nonetheless, Japan has been the most skeptical major Western nation when it comes to ATBMs. The reasons are different from the Chinese case, but no less compelling.

Unlike China, Japan has not been a major spender on military forces. Some have described Tokyo's heavy reliance on the U.S. nuclear umbrella and U.S. military forces as a "free ride." (Japan is host to 119 U.S. military facilities and 45,000 U.S. troops.) Certainly this reliance does allow Japan to spend far less on its own military. Nevertheless, as the world's second-largest economy, Japan ranks among the world's top ten military powers even when it spends only 1 percent of its GNP on its armed forces.

Yet Japan's military policy remains muted. If Japan genuinely did have a high perception of threat, as its official statements occasionally suggest, then it certainly acts in perverse ways. Its air defenses have remained notoriously backward, and its armed forces are equipped with less than the latest hardware. In reality, Japan simply does not perceive an imminent Soviet threat that would justify ATBMs.[5]

As in the case of China, Japan's attitude is partly an act of faith, partly an assessment of objective conditions. As a legacy of World War II, Japan was initially discouraged by its allies and neighbors from a major military effort. The war also had a traumatic effect on Japan itself, making military affairs a less honorable pursuit and nuclear status all but impossible. As a consequence, Japan became dependent on the United States for security and now recognizes it is unable to defend itself without U.S. support — regardless of its own assessment of the Soviet threat. Objectively, as in the case of China, the targets of military significance in Japan lie far from the main Soviet missile fields. Thus, like China, Japan remains more concerned with SS-20s and Backfire bombers than with SS-21s, SS-22s, and SS-23s. Although Japan has acquired a new Patriot anti-aircraft system from the United

States, Patriot is far from having an effective anti–ballistic missile capability.[6] Japan is unlikely to see the ATBM problem as especially pressing in an otherwise nonurgent military budget.

More important, Japan, like China, tends to see security policy in broader terms than merely a narrow calculation of the balance of armed forces. In recent years Japan has articulated more succinctly its long-held belief that security must be understood "comprehensively." Much as China emphasizes the "correlation of forces," Japan believes that a proper perspective on the balance of power must encompass broader economic and social factors.[7] Thus a preoccupation with SS-21s, SS-22s, and SS-23s would be seen by Tokyo as excessively narrow, and Japan might be better off spending on economic aid to ASEAN than on developing ATBMs.

HOW MUCH DEFENSE IS ENOUGH?

Even if the sense of threat in Beijing and Tokyo were higher, greater emphasis on missile defenses would still lack appeal. The essential argument for ATBMs is a curious variation on deterrence by denial. If the threat from Soviet missiles is entirely conventional, then defense against that threat would be akin to defense against conventional attack by aircraft. Any state determined to provide air defense might therefore be interested in ATBMs. By helping to deny the adversary his conventional objectives, ATBMs could also raise the nuclear threshold: A robust conventional defense would help avoid early resort to nuclear weapons by a desperate defender. If Soviet shorter-range missiles are viewed as principally a nuclear rather than a conventional threat, then ATBMs could play a role in nuclear war-fighting and damage limitation.

The question is, Do either China or Japan see a role for deterrence by denial, through ATBM defense? The Chinese case is the more ambiguous of the two. China, like NATO, faces an enemy that is better-armed conventionally. On the one hand, as suggested earlier, China can take some comfort in the fact that for reasons of geography, shorter-range ballistic missiles would be less useful to the Soviets in a conventional attack—and hence, ATBMs would be less useful to China.

On the other hand, China seems to appreciate that its conventional weaknesses might compel it to go nuclear, and first, if conventional war comes. China has regularly pledged that it would not be the first to use nuclear weapons in war, and officially at least, China has not deployed any tactical nuclear weapons. Yet in reality Chinese military exercises have simulated the first use of nuclear weapons, and recent Chinese nuclear tests suggest a program to develop tactical weapons. Thus, China does seem to understand the problem of keeping the nuclear threshold high. Moreover, China (like the Soviet Union) has long adhered to a doctrine of deterrence by denial. It has a sophisticated civil defense program, and it could have more hope than most states of "surviving" a nuclear war because 80 percent of its population lives in the countryside.[8]

Despite all this, China has never had a sophisticated anti-aircraft defense network. This gap in its deterrence by denial is no doubt related to the belief that because the majority of the population is rural, it is therefore safe from attack. China's own retaliatory nuclear capability is increasingly moving out to sea, where it has no need for the protection of an anti–ballistic missile defense.

Perhaps most important, however, Chinese strategy has never been as full of the complexities that Western strategists excel at developing. The notion of nuclear thresholds and limited nuclear was has never been seen by China as realistic. The risks and conduct of war depend, in the Chinese view, on grander forces and are far less subject to scientific planning. This simplistic strategy, however, may have merely been part of the Maoist legacy that is now being discarded. Certainly Chinese strategists now discuss types of weapons and modern strategies of the nuclear age in a new way. But China still seems far from the technology-fetish of modern Western states that created the ATBM scare in the first place.

Japan has a less complicated view of these matters. As the only victim of nuclear attack in history, it knows its vulnerabilities all too well. Even a small conventional war in Japan would devastate a country of its size and population density. The security task, as Japan sees it, is to deter any Soviet attack, nuclear or conventional. Because Japan has forsworn the possession of its own nuclear weapons and that commitment remains deeply popular, Japan must rely for security on the United States and U.S. nuclear deterrence.[9] Necessarily this means that Japan tends not to draw the fine distinctions between conventional and nuclear conflicts that are so prominent in Western arguments for ATBMs. Moreover, Japan's deep abhorrence of nuclear war paradoxically makes it one of the strongest supporters of pure deterrence by punishment. The notion of a nuclear war-fighting strategy is anathema to the nation that suffered severely at Hiroshima and Nagasaki. If (for reasons of geography) Soviet ballistic missiles are assumed to pose a nuclear rather than conventional threat to Japan, then deployment of an ATBM system against them would imply that fighting a nuclear war is possible and that it is useful to discuss levels of bearable damage. Neither position would be politically tenable in Japan.

Thus Japan and China, albeit for different reasons, see no need for an ATBM system as a component of their nuclear or conventional armed forces.

ATTITUDES TOWARD THE SDI

If the cynics are right about ATBMs—that they are not desired in themselves but rather as a quick route to a rudimentary SDI—then there is even more reason for the Chinese and Japanese to oppose ATBMs. China's view of SDI is clear and hostile.[10] Although China has adopted a variant of deterrence by denial, it has relied on a minimum nuclear retaliatory capability to ensure the opponent's caution. An effective SDI would undermine Chinese deterrence, and there are signs that China is concerned about such an eventuality. Recent interest in in-flight refueling, greater emphasis on SBLMs, and advances in cruise missiles all suggest that China's response to superpower strategic defenses would be to evade the defenses by "underflying" them. China has not developed its own defensive components—for example, by expanding its civil defense program. As already noted, rural China has seen little reason to invest in sophisticated air defense because defending the countryside is impossible. Therefore China is unlikely to be interested in ATBMs as a route to SDI, for it is a road China does not want to travel.[11]

China's attitude to the European Eureka project has also suggested scant support for ABM or ATBM defenses. Although China has praised the Europeans for trying to unite themselves in opposition to U.S. technical and economic domination, China has not praised the military application of the project. To some extent, Japanese reaction to Eureka has been similar, although Japan has an even more active stake in competition with the United States for new technologies and markets.

Japan, as a U.S. ally, cannot afford to be hostile to a pet project of the U.S. president. A Japanese prime minister such as Nakasone who prized his close relations with "Ron" was even less likely to repudiate the idea of SDI openly. But Japanese actions on SDI speak louder than words.

Japan, however, is interested in technological spin-offs from SDI. As a major power in the forefront of modern technology, Japan cannot afford to sit out the SDI research game, and Japanese industry has been looking for opportunities to cooperate with United States corporations in the SDI market. But unlike the United States' other close allies, Japan held back from agreement on participation of Japanese firms and the sharing of SDI research products until mid-1987. Japan watched as NATO allies gradually fell into line by, for all intents and purposes, surrendering claim to the exploitation of technological benefits that derive from SDI research. When agreement with the Department of Defense was finally struck in July 1987, Japanese firms were assured that they would retain all rights to technologies they brought to SDI research and would be granted free licenses to use technologies developed under SDI contract.[12]

Japan's own air defense is notoriously porous. Yet only one Japanese firm was involved in bidding for early ATBM research. MMI, in conjunction with Raytheon, unsuccessfully bid for a contract, and nothing has been heard of the Japanese since.[13] Few Japanese officials even discuss the ATBM issue, although various U.S. officials have tried to get them interested.[14] For Japan, SDI and its variants are primarily of technological interest, but like China, it sees more threat than promise in SDI.

As long as the SDI research remains in its infancy, Japan runs few risks in its hard line. If the program should survive a change of presidents, and if important technology does begin to spin-off, then Japan may well take a more active part in SDI research. But in military terms Japan, like the NATO allies, is likely to be skeptical about the possibilities for strategic defense. As a close neighbor to the Soviet Union, Japan's warning time of an SS-20 attack would be small, and the threat that Japan faces from cruise missiles is strong. A U.S. SDI that protected U.S. cities might make it more likely that the United States would risk Houston for Hiroshima. But then unlike the Europeans, Japan has never questioned the stability and strength of the U.S. nuclear umbrella.[15] The real concern from Japan's point of view is that money wasted in the West on SDI will not be available for conventional weapons, and especially for naval forces, that would be more useful in assuring Japan's security.

THE ARMS CONTROL CALCULUS

Some of the arguments offered on behalf of ATBMs are especially cynical, among them assertions that ATBMs are especially vital in a world of superpower nuclear parity brought on by arms control or that ATBMs are not violations of arms control agreements regulating strategic defenses. Such arguments have been made in the European context, and some U.S. government officials have made them to the Japanese as well.[16] In the East Asian context, there has been no serious interest in such arms control controversies. This is not to say that arms control does not take place in East Asia, but rather that it is more tacit than formal and more concerned with building confidence than in creating elaborate disarmament regimes.[17] The recent reduction of tension along the Sino-Soviet frontier is a case in point, and it stands in marked contrast to the unproductive negotiations on Mutual and Balanced Force Reductions (MBFR) in Europe.

Naturally, there are close linkages between European and East Asian arms control issues. For example, both China and Japan have been concerned that any agreement on medium-range nuclear weapons in Europe not simply shift the weapons to East Asia (though since the Andropov days, the Soviet Union has made it clear that it had no intention of simply shifting its SS-20s to Asia). China and Japan did not demand to be involved formally in the arms control process and indeed backed away from any such suggestion. They took for granted that roughly one hundred Soviet SS-20 launchers would be aimed at them, and they saw little reason to take a formal part in arms control as long as their basic security objectives were achieved. This was not just an effort to get a "free ride" on arms control. It reflected a less legalistic and more practical approach to the purpose of arms control, where the object is genuine security, not a formal piece of paper. Japan expressed its interests via its U.S. ally, of course, and Japanese periodicals offer accounts of arcane nuclear arms negotiations, refreshing if only for their ability to discern the essentials from the ephemera. Yet as a nonnuclear power, Japan was never likely to be very interested in the details of arms control.

China, on the other hand, is a nuclear power. But like other medium powers, China is not particularly interested in arms control unless the superpowers prove willing to make deep cuts in their arsenals. In the 1980s the Chinese grew more sophisticated in their analysis of arms control, but they steadfastly refused to see the merit in direct involvement. Because its military strategy rests on deterrence by denial and diversified forces, China has often been bemused by and dismissive of European and superpower obsessions with "overkill" and obscure war-game scenarios. Arms control was often dismissed as merely another forum for superpower contention, where neither side was serious about reaching an agreement.

Thus, for both China and Japan, the value of ATBMs as a bulwark of security in a world constrained by arms control is not especially relevant. Arms control, in their judgment, should not require such convoluted strategies, and if it does, then it is not a game worth playing. If ATBMs are to be justified, a more positive rationale is needed. These backdoor arguments to ATBMs merely confirm both countries' skepticism.

CONCLUSION

It is hard to think of two countries in Asia more different than China and Japan. Yet for all their differences, they share a remarkably similar disdain for ATBMs.

The common element in Chinese and Japanese approaches is a certain "laid back" attitude, a diminished sense of peril that shares little of the West's narrow obsession with technological imperatives and security based on finely calibrated military balances. As long as neither country has expectations of using its armed forces offensively further afield, neither will be terribly anxious about obtaining the latest in military hardware. They will be satisfied with variations of deterrence, achieved at minimum levels of armed forces. As in many contemporary economic issues, perhaps this too is a lesson the West Europeans might learn from East Asia.

NOTES

1. David Goodman, Martin Lockett, and Gerald Segal, *The China Challenge* (London: Chatham House Paper No. 32, 1986).
2. Gerald Segal, "Sino-Soviet Relations After Mao," *Adelphi Paper* no. 202 (London: International Institute for Strategic Studies, 1985), and "Sino-Soviet Arms Control," in Gerald Segal, ed., *Arms Control in Asia* (London: Macmillan, 1987).
3. Ellis Joffe, *The Chinese Army After Mao* (London: Weidenfeld, 1987).

4. Joffe, *The Chinese Army After Mao*, and Liaowang, 22 December 1986 in British Broadcasting Corporation, *Summary of World Broadcasts, Far East*, 8453, BII, pp. 7–9.
5. Malcolm McIntosh, *Japan Re-Armed* (London: Frances Pinter, 1986).
6. J.W. Chapman, R. Drifte, and I.T.M. Gow, *Japan's Quest for Comprehensive Security* (London: Frances Pinter, 1983).
7. Chapman *et al.*, *Japan's Quest*, and Brian Bridges, "Japan's Interests and Security Policy in the Pacific Basin" in *Brassey's Defence Yearbook* (London: Brassey's, 1986).
8. Gerald Segal, "Nuclear Forces," in Gerald Segal and William Tow, eds., *Chinese Defense Policy* (London: Macmillan, 1984). For recent comments, see *Liberation Army Daily* in *Summary of World Broadcasts, Far East*, 12 November 1986 and 23 July 1986, for an account of a meeting on defense strategy.
9. Terumasa Nakanishi, "U.S. Nuclear Policy and Japan," *The Washington Quarterly*, Winter 1987, pp. 81–100.
10. Bonnie Glaser and Banning Garrett, "Chinese Perspectives on the Strategic Defense Initiative," *Problems of Communism*, no. 2, 1986; John Garver, "China's Response to the SDI," *Asian Survey*, November 1986, pp. 1220–1239; and Alastair Johnston, "China and Arms Control," *Aurora Papers* no. 3 (Ottawa: Canadian Centre for Arms Control and Disarmament, 1986). China has become so concerned with the SDI issue that by 1987 it was even joining the Soviet Union in denouncing the U.S. program. China's comments on superpower strategic arms talks began to blame the United States for the deadlock at Geneva and for trying to gain advantages in strategic weapons. See Huang Tingwei and Song Baoxian, "Disarmament: New Aspects of an Old Issue," *Beijing Review*, no. 3, 1987, pp. 24–25.
11. Yao Wenbin, "Soviet Military Deployments in the Asia-Pacific Region" in Richard Solomon and Masataka Kosaka, eds., *The Soviet Far East Military Buildup* (Dover, Mass.: Auburn House 1986), pp. 97–105. China has recently begun to explore the military uses of outer space, but it is clear that discussions on such uses are at their very earliest stages. See *Liberation Army Daily*, 2 January 1987 in *Summary of World Broadcasts, Far East*, 8467, BII, p. 7.
12. *New York Times*, 22 July 1987.
13. *Jane's Defense Weekly*, 11 October 1986.
14. From interviews undertaken by Reinhard Drifte for a project on Japan's defense technology by the International Institute for Strategic Studies, London. I am grateful to Reinhard Drifte for this information.
15. See generally Richard Solomon and Masataka Kosaka, eds., *The Soviet Far East Military Buildup* (Dover, Mass.: Auburn House 1986), and especially the chapter by Masataka Kosaka, "Theater Nuclear Weapons

and Japan's Defense Policy," pp. 123–140.
16. U.S. Assistant Secretary of Defense Richard Perle, cited in *Daily Yomuri*, 16 April 1986.
17. Douglas Stuart, "The International Context of Asian Arms Control," in Gerald Segal, ed., *Arms Control in Asia* (London: Macmillan, 1987).

12 PERSPECTIVE AND COMMENTARY
ATBMs
An Opportunity for the Alliance
François DeRose

The possibility of defense against ballistic missiles may be the most significant event thus far in the life of the Atlantic Alliance, in three respects: as a challenge to four decades of Alliance strategy; for its repercussions on U.S.-European relationships; and for its impact on relations with the Soviet Union. Unquestionably, nuclear weapons opened a new era in the age-long duel between sword and shield. In a sense, nuclear weapons perform both functions—a sword in military terms, a shield in political terms—by introducing a balanced and therefore reasonably stable deterrence. The result has been remarkable stability in areas where the nuclear camps are face to face, as in Europe. No less remarkable is the instability elsewhere, where the Soviet Union, having apparently mastered the art of indirect strategy more successfully than the Western powers, has been able to alter the political map of the world to its benefit. These facts are based on the recognition that nuclear weapons would make war no longer "the continuation of policy by other means" because the fruits of eventual victory would not be worth the price of acquiring them and on the fear that nuclear exchanges, once begun, might escalate to the absurd.

Such assumptions, agreed on among the Allies, led to the adoption of the strategy of flexible response when the older strategy of massive retaliation became untenable. Originally based on the balance between U.S. superiority in the nuclear field (strategic and tactical) and Warsaw

Pact superiority in conventional armaments, flexible response has remained in force, even though that "balance of imbalances" disappeared as the Soviet Union gained parity in strategic weapons and superiority in short- and medium-range theater systems. In part, flexible response has been sustained by the fact that no better strategy was conceivable. But it has also survived because it has been impossible to protect military forces and populations, either by destroying all enemy weapons or by sheltering tens of millions of people and economic assets. Deterrence, with its inherent risk that any theater conflict in Europe would escalate to strategic nuclear weapons, was the only conceivable policy for overcoming the geographical "decoupling" between allies separated by an ocean.

Inevitably, first reactions to the ATBM issue would be largely influenced by the reactions provoked earlier by SDI, which in turn were the result of growing discrepencies between European and U.S. views over the role to be played by nuclear weapons in the mechanism of deterrence and defense. These differences had already been made plain by Henry Kissinger's statement in Brussels in 1979, warning the Europeans not to expect the United States to inflict strategic destruction on the Soviet Union in the event of aggression against Western Europe. Even if "no first use" proposals have never been endorsed at responsible political and military levels in Washington, there is little doubt that Europeans regard the threat of "going nuclear," even rather early if need be, as the main foundation of deterrence. The Americans, in contrast, think that the capacity to defend ourselves at all levels is a safer security bet than the threat of collective suicide.

All this simply underlines the unique position of nuclear weapons in the political as well as military relationships among Western allies. And it accounts for the commotion created by President Reagan's sudden announcement of a policy to render nuclear weapons impotent and obsolete.

It can be argued, of course, that had the Europeans been previously informed of the president's March 23, 1983, speech, their reaction would likely have been no different. And it is probable that had President Reagan known in advance of European objections, he would have gone ahead all the same, and the crisis might have been even more serious. Nevertheless, let us take note of two facts: First, the political impact of the president's proposal is being felt, perhaps decades before the military consequences can be verified; and second, contrary to precedent, the consequences for strategy and arms systems are being discussed and analyzed long before feasiblity can be ascertained.

The emotion felt in Europe stems from the fear that the president's SDI proposal was nothing less than confirmation that the United States does not intend to initiate the use of nuclear weapons in defense of the Old Continent, as long as the Soviets refrain from nuclear use. If the European fear was confirmed, then the whole concept of deterrence would be condemned, and with it the future independence of Europeans. This feeling was so strong that it obscured the related question of whether antimissile defense could be conceived for the NATO theater in Europe. Many, jumping to conclusions in complete ignorance of the facts, anticipated a situation where the United States and the Soviet Union would achieve complete invulnerability for themselves, while their allies would remain helplessly exposed to all kinds of weapons.

There is no use crying over spilled milk. Yet the damage thus incurred in the Alliance probably could have been spared if a less ambitious and revolutionary objective had been proposed for SDI: building defenses against a Soviet disarming first strike, at both the strategic and theater levels. Although less glamorous and less impressive than ridding the world of nuclear fear, this objective might have proved more compatible with past agreed policy and more difficult for the Soviets to criticize. And it probably lies closer to what will eventually be achievable. Above all, defense systems designed to thwart a Soviet first strike might have been more readily adapted for the protection of U.S. allies and forces abroad. Put another way, such defenses might have provoked fewer fears that the United States would become decoupled from its European (and Japanese) allies.

Responsibility for mistakes probably must be shared equally on both sides of the Atlantic. On the one side, the Europeans found themselves more in agreement with the criticisms of SDI put forward by Moscow, much to the resentment of Washington. On the other side, the United States nonetheless proved unready for genuine cooperation with her allies, with the Department of State going as far as to warn the Europeans against concerting their attitude toward the issue within the Western European Union.

So much for the past. We shall now try to see how the ATBM problem presents itself as a parameter of interalliance relationships. The first question is whether there is a case for ATBM being approached as a special problem, distinct from SDI.

This is not the place to guess or evaluate the technical probability of intercepting and destroying short- and medium-range missiles. But it is pertinent to note that the whole of Western Europe is threatened by Soviet missiles that are not limited in numbers, in the way that NATO's Pershing II and cruise missiles are. These Euromissiles are the only ones deployed on our side that can hit the real enemy, while NATO's other, shorter-range delivery vehicles could only attack targets in the satellite countries—countries that, we should not forget, are our European brothers and cousins.[1] Finally, in view of the very high density of urban centers on our side, the consequences of a Soviet attack on NATO's military forces may be almost indistinguishable from an attack on population centers, which makes our vulnerability that much greater.

All this amounts to saying that the latest developments in delivery systems increase the vulnerability of Western Europe, and that the countermeasures NATO can take in offensive weapons do not really compensate for the deterioration that has occurred in the balance between the two alliances in Europe. This in itself should be an incentive for NATO to examine whether ATBMs could obviate or correct the untoward effects of these conditions. We have even more incentive if we admit that the Soviet Union is busy preparing for the defense of its territory and forces deployed abroad, against weapons of all categories. We know that Soviet antiair defenses would make penetration by NATO's manned aircraft extremely costly. We know also that the Soviet Union has made use of all possibilities allowed by the ABM Treaty (and maybe more) to protect the Moscow area against intercontinental missiles. It would be against every lesson we have learned about the Kremlin's approach to security issues to imagine that the Soviets would not try to seal off any remaining gap in its defenses that the West might exploit.

This is of paramount importance from the point of view of crisis management. In the days of direct strategy and open warfare, what mattered in the long run were the potentials (human and material resources, industrial, scientific, and technological capabilities) that each side could mobilize and bring to bear on the enemy over time. In the era of indirect strategy and crisis management to which we are fortunately bound today, what matters is what is immediately available on both sides. Now, if worse came to worst in any future crisis and we knew there were no defenses on our side against enemy short- and medium-range rockets, but that defenses protected the Warsaw Pact against similar NATO weapons, it is difficult to believe we would be in an equal position to negotiate the crisis. After all, resolving a crisis depends, in the last resort, on the capacity to resist your opponent's will.

With or without ballistic missile defense, the strategy of the Soviet Union remains that of victory without war. The business of the Western powers is *not* to match the power of the Warsaw Pact, especially in numbers, let alone to be able to win a prolonged war. NATO's purpose must be to command sufficent means to make the Soviet leaders doubt that they can implement their strategy in war and consequently also doubt that they can impose their will in crises. On our side, we must be reasonably sure that the balance is not so adverse that we are unable to resist Soviet pressures except at the risk of suicide. And this might well be our lot, if Soviet ATBMs gave them relative security.

The reasons for finding out whether ATBMs are feasible seem, therefore, well established. ATBMs would be neither a substitute for nor an alteration of NATO's current defense and deterrence concepts. They would be part of the political posture we must build up in order to be able to hold our own, not only in any crisis but also in day-to-day dealings with the other camp.

This being so, the question arises whether there is a case for studying the ATBM problem separately from SDI, or whether ATBM programs should be subsumed within the SDI. The answer, however provisional in the present state of the art, calls probably for technical and political considerations. The nontechnician might hope that the boost-phase defenses being examined in the SDI will prove totally efficient against missiles of all ranges since this would ensure the security of Europe and Japan as well as that of the United States. The political adviser would be more cautious, however, and would consider it safer to assume that SDI systems will prove less efficient against SS-21s, SS-22s, or SS-23s than against intercontinental missiles and that NATO ought to consider now what, if anything, could be done about it.

What has been said earlier about the importance of a certain degree of parity in vulnerabilities between East and West also applies within the Alliance. To be sure, Europe is vulnerable to all kinds of weapons, whereas the United States and the Soviet Union are exposed only to nuclear ones. But if a situation should develop where a defense against nuclear weapons could be built for the two superpowers, with nothing of the sort for their allies, then NATO would experience a decoupling of vulnerabilities that would, for all intents and purposes, invalidate the recoupling effect that was sought through the recent deployment of Euromissiles. ATBM defenses for Europe therefore should not be considered as merely a subsidiary issue within the SDI, receiving its solution as an afterthought. Maintaining the "parity of vulnerabilities" within the Alliance is a major political problem that, if not attended to properly, could well undermine Western unity more seriously than any other difficulty encountered so far.

The fact that to this day, there is no organization or structure entrusted with the responsibility for studying the ATBM issue, neither in Europe nor in the United States, is a real cause for amazement. The only dimension of the matter that has been discussed so far is whether and how Europeans could take part in SDI research. And how disorderly the European answers were is well known. Never was it considered, apparently, that Europe (and Japan, for that matter) might be threatened by a specific menace, which should have a distinctive response. To be sure, the United States also has an interest in ATBMs, to provide protection for the forces it maintains abroad, in Europe and elsewhere. But even if ATBMs emerged as a byproduct of U.S. research and development on SDI, and if they were deployed in Europe (at European expense, perhaps) but operated under complete U.S. leadership and responsibility, this would hardly be conducive to the development among Europeans of a sense of responsibility for their own security. The feeling that in the last resort, this responsibility rests with the United States is already too strong on this side of the Atlantic and is resented on the other. If ATBM becomes an almost exclusively U.S. achievement, it will only exacerbate a situation that is already unsatisfactory.

As far as SDI is concerned, there is little doubt that for various reasons, the part played by Europeans will be extremely limited, if not negligible. Some of these reasons (political, financial, industrial, and so forth) need not be gone into here. Let it simply be said that Europeans should not complain when they are left out of an enterprise that elicited such misgivings on their part to begin with—nor are the Americans entitled to criticize their European partners for not "pulling their weight" if Europeans are deliberately excluded from the most promising avenues of scientific and technological developments within the SDI.

There is a far broader aspect to this problem, with important cultural connotations well beyond ATBMs or the SDI. It concerns the role Europeans will play in the scientific and technological developments of the coming era. Modern science was born in Europe, and for many centuries modern science ensured European supremacy throughout the world. Now that many scientific programs require enormous means, both in human terms and financial outlays, many branches are beyond the resources that individual European countries can make available. What is at stake, fundamentally, is whether the Europeans will continue to be equal partners with the United States in at least some areas of advanced knowledge or will drop out of the scientific race altogether. What is involved ultimately is continuing European influence over the development of a civilization that is largely their own.

The days are not far past when enlightened U.S scientists such as Robert J. Oppenheimer and Isidore Rabi were extremely influential in the creation of CERN (European Organization for Nuclear Research), which allowed Europe to remain abreast with the United States and Soviet Union in basic nuclear physics. They felt, and so did the wider U.S. scientific community, that it was fundamentally unhealthy for the United States alone to carry the responsibilty for advancing basic science in nuclear physics. The Eurospace and Ariane programs for space exploration continue in that same spirit. Perhaps Eureka will also produce significant results. To be sure, not all these ventures are concerned with meeting military requirements, although we nonetheless have the same interest in their success. And if the European states fail to show the interest they should in mastering new technologies, the Americans should not be held responsible. Yet we shall all be the poorer if European intellectual resources are not tapped for a competition that may decide the future of our common civilization and culture.

Coming back to ATBM issues, it may transpire that defenses against short- and medium-range ballistic missiles prove more efficient and reliable than against long-range ones, or they may prove less so. In the first case, no problem would be created among the allies, at least as far as their common stake in security in Europe is concerned. The second possibility, however, might raise a political problem that would require delicate management. For the moment, we do not know which outcome will occur, so we are all equally concerned in investigating all possibilities.

One wishes, therefore, that the Europeans had taken up or will take up the problem of ATBM defenses in cooperation with the United

States, but as a special responsibility toward themselves and toward the Alliance as a whole. This does not mean harboring the ambition or illusion of duplicating the SDI. It is a fact of life that we on the Old Continent do not have the capacity for research and development on space-based defenses that would operate in the boost and midcourse phases of enemy missile trajectories. But systems for interception of short- and medium-range missiles during the reentry phase are probably within our possibilities.

It is regrettable that Western European governments did not get together to consider the threat aimed directly at their countries that, if not checked, might weaken the deterrence posture on their half of the continent. Were they to do so, France, although not part of the integrated military system, would have the same interest in participation. Let it be recalled that when General de Gaulle withdrew French forces from NATO's integrated military structure, he was careful to maintain France's participation in the Alliance's integrated air defense network (NADGE). What was felt necessary to cope with the menace of supersonic aircraft is even more in order against missiles that take less than ten minutes to reach their targets.

The advantages to be gained by such a joint effort would not be limited to the military field. European leadership in such a major project of interest to all allies would be a form of political revolution in interallied relationships, opening the way to greater European influence on questions of common security concern. The problem of a fair balance of influence within the Alliance is as old as the Alliance itself. It is only natural, as long as nuclear weapons play the decisive role in NATO strategy and these weapons are predominantly American, that U.S. views be most generally predominant when discussing defense concepts. On the other hand, European countries provide between 70 and 80 percent of the land and air forces that would be under SHAPE command in case of hostilities. And we know that at SACEUR's insistence, conventional forces are to play an increasing part in the deterrence and defense posture of the Alliance. It would only be natural, if the nuclear threshold is going to be substantially raised (which means less reliance on early use of nuclear weapons), that the influence of those who will make this shift possible should also be raised accordingly.

If, in addition, ATBM defenses would make the nuclear menace of the enemy less pressing, and if these defenses were largely due to the positive contribution of European nations, they should receive their due of influence in military and political deliberations. It is up to them to see it that way and to act accordingly.

And that, of course, applies to France as well. It is pointless to expect that the Paris government might or could return to the integrated NATO organization. But practically all French political parties, except the dwindling Communists, say they are in favor of increased cooperation with the allies, especially with the Federal Republic. And "extended air defense" is high on the list of cooperative projects. Time will tell whether this cooperative spirit will yield no more than a joint arms production project, such as the many we have seen over the past decades, or whether it will yield a new broad political move that provides the impetus needed to reorganize Europe's status within the Alliance on a basis of greater responsibility. ATBMs, in view of the importance of what is at stake, could be a starting point for such a change, if we have the vision and will to bring it to life.

Whatever the future of ATBMs, it is pertinent to consider on the one hand the likely position of the Soviet Union with respect to its own defense and that of its allies and, on the other, the probable Soviet reaction to an effort on our side to develop ATBM defenses. We know that Warsaw Pact defenses against manned aircraft are extremely powerful and constantly being improved and that the Kremlin has made full use of the 1972 ABM Treaty to construct and modernize its ABM protection around Moscow. If we remind ourselves of all the evidence that shows the Soviets' continuing activities in research on ballistic missile defense, there can be little doubt that ATBMs are also on their drawing boards. Whether they really believe that the West could, one day, initiate an attack out of the blue is debatable. But we know that the Soviets' strategy and the theme of their maneuvers are geared to scoring an immediate disarming blow against NATO forces.

Hence, there is little doubt that the first priority of the Soviet Union is to protect the territories of its allies and its own western districts where the bulk of the Warsaw Pact forces are stationed, and where the lines of communications, the depots, and the air bases — in short, the logistic assets that first-echelon forces and reinforcements would be dependent upon to conduct their operations — are found. And that necessarily means ATBMs.

In all likelihood, a U.S.-European program to develop ATBMs would be denounced by Soviet propaganda as a part of the sinister SDI project and a new step in the arms race. Such denunciations, however, would lack the juridical basis provided by the 1972 ABM Treaty, since that treaty does not restrict defenses against short- and medium-range missiles. At this juncture it must be recalled that while the USSR was fighting against the deployment of Pershing II and cruise missiles, she was also busy deploying SS-20s and preparing the deployment of SS-21s, SS-22s, and SS-23s. The Soviets were so determined to have it their way that they even refused NATO's "zero option" arms control proposal, although it would have suppressed the threat to Soviet territory from NATO's medium-range missiles. Had the Soviets won on that point, Western Europe would have been threatened by all four types of Soviet ballistic missiles, while being deprived of the only medium-range missile capable of reaching Soviet territory. In other words, the asymmetry of vulnerabilities that exists through geography would have been completed by an agreed asymmetry in arms deployment.

If keeping this asymmetry in vulnerabilities remains the Kremlin's objective, we must expect that the Soviets will muster against NATO's potential deployment of defensive systems the same opposition they showed to actual deployment of offensive ones. And we might as well prepare for a quarrel on the matter. But the outcome of the Euromissiles crisis, and the fact that Mr. Gorbachev has now accepted the zero option, prove that we have nothing to lose by going ahead with what we think necessary for our own security. All the more so because in the field of ATBMs we probably lag behind Soviet programs. Moreover, we should not allow ourselves to be hamstrung in deciding the course we want to follow merely because arms control discussions are proceeding at Geneva. Eventually, ATBMs would have to be included in arms control arrangements, if we are to reach a settlement that would bring a genuine easing of tensions between East and West. But as long as the Geneva negotiations remain focused on space-based defensive systems, we are free to concentrate on terminal-phase defenses against short- and medium-range missiles. It would be ill-advised for us to start limiting our freedom of thought, and even more so our freedom of decision on ATBMs, by speculating on what Moscow's reaction might be. We will be much better off in any eventual talks on arms control if we start from well-defined security positions.

Let us also dispose of the argument often used against ballistic missile defense that it would only result in deployment of more offensive weapons to saturate whatever defenses might be built. Short- and medium-range missiles that the Red Army can field are not limited in numbers by any agreement such as SALT I or II. Furthermore,

SS-21s, SS-22s, and SS-23s were deployed at a time when ATBM defenses in Western Europe were not even under consideration. Both these facts demonstrate that Soviet decisions about offensive missile deployments are not conditioned either by arms control considerations or by the deployment, on our side, of this or that type of defense.

Let us not indulge in daydreaming. Competition, rivalry between Marxism and free democracies will go on, and military force will remain in the background as a guarantee to each side of the restraint and wisdom of the other. The problem is to find a formula that gives us the same result without a ruinous and really absurd race for supremacy. It is unlikely, in this respect, that the elimination of nuclear weapons as envisaged by Mr. Reagan and Mr. Gorbachev — though each approaches it along a different path — is the proper formula. The time scale proposed by the Russian leader ignores all lessons of talks held so far on this subject. And the hope of the U.S. president that nuclear weapons can be made obsolete seems to ignore historical experience, where weapons become obsolete most often when more efficient weapons appear. Both statemen seem to sin by optimism, the master of the Kremlin by expecting too much from human goodwill, and the host of the White House by betting too much on the miracles of technology. Mr. Reagan's vision would require that research on defense be 100 percent successful, while research on countermeasures proves 100 percent unsuccessful — too unlikely an outcome to be made the basis of security.

The period of "no war" brought about by the certainty of devastating nuclear retaliation has now lasted for forty years. It seems to show that we have learned we must live side by side if we want to live at all. But deterrence, blessed as it is, is based on mutual fear, which in turn breeds arms races. What we would prefer is a situation where we could gradually muzzle the nuclear monster while searching for a less tense and more trustworthy state of security. Ballistic missile defenses could provide the new element on which such a transformation could be built. But this transformation would require that both sides acknowledge their common danger, the danger which fuels arms races: a disarming attack, striking like lightning from a blue sky.

Assuming that both sides could agree that this was the peril and that both sides shared a common interest and advantage in averting the danger, it seems possible to achieve our goal of a new basis for security by combining gradual reduction of nuclear weapons with simultaneous deployment of SDI and ATBM defenses. Nuclear warheads and delivery systems would be gradually, but in the end drastically reduced to a small proportion (10 to 20 percent) of what they are now. At the same time, ballistic missile defenses would be deployed, calculated so as to ensure the interception and destruction of a sufficient number of enemy weapons to foil a counterforce attack. Any aggression would then lose its rationale, and the capacity to carry out a disarming first strike would no longer have a paralyzing political influence. Civilian targets and economic assets would not have to be protected in this situation, for if some or all strategic weapons remaining after reduction were directed at these targets, the victim of aggression would always have the capacity to retaliate. MAD would remain in force, and indeed an attack under such conditions would be even more absurd than today.

The same arrangement covering offensive and defensive weapons would be applied to Europe, on both NATO and Warsaw Pact territories. Here again, an attack with no warning by either side would be pointless because it would not destroy the fighting capacity of the defender, whether nuclear or conventional, strategic or tactical.

Plans developed along these lines would seriously depart from the paths so far followed in arms control discussions. The interesting point is that this approach is based on the anticipated successful outcome of research on antimissile defenses and can combine drastic reductions in offensive weapons with the preservation of deterrence. Fears expressed at the prospect of a disappearance of deterrence would no longer be justified, nor would be the anxiety by any camp of being suddenly knocked out. Last but not least, monitoring compliance with an agreement to reduce opposing forces to equal levels (of whatever magnitude) will always be more reliable and tolerant of possible minor errors than monitoring a commitment to the complete elimination of any type of armament.

This new security regime could only be achieved if a certain degree of defense proved to be obtainable against missiles of *all* ranges. But if such defenses are feasible, an opportunity would be opened to change considerably the long-term political relationship within the Alliance and toward the Soviet Union.

If defenses against missiles of *all* ranges are not feasible, then within the Alliance, several outcomes are possible. Should SDI prove effective but not ATBMs, feelings would become very strong among Europeans that the Alliance was no longer based on shared vulnerabilities, and that Europe had become decoupled from U.S. strategic systems. The argument is sometimes put forward in U.S. quarters that if U.S. territory were protected from Soviet missiles, we would return to the situation in the 1950s, when an invulnerable United States could offer full protection to her allies. The argument is not very convincing. In those remote days, U.S. invulnerability was matched by Soviet vulnerability, which made the Alliance's massive retaliation doctrine credible. It would hardly be attractive to the Europeans now to stand defenseless while *both* superpowers are protected by missile defenses.

The situation would be quite different if both SDI and ATBM prove reliable, especially if the Europeans had taken a substantial part in the research and development of their own missile defenses. Not only would the sense of shared protection against common dangers be enhanced but, as noted, the Europeans could hope for greater role in the military leadership and political responsibilities within the Alliance. That could be the beginning of a new and better balanced relationship within the Western world.

As for relations with the Soviet Union, it remains to be seen if anti–ballistic missile technologies will herald a major change in the arms control talks. As useful as these negotiations are, as long as they focus only on quantitative reductions in offensive weapons there is little chance they can bring about a major breakthrough to less antagonistic relations. The situation would be quite different, however, if missile defenses combined with reductions in offensive weapons established a common sense of security against sudden attack or the adversary's wickedness or bad faith. In such a situation, it would be the configuration of military forces that would breed confidence, a confidence based on the "facts of life" rather than on the inevitably questionable motives of the other party.

If such a world came about, it would mean that thanks to the technologies of missile defense, East-West relations could enter a new phase, where the elements of reciprocal fear would progressively diminish, making room for a more relaxed approach to other problems. ATBMs would prove to be an opportunity rather than a liability in the longer-term political relationships within the Alliance and with the Soviet Union. But perhaps all this would require that the Russians be very different from what they are today — and that we ourselves be very different as well.

NOTES

1. This chapter was written before the 8 December 1987 agreement between the United States and the Soviet Union was signed in Washington, eliminating INF missiles from the territory of Europe and the USSR. This treaty, by removing the only U.S. ground-based missiles capable of reaching Soviet territory from Europe, eases Moscow's ATBM problem while increasing the asymmetry in vulnerabilities on the Old Continent.

13 PERSPECTIVE AND COMMENTARY
Of Allies and ATBMs
Josef Joffe

For a European power, it is hard not to think about a defense against tactical ballistic missiles (ATBM) and, indeed, against all kinds of hostile flying objects targeted in an East-West direction. And among the European members of NATO, a country like the Federal Republic must think hardest of all about ATBMs and an "extended air defense," as the official term of the day has it—for the usual and well-known reasons.

The Federal Republic is situated on the front line of potential conflict in Europe. It shares a 1,000 mile border with two countries of the Warsaw Pact. West Germany hosts the highest concentration of peacetime military power in history and the largest portion of interesting targets—from nuclear weapons depots to C^3I—that NATO has to offer. And if war does break out, the FRG is destined to be its prime venue and victim.

Arrayed on the other side of the Elbe and beyond is a threat of increasing size and sophistication, geared to the swift destruction of the Alliance's "time-sensitive" targets with conventional, chemical, or nuclear means.[1] In addition to its frontal aviation (500 medium-range and 2,500 attack bombers), the Warsaw Pact is said to have deployed some 1,400 short-range ballistic systems (with ranges from 70 to 500 km). In a forward position, these missiles could well take care of the tasks assigned to the SS-20, which stood at the center of the Great

Euromissile Debate of the late 1970s and early 1980s. What might these tasks be?

As one authoritative observer has it, there are nine major C^3 centers in the Central Region. There are eighty nuclear weapons sites.[2] There are twenty-five reinforcement facilities. There are about 132 targets offered by surface-to-air missile (SAM) belts. And there are, finally, about thirty-five additional air-defense nodes: interceptor airfields and communication/surveillance centers.[3] All of this adds up to some 280 time-urgent targets whose destruction (theoretically within minutes rather than hours or days) would practically obliterate NATO's ability to mount a coordinated defense "up front." Nor would it seem difficult for some 1,400 shorter-range Warsaw Pact systems to live up to that task, let alone in conjunction with the Pact's frontal aviation.[4]

By implication, then, the West faces a problem that echoes the beginnings of the Great Euromissile Debate *circa* 1977, when Chancellor Helmut Schmidt delivered his notorious IISS speech. The key sentences in that address read: "SALT neutralizes [American and Soviet] nuclear capabilities. In Europe, this magnifies the significance of the disparities between East and West in nuclear, tactical and conventional weapons. . . . We in Europe must be particularly careful that these negotiations do not neglect the components of NATO's deterrent strategy."[5]

Since the nuclear debates of the Alliance always focus on the same issues, though in different guises, it is instructive to compare and contrast 1977 with 1987. Ten years ago, Schmidt reacted to the classic problem of the "three balances": the nuclear-strategic, the nuclear-regional, and the regional-conventional. SALT II, he postulated, took care of only the strategic balance, thus not only bypassing the two regional problems but in fact *exacerbating* them. Put differently, he was haunted by the specter of "communicating security valves," whereby stability at the top would *necessarily* diminish security at the bottom. With strategic weapons neutralizing each other by formal agreement, Soviet superiority—indeed, a monopoly[6]—on the theater level would weigh that much heavier, posing a separate threat against Western Europe that was no longer compensated, as in the 1960s, by a U.S. advantage on the global-strategic level.

Today, that issue has returned in a new guise—and one rung lower on the ladder of nuclear escalation. At Reykjavik in October 1986, Gorbachev put the "zero-solution" for Intermediate-Range Nuclear Forces (INF) on the table; in December 1987, "double-zero" for all missiles with ranges between 500 and 5,000 km was enshrined in the INF Treaty. Were all the INF forces of NATO and the Warsaw Pact to go, while shorter-range systems remained, the Germans (though not all of NATO Europe) would be in a position analogous to the situation prior to the INF counter-deployment (as of late 1983). As the West German Defense Minister Manfred Wörner put it: "[On the SRINF level[7]] the Warsaw Pact possesses an insufferably high superiority of ten to one. For us, it makes no difference whether we are threatened by an SS-20 or SS-23 or Scud. All of them reach our territory."[8]

French Foreign Minister Jean-Bernard Raimond outlined the next level of the problem: What happens if short-range systems are eventually eliminated too? That would signify the "complete withdrawal of American nuclear forces [from Europe and] create a serious situation. In effect, there already exists an imbalance of conventional forces and chemical weapons in favor of the Soviets, and this withdrawal of American nuclear forces would engender a formidable politico-strategic instability in case of crisis."[9] NATO's foreign ministers, meeting at Brussels at the end of 1986 merely put the issue more diplomatically. The "reduction of nuclear weapons" by the Big Two "would enhance the importance of removing conventional imbalances."[10]

In short, there is no escape from the "Schmidt Syndrome," defined by the oldest of NATO's dilemmas: When it comes to the basics of West European security, everything is linked. That problem could almost be cast in the form of a law: The stabilization of one level via arms control necessarily destabilizes the next one down. Yet in contrast to the late 1970s, there is now an additional layer to the problem, and it goes by the name of SDI.

Actually, that dilemma too is familiar, and it stems from a classic ambivalence of the European allies. Strategic defenses are supposed to render the United States more invulnerable to a Soviet attack. Even a modest shield—one that would destroy X percent of incoming warheads—would discourage a first/disarming strike because the aggressor could never calculate with any confidence which of his warheads would penetrate and thus which of the defender's second-strike weapons he would actually manage to preempt. Such an attack would be irrational by definition because it would have to proceed on the prospect of random destruction, rather than on a rational calculation of force-exchange ratios.

In theory, even such an X-percent solution to U.S. vulnerability ought to reassure the nonnuclear allies. At least it ought to reassure all those who, for the past twenty years, have argued that the U.S. deterrent threat has been devalued by the United States' vulnerability to Soviet strategic strikes. If this argument is correct, then it should also be true that a less vulnerable United States is also a more reliable guarantor. Less exposed to Soviet counterblows, the United States ought to be less hesitant to wield its nuclear weapons on behalf of its European clients.

In practice, of course, the SDI does *not* reassure the nonnuclears. In fact, there is a perverse logic that has animated European deterrence thinking since the loss of the U.S. nuclear monopoly. Although that logic is never openly acknowledged, the nonnuclears seek safety in a patron who, having lost his nuclear immunity, must be just as vulnerable as they are.[11] Nonnuclear allies are haunted by the nightmare of a war that might start and end in Europe, a war that would spare the homelands of the superpowers while turning Europe into the sole arena of "limited" war. Hence the relentless European search for "coupling" (the most recent instance being the INF deployment), which is just another word for the homogenization of risks and the extension of vulnerability across the Atlantic divide and, of course, across the Soviet border. Nor is it so strange that the weak should seek safety in the exposure of the strong. Precisely because the suicidal character of nuclear weapons threatens to render all obligations null and void during the moment of truth, the Europeans have perennially pressed for strategies that chain the possessors and the protected to a common nuclear fate and that guarantee that an attack on Europe is an attack against the United States.

While a perfectly invulnerable United States would theoretically make for perfect extended deterrence, the West Europeans assume neither to grow from the SDI. The Soviets have been working on their version of "exotic" strategic defenses since the late 1960s, so it would be only a matter of time until both superpowers had acquired shields of sorts. That situation evokes Western Europe's classic nightmare: a United States still vulnerable enough to be self-deterred by the risks of first-use on behalf of the allies, yet just sheltered enough to evade entrapment in global war. In a bilateral state of imperfect strategic defenses, both superpowers would muster just enough denial capabilities to discourage an attack on themselves but not enough offensive strength to deter aggression against clients. Put differently, as MAD (Mutual Assured Destruction) shades off into MAS (Mutual Assured Survival), assurance would not come to the nations in between. They seek safety in deterrence-by-punishment, not in deterrence-by-denial that would accrue only to those who possess the wherewithal for strategic defense.

Thus the Europeans ask: Where would the giants do battle, if not in arenas unsheltered by strategic defenses—and how, if not with weapons unblunted by SDI? Europe's ancient nightmare is a war fought in Europe, and Europe only—and against superior conventional forces in the East, no longer held in check by America's first-use threat. Worse, the conventional nightmare is wrapped up in a nuclear one. Soviet strategic defenses would badly degrade those (strategic) "selective options" that NATO doctrine hopes to employ in the escalation process, while the U.S. shield would close off similar Soviet options against the United States. If so, battlefield weapons might move to center stage with their role doubly enhanced: liberated from the restraints of escalation and untrammeled by the defenses that devalue their strategic cousins.

For the European allies, the best of all possible deterrence worlds was a U.S. nuclear monopoly, which obtained until the beginning of the 1960s. This world is no more and will not be again. In the shadow of MAD, there is only a second-best solution: a United States that is just as vulnerable as its allies are, hence a world where the United States is destined to be embroiled from the very beginning in any war that breaks out in Europe. According to this logic, which is the logic of all client states, the Soviet Union will be deterred once it cannot count on a war that remains limited in intensity and geographical scope.

In a mixed MAD/MAS world—the most realistic assumption for the 1990s and beyond—there is the third-best solution of SDI plus EDI: strategic/exoatmospheric defenses that reach down as low as the Soviet SS-23, plus regional/endoatmospheric defenses that would do battle against short-range missiles such as the SS-21 and the Warsaw Pact's air armies.[12] The key idea behind EDI or ATBM is to close the gap that might be left unprotected (and appear all the more inviting) by U.S. space-based defenses. And here, the West Germans (and, at one step removed, the Dutch and Belgians) face the excruciating problem of their geography: To the extent that strategic defenses neutralize the long-range threat and perhaps nuclear weapons in general, war might concentrate on the conventional/tactical battlefield that is West Germany.

This unpleasant contingency—plus the time-proven needs of dependents to gain some role in the decisionmaking process of their patrons—has informed the FRG's politico-military interest in the SDI.

Cooperation with the United States might open up a two-way street for the transfer of exotic technology, yielding both hardware and software for an ATBM application in Europe. Indeed, West Germany's interest in formalizing cooperation precedes the U.S. push for it since late 1984. Worried that the United States would merely milk West Germany's considerable technological base without paying due attention to Allied needs, Bonn insisted on a measure of governmental supervision once the SDI Office set out to recruit high-technology firms in Western Europe.[13]

Moreover, in some respects, the technical problems of ATBM look less daunting than those of SDI. The boosters of tactical missiles do not separate from their warheads, hence their relatively large radar cross-sections should make detection easier. Second, decoys seem to make little sense on a tactical missile because "discrimination" is assured by atmospheric drag. Third, tactical missiles are slower than their strategic cousins because they spend much or all of their time within the atmosphere and because their shorter trajectories limit their maximum speed. Fourth, conventionally armed tactical missiles would yield even more time to the defender because, given the limited lethal radius of their warheads, they can be attacked close to target.[14]

Finally, there is a good politico-strategic reason for a defensive system in Western Europe: Given NATO's obvious political constraints, it cannot go for an Israeli-style "pre-boost phase defense," that is, for a preemptive strike against the Warsaw Pact's ballistic/airborne assets. Yet while the military imperatives clearly point in the direction of an ATBM system, the political ones do not. Once U.S. policy on SDI had reached the stage (in late 1984) when it began asking for European and Japanese adherence to the project, the old battle lines in and outside the Federal Republic were promptly redrawn.

Social Democrats and Greens began to express categorical opposition to the SDI in general and to any West German participation in particular. According to Egon Bahr, the SPD's spokesman on arms control matters, the West Germans would gain nothing but "a burden of responsibility, with all the consequences [such a step] would have for our relations with Eastern Europe" and, by implication, the Soviet Union.[15] The Free Democrats, Chancellor Kohl's junior coalition partners, opted for a position of noncommitment that, as time went on, began to tilt toward evident distaste for both the project and West German involvement in it.

With Gorbachev's accession in March 1985, the Federal Republic was once more confronted with the classic bane of its foreign policy. Toward the United States, the Soviet Union began to define the renunciation of the SDI as the price of superpower arms control; toward the West Europeans, and the Federal Republic above all, abstention from the U.S. program was demanded as proof of detente-minded realism.[16]

And thus the Kohl government was once more caught in a classic squeeze. Given the direction of the forces acting on German policy, the outcome was no longer difficult to predict. To begin with, Foreign Minister Genscher demonstratively began to lengthen the distance between his Liberal Party (FDP) and SDI. His basic objective was, and remains, a maximum pace and scope for Ostpolitik consistent with the Federal Republic's basic obligations to the United States and the Western alliance.[17] Given the latter, Genscher chose to articulate his opposition to SDI in terms of the traditional doxology of German security. Though Europe must "not be decoupled from technological innovation," it was just as crucial not to tamper with prevailing doctrine as long as there is "no better strategy of war-prevention." *En clair*, that meant: Let us beware of undermining "flexible response" and MAD through departures like strategic defenses. Finally, he invented an elegant counter to SDI in the guise of Eureka (European Research Coordination Agency) and let the French take credit for the idea. Eureka had a twofold advantage over SDI. Defined as a civilian high-technology effort, it would not provoke the Soviets. Moreover, it had the blessing of the strongly anti-SDI Mitterrand government, and hence it had a character that was not so much anti-American as pro-European.

And soon, Chancellor Kohl himself began to modify his early enthusiasm for SDI. In a widely noted address to the annual Wehrkunde Conference in Munich in February 1985, Kohl had still expressed guarded approval.[18] By May, however, Kohl began to tone down his endorsement of the American SDI venture. "We cannot predict today," he said, "whether [SDI] will prove to be an alternative means of preventing war and a way to reduce dependence on nuclear weapons. . . . SDI implies opportunities and risks for the North Atlantic Alliance at the same time."[19] By year's end, the government was still talking about "political support" for the "U.S.-initiated" SDI "*research program.*" On the other hand, it did "not aim for state-to-state participation" and would therefore not "furnish any public funds for cooperation projects." Previously widely celebrated, the presumed spin-offs for civilian R&D and ATBM were no longer mentioned. Instead, the "strategic and arms control implications of SDI research" had moved to the "foreground." To blunt any possible anti-Soviet edge, the government reaffirmed its "demand that SDI research had to lead to *cooperative* solutions," meaning not to a renewed arms contest but to arms control.[20] Significantly, Defense Minister Wörner no longer used the term "European Defense Initiative," speaking about "extended air defense" instead.

Those were precisely the principles that informed the "Memorandum of Understanding" (MOU) signed by the Federal Republic and the United States on March 27, 1985.[21] To evade even the slightest hint of a military commitment, the MOU was signed not by the defense minister (as it was signed by Secretary of Defense Caspar Weinberger on the U.S. side) but by Economics Minister Martin Bangemann. With respect to patents, technology transfers and classification procedures, the MOU added nothing that had not already been sanctified by bilateral treaties reaching all the way back to the 1950s.[22] Finally both countries promised to share development applicable to "conventional air defense."[23]

That Memorandum of Understanding closed the most recent chapter in the making of West German SDI/ATBM policy—which is less of a policy than a finely tuned dilemma. Though the Federal Republic has a distinct interest in defenses that would inhibit the threat posed by Soviet shorter-range missiles, especially in the post-Reykjavik era haunted by various "zero-solutions," there are stringent diplomatic and domestic imperatives militating against an active ATBM role.

Above all, there is a permanent detente imperative that any West German government must obey—both for internal and external reasons. To reduce its excruciating dependence on the United States, the Federal Republic must reduce its demand for security *made in the USA*, and this requires a policy of partial propitiation toward the Soviet Union, which endows Moscow with a partial veto power over West German strategic choices. Moreover, West Germany is also a *demandeur* vis-à-vis the USSR. Given its unresolved national problems, the FRG needs access and a measure of influence over its semihostile brother, the GDR. Because the Soviet Union holds the key to East/Central Europe, the FRG cannot afford to alienate Moscow with security choices the latter regards, or pretends to regard, as provocative. Finally, the FRG's national aspirations in the East can only flourish in a climate of detente—which allows the GDR and its East European allies to discretely loosen the ties of bipolarity binding them to their bloc leader. Conversely, that objective collides mercilessly with the reassertion of bipolarity in the West, hence with moves that would strengthen NATO with SDI/ATBM-type ventures.

These imperatives have been well internalized by all significant actors on the West German domestic scene: Social Democrats, Free Democrats, and even Christian Democrats. The strengthened role of the Free Democrats and Foreign Minister Genscher in the wake of the 1987 election (who had campaigned on a platform of Ostpolitik and detente[24]) was not destined to increase the Kohl government's attachment to SDI and ATBM in the four years to follow. And so the government's course seems mapped out well in advance. West German defense industries will work quietly on ATBM/extended air defense solutions, and the government will concentrate on SRINF arms control—all the while hoping with bated breath that the real world will take care of the Reykjavik dream of a Europe denuded of U.S. nuclear weapons.

NOTES

1. Assuming that all INF with ranges between 500 and 5,000 km are withdrawn according to the Washington Treaty of December 1987, the tally of short-range TBM launchers would look as follows:

		USSR	Non-USSR Pact
Frog-3/-5/-7	(70 km)	650	400
SS-21 Scarab	(120 km)	130	8
SS-1c Scud B/C	(300 km)	580	155
Totals		1,360[a]	563

		U.S.	Non-U.S. NATO
Lance	(110 km)	50[b]	51
Pluton	(120 km)		32
Totals		50	83

[a]Of which about 380 are assumed to be stationed with Soviet forces in Poland, Czechoslovakia, and the German Democratic Republic, with the remainder in the Soviet Union west of the Urals.
[b]Of which 36 are stationed in Europe.
Source: International Institute for Strategic Studies, *The Military Balance 1987–88* (London: IISS, 1988), Tables 1 and 2.

2. This estimate by Dennis Gormley (see note below) seems a bit high; 50 or less are more likely.
3. Dennis M. Gormley, "A New Dimension to Soviet Theater Strategy," *Orbis*, Fall 1985, p. 560.
4. On the NATO side, there are seventy-two West German Pershing IAs, to be eliminated by the mid-1990s. In addition, the Federal Republic, the Netherlands, Belgium, and Italy together deploy fifty-one Lance missiles (with a range of 110 km). The nuclear warheads for all these missiles are controlled by the United States. France disposes of thirty-two Plutons (with a range of 120 km).
5. Helmut Schmidt, "The 1977 Alastair Buchan Memorial Lecture," 28 October 1977, in *Survival*, January/February 1978, pp. 2–10.
6. Then, that monopoly consisted of a Soviet SS-4 and SS-5 medium-range potential, which was in the process of being dramatically enlarged by the triple-warhead SS-20. By contrast, the United States had withdrawn the last of its European-based medium-range missiles in the wake of the Cuban Crisis. The last "Eurostrategic" weapon of the United States, the Mace-B cruise missile, was withdrawn from Europe in 1969.
7. The acronym *SRINF* stands for the official oxymoron "shorter-range intermediate-range nuclear forces."
8. "Die NATO bleibt auf Atomwaffen angewiesen," interview with *Die Welt*, 17 November 1986.
9. Interview with *Le Quotidien de Paris*, 22 January 1987.
10. "Declaration on Conventional Arms Control," as cited in *Frankfurter Allgemeine Zeitung*, 12 December 1986.
11. See Josef Joffe, "Nuclear Weapons, No-First-Use, and European Order," *Ethics*, no. 3, 1985, pp. 614 ff.
12. *EDI* stands for European Defense Initiative, and it is no coincidence that a German defense minister, Manfred Wörner, was the first to launch the idea. See Manfred Wörner, "A Missile Defense for NATO Europe," *Strategic Review*, Winter 1985/86, pp. 13–20. Subsequently, Wörner dropped the term EDI in favor of "extended air defense."
13. Apart from German industry's traditional excellence in the fields of optics, there are weapons manufacturers like Messerschmidt-Bölkow-Blohm which offer state-of-the-art tracking and guidance technologies.
14. See Gregory H. Canavan, *Theater Applications of Strategic Defense Concepts* (Los Alamos, NM: Los Alamos National Laboratory, 10 January 1986).
15. Egon Bahr, "Die Bonner Entscheidung zu SDI muss nein heissen," *Vorwärts*, 18 May 1985. *Vorwärts* is the official publication of the SPD.
16. If Bonn were to decide in favor of SDI "in any form whatsoever," wrote *Pravda* on 5 September 1985, then the Federal Republic "would have to assume a great burden of responsibility for the grave consequences of such an act and for all the disadvantages resulting from it." The Soviet

Party newspaper accused the Bonn government of "following unconditionally in the wake of Washington's adventurism." See also "Moskau warnt Bonn wegen SDI," *Süddeutsche Zeitung*, 6 September 1985.

17. Domestic politics played at least as important a role. A small party, which has repeatedly faced the perils of extinction at the polls (because it might not clear the 5 percent hurdle mandated for parliamentary representation), Genscher's FDP has always sought to exploit political terrain left unplowed by its senior coalition partner. While in coalition with the SPD (1969–82), the FDP steered a course visibly to the right of the Social Democrats. When the FDP joined the Christian Democrats in 1982, it soon shifted leftward, especially in foreign policy, with Foreign Minister Genscher posing as trusty guardian of "continuity" (meaning as guarantor of detente and Ostpolitik) against the CDU/CSU right. In that role, the FDP hopes to attract the votes of those who are alienated by radical tendencies in the SPD but who also prefer a more pliant policy toward the East. A critical/rejectionist stance toward SDI appeared as a nice way to maximize votes at home while increasing the scope of diplomatic maneuver in the East.

18. On the one hand, Chancellor Kohl underlined his preference for MAD, that is, the "maintenance, on both sides, of a high and unacceptable risk attached to a first strike" plus "renunciation of superiority," meaning that "technological developments on either side must not destabilize the relationship of the great powers." On the other hand, he followed U.S. cues by proclaiming his attachment to the principles of MAS, that is, the "search for an improvement of war-prevention capabilities through the introduction of defense elements into the strategy of deterrence" and the "establishment of a new relationship between offensive and defensive weapons by recourse to available new technologies." See Chancellor Kohl, "Die Bundesrepublik Deutschland und Europa im Nordatlantischen Bündnis," Address to the 22nd Wehrkunde Conference, Munich, 9 February 1985. Presse- und Informationsamt der Bundesregierung, *Bulletin*, 14 February 1985.

19. In an address to NATO parliamentarians in Stuttgart, 20 May 1985, as quoted in William Drozdiak, "Kohl Hedges Support for 'Star Wars'," *Washington Post*, 21 May 1985.

20. See the resolution of the Cabinet on 18 December 1985, reproduced under the title, "Die Regierung will keine staatliche Beteiligung," *Süddeutsche Zeitung*, 19 December 1985 (emphasis added).

21. By April, the text of the "secret" Memorandum of Understanding had been leaked to the press. The first to publish it was the *Kölner Express* on 18 April 1986. An English translation appears in Ivo Daalder, *The SDI Challenge to Europe* (Cambridge, Mass.: Ballinger, 1987), pp. 112–124.

22. A rare element of novelty was introduced with respect to tendering procedures, where both sides pledged to "facilitate" fair and equal competitive conditions.
23. For an analysis, see Josef Joffe, "Geheimnisverrat ohne Geheimnisse," *Süddeutsche Zeitung*, 19 April 1986. It is instructive to note what Kohl's critic, the Bavarian prime minister and leader of the CSU Franz-Josef Strauss, had to say about the tactics of the Bonn government: "During the Wehrkunde Conference in 1985, the Chancellor clearly affirmed his support for the SDI project and for German participation in it. A bit later, the Foreign Minister [Genscher] uttered very skeptical opinions. Thereafter, the Chancellor had trouble harmonizing his position with that of the FDP Foreign Minister.... In the U.S., it was not easy for Mr. Bangemann [the FDP economics minister] to explain why it was he, of all people, who was charged with the negotiations, what his brief was, and which enigmas of German domestic or coalition politics were at work here." See Josef Joffe and Christian Schütze, interview with Franz-Josef Strauss, *Süddeutsche Zeitung*, 25–26 January 1986.
24. The FDP increased its share from 7 to 9.1 percent of the vote, while that of the CDU/CSU dropped by a thudding 4.5 percent.

Index

Abrahamson, James, 213
ABM Treaty, 133, 179–180, 184, 187–190, 288, 293–294; and ABM/non-ABM systems, 180–183, 190–195, 202–203; and ATBMs, 7, 16, 217; and Europe, 179, 183, 187–189, 203, 227, 228, 245, 251, 258; and Patriot system, 223; radar limitations in, 38, 181–182, 193, 194–196; and SAM systems, 181; and SDI, 214; and Soviet Union, 187–189, 293; systems covered by, 184–187; and TBMs, 180; and United States, 180–183, 185, 187–189, 194; verification of systems, 200–201, 227. *See also* Anti-ballistic missiles (ABMs)
Advisory Group for Aerospace Research and Development (AGARD), 161, 162, 220, 244
Aerospace Application Study (AAS-20), 161
Agreed Statements, 185-186
Air Defense Program Plan 90 (ADPP90), 223
Air defenses, NATO, 74, 127–128, 158–159, 165–166, 170, 201–202, 209, 219, 223, 244, 288; active/passive, 10, 15, 16, 22–27, 49–52, 86, 159, 221, 226–228; dual anti-aircraft/anti-TBM, 29, 31; "extended," 9, 11–13, 15, 210, 219–220, 222–225, 240, 243, 244, 299; funding for, 149; ground-based, 74, 224; layered, 11–12, 240; modernization of, 10, 21, 174; Air Defense Ground Environment (NADGE), 165, 257, 292; passive, 137–142, 143, 146, 149, 151, 200, 220, 224, 225; Patriot-like operations, 27–39; research, 161-162; and SDI, 215; Soviet challenge to, 162–171; and U.S. Army, 224; vulnerability of, 71–75, 127, 136–142, 221. *See also* Anti-tactical ballistic missile (ATBM) defense strategy, NATO; Defense strategy, NATO; Radar
Air defense strategy, U.S., 222–225
Air defense systems, Soviet: SA-2, 91; SA-4, 91; SA-X-12, 180, 183; SA-X-12A/Gladiator, 182; SA-X-12B/Giant, 91, 182.
Air Force, U.S., 161, 222, 223–225
Airborne Optical Adjunct (AOA), 151
Airborne Warning and Control System (AWACS), 51, 74, 165

312   INDEX

Airfields, NATO: as target, 3, 7, 72–73, 77, 94, 101, 112–121, 127, 128, 146, 166, 219, 221, 300
Airfields, Soviet, 159
AirLand Battle doctrine, NATO, 82–83
Alliance. *See* NATO
Allied Command Europe (ACE), 158, 160
Anti-tactical ballistic missile (ATBM) defenses, NATO, 9–11; 16, 18, 37–38, 84, 133, 201, 215, 221, 303, 307; and arms control, 15–17, 86, 179, 227–228; and available technologies, 13; and BMD, 211, 212; constraints on, 225–233; cost of, 173–175; countermeasures, 23, 24, 39–45; dual nuclear/conventional, 148; and East Asia, 273–282; European reaction to, 237–238, 241–259, 287–288, 290, 291–292; external surveillance, 45–49, 51–52; funding for, 226–227; issues and debate, 12–13, 14–15, 21–22, 57; and Japan, 273, 275–279; and Middle East, 262, 264–267, 270–271; nuclear dispersal option, 73–74, 78–79, 84, 144–145; passive, 217; Patriot-like operations, 27–39; politics of, 238–241; radar capabilities, 31–39; research, 146, 149–151, 213–214; resource implications, 17–18; Soviet challenge to, 162–171, 293; Soviet response vs. arms control, 15–17; and SDI, 149, 150, 179, 210–211, 229, 230, 241–259, 286, 289, 295, 297, 307; strategic issues, 12–13; technical areas, 22–27, 49–52, 304; technological issues, 14–15; and U.S.-European relations, 229–230. *See also* Air defense strategy, NATO; Defense strategy, NATO; Radar
Anti-tactical ballistic missile (ATBM) defenses, Soviet, 16, 57–58, 79–80, 289; antinuclear capability, 172; capabilities, 16, 79; deployments, 79–80, 82; future of, 82–87; geographic context, 80–82; offensive, 79–80; radar used in, 46; SA-10, 16; SA-12B, 79; SA-X-12, 16. *See also* Air defense strategy, Soviet; Defense strategy, Soviet; Radar

Anti-tactical ballistic missile (ATBM) defenses, U.S., 225–233
Anti-ballistic missile defenses (ABMs), 37–38, 50–52; definition of, 180, 183, 188, 189; and Middle East politics, 262, 264–267; technical characteristics of, 50–52; testing of, 192–193, 203. *See also* ABM Treaty
Anti-tactical ballistic missiles (ATBMs) antinuclear defense role, 146–149; arms control implications of, 7, 15–17, 86, 179, 227–228, 240–241, 294; debate, 2–3, 223–225, 227, 237–238; definition of, 2; deployments, 172; future of, 293; limitations on, 195–202; and military services, 255; research, 217, 228; and SDI, 83, 217, 257, 295, 297; as target, 293; technical characteristics of, 50–52; technology, 22, 179, 217, 228
Antiradiation missiles (ARMs), 143
Antisimulation, 44–45, 48
Arab states, 262, 263, 265, 266; and ABM/ATBM debate, 267–269; and Israel, 265–269, 270–271; and Soviet Union, 268
Ariane program, 291
Arms control, 210; and ABM technologies, 297; and ATBM/TBM policy, 7, 15–17, 86, 179, 227–228, 240–241, 294; and deterrence, 296; and European security, 301; Geneva Conference, 240, 249, 294; and technology, 83; verification of systems, 249–250; violations of, 182; "zero option" proposal, 294, 300–301, 306. *See also* ABM Treaty; Intermediate-range Nuclear Forces (INF) negotiations and agreements
Army, U.S., 222, 223–225, 227
Aron, Raymond, 164
ASEAN, 277
Assault Breaker program, 134
Atlantic Alliance. *See* NATO
Attack options: chemical, 83, 94, 219; deep, 82; limited nuclear, 83, 146–149; nonnuclear, 93; saturation, 15, 85–86, 147, 173, 223; suppression, 85; surprise, 5, 21, 71, 94, 101, 113, 135, 170, 171, 175,

197–199. *See also* Follow-On Forces Attack (FOFA)
Attrition rates for aircraft, 71–72

Bahr, Egon, 304
Ballistic Missile Early Warning Radars (BMEWs), 181
Ballistic missiles, NATO and U.S., 172, 301; and ABM Treaty, 191, 195; accuracy of, 94–97; definition of, 183–187; deployments, 69, 79; flight time, 77; Honest John, 96, 202; INF, 17; Lance, 27, 95, 199; Pershing I, 96, 112; Pershing II, 17, 27, 30, 35–37, 67, 69, 79, 86, 96, 97, 183, 222, 288, 301; as target, 86; terminal guidance systems, 67; verification of, 200–201
Ballistic missiles, Soviet: accuracy of, 67, 94–96; character of, 6–11; conventionally–armed, 74; dual–capable, 62–63, 66; improvements in, 1–2, 66–67, 69; nonnuclear, 7; nuclear, 6. *See also* Tactical ballistic missiles (TBMs) Soviet
Bangemann, Martin, 306
Belgium, 160, 166, 175, 303
Bombers, Soviet. *See* Air defense systems, Soviet
Britain, 79, 239, 247; antinuclear policy, 239; ATBM issue in, 246–248, 251, 259; and NATO defense strategy, 174; nuclear doctrine, 5–6; nuclear forces, 197, 200, 247, 254, 255; research collaboration in, 254–256; SLBMs, 35, 37; and SDI, 14, 246–247, 251, 253
Brussels. *See* Belgium
Brussels Treaty, 256
Bülow, Andreas von, 229
Bundy, McGeorge, 219

Carter, Ashton, 191
Carter, Jimmy, 223, 232
CENTAG, 163
CERN (European Organization for Nuclear Research), 291
China, 273–282
Chirac, Jacques, 250
Christian Democrats (West Germany), 307

Christian Social Union (CSU), 242
Circle of equal probability (CEP), 67, 95–96, 128, 147
Clausewitz, Karl von, 164
Cohen, William, 216
Command, control and communication (C^3) centers, NATO, 159; as target, 3, 7, 74, 122–127, 128, 143, 144, 165, 166, 219, 221, 299–300
Conceptual Military Framework (CMF), 157–160, 162, 168, 215, 220
Conference of National Armaments Directors (CNAD), 221
Congressional Research Service (CRS), 94
Conventional Defense Improvements (CDI), 159–160
Conventional forces, NATO, 1, 3, 62, 157–160, 161, 162, 218–219, 226, 246, 292; ground, 167, 169–170, 171; improvements, 161, 209, 226, 232, 245; munitions, 70; technology, 243–244
Conventional forces, U.S., 5
Conventional forces, Soviet, 57–58, 70–71, 218–219, 227, 232, 286
CounterAir, 92, 161, 220
Countermeasures, 23, 24, 39–45, 50; antiradar, 32; electronic, 37, 50; NATO, 37, 221
Crisis management, 288–289
Cruise missiles, 42–43, 95, 99, 128
Czechoslovakia: Soviet deployments in, 60, 66, 67, 78, 81–82

Daalder, Ivo, 213
Damage repair facilities, 10
Dean, Jonathan, 215
Decoys, 23–24, 25, 37, 44–45, 47, 84, 143, 191, 304; against SS-21, 45; transmitters, 103. *See also* Jamming, electronic; Radar
Deep attack strategy, 82
Defense Planning Committee (DPC), 157, 161
Defense strategy, NATO, 7, 9, 80, 82–83, 289, 292; allocation of forces, 165; conventional force planning, 1, 3, 62, 157–160, 161, 218–219; counterforce capability, 37, 221, 288; debate issues, 7–8; escalation, 17, 80, 87, 148, 171–173; first-use option, 62, 218, 286; flexible response, 3–6,

57, 60, 156–157, 164, 171, 197, 202, 203, 237, 240, 246, 285–286, 305; forward defense, 3, 158–159, 165, 167; multilayered, 151, 240; nonprovocative, 164; objectives of, 158–159; offensive/defensive, 158, 162; retaliation, 147, 285, 297; selective strike options, 171–172, 173, 197; TBM-focused, 9. *See also* Air defense, NATO; Anti-tactical ballistic missile (ATBM) defenses, NATO

Defense strategy, Soviet, 57–59, 74, 78, 80, 84–85, 289; chemical weapons, 63; conventional-only options, 62–71, 83; escalation, 60–63; exploitation of NATO vulnerability, 71–74; first-use option, 64; improvements in, 64–67, 74; massive nuclear use option, 59–60; missile role in, 75–79; modernization of forces, 64–65, 82; nuclear options, 62–63, 64; offensive, 79–80; preemptive action, 65; surprise action, 65; target planning, 72, 73–74, 78. *See also* Air defenses, Soviet; Anti-tactical ballistic missile (ATBM) defenses, Soviet

Defensive Counter Air (DCA), 158, 159, 167

De Gaulle, Charles, 248–249, 292

Demilitarization of space, 249

Denmark, 166

De Ruiter, Job, 161, 245–246, 247

Detection of targets. *See* Radar

Deterrence, 5, 6, 147, 156, 172, 239, 247, 286, 287, 295, 300; and arms control negotiations, 296; credible, 158; extended, 172, 210, 212; and first use, 164; and missile systems, 190; and NATO, 289; by punishment, 303; and Western Europe, 292. *See also* Defense strategy, NATO, flexible response

Discrimination of targets, 23–24, 27, 51–52, 305. *See also* Radar

Dispersal of forces, NATO, 10, 73–74, 78–79, 84, 159, 170, 175

Durch, William, 183

East Germany: Soviet air deployments in, 78, 81–82; Soviet ground deployments in, 60, 61, 66, 67, 69, 71

Egypt, 202, 263, 267

Enders, Thomas, 188, 189, 233n

ESECS (European Security Study), 219, 220

Esprit program, 253

EUREKA (European Research Coordination Agency), 14, 211, 250, 253, 257, 279, 291, 305

Euromissiles, 288, 290, 294, 300

Europe. *See* Western Europe, *specific countries*

European Defense Initiative (EDI), 211, 214, 221, 238, 240, 242–243, 253–254, 303, 306; and Middle East politics, 265; tripartite agreement on ATBMs, 254–256

Eurospace program, 291

Exoatmospheric Reentry Vehicle Interceptor Subsystem (ERIS), 151

Explosives. *See* Munitions

Fletcher Panel, 214

Flexible response. *See* Defense strategy, NATO, flexible response

Follow-On Forces Attack (FOFA), 5, 82, 113, 135, 141, 142–143, 146, 158, 159, 169, 174, 220, 221

Foster, John, 181, 186, 189

France, 79, 162, 166, 239, 293; absence from NATO, 3, 239, 257, 292; air defense of, 257; ATBM issue, 217, 248–251, 259; conventional forces, 249; EUREKA initiative, 14, 211, 250, 253, 257, 279, 291, 305; nuclear forces, 197, 200, 247, 249, 254, 255; research and development programs, 222, 254–256; and SDI, 14, 214, 246, 248–251; SLBMs, 35, 37

Free Democrats (West Germany), 243, 244, 304, 307

Frontal aviation, Soviet, 65, 66, 78, 299, 300; Fitter D/H, 65; Flogger D/J, 65; M16–27, 65; SU-17, 65; SU-24, 65, 66; SU-25/Frogfoot, 169. *See also* Air defense strategy, Soviet; Long-range aviation, Soviet

Geneva Conference on Disarmament, 240, 249, 294

Genscher, Hans-Dietrich, 243, 244, 307

INDEX   315

Global Positioning Satellite System, 34
GLONASS system, 34
Golan Heights, 268
Gorbachev, Mikhail, 180, 239, 245, 294, 295, 305; zero solution proposal, 300–301
Gormley, Dennis, 167, 169, 173, 199
Greenwood, David, 253
Ground forces, Soviet, 59, 60, 63, 65, 67

Hardening of targets, 10, 122–123, 159
Hassel, Kai-Uwe von, 242
Hawk interceptor missiles, 74, 144, 222; deployment of, 10, 166; radar, 77; as target, 165
Helicopter forces, 170
High Endoatmospheric Interceptor (HEDI), 151
Hoffman Panel/report, 13, 212, 214, 242
Holst, Johan, 212
Hunter, Duncan, 184, 216

Iklé, Fred, 184
Independent European Program Group (IEPG), 221, 257
Inertial guidance systems, 134
Interceptors, 24–39, 40–41, 44, 185, 188–9, 193. *See also* Hawk interceptor missiles; Patriot interceptor missiles
Intercontinental ballistic missiles (ICBMs): arrival speed, 30, 37; ballistic trajectories, 37; limitations on, 251; reentry speed, 186, 194; as target, 200; technology, 231–232
Intermediate-range ballistic missiles, 172, 192, 215, 231, 232. *See also* Medium-range ballistic missiles (IRBMs), Soviet; Tactical ballistic missiles (TBMs)
Intermediate-range nuclear forces (INF), 219, 222, 301, 302; negotiations and agreements, 17, 67, 69, 172, 195–197, 200, 203, 209, 215, 217, 227; anti-INF movement, 232; double zero proposal, 180; European reaction to, 216; limitations, 180; verification of systems, 180; zero solution proposal, 300–301
Iraq, 202, 263, 269–270
Iran, 202, 263, 269–270
Israel, 80, 81, 103; and ABM/ATBM debate, 264–267, 270; and Arab states, 265–269, 270–271; nuclear forces and doctrine, 202, 263, 266; superiority in Middle East, 262, 263, 265–266, 268, 270; and SDI, 265, 304; war with Syria, 217, 262, 266, 268; and United States, 262
Italy, 14

Jamming, electronic, 10, 23, 25, 39–42, 46–48. *See also* Radar
Japan, 81, 217, 273, 276–282, 287, 289, 290, 304
Joint Surveillance Target Attack Radar System (Joint STARS), 51
Jump Command Post (JUMP), 124

Keepout zones. *See* Radar, range (keepout zone)
Kennan, George, 219
Keyworth, George, 214
Khrushchev, Nikita, 59
Kissinger, Henry, 232, 286
Kohl, Helmut, 242, 243, 252, 304, 305, 307

Laird, Melvin, 183
Large phased-array radars (LPARs), 181, 182. *See also* Radar
Lebanon, 268
Libya, 202, 263
Long-wave Infrared Sensors (LWIRs), 23–24, 46, 48
Low Altitude Defense System (LoAD), 222

McNamara, Robert, 219
Main Divisional Command Post, U.S., 124
Main Operating Bases (MOBs), NATO, 137, 139
MC-299, 220
Medium-range ballistic missiles (IRBMs), Soviet: SS-2, 79; SS-4, 79, 231, 232; SS-5, 231, 232
Middle East, 259. *See also specific countries*
Military policy, Soviet, 8, 60, 161, 162
Mines, 141
Missiles (general discussion). *See* Anti-ballistic missiles (ABMs) (general discussion); Anti-tactical ballistic missiles (ATBMs) (general

discussion); Intercontinental ballistic missiles (ICBMs) (general discussion); Intermediate-range ballistic missiles; Intermediate-range nuclear forces (INF) (general discussion); Tactical ballistic missiles (TBMs) (general discussion)
Missiles, NATO. *See* Anti-tactical ballistic missile (ATBM) defense strategy, NATO; Anti-tactical ballistic missiles (ATBMs); NATO; Ballistic missiles, NATO and U.S.
Missiles, Soviet. *See* Anti-tactical ballistic missile (ATBM) defense strategy, Soviet; Anti-tactical ballistic missiles (ATBMs), Soviet; Medium-range ballistic missiles (IRBMs), Soviet; Short-range ballistic missiles (SRBMs), Soviet; Tactical ballistic missiles (TBMs), Soviet; Submarine-launched ballistic missiles (SLBMs), Soviet; Surface-to-air missile (SAM) systems, Soviet
Missiles, U.S. *See* Anti-tactical ballistic missile (ATBM) defense strategy, U.S.; Ballistic missiles, NATO and U.S.; Hawk interceptor missiles; Patriot interceptor missiles; Submarine-launched ballistic missiles (SLBMs), U.S.; Surface-to-air missile (SAM) systems, NATO and U.S.
Mitterrand, François, 305
Mobility, 10; of forces, 169; of targets, 128, 134, 135, 143, 159
Multi-Lateral Force (MLF), 209–210, 215, 230–231
Multiple independently targetable reentry vehicles (MIRVs), 5, 84
Multiple Launch Rocket System (MLRS), 219
Munitions, 123; earth-penetrating, 122, 133; combined effect, 143; fragmentation, 97; fuel-air explosive (FAE), 99; shaped charge, 98–99, 123; on TBMs, 97–101
Mutual Assured Destruction (MAD), 296, 302, 303, 305
Mutual Assured Survival (MAS), 302, 303
Mutual and Balanced Force Reductions (MBFR), 281
MX missile, 220

Nakasone, Yasuhiro, 279–280
Nasser, Gamal, 263
National Air Defense Troops, Soviet, 65
Nato, 5; balance of influence in, 292–293; decisionmaking process, 71, 170, 173–174; European role in, 237, 293; military doctrine, 155, 220; nuclear arsenal, 62, 73, 82; nuclear doctrine, 5, 16, 149, 289, 303; nuclear superiority, 156–157; operational doctrine, 162–163; political solidarity in, 5–6; research programs, 146, 147–151; security doctrine, 2; U.S. role in, 238; zero option proposal, 294. *See also* Air defense strategy, NATO; Anti-tactical ballistic missile (ATBM) defense strategy, NATO; Defense strategy, NATO
NATO Air Defense Committee (NADC), 161
NATO Air Defense Ground Environment (NADGE), 165, 257, 292
Navy forces, NATO, 159
Netherlands, 14, 245, 246, 254, 256; deployments, 166, 168; and NATO defense strategy, 174, 220, 303
Neutron bomb, 232
Nike Hercules, 166
Nitze, Paul, 186
North Korea, 202
NORTHAG, 163
Nuclear forces, NATO, 166, 289
Nuclear parity, 60, 64, 210, 281, 289
Nuclear Planning Group (NPG), 211, 212, 231
Nunn, Sam, 216, 219, 226

Offensive Counter Air (OCA), 158–159, 165
Offensive Counter Air, Soviet attack on NATO airfields, 3, 7, 72–73, 77, 94, 101–102, 113, 119–122, 127–128, 146, 166, 219 221, 300; capabilities, 99–100, 219, 221, 227; combined arms operation, 58, 163; conventional, 82; mass strikes, 76–79; offensive, 61, 167, 169;

overlapping, 79; superiority of, 167; vulnerability of, 75
Operational doctrines, 162–164
Operational maneuver groups, 64
Oppenheimer, Robert J., 291
ORACLE mine sweepers, 141
Otrag, 263

Panel on Air Defense Philosophy (PADP), 161
Panel on Air Defense Weapons (PADN), 161, 162
Patriot interceptor missiles, 25, 166, 192, 222, 276–277; and ABM Treaty, 223; air defense by, 27–39, 74; ATBM capability, 192; cost of, 137, 168, 226; deployment of, 10, 166; dual-mode, 83, 257; mobility of, 150; radar, 31–32, 33, 38, 40–43, 46, 50, 150, 194; as target, 165; upgrading (nuclear arming) of, 50, 84, 85, 143, 168, 192, 219, 220, 222–223, 226, 228, 229, 257, 265
Perle, Richard, 215
Persian Gulf, 263–264, 269–270
Philips electronics (Dutch), 246, 256
Poland, 66, 78
Polaris missile, 232
POMCUS sites, NATO: as target, 63, 145–146, 167–168
Precision Location Strike System (PLSS), 51
Probability of kill, 24, 102–104, 106–107
"Provisional Political Guidelines," 171

Quayle, Dan, 216, 217, 226

Rabi, Isidore, 291
Radar, 22–23, 25–26, 30, 51, 305; ABM Treaty limitations on, 38, 193, 194–195; ATBM, 37; Radar Cross Section (RCS), 33–35, 37, 38, 45; definition of, 185; discrimination of decoys, 23–24, 41; early warning, 181, 194, 195; ground-based, 46, 150, 195; Hawk, 77; keepout zone (*see* range); limitations on, 181–182, 185; Patriot, 31–32, 33, 38, 41–42, 46; 49–50, 150, 194; phased-array, 46–47, 181, 182; and probability of kill, 106–107; range (keepout zone), 27–29, 30–31, 33–35, 37, 148, 150,
186; and reentry speeds, 186; research, 150; search function, 30–39, 42; silence, 103, 143; Soviet, 185; surveillance, 45–49, 75, 165; as target, 103–104, 126, 127, 128, 194; TBM detection by, 25–26; and technical distinctions between missiles, 37–38. *See also* Jamming, electronic
Radio communications, 125
Raimond, Jean-Bernard, 301
RAND's TSARINA model, 140
Raytheon Corporation, 280
Reagan, Ronald, 223, 229, 237, 244, 245, 295; and arms control, 182, 184; and SDI, 2, 12–13, 14, 161, 179, 203, 211, 237–239, 240, 242, 246, 249, 252, 280, 286
Reinforcement facilities, NATO, 166, 167–168
Reykjavik summit, 179, 216, 237, 239, 252, 256, 300, 307
Rogers, Bernard, 160, 161, 220–222, 243, 244
Roland missile system, 227

SAFEGUARD point defense system, 212
Salt I, 82, 184, 294, 300
Salt II, 257, 294, 300
Saturation strategy, 15, 85–86, 147, 173, 223
Saudi Arabia, 269
Schlesinger, James, 181, 232
Schmidt, Helmut, 300, 301
Sea-based Anti-Ballistic Missile Intercept System (SABMIS), 211
Sensor technologies, 253. *See also* Radar
SENTINEL area defense system, 211, 212
SHAPE, 171, 292
Short-range ballistic missiles (SRBMs), Soviet, 66, 69, 75, 299, 300; accuracy, 2; and arms control, 86, 191, 195, 196–202, 217; deployments, 81, 82; exports to Third World, 80; Frog 3/7, 60, 202; Frog-7, 61, 67, 202; production rate, 69–70; refire times, 78; SS-12 Scaleboard, 79; Scud A/B, 60; Scud-B, 61, 67–69; Scud-C, 66, 67–69, 70, 202; verification of, 200–201

Short-range ballistic missiles (SRBMs), third party, 202
Short-wave infrared (SWIR) sensors, 46, 48–49. *See also* Radar
Smart weapons, 3, 128, 134–135, 219
Smith, Gerard, 183, 219
Social Democratic Party (SPD) (West Germany), 242, 245, 304, 307
South Korea, 81, 202
South Yemen, 202
Soviet Union: and ABM Treaty, 187–189, 293; and East Asia, 274–276; and Middle East, 261, 262, 268; and NATO defense strategy, 162–171, 293; nuclear doctrine, 8–9, 147; and SDI, 305; and West Germany, 306–307. *See also* Air defense strategy, Soviet; Anti-tactical ballistic missile (ATBM) defense strategy, Soviet; Defense strategy, Soviet
Space program, European, 249–250, 291
SRINF, 307
Standing Consultative Commission (SCC), 182, 203
Stealth missiles/technology, 22, 35, 43, 50
Storage sites, NATO: as target, 3, 7, 77, 144–145, 166, 199–200, 217, 299–300
Strategic Air Armies, Soviet, 66
Strategic Defense Initiative (SDI), 2, 58, 83, 133, 237, 238–239, 240, 301; and ABM Treaty, 214; and ATBM defense, 149, 150, 179, 210–211, 229, 230, 241–259, 286, 289, 295, 297, 307; deployments, 16; European response to, 3, 12, 14–15, 18, 57, 83, 213, 214–216, 229, 241–245, 249, 287, 290–291, 296, 304, 305; extension of, 11–13, 15; funding for, 217, 221, 223; and Israel, 265; military implications of, 286; and NATO air defense strategy, 215; political implications of, 247, 284; and Reagan, 2, 12–13, 14, 161, 179, 203, 211, 238–239, 240, 242, 246, 249, 252, 280, 286; research, 215, 221, 238, 246–247, 250, 252, 253, 280, 290, 305–306; sensors, 194; and Soviet technology, 83; technologies, 11, 14–15, 51, 150, 211, 212–214, 217, 221, 253, 280; U.S. support for, 3, 211–218, 227, 229; and West Germany, 14, 214, 249, 251, 252, 303–304
Strategic Defense Initiative Organization (SDIO), 213–214, 216, 218, 220–221, 222, 225, 250, 304; funding for, 223; research programs, 215, 216–217, 221
Strategic Rocket Forces (SRF), Soviet, 59, 65
Strauss, Franz-Josef, 242
Submarine-launched ballistic missiles (SLBMs), Soviet: SS-N-5, 184; SS-N-6, 184, 187
Submarine-launched ballistic missiles (SLBMs), U.S., 172, 184, 192, 194; Trident, 35, 36, 37; Trident II, 247
Submunitions: dispersal of, 135, smart, 128, 134–135. *See also* Tactical ballistic missiles (TBMs), submunitioned-armed
Supreme Allied Commander, Europe (SACEUR), 5, 160, 163, 175, 220, 222, 292; attack strategy, 158; and SLBMs, 197; U.S. deployments to, 172
Surface-to-air missile (SAM) systems, NATO and U.S., 76, 166, 257; ATBM capability, 51, 143, 180, 181, 183, 194; defense (SAM-D), 37–38, 43, 77, 78, 180, 186, 189, 222; deployments, 166, 189, 199; mobility of, 74; modernization of, 10; "son" of, 11, 210; as target, 142–144, 146, 167, 169, 300; upgrading of, 141; vulnerability of, 77. *See also* Anti-tactical ballistic missile (ATBM) defense strategy, NATO
Surface-to-air missile (SAM) systems, Soviet: SA-5, 173, 181–182; SA-10, 173. *See also* Anti-tactical ballistic missile (ATBM) defense strategy, Soviet
Surprise attack. *See* Attack options, surprise
Surveillance systems, 45–49. *See also* Radar
Syria, 80, 81, 104, 202, 263; war with Israel, 217, 262, 266, 268

Tactical Air Armies (TAA), Soviet, 66

Tactical ballistic missiles (TBMs) (general discussion): accuracy (CEP), 27, 96, 98, 100, 102–103, 128, 133, 135, 149; arrival speeds, 104–105, 193; chemically- armed, 28, 99; conventionally- armed, 97–99, 128, 135–136, 148, 150; damage expectancy of, 102; detection range, 39; limitations on, 180; maneuverability, 34; reentry speeds, 186, 192; submunitioned– armed, 94, 99–100, 104–107, 108–113, 118–121, 127, 128; terminal guidance, 34; terrain–sensitive, 96–97

Tactical ballistic missiles (TBMs), Soviet; arms control limitations on, 69, 70, 128, 195, 196–202; attack advantage and objectives, 17, 101–103; ballistic trajectories, 30–31; bombing capabilities, 100–101; effectiveness against NATO airbase targets, 113–122, 136–142; effectiveness against C^3 facility targets, 122–127; effectiveness against SAM site targets, 140–142; exports of, 80–81; force levels, 122, 128; improvements, 128; launchers, 139; non-European deployments, 202; nuclear-armed, 146–149; and radar detection, 50–51; numerical superiority, 157; SS-12/22, 2, 17, 30, 35–37, 42, 49, 57, 66, 67, 69, 70, 79, 81, 93, 96, 97, 122, 167, 240, 248, 265, 291, 294–295; SS-20, 2, 17, 30, 35–37, 61, 183, 184, 185–187, 190, 231, 240, 265, 275, 281, 294, 299–301; SS-21, 2, 30, 45, 48, 57, 66, 67, 80, 82, 93, 96, 97, 122, 167, 187, 202, 217, 238, 265, 289, 294–295, 303; SS 21/Frog, 199, 202; SS-23, 2, 17, 30, 35–36, 42, 49, 66, 72–73, 82, 93, 96, 97, 122, 167, 187, 240, 265, 289, 294–295; SS-25, 187; submunition-armed, 94, 104–113, 118–122; vulnerability of, 94

Tactical Operations Command Post (DTOC), 126

Taft, William Howard IV/Taft directive, 225–230

Targets, 26–27, 94–95, 143–144, 146; detection of, 22–23, 135; discrimination of, 23–4, 27, 51, 304; fixed, 136; hardening of, 10, 122–123, 159; and interceptor guidance, 24–26; mobile, 128, 134, 135, 143, 159; probability of kill against, 24, 102–104, 107; protection of, 136; tracking of, 24, 30, 98, 51; types of, 101–102; vulnerability criteria, 133–136. *See also* Airfields, NATO, as target; Command, control and communication (C^3) centers, NATO, as target; POMCUS sites, NATO, as target; Radar; Surface-to-air missile (SAM) systems, NATO and U.S., as target; Storage sites, NATO, as target

Technology: and arms control, 83; ABM/ATBM, 22, 179, 217, 228, 267–268, 297; conventional, NATO, 243–244; conventional, Soviet, 64, 70–71, 83; defense, Western, 7, 13, 21, 50–51; emerging, 157, 161, 201, 210, 246; guidance, 93; ICBM, 231–232; information, 253; interceptor, 150; jamming, 41–42; missile, NATO, 155; missile, Soviet, 2, 8, 133; missile, U.S., 2; new system, 174–175, 262, 291; propulsion, 93; research, Soviet, 70, 146; research, U.S., 14; SDI, 11, 14–15, 51, 150, 211, 213–214, 217, 221, 253, 280; sensor, 253; sharing/transfer, 216, 250, 253, 254

Teller, Edward, 213
Terrain-matching sensors, 134
Thatcher, Margaret, 246, 247, 252
Thor-Jupiter program, 231–232

Unilateral Statement B, 186
United States: arms control policy, 259; ATBM strategy, 225–233; ATBM support, 218–225; ATBM vs. SDI debate, 210–211, 247; -European ATBM program, 293; and Japan, 276, 278, 287; and Middle East, 261, 262, 267; nonnuclear allies of, 302; nuclear monopoly, 302, 303; SDI support, 3, 211–218, 227, 229; security, 289; technological superiority, 227; vulnerability of, 301–302

Ustinov, Dimitri F., 65

War, conventional, 5, 60
War, nuclear: limited, 60, 173, 302–303
War scenarios: ATBM/TBM, 147–148; short-warning attack, 85–86; surprise attack, 5, 21, 71, 94, 101, 113, 134, 170, 171, 175, 197–199
Warheads. *See* Munitions
Warsaw Pact: conventional superiority, 156–157; target acquisition system, 62; TBM advantage, 17. *See also* Air defense strategy, Soviet; Antitactical ballistic missile (ATBM) defense strategy, Soviet; Defense strategy, Soviet; Soviet Union; *specific countries*
Weapons (general discussion): biological, 63, 94, 99, 126; chemical, 28, 63, 94, 99, 126, 268, 301; smart, 3, 127, 134–135, 219; space-based, 13; standoff, 219
Weinberger, Caspar, 157, 214, 246, 306
West Germany, 18, 239; antinuclear policy, 239; ATBM issue in, 217, 241–245, 247–248, 251, 252, 259, 299, 303, 304–306; and EDI, 242–243, 265; military land use, 139, 142; and NATO defense planning, 157, 220, 222; nuclear forces, 200, 254; research and development programs, 232, 254–256; and SDI, 14, 214, 249, 251, 252, 303–304, 304–306; and Soviet Union, 306–307; as theater of conflict, 86, 303; U.S. forces in, 166
Western Europe: arms acquisition, 257; arms control issues in, 281; ATBM debate in, 237–238, 241–259, 287–288, 290, 291–292, 304; and SDI, 3, 12, 14–15, 18, 57, 83, 213, 214–216, 229, 241–245, 249, 287, 290–291, 296, 304, 305; and SDI research, 253, 290; security and defense requirements, 209, 211–212, 230, 237–238, 249, 259, 288, 289, 291–292, 295–296, 301, 304; space program, 249–250; as theater of conflict, 59, 61, 165; -U.S. relations, 229–230, 237–238
Western European Union, 256, 287
Wickham-Gabriel Memorandum of Agreement, 223–224
Wilson, Pete, 216, 217
Wörner, Manfred, 133, 301; ATBM defense proposal, 161, 220, 227, 247, 248, 252, 306; and NATO defense planning, 172; and SDI, 243–245, 246

Zero solutions for defense, 180, 294, 300–301, 306

ABOUT THE EDITORS

Donald L. Hafner is an associate professor of political science at Boston College. He received his Ph.D. in political science from the University of Chicago. In 1977–78 he worked with the U.S. Arms Control and Disarmament Agency, serving as an adviser with the U.S. SALT delegation in Geneva and as an analyst on strategic and antisatellite arms control policies. He has written extensively on antisatellite and other defense issues and was co-editor of the American Academy of Arts and Sciences study, *Weapons in Space*.

John Roper is the editor of *International Affairs* and a research fellow at the Royal Institute of International Affairs. He is co-founder of the Social Democratic Party in Britain and a former member of Parliament (Labour, 1970–81; Social Democratic, 1981–83). He is a graduate of Oxford University and was a member of the faculty at the University of Manchester from 1962 to 1970. He served as Labour Party front bench spokesman on defense issues from 1979 to 1981 and was chairman of the Committee on Defense Questions and Armaments of the Western European Union from 1977 to 1980.

ABOUT THE CONTRIBUTORS

Alain Baer is a retired general of the French Air Force and a former fighter pilot. He is currently serving as a consultant and expert in defense matters to several organizations and business firms. His articles on defense matters have appeared in *Défense Nationale*.

James Bonomo is a member of the research staff of the engineering and applied sciences department of the RAND Corporation in Santa Monica, California. He holds a Ph.D. in physics from the University of California at Berkeley. His work at RAND has dealt with analysis of the technical feasibility of proposed military systems, concentrating on surveillance and guidance systems.

Jeffrey Boutwell is a policy analyst at the American Academy of Arts and Sciences, and is a co-editor of *Weapons in Space* and *The Nuclear Confrontation in Europe* and the author of a forthcoming book, *The German Nuclear Dilemma*.

Shahram Chubin is the director of research for the Program on Strategic and International Security at the Graduate Institute of International Studies, Geneva. His recent publications include *India and the Great Powers* and *Soviet Policy Towards Iran and the Gulf*.

Ivo H. Daalder is a research associate at the International Institute for Strategic Studies, London, and a Ph.D. candidate in political science at the Massachusetts Institute of Technology. He is the author of *The SDI Challenge to Europe* as well as a number of journal articles dealing with European security, NATO, and arms control.

François de Rose is an ambassadeur de France and served as France's permanent representative to the North Atlantic Council from 1970 to 1975. He is a member of the Trilateral Commission and of the Council of the International Institute for Strategic Studies. His publications include *La France et la défense de l'Europe* and *European Security and France*.

Sir James Eberle is the director of the Royal Institute of International Affairs, London. He is a retired admiral of the Royal Navy, having graduated from the Royal Naval College at Dartmouth prior to serving in the Pacific theater in World War II and in the Korean War. Sir James served as commander-in-chief, fleet (UK). He retired from active duty in 1983.

Dennis M. Gormley is a vice president of Pacific-Sierra Research Corporation, a subsidiary of Eaton Corporation, in Washington, D.C., where he specializes in Soviet military policy. Previously, he was head of foreign intelligence at the U.S. Army Harry Diamond Laboratories in Washington, D.C. His articles on Soviet military programs have appeared in *Orbis, Survival,* and *Washington Quarterly*, among others.

Josef Joffe is a columnist and foreign editor of the *Süddeutsche Zeitung* in Munich. He received his Ph.D. in government from Harvard University. He has written widely on Germany, international relations, strategy, and arms control. His most recent book is *The Limited Partnership: Europe, the United States and the Burdens of Alliance*.

Catherine McArdle Kelleher is a professor in the School of Public Affairs and director of the Center for International Security Studies at the University of Maryland. She is the author of *Germany and the Politics of Nuclear Weapons*, co-editor of *Nuclear Deterrence: New Risks, New Opportunities*, and co-editor of *Evolving European Defense Policies*.

Benoit Morel is a faculty member in the Department of Engineering and Public Policy at Carnegie-Mellon University. He was previously a science fellow at the Center for International Security and Arms Control, Stanford University; a senior research fellow at the California Institute of Technology; and an adjunct professor of physics at the University of Southern California. He received his doctorate in theoretical physics from the University of Geneva, Switzerland.

Theodore A. Postol is currently a senior research associate at the Center for International Security and Arms Control, Stanford University. Previously he served in the U.S. Department of Defense as scientific adviser to the Chief of Naval Operations, and with the U.S. Office of Technology Assessment. He received his doctorate in physics and nuclear engineering at the Massachusetts Institute of Technology.

David Rubenson is a member of the research staff of the engineering and applied sciences department of the RAND Corporation in Santa Monica, California. He holds an M.S. degree in physics from the University of Pennsylvania. His work at RAND had dealt with assessing the utility of advanced technology weapons systems, including space surveillance and missile defense systems.

Gerald Segal is the editor of the quarterly journal *The Pacific Review* and a lecturer in politics at the University of Bristol, Great Britain. He is the author of *Defending China* and *Sino-Soviet Relations After Mao*. He is also the editor of *The Soviet Union in East Asia* and co-editor of *Chinese Defense Policy*.

Peter Volten is a professor of military history at the University of Utrecht and was recently a research fellow at the Netherlands Institute for International Relations, Clingendael, the Hague. He is a senior civil servant in the Netherlands Ministry of Defense and has written widely on defense and military matters. Among his most recent publications is *Brezhnev's Peace Program: A Study in Soviet Domestic Political Process and Power*.

Phil Williams is a senior lecturer in international relations in the Department of Politics, University of Southampton in Great Britain. He is the author of *Crisis Management, U.S. Troops in Europe*, and *The Senate and U.S. Troops in Europe*. He is a co-editor of *The Carter Years: The President and Policy Making*, a co-author of *Contemporary Strategy*, Volumes 1 and 2; and co-author of *Superpower Detente*.

RAYMOND H. FOGLER LIBRARY